This book is a gift to

_____

from

_____

5215 North O'Connor, Suite 200 | Irving, TX 75039 | www.hbcutoday.net

Publisher: Black Educational Events, LLC

Editorial Director: J.M. Emmert

Editorial Staff: Meta Williams, Nancy Laichas, and Rebecca Larson

Cover and Interior Design: Jennings Design/www.jenningsdesignonline.com

Published by BEE Publishing, a division of Black Educational Events, LLC.

The artwork on pages xviii, 2, 20, 44, 64, 276, and 292 are reproduced herein courtesy of Bernard Kinsey. Artwork photography by Manuel Flores and John Sullivan.

 Black Educational Events, LLC

5215 North O'Connor
Suite 200
Irving, TX, 75039
U.S.A.
www.blackeducationalevents.com

BEE Publishing is a trademark of Black Educational Events, LLC.

To order additional copies, go to www.hbcutoday.net.

Printed in the United States of America

ISBN-13: 978-0-615-29383-7

LCCN: 2009904194

Your Comprehensive Guide to Historically Black Colleges and Universities

HBCU

TODAY

Dedicated to the 104 Historically Black Colleges and Universities that have served the social, cultural, and educational needs of America's young men and women for the past 170 years.

CONTENTS

EDITOR'S NOTE

Dear Reader:

Our goal with the publication of *HBCU Today* is to raise awareness of the rich traditions and educational relevance of our nation's 104 Historically Black Colleges and Universities (HBCUs). As the majority of these institutions are located east of the Mississippi, students and parents in many regions of the country are not aware of the wonderful opportunities that can be found at HBCUs. It is our hope that this comprehensive guide will illustrate the many benefits they have to offer, as well as assist you in the college selection process.

The advertisements you see throughout the book are from preferred providers only. Their services and products will add value to your decision-making process as a student, parent, or counselor.

We hope you enjoy *HBCU Today*. For more information and additional resources, please visit www.HBCUToday.net.

J.M. Emmert
Editor

The Kinsey Collection

As you read through the book, you will notice selected art works. These reproductions are from The Kinsey Collection, a group of African-American art, books, and manuscripts that document and tell the remarkable story of African-American triumphs and struggles from 1632 to the present. As we strive to educate and inform about our nation's HBCUs, we also wish to make known the culturally rich history of African-American artists. For more information on the Kinsey Collection, please refer to page 292.

FOREWORD

by Dr. George C. Wright,
President, Prairie View A&M University

© 2003 Gittings

There is something special about the designation Historically Black College and University. These 104 institutions share a pride and purpose that over time has been modified and altered but remains consistently grounded in one mission—educating African Americans. As the president of Prairie View A&M University, I can attest to the uniqueness of our designation.

Since 1837, when the oldest HBCU, Cheyney University of Pennsylvania, opened its doors, HBCUs have contributed to the rise of black professionals, business leaders, teachers, nurses, artists, and engineers. While comprising only 3 percent of the nation's approximately 3,700 institutions of higher learning, these academic institutions are responsible for producing more than 50 percent of African-American professionals and public-school teachers. According to the United Negro College Fund, HBCUs award more than one-third of the degrees held by African Americans in natural sciences and half of the degrees in mathematics. But an HBCU education doesn't end with the award of a degree.

Organized by churches, missionary groups, and philanthropists, HBCUs have helped shape students who often could not be educated at other institutions because of the color of their skin. Legislation has changed since 1837, but current HBCUs still have a similar and vital role consistent with the early days. They often educate and support students who need further academic development or lack financial resources. But even further, schools like Central State University or Fisk University provide young men and women the opportunity to gain a greater sense of identity.

I consistently talk with students about the "value of an education," especially an education that takes place outside of the classroom. The unique social experiences that occur on an HBCU campus are unmatched by other academic institutions. The culture and rich history adjacent to rigorous academic programs and community service opportunities allow students who attend schools like Dillard University or Morehouse College to see beyond the walls of a classroom and into the streets of their local community and communities around the world.

At Prairie View A&M University, we have several initiatives that help us maximize our value as a resource to our community. A faculty member is working to research disparities in health that exist within minority and majority populations, particularly in rural areas. Additionally, engineering students are working to find new ways to keep future astronauts and their flight instruments safe from harmful radiation while in space. The University also works closely with the National Urban League and provides support to the local school districts by way of mentors and volunteers. Prairie View A&M University has partnered with the Federal Democratic Republic of Ethiopia to improve animal health and provide training for sheep and goat producers. Indeed, I am sure that many other HBCUs have similar alliances with global organizations and political leaders and partnerships with foundations and members of the community that they support.

Historically, HBCUs have been a place of respect and dignity. Graduates of schools like Langston University, Arkansas Baptist College, and Denmark Technical College carried themselves differently. They held a sense of pride about their accomplishments, and they labored with purpose. These students had goals and supported one another in spirit, all while recognizing their historic past. HBCU faculty and administrators support students in their efforts by being accessible, caring, and supportive.

As an historian, I am interested in the changes that have occurred over time. It intrigues me that HBCUs have served as the archivists of African-American history. Throughout the years, HBCUs have contributed greatly to society through award-winning writers, athletes, scientists, and researchers, and show-stopping marching band techniques. With limited resources, HBCUs have provided opportunities for young men and women to develop confidence and become productive leaders who are socially and economically responsible. Famous graduates like entrepreneur and philanthropist Oprah Winfrey, U.S. Supreme Court Justice Thurgood Marshall, movie producer Spike Lee, and poets Langston Hughes and Nikki Gionvanni are testaments to the talent HBCUs have produced. ⚏

PREFACE

© 2008 Chris Williams

This publication was borne out of my personal life experience as well as the knowledge gained from producing the Angel City Classic, the largest HBCU event held west of the Mississippi, in Los Angeles, California.

Over the past 40 years, I have been blessed with many gifts, including the gift of family and the opportunity to receive an education that allowed me to be able to compete and work in an ever-changing and competitive society. In late 2005, I decided to retire from the corporate world and devote the rest of my life to causes near and dear to my heart. While many were worthy, one cause lit an enthusiastic fire that has since been raging inside me: the plight of minority youth in urban areas all across America.

I had become increasingly dismayed that the high school dropout rates in urban geographies were fast becoming a blinking red warning light on America! Never before had we experienced such high numbers—dropout rates were, and still are, exceeding 50 percent in many school districts. This was extremely disheartening to me and many others across the nation. In fact, former Secretary of State Colin Powell once declared it a threat to our national security.

When I graduated from high school in Richmond, Virginia, in 1961, the dropout rate was, to the best of my estimate, probably less than 5 percent and certainly no more than 10 percent. Most of my friends were encouraged to continue their education at the many institutions that embraced us and inspired us as young African Americans—our Historically Black Colleges and Universities. I was fortunate enough to be awarded a scholarship to Hampton University, but I chose to pursue a new and exciting opportunity that was then becoming available in the early 1960s—the opportunity to attend a prestigious university outside my home state.

The opportunity to attend of a top five engineering school was appealing to me. However, life in the 1960s was a time of social unrest, with lines drawn between races, and what was afforded to some was not always available for others. My counselors advised me that if I chose to go to college outside of my home state rather than apply to some of the prestigious institutions within the state which were just beginning to accept minorities, that I might be eligible for assistance from the state that would fund, all or part, of my tuition and housing costs. In my case, I chose to take advantage of the opportunity to study outside of my home state. I chose a top five engineering school and spent five plus years receiving a great education in my chosen field, but I also reflect upon those days as being a "social dropout."

Because of this experience, I decided that my children would be exposed to our HBCUs. While the choice was ultimately up to them, I am proud to say that both my son and daughter are graduates of an HBCU— Hampton University and Howard University, respectively. I have witnessed in both of my children, as well as in my nieces, the fruits of educational and cultural experiences that could **only** be gained at an HBCU!

This publication is dedicated to supporting awareness and relevance of our HBCUs. It is my hope that minority youth, particularly in urban areas, will realize there are institutions that will embrace them and treat them as family! **Ħ**

Because of this experience, I decided that my children would be exposed to our Historically Black Colleges and Universities.

John T. Fleming

John T. Fleming
President & CEO
Black Educational Events, LLC

© 2008 Chris Williams

For many, there's a mystique associated with HBCUs. Many don't quite understand what they are or believe that they are "equal" to other major universities. Some don't know that they even exist. Some say that one homecoming is the same as any other, one student union is no different from the next, or one class is just like the next. Most jump onto that college campus with high expectations and an eager ambition to learn something new. I made that jump at Hampton University. With the many expectations I had and the assumptions of what it would be like, nothing could have prepared me for what this school really was like. Even with a grandfather who taught there, the "idea" of what an HBCU was and knowing that the back of the school's campus ended on a beautiful ocean view; I was not prepared for what would come next.

Hampton University took on a fairy-tale-like feel that was part completely unbelievable and another part simply awe-inspiring. The student union was more than a place that served food. It was a Thanksgiving dinner table, where people studied, laughed, celebrated and even cried together like a young boisterous family. Homecoming became a reunion, where current students and alumni celebrated being raised under the same roof with a mutual respect for all things associated with Hampton University. A constant display of Greek colors signified community strength, service, pride, and common bonds. Everywhere one could look there was an invisible cloud of excellence. My teachers challenged me to not only be better, but also prepared me to be a productive and positive black male role model upon graduation. This challenge, they told me, was my primary responsibility and a life-long commitment asked of me on behalf of the university. The classroom was no longer a place of torture for me as a student, but actually a place for disseminating current information, sharing current news from politics to parties, and discussing new ideas. This was an unbelievably *strong* network. The only time I ever felt anything like this was when we would travel to other HBCUs. There is something unique that can't be explained. It had to be experienced in order to be truly understood. I found nothing similar at other schools, and, believe me, there was a major difference.

My HBCU family will forever be my catalyst for productive growth.

I would argue with anyone that pound-for-pound Hampton University and all HBCUs offer an extremely dynamic education that surpasses that obtained by the largest schools in the nation. Compare classroom size to student/teacher ratio, tuition costs, community, and alumni support, and, most importantly, the attention to detail placed on a young *person*—not just an accepted "applicant."

HBCUs are not a reflection of the real world?

I argue that I bleed just like the next man. These schools are as real as it gets and, better yet, even more insightful in preparing you for masked realities. I graduated in four years with a bachelor's degree in mass media and continued what would become a ten-year career in radio, later receiving my MBA. Today, with additional programs added and recent improvements, I would not hesitate to do it all over again in exactly the same manner. Hampton University will always be my "Home By the Sea" and my HBCU family will forever be my catalyst for productive growth.

Because of my respect and value for family, my focus now resides in HBCU Today and the remaining Black Educational Events projects centered on building community strength. It is important for us to understand how HBCUs have reared, preserved, and produced many generals that have ignited change so precisely and strategically that we're living in a time where we are witness to our first black president. This wasn't a recent campaign; it was something with origins that can be traced directly back to our nations HBCUs as they laid this foundation of hope when others would not.

This publication is dedicated to the mothers, fathers, sisters, brothers, uncles, aunts, and best friends who have pushed me as well as to the future prosperity of HBCUs. It is also dedicated to *you*—our future leader—who may find that light at the other end of the tunnel through the information provided within these pages. ⊞

John T. Fleming III, M.B.A.
Executive Vice President
Black Educational Events, LLC

When I arrived at Howard University in the summer of 1988, I did not fully understand the impact that historic institution would have on my life. For my primary and secondary schooling, I attended public and private schools in a predominantly white suburb. I had grown accustomed to being the only person of color in many of my classes. I had focused on academics and worked very hard to get good grades. I had many friends of many different races. Still, something was missing. It was that inner voice and the wisdom of my parents that led me to explore HBCUs.

With an interest in journalism, I gravitated to Howard University and the Washington, D.C., area. On my visits to campus, I was struck by the sense of family felt in the dormitories and in the classrooms. Not only were professors challenging students to think deeply in their search for answers, but the entire classroom was filled with beautiful black people!

As an undergraduate student at Howard, I felt like there wasn't anything I couldn't accomplish in this stimulating learning environment. For the first time, there were no stigmas that I had to fight through. On our first encounters, my teachers did not classify me as academically inferior based upon the color of my skin. Instead, I had professors who celebrated my intellect and pushed me to work harder. They genuinely cared about my success. I felt like I was an integral part of the institution.

I know firsthand the value that HBCUs can have on higher learning experiences. I'll encourage [my daughter] to explore Howard because there is no question in my mind that HBCUs are more than worth it!

Some of my closest friends today are ones that I met during my four years at Howard. I learned how to balance my academic demands and find time to enjoy other hallmarks of the black college experience, including Greek step shows, football games, and dances.

Since graduating from Howard University with honors, I went on to receive a master's degree in education from the University of Pennsylvania as well as a master's degree in administration from Bank Street College. I currently work as an administrator in a private school in New York. I believe the proof of the power of HBCUs lies in the success of each and every graduate.

Today there are 104 HBCUs that count among their graduates trailblazers such as W.E.B. Du Bois (Fisk University), Thurgood Marshall (Lincoln University and Howard University), Toni Morrison (Howard University), and Martin Luther King, Jr. (Morehouse College). This is a far cry from the boxcars and basements that housed the first black colleges in the late nineteenth century. I think Mary McLeod Bethune, one of the nation's foremost black educators, would be very proud.

So where do we go from here? If you are an alum of an HBCU, it is important to keep telling your story and encouraging others to explore HBCUs. It is also equally important to continue to make financial contributions to support HBCUs. If you are a student exploring HBCUs for the first time, seek resources such as this to gather as much data as possible. Most importantly, visit the schools of interest and take the time to observe classes and walk around campus.

As the mother of an eight-year-old daughter growing up in a suburb that looks all too familiar to me, I know firsthand the value that HBCUs can have on her higher-learning experiences. I'll encourage her to explore Howard because there is no question in my mind that HBCUs are more than worth it!

Kassandra Fleming Hayes, M.Ed.
Director of Admissions
The Cathedral School, New York

ACKNOWLEDGMENTS

Many people were involved in the production of this publication, and it is to them that I am indebted for their hard work and devotion to creating a concise research tool that will serve as an invaluable resource to students.

Specifically, I want to thank the following individuals for their tireless efforts: Meta Williams, Nancy Laichas, Erica Jennings, and Judith Emmert.

Finally, I would like to thank all of my family and friends. Your friendship, encouragement, guidance, and advice provided me with the stamina to stay the course and complete this work. This book is a result of our collaboration and our joint commitment to bring forth a better understanding and awareness of our HBCUs.

John T. Fleming

INTRODUCTION

"This is our moment. This is our time to put our people to work and open doors of opportunity for our kids; to restore prosperity and promote the cause of peace; to reclaim the American Dream and affirm that fundamental truth—that out of many, we are one; that while we breathe, we hope; and where we are met with cynicism, and doubt, and those who tell us we can't, we will respond with that timeless creed that sums up the spirit of a people: Yes, we can!"

—President-Elect Barack Obama
Grant Park, Chicago, November 4, 2008

The above words, spoken by then-President-Elect Barack Obama upon winning the presidency of the United States, are a true reflection of the greatness of America and its promise of equal opportunity for all. Even as all Americans celebrate the election of our first African-American president, it behooves us to also reflect on the journey of African Americans in this country. It is one that starts with the forced migration of a people from a motherland to an unknown world ... to subsequent slavery and the ensuing struggle to become free of the chains that bound ... to the new taste of freedom and the unquenchable thirst for learning. That journey's end was the result of courageous, well-educated leaders such as Frederick Douglass, whose influence and eventual friendship with President Abraham Lincoln helped bridge the great divide between white and black, and set a new course for this nation.

The mission associated with this book is this: to enhance awareness of the cultural and educational opportunities offered at our HBCUs, and to show, through articles and profiles, that these great institutions, which have contributed so much to the journey of a people, are as significant and as relevant today as they were when they were first established.

Therefore, we dedicate this book not only to our HBCUs for all that they have contributed to the journey, but also to two other forces that made a significant difference along the way and continue to contribute to the growth of our people today—the African-American Church and the African-American Media. When viewed collectively, these three forces, in our view, are the cornerstones for the continued spiritual, academic, and social development of African Americans.

1. **The African-American Church:** The formation of the first churches was out of necessity—to maintain faith while enduring the most severe challenges—ones that often led to forced hardship and premature death. Without faith, the people perish. Faith kept African Americans alive and full of hope in the darkest of times. The early churches were also, in many cases, the key to creating the first HBCUs.

2. **Historically Black Colleges and Universities:** These schools embraced African Americans when others would not. Without education, the people are doomed to chains forever, shackled by a mental slavery.

3. **African-American Media:** These entities told our stories when no others would. Without light, the people are blinded to the truth. The African-American Media have kept our communities informed even as they have struggled to survive.

And so, we gratefully acknowledge the participation of these three forces in enabling the people to flourish in a foreign land—and experience the election of one of its own as president of the United States of America!

Georgia Youth, 1934
Hale Woodruff
Linocut
17" x 13.25"

Part I:
HBCU Perspectives

The following articles provide insight into the rich historical traditions and cultural impact that HBCUs have left on our educational system and American society as a whole.

Stories on the past, present, and future of HBCUs, as well as insights into the life on campuses—including sports and Greek life—are presented.

We have also included articles on selected programs at eight HBCUs that are allowing students to forge careers in various fields. While these selections represent just a few of the hundreds of programs available, it is our hope that you will gain an understanding of the quality educational opportunities that await you.

HISTORY

Landscape, Autumn, ca. 1865
Robert Scott Duncanson
Oil on board
16.75" x 13.25"

Photo courtesy of Howard University

HBCUs PAST, PRESENT & FUTURE

by Hamil R. Harris

Although students had not yet returned to the Howard University for fall classes, Phil Dixon, chairman of the Journalism Department, was working hard in his campus office and listening intently as Tamika Smith tapped a computer screen and played her radio report about an elderly woman in Las Vegas whose gambling addiction pushed her to the edge of suicide.

Smith, who made the audio report during the National Association of Black Journalists Convention in Las Vegas, is a member of the Howard University Class of 2007. She has earned her degree in broadcast journalism and is preparing to enter the workforce. The report she produced was played nationally on National Public Radio's Next Generation Radio.

"Howard University gave me my life," says Smith, a 22-year-old native of Miami, who had a change of heart about the military after she was offered a scholarship to attend Howard. "I was about to go off to Iraq. I had signed up for the military. I wanted to go to college, but I didn't know how. When I came here, it was the best decision I have ever made in my life."

From freed slaves to a young lady from the streets of Miami, HBCUs have snatched young minds from the brink of despair and given them opportunities for higher learning for decades. Today, Jim Crow is dead, legalized segregation is over, and there is an appearance that the career playing field of success is level. However, professors like Dixon know better. They continue to compete for the brightest minds among us while other bright minds flock to them. For some, education is not about grades but simple economics. They don't have the money to go to college. It is for this reason that HBCUs are more important today than ever.

According to the National Association of Equal Opportunities in Education, HBCUs are disproportionately educating students who come from families with low to moderate incomes. One hundred percent of enrolled students are eligible for the Pell grant in at least five HBCUs—an economic barometer since this award is given to students with low to moderate incomes.

But HBCUs are not just educating students who wouldn't have a chance to go to college otherwise. HBCUs are producing the highest number of African-American Ph.D.s per capita and, according to Grambling University President Horace Judson, at a time when the United States is falling behind China and India in producing engineers and scientists, universities like Grambling have tailor-made their missions to be on the international stage.

"I have a Ph.D. in chemistry, I went to Cornell and Lincoln University, and my provost has a degree in nuclear physics from Morehouse," Judson told *HBCU Today*. "My mission as the president of an HBCU in the twenty-first century is to recognize that it is not an industrial age, but an informational age. The issue today is not whether or not we can get a job in corporate America, the issue is can we be effective and produce in whatever pursuit we choose in the global economy."

From Grambling to Howard, excitement is in the air on the campuses of HBCUs cross the country. With 12,000 students and an endowment of nearly $400 million, Howard University remains one of the top HBCUs in the country. Among the distinguished alumni at the Washington, D.C., institution founded in 1867 are former Ambassador Andrew Young, actresses Debbie Allen and Phylicia Rashad, former Supreme Court Justice Thurgood Marshall, and Black Panther Stokely Carmichael. Howard University leads the country in turning out African-American Ph.D.s.

Making the Choice

As Tamika Smith talked, Phil Dixon smiled without saying a word. Before coming to Howard, he was an award-winning editor at the *Philadelphia Inquirer* and then at the *Washington Post*. Dixon gave up daily journalism to teach future journalists at Howard. "Students like this make it worth it," he says. "You have students who come here who could have gone anywhere. Sometimes parents bang their heads against the wall because the students will get a full ride to MIT or somewhere else and they will say, 'I didn't want to go there, I wanted to come here.'"

Howard is filled with talented students, and some give up lucrative scholarships to larger, state-funded schools to attend this private HBCU. Courtney Holland, 19, a Howard sophomore from Miami, said when she graduated from high school her parents insisted that she cross the Florida state line when it came to going to college. "I said if I am going to indulge in a worthwhile experience then Howard University could provide the best experience," she says.

Holland, who is majoring in accounting, said her decision was costly because she had received a Bright Futures Scholarship that covered 75 percent of the costs if she attended any college in the State of Florida. "Ninety percent of my classmates were going to Florida State University and Florida, but I said that I have all my life to be in a predominantly white world," Holland says.

Even though Ed Holland, a Miami Certified Public Accountant and business owner, graduated from Florida State University with a degree in accounting in 1981, he respected his daughter's decision.

"I think the beauty of it all is that we have a choice today," Holland says. "We fought hard as a people to have a choice, and it was her choice. My wife graduated from Virginia Union, my brothers graduated from Morehouse, and now my daughter Courtney is majoring in accounting at Howard. She specifically wanted to go to Howard because she would be pushed to excel."

Dr. Paula Matabane can relate to Holland's attitude toward HBCUs. Even though she received a B.A. from the University of Pennsylvania and a master's from Stanford University, she came to Howard, where she earned a Ph.D. and master's of divinity. "The University of Pennsylvania, an Ivy League school, prepared me superbly to become an intellectual scholar," Dr. Matabane said, "but the issue of my identity, my place in the world as a scholar and the essential experiences that shaped me, including the experiences and wisdom of my once-enslaved ancestors, were not only ignored but actively discredited.

"Sometimes I look back on my undergrad years and regret not pursuing certain areas of experience," she said. "There was no encouragement to see value in the world I came from or to understand how it formed who I was, who I could be, and how I might make the larger world a better place. At Howard, students are encouraged to bring the totality of themselves into dialogue with their intellectual growth."

HBCUs: A Look Back

Quality HBCU educational experiences are found not just in large, well-endowed private schools like Howard, Hampton or Tuskegee. From North Carolina A&T to

> ## "While all of these institutions were created for the education of freed slaves, they are needed today more than ever to educate all kinds of marginal people, regardless of their race."
>
> —Dr. Barbara R. Hatton, former president of South Carolina State University

Grambling State University, there are strong HBCUs across the country. Many of these state schools were created as "land grant" institutions after the Civil War to educate freed slaves. Today, although their missions have broadened, schools like Florida A&M, Prairie View A&M, Jackson State, Texas Southern University, and Alabama State University still carry the proud HBCU name and traditions.

Prior to the Civil War, it was against the law for slaves to be educated. Although there were exceptions, like self-educated Frederick Douglass, there were almost no formal educational opportunities for people of color. In the early 1830s, a group of Philadelphia Quakers started to educate some blacks at Oberlin College in Ohio and Berea College in Kentucky, but it would take decades of court battles and congressional laws for change to come.

Following the Civil War, Congress passed the 13th Amendment abolishing slavery. In 1862, Senator Justin Morrill led a movement to train Americans in the applied sciences, agriculture, and engineering. The Morrill Land-Grant Act gave federal lands to the states for the purpose of opening colleges and universities. Initially, few opportunities were created for freed slaves, but three decades later, the freedmen finally got their chance when Congress passed the second Morrill Land-Grant Act of 1890.

In the wake of the Morrill Land-Grant Act of 1890, sixteen black institutions opened after they received land-grant funds. The American Missionary Association (AMA) and the Freedmen's Bureau would continue to set up colleges for blacks, and between 1861 and 1870, the AMA founded seven black colleges and thirteen normal (teaching) schools. These institutions would become the bedrock of black higher education. For the next fifty years, HBCUs

would flourish. Although funds were low and students often needed financial support from family and friends, they were getting something more than could be placed in a bank.

In 1928, HBCUs gained more support when the Southern Association of Colleges and Schools began to accredit some schools. Even though the Great Depression and World War II crippled many black institutions, most kept their doors opened thanks to churches, a growing black community, philanthropists, and a new organization called the United Negro College Fund.

In 1954, the historic case Supreme Court Brown v. The Board of Education of Topeka, Kansas, ruled that the nation's "separate but equal" system of education was unconstitutional. The case was won by a group of lawyers trained at Howard University that included a young lawyer by the name of Thurgood Marshall. A decade later, Congress passed the Civil Rights Act of 1964 that gave the federal government greater power to enforce desegregation.

In 1965, the federal government provided additional funding to HBCUs through the Higher Education Act. Then came *Adams v. Richardson*, a Supreme Court decision that found ten states in violation of the Civil Rights Act for supporting segregated schools.

While HBCUs gained in influence and resources because of government mandates and court decisions, in the last two decades, court-issued rulings have threatened the existence of some state-funded HBCUs that have duplicate programs as other state institutions often located in the same areas.

In 1992, the United States Supreme Court ruled in *United States v. Fordice* that dual and segregated educational systems were unconstitutional; since that time, many HBCUs have become more diverse than ever.

A Culture of Inclusion

Dr. Barbara R. Hatton, former president of South Carolina State University, points out that institutions like Florida A&M, Tuskegee, Alabama A&M, South Carolina Sate, and North Carolina A&T have done well because they were federal land-grant institutions dedicated to educating freed slaves. "In the old segregated days you had white land-grant institutions and black institutions, and that funding still exists today," she said.

Even though African-American students have more educational options than ever, many continue to choose HBCUs. Leah Dixon had a briefcase full of college admission letters, but the twenty-year-old from Hampton, Virginia, traveled a few miles away from home and enrolled at Norfolk State University in an historic city that is home to one of the test cases for the landmark *Brown v. Board of Education* desegregation case.

Austin Cobb also had plenty of choices for college, but the nineteen-year-old from Philadelphia headed to Alabama, to Tuskegee University, because he wanted to major in animal science.

And although 19-year-old Paul Henry just wanted to leave New Orleans and go into the Air Force after Hurricane Katrina, a family member convinced him to go to college, so he attended Tuskegee University because he knew he wouldn't be treated like just another student.

Today, the mandate is strong and the mission is undaunted on HBCU campuses across the country. According to each of these students, attending an HBCU has been a life-changing experience that began on the day they arrived on the campus with a big trunk and too many warm sweaters.

Leah Dixon said she went to Norfolk State because, "I got a chance to be around a culture like no other." Cobb is fulfilling his dream of majoring in animal science "because of the warmth of the faculty and staff," and Henry is glad that he didn't go into the Air Force or another school because, "They care about you [here] while at another university you might be just another name."

Rev. Grainger Browning is pastor of the 10,000-member Ebenezer African Methodist Episcopal Church in Fort Washington, Maryland, one of the most affluent predominantly black jurisdictions in the country. Even though his children and many young people in his church could afford to go to any school, Browning is a strong supporter of HBCUs. His father was a professor at Hampton University in the 1960s, and today his son attends Morehouse, and his daughter is a student at Hampton University.

"It was always clear that I was going to Hampton to be free of not having to deal with racism," said Browning. "It changed my life. I had never been in a position of leadership. You have to be able to go as far as you can with nothing being able to stop you but you."

Impact on History

While alumni and students talk about their affinities for HBCUs, these institutions offer more than warm and fuzzy anecdotes of success. The glaring reality is that without the role and function of HBCUs, the landscape of America would be quite different. Had it not been for the desire of Heman Marion Sweat and a rejection letter from the University of Texas Law School, there would not have been a Texas Southern Law School. Had there not been a Dr. Benjamin Mays at Morehouse, there might not have

been a Martin Luther King, Jr. Had there not been a George Washington Carver at Tuskegee, there might not have been a Skippy peanut butter or a Ponds cold cream.

The nation's 104 HBCUs are having an impact beyond just educating young people. According to a 2006 report released by the National Center for Educational Statistics, the combined spending of all 101 HBCUs was $6.6 billion in 2001, and of this amount, 62 percent was spent by public HBCUs. Collectively, HBCUs would rank 232 on *Forbes* Fortune 500 companies. The report goes on to say these schools are not just producing graduates—they have a tremendous economic impact on the communities in which they are located.

According to the report, the 104 HBCUs pumped $4 billion in the labor economy, creating 180,142 full- and part-time jobs. The impact of these institutions was particularly significant in smaller communities. For example, in Tuskegee, Alabama, Tuskegee University hires more than 2,100 workers and accounts for 24 percent of the town's entire labor force. The job picture is similar in Grambling, Louisiana, where Grambling State University employs about 10 percent of the town's workforce.

The 10 largest public HBCUs that are having an economic impact in their community include Florida A&M ($432 million), North Carolina A&T ($298 million), Tennessee State University ($289 million), Southern University ($267 million), Texas Southern ($254 million), Morgan State University ($252 million), Jackson State University ($249 million), Prairie View A&M ($231 million), Norfolk State University ($194 million), and North Carolina Central ($178 million). The largest private schools economically are Howard University ($1.2 billion), Hampton University ($227 million), Clark Atlanta University ($227 million), Meharry Medical College ($173 million), and Xavier University of Louisiana ($154 million). The report also states that the Morehouse School of Medicine and Morehouse College accounted for $212 million combined.

HBCUs Today and Tomorrow.

Dr. Barbara R. Hatton says if HBCUs are to thrive in the future they must obtain additional resources, reassess their core missions, and adapt to changing times.

"The truth is unless some of these institutions can redirect themselves to the original mission while at the same time refitting that mission to today's culture and needs, some of them will not survive," Hatton said. "While all of these institutions were created for the education of freed slaves, they are needed today more than ever to educate all kinds of marginal people, regardless of their race."

From Grambling to North Carolina A&T and from Tennessee State to Florida A&M, every fall thousands of alumni and fans returned to their old schools to enjoy all of the bands, fashion, and pageantry of black college football games. University officials point out that these stadiums are filled with African American professionals who earned degrees from HBCUs, and many of these people would have never gotten a chance to attend college had it not been for the efforts of an HBCU.

When many people think about Grambling University they often bring up the name of legendary football coach Eddie Robinson and all of the great football classics that the team has been part of over the years, but Grambling is more than just a football power or a Saturday afternoon experience. The university offers seventy-five undergraduate and graduate degree programs through their colleges of Business, Education, Arts & Sciences, Professional Studies, and School of Graduate and Research. In addition, Grambling has the only doctoral program in developmental education in the nation.

From the opening of its new Center for Mathematics Achievement in Science and Technology—that was funded by a $2.4 million National Science Foundation grant—to the creation of the Summer Institute on World Literature that, in 2007, featured eight prominent literature scholars from across the country who spent several weeks discussing the works of Homer, Dante, Christine de Pizan, and Shakespeare, there is plenty of action going on at Grambling away from the football field.

Grambling, under the leadership of President Horace Judson, has been on the move since he arrived three years ago. Some of Judson's projects include increasing the diversity of the student body, crafting a master plan for the institution, and overseeing the construction of Tiger Village, a state-of-the-art, 1,200-bed, apartment-style dormitory that opened in the fall of 2007. In addition, Judson and his administration embraced new academic standards handed down by Louisiana's Board of Regents that actually raised admission requirements for students coming to the school.

"The real strength of American higher education is diversity," Judson told *HBCU Today*. "We come at diversity from a different angle. We can't forget that 60 percent of the world is not white and not Christian. Our goal is to be very relevant in the global community. Since I have been here, we have increased the number of international students from forty to more than 300. We have a mission not just to educate African-American students but to help our students achieve cultural competence."

Judson went onto say that students from thirty different countries are now matriculating at Grambling and 40 to 45 percent of the school's faculty is non-African American. He says while the university is proud of its rich history and legacy, it is equally important that they know the Grambling that extends far beyond the football field and the famous football teams that made the late Eddie Robinson the winningest football coach in history.

"It is critically important for people to know that throughout our history, Grambling has been about the pursuit of academic excellence, but the broad society has not looked at us in that way," Judson said. "Our focus is to strengthen our academic programs. We are going to make those programs stronger and stronger. We are focusing on national problems."

Overcoming Challenges

While HBCUs provide a tremendous opportunity, they also have a big challenge of gleaning critical resources to keep their doors open. "There is a tremendous pressure on small private colleges because of the cost of education today," Judson said. "Their financial support has eroded because of the way they used to get their money from the churches; today there is also a tremendous competition for students."

But despite this challenge, Judson says larger private institutions show that it can be done. He pointed out that institutions like Howard, Hampton, Morehouse, and Spelman have been successful not just because they have great academic reputations, but the leaders of these schools have worked for decades to build large endowments, with the money for these schools generated from the interest of these funds. He says the key for all HBCUs is to adapt to present times because the mission has changed.

Although Grambling is a public school, Judson says it still is important that funds be raised to finance school programs. He has established an endowment and would like to raise $30 million to fund the university's programs. "We are an institution now that is relevant for the twenty-first century," Judson says. "We are inclusive, and we are more effective in the way that we function, providing strong and effective leaders who are also culturally competent." ⌶⌶

Hamil R. Harris is an award-winning writer and reporter for The Washington Post.

HBCUs: OUR PROUD HERITAGE

by Rev. Eric Lee

The following is a speech given by Reverend Eric Lee, President and CEO of the Southern Christian Leadership Conference of Greater Los Angeles, on Martin Luther King, Jr.'s birthday on January 13, 2008.

In 1837, Cheyney University was founded and later designated as the first Historically Black College and University. It wasn't until 1865, at the end of Civil War and passing of the 13th Amendment ending slavery, that the establishment of the HBCUs continued with the pace necessary to meet the growing need and desire of African Americans to participate

History shows that when our people are lifted up, the entire nation—even the world—will be lifted up.

in the pursuit of academic excellence. The social and economic conditions that African Americans existed in gave birth to the mission, purpose, and motive of the Historically Black Colleges AND Universities.

Rev. Eric Lee, President/CEO of the Southern Christian Leadership Conference of Greater Los Angeles

The universal mission of HBCUs is to provide quality educational environments for African Americans. The purpose was to ensure that the educational experience reflected the cultural pride and historical greatness of our existence and that the curriculum was culturally relevant to African-American experiences. The motive was to develop productive, creative, intellectually engaging, socially responsible, morally centered black folk who would contribute to the land that our ancestors were brought to … contribute to a land and nation that, at that time did not offer its citizens of color equal educational opportunity.

The result of the birth of Historically Black Colleges and Universities was W.E.B. Du Bois from Fisk University; Toni Morrison, Nobel Laureate and Pulitzer Prize-winning author and Zora Neal Hurston, author, both from Howard University; Hildrus Poindexter, physician and scientist, and Langston Hughes, poet and playwright, both from Lincoln University; Thurgood Marshall, first African-American United States Supreme Court Justice, Lincoln University and Howard Law School; Spike Lee, filmmaker, and Samuel L. Jackson, actor, Morehouse College. My cousin, Maynard Jackson, mayor of Atlanta, Morehouse College and North Carolina Central; L. Douglas Wilder, first African-American governor of Virginia, Virginia Union University and Howard Law School; Medgar Evers, Freedom Rider—NAACP, Alcorn College; and as we remember the 40th anniversary of the assassination of Dr. Martin Luther King, Jr., and celebrate his life and legacy, we must remember that he is a son of Morehouse College.

Historically Black Colleges and Universities were birthed out of necessity to provide African Americans with a vehicle to demonstrate our greatness, our excellence, and our value and worth to this world. As we are in 2009, forty years after the assassination of Dr. Martin Luther King, Jr., … forty-four years after the *Brown vs. the Board of Education* decision strik-

ing down the concept of a separate but equal education … forty-four years after the civil rights legislation banning segregation in education, we find that the necessity of providing our people with a vehicle to demonstrate our greatness is more critical now than ever before.

When the University of California at Los Angeles admits only ninety-six African-American students out of 5,000 freshman in a fall 2006 class, twenty of which were recruited athletes, and claim that they cannot find academically qualified students but can find them to generate revenues by running up and down a football field, basketball court, or around a track, HBCUs are needed now more than ever before. And, when we send our ninety-six sons and daughters to an environment where they are not welcome, or considered the products of entitlements, we need to reassess whether the academic experience will benefit or harm our children.

When public schools K–12 are experiencing a 50–60 percent dropout rate, HBCUs are needed more now than ever before to reach out to our communities and our children with the mission of providing a quality educational environment and the purpose of making the curriculum culturally relevant. The history of our struggle in this country will not permit us to fail our children. The history of our struggle will only permit us to push our children to go further than the previous generation.

When our children and communities are seeking to recapture our identity as a proud and noble people with moral integrity, HBCUs are needed more now than ever to provide us with the vehicle of restoration. The education provided by Historically Black Colleges and Universities is more than an intellectual exercise. HBCUs provide our children with the necessary cultural education that ultimately reclaims, restores, and retains our proud heritage.

In conclusion, we must recommit ourselves, churches, community-based organizations, civil rights organizations, and Historically Black Colleges and Universities to working together to uplift our people. History shows that when our people are lifted up, the entire nation—even the world—will be lifted up.

Historically Black Colleges and Universities should not be considered the alternative education for our children, but the *imperative* when seeking institutions of higher learning! ▞

HISTORY

HBCU ALUMNI SHARE SUCCESS:
Breeding Ground for Excellence in Life

by Erin Casey

Though his football skills in high school were impressive, as a young black player with only a few years of the sport under his belt, Walter Payton wasn't heavily recruited by major universities. So instead of attending a larger school, Payton chose an historically black school close to home, Jackson State University. For Payton, the decision was a smart one.

While some people speculate Payton would have received greater notoriety early on had he attended a larger, well-known university, his outstanding academic and athletic performance put him in the spotlight. He broke an NCAA record, rushing for sixty-five touchdowns during his college career. He graduated from Jackson State with a bachelor's in communications in 1975 and was the Chicago Bear's first-round draft pick that season.

The football legend left his mark on the sport and the world around him. During his thirteen-year career with the Bears, Payton amassed ten NFL records. He was known his success and for the way he carried himself, both on and off the field. Outside of football, Payton was a both a businessman and a philanthropist. His business interests included real estate, construction, restaurants, and auto racing. In 1998, Walter and his wife, Connie, began the Walter and Connie Payton Foundation to help abused, neglected, and underprivileged children in Illinois. Payton's legacy of strength and determination live on through his memory long after cancer took his life

Payton's story is echoed by millions of successful HBCU graduates. Professional athletes, congressmen and women, business leaders, entertainers—countless successful men and women across the nation and around the world got their start at HBCUs. Without a doubt, these traditionally smaller but culturally rich schools provide students with a well-rounded education and a strong foundation on which to build a successful future.

One HBCU alumni is arguably one of America's most influential people. Oprah Winfrey's focus on speech communications and theater at Tennessee State University set the stage for her unparalleled career. Winfrey grew up poor but was an avid learner who, even as a toddler, loved the center stage. Despite a rocky start, Winfrey has far surpassed others' expectations.

Her delivery of a short speech titled "The Negro, the Constitution and the United States" earned Winfrey a $1,000 scholarship, which opened the door for her to attend Tennessee State University. At age nineteen, during her sophomore year and on the advice of one of her professors, she accepted a job as the co-anchor for a CBS affiliate in Nashville and began her television career.

In the decades that have followed, Winfrey's career as a talk show host, entertainer, and phenomenally successful businesswomen and philanthropist has cemented her place in history. And like so many HBCU graduates, Winfrey remembers the challenges she faced by using her wealth to help others.

Why Attend an HBCU

For some students, HBCUs' lower tuition rates make the dream of attending college more financially attainable. Smaller class sizes and the opportunity to connect with both students and teachers appeals to others. And many black students are drawn to HBCUs because of the unique environment they provide.

That environment was one reason District Heights, Maryland, Mayor James Walls, Jr., a Bowie State University graduate, chose to attend an HBCU. "I graduated from Gwynn Park High school, which had a larger white population, and I wanted to be in a different environment," Walls said. "For me, the best setting was an HBCU. I chose Bowie State and found it to be quite rewarding."

At Bowie State, Walls found small class sizes, which gave him the opportunity to get to know the faculty. "There weren't 500 people in my introductory courses like there are at some schools," Walls said. "I got an opportunity to do a lot of networking, and the faculty members were very helpful and friendly. One of the vice

STRONG FOUNDATION, BIG SUCCESS

Countless HBCU graduates have used their college experience as a launch pad and achieved amazing success. The list of notable HBCU graduates is extensive, and knowing that attending an HBCU had a role in their rise is a great marketing and recruiting tool. Following are just a few of those who have made a name for themselves:

In 2004, *People Magazine* listed Kenny Leon as one of the 50 Most Beautiful People, but looks aren't the only thing this prominent, Tony award-winning, Broadway director is famous for. He is the co-founder and artistic director of True Colors Theatre Company and principal of KLProductions. Leon graduate from Clark University with a degree in political science and a minor in theatre.

Novelist and editor Toni Morrison graduated from Howard University with a degree in English in 1953. She was awarded the Pulitzer Prize for fiction for her 1988 novel, *Beloved,* and in 1993 she became the first African-American woman to receive the Nobel Prize for literature.

R&B songstress Sunshine Anderson was discovered while she was humming a song, waiting in line in the cafeteria at North Carolina Central University where she received a bachelor of science degree in criminal justice.

Earl G. Graves, founder and publisher of *Black Enterprise,* received a bachelor of arts degree in economics from Morgan State University in 1958. His admirable and entrepreneurial career, like his magazine, serves as an inspiration to many. In 2002, *Fortune* named Graves one of the 50 most powerful and influential African Americans in corporate America. He supports higher education and equal opportunity and has donated more than $1 million to Morgan State University. In appreciation, Morgan State renamed its business and management school the Earl G. Graves School of Business and Management.

Erykah Badu, one of the best American neo-soul, R&B/hip-hop artist whose work crosses over into jazz, studied theater at Grambling State University. She is best known for her singles "You Got Me," her collaboration with The Roots, as well as her own songs "Tyrone," "Next Lifetime," "On & On", and "Clevah." Her lyrics are highly personal urban philosophies that throw emotional challenges in the face of the listener.

Actress and singer Taraji Henson, who worked as a cruise ship entertainer and at the Pentagon before becoming an actress, holds a degree in theater arts from Howard University. Henson has appeared in such films as *Baby Boy* (2001), *Hustle & Flow* (2005), and *Four Brothers* (2005), and was a cast member on Lifetime Television's *The Division.*

Singer, songwriter, actress, and five-time Grammy winner Toni Braxton has had a roller-coaster career. Despite many challenges, Braxton, who attended Bowie State University, made history when it was announced in May 2006 by the Flamingo Hotel and Casino in Las Vegas that Braxton would replace Wayne Newton as the casino's new headlining act starting August 2006. The show, "Toni Braxton: Revealed," became the first headlining show from an African-American performer in Vegas to enter the Top 10 Vegas show's charting and was extended several times.

presidents was a young African-American male who took me under his wing, mentored me, and gave me a job working in student services."

Walls made the most of his undergraduate experience. He was involved in the student government association, was the campus NAACP president, and was a resident advisor in one of the dorms. He was (and remains) an active member of the Iota Phi Theta Fraternity (ΙΦΘ). "I had an opportunity to experience what I think college life should be. I was surrounded by good people, people who were genuinely concerned about me and my educational goals," he says.

Walls received a bachelor of arts in history and pre-law and went on to earn a master's in arts and doctor of ministry in pastoral counseling degree from Richmond Virginia Seminary. His education has served him well. At age twenty-eight, Walls made history in May 2006 when he was elected mayor of District Heights—the youngest mayor ever to be elected in that state.

Many students, like Walls, appreciate the close-knit atmosphere of HBCUs. "If someone is looking for a place that is more personal, a warm atmosphere, an HBCU like Bowie State might be a good option," Walls said. "Sometimes it's better to be in a smaller environment where people can pay attention to you and your growth. Their main intention is to help you succeed. They take a personal interest in each student, and it's up to the student to decide what to do with that." ⊞

HISTORY

RIGHT HERE, RIGHT NOW:
Belle—A Clarion Call for Excellence and Equality

by Dr. Julianne Malveaux

The following text is from the March 29, 2008, inaugural remarks of Dr. Julianne Malveaux, upon her installment as the fifteenth president of Bennett College For Women.

I am humbled today as I reflect on the history and heritage for which I am truly blessed, the history and heritage that I honor and that led me, in so many ways, to this role at Bennett College for Women. Many years ago, I met Dr. Dorothy Irene Height in an airport terminal. At the time, I was contemplating pledging Delta Sigma Theta Sorority. I was all of nineteen, and I had no way of knowing that this gracious and extraordinary leader would become and remain such an important part of my life. Dr. Height reminds us "black women don't do what they want to do, but what they have to do." Thank you, Dorothy Height.

Susan Taylor and I also go "way back," and the constant between us has been the way I have always been touched by her grace, gentle spirit, and uplifting words. Sue has chosen a new path and committed her substantial energy to service of our at-risk youth through her National Mentoring Cares Movement, and our nation will be grateful for the difference that she makes.

Dr. Maya Angelou, whose rich love and resonant voice has been such a blessing to all of us. We thank you and acknowledge your generosity to Bennett College for Women. Dr. Maya serves on our board of trustees and continues to inspire all who come to know her.

Mrs. Cora Masters Barry, whose tenacious zeal for transforming young lives, is infectious. Her youth advocacy has made a tremendous difference to so many, including some present here today.

We have to look back to move forward. To prepare for this speech, it will surprise few to learn that I started with my nose in a book. I specifically set a day aside to read Paula Giddings' excellent new biography of Ida B. Wells, *Ida: A Sword Among Lions*. Why Ida B. Wells? Because in so many ways her story, speaks to the passion for justice, the resilient

Dr. Julianne Malveaux, 15th President, Bennett College For Women

determination to be heard, the audacity to believe that pen and voice make a difference, the temerity to conquer every challenge. The Ida B. Wells story is the African-American woman's story, a story of determination, of achievement against all odds, a story of overcoming so very much in order to make a lasting contribution to a people. Ida B. Wells was born in 1862; Bennett College in 1873. What is the connection?

The Bennett story formally began in 1873, but it really began the first time that enslaved women demanded knowledge, the first time that—despite the law—somebody taught somebody else to read. We may not know the names of the teachers or the students because history belongs to those who write it; history too often swallows black women's lives. But there is Phyllis Wheatley, our first published poet. Who taught her? There is Maria Stewart, the first black woman to lecture about women's rights, especially the rights of black women, and the first black woman public speaker. And there is Harriet Jacobs, the Edenton, North Carolina, enslaved woman who wrote *Incidents in the Life of a Slave Girl* in

1861. How did this woman, born in North Carolina in 1813, manage to learn to read, to write, to publish? In her book, *Self-Taught: African American Education in Slavery and in Freedom,* UNC Chapel Hill Professor Andrea Williams writes that the law prevented enslaved people from learning, but we did it anyway.

This excitement of dissatisfaction, the will to read, to break the law to read, were the very seeds harvested when former slaves sat in the unpaved basement of St. Matthews church and planned the development of this college.

This excitement of dissatisfaction was the forerunner, the foundation, of the clarion call that is issued today, an urgent call for all of us to move closer to excellence and equality, right here, right now.

What is the urgency? These times dictate an urgency. Our country will suffer economically unless we choose to invest in the educational enterprise, to value what every single brain brings to the table. Of course, we have come a long way. But China, India, and Eastern Europe out-produce the United States in math, science, and engineering. Our economy is shedding jobs as millions contemplate home foreclosures and bankruptcy. More than 8 million Americans who want work can't find it.

There are not enough words to fully describe my immediate predecessor, Dr. Johnetta Betch Cole. The sister had fully contributed in her brilliant leadership of Spelman College and in her contribution to her field of anthropology. Her book, *Gender Talk,* importantly looked at the discrimination that exists into our own black community, a sexism that is woven into the very fabric of our being. Was that enough? No, Dr. Cole came out of retirement to lead Bennett College during its time of need. She tirelessly traveled from city to city, raising money and awareness of our beloved oasis. She established a diversity institute that, though now independent from the college, has left a series of signature programs on campus, including a diversity lecture series, a professor of diversity in residence, and a group of diversity scholars. Dr. Cole rescued Bennett College at one of its bleakest periods in history. We are forever grateful.

We issue a clarion call for excellence and equality at a time when our nation seems to be moving away from both. We make excuses for financial institutions but impose standards on our nation's colleges and universities. If Bear Stearns can get a bailout, can Bennett get a break on some of our financing? We have zero tolerance for children who act out but due process for grown folks who ought to know better. We have state-of-the-art jails and crumbling schools. So where do we go from here? How do we move our college

from good to great? What special skills must young women have as they move into the 21st century? How will our college look in a decade?

We move forward, embracing excellence, equality, and the ferocious pace of change that is transforming our world. We move forward, dedicated to the finest forms of communications excellence, teaching, and speaking and writing, organized in learning communities and campus sister circles, such as those we started this semester to discuss Zora Neal Hurston's *Their Eyes Were Watching God* as part of the Big Read Program. We understand fully that communications skills are at the base of this endeavor.

We move our college from good to great by implementing academic programs, which reflect the challenges our students will face in the future. In order to do this, we must raise funds for endowed chairs, we must attract and retain the best faculty, the best students and administrators. We must invigorate campus life by renovating our buildings and planning for the construction of dormitories, a performing arts center, and additional classroom space. We must increase our investment in and use of technology.

We move from good to great understanding that political, social, cultural, spiritual, and economic ties bind us to people around the world, and our curriculum must reflect that. We build our global studies program so that Bennett Belles are global Belles. We have begun to build this year, with our visiting professor Cheryl McQueen providing a lecture series on China. Additionally, members of our team, Provost Marilyn Mobley, Dr. Gwenn Bookman, Cinnamon Hunter, and others have been actively engaged in the Salzburg Center, improving our capacity in global studies. Yesterday, Rosa Whitaker, one of our Women with the Audacity to Excel Honorees, offered to work with us on our global studies offerings. And we are grateful for the involvement of former Assistant Secretary of State for Africa, Constance Berry Newman, in the work of Bennett College.

We must learn the world even as we cease to lead the world. The dollar is no longer king—more people hold euros than dollars. Our economy is decoupling from markets overseas, with global economies growing by as much as 10 percent while ours stumbles along with 2 or 3 percent growth, at best. And trade accounts for as much as 20 percent of our GDP. Once, other economies were dependent on us. Soon, if we are not careful, we will be dependent on others. Indeed, once a U.S. recession could signal challenges around the world. Now, with a rising Chinese middle class, that country could be unaffected by a recession in this country.

How do we move our campus from good to great? By embracing the mandate of global studies and preparing our students for a global world. To prepare our students for a global economy, we must also expose them to entrepreneurial possibilities. Indeed, as the economy fails to generate enough good jobs, it is critical that creative souls understand the value of entrepreneurship in developing opportunities both for self and community. African-American women own fewer than 2 percent of our nation's businesses, yet we again stand on powerful shoulders as we develop entrepreneurial acumen. The Madame C.J. Walker story is well-known. Less well-known is Maggie Lena Walker, the Richmond woman who, in 1903, formed the St. Luke Penny Savings Bank, which is now the Consolidated Bank and Trust Company, the oldest continually African- American-operated bank in the United States. Cathy Liggins Hughes took one radio station and turned it into a publicly traded, multimedia empire of seventy stations, the largest African-American-controlled media company in the nation. This is the entrepreneurship our students must emulate, and we are committed to exploring an academic and practical foundation for that.

How do we move from good to great? We are building an oasis, a sacred space where women can grow and learn and thrive. We are building a national center for African-American women, we can study those issues that affect us and, that by extension, shape the world. In this political context, one of my foci has been the third burden that African-American women face, the extent to which it is foolhardy to ask African-American women to choose between race and gender as they make political, economic, and social decisions. Race and gender only partly explain African-American women's reality.

We do this work with our history as a backdrop, the backdrop of belle, of Bennett Belle. What does it mean to be a Belle in the twenty-first century? It means to be distinguished, impactful, focused, and transformative. The Belle once distinguished herself with her hat and gloves worn, once even brandished, like armor. Hats and gloves meant respectable. Hats and gloves were a way to insist, no, to demand, respect. Hats and gloves on black women in the '20s, '30s, and '40s were a signal to the outside world. "We learned your rules, we played your game, now give me my respect." Hats and gloves here at the Carolina Theatre, where once we had to enter through the side door to a segregated balcony if we wanted to enjoy a movie.

Hats and gloves were a cry, an utterance, and a cleverly disguised revolutionary act. A clarion call in and of themselves. An insistence for equality, for excellence. A way to excite dissatisfaction. They were the educated woman's way of speaking in the words of Sojourner Truth, "Ain't I a woman? I have plowed and planted and not a man could head me, and ain't I a woman?"

Consider Willa Player. Taking homework to jail, the demure, pristine, gloved Willa Player, the gentle manner no mask for her commitment to her college, commitment to our people. Consider Ida B. Wells. Always fighting. Always impeccably attired. Gloves, protection. Gloves, part of Paul Dunbar's mask—"we wear the mask that grins and lies that hides our cheeks and shades our eyes." The mask. The gloves. The bellow. The bell. It takes no gloved hand to ring the bell today. We don't need hats and gloves as armor.

Now we are armed with our intellects, with our educations, with our excellence, our academic achievement, our commitment to no less than the transformation of a society that places a third burden on our shoulders.

Bell. An instrument that produces a ringing sound when struck. My sisters, we have been struck. We are struck by economic injustice and by struggles for educational access. Each of you is struck every day by the inhospitable way in which women, and especially African-American women, are marginalized by a culture that has reduced us to hip-swaying, neck-rolling caricatures. Struck by the gratuitous violence that so many of us are subjected to—can somebody say Megan Williams—and the extent to which male leaders turn silently away from this violence. And we respond with a ringing sound. A ringing sound of activism. A clarion call of commitment. I've been called a firebrand, and I claim that. On fire for Bennett. On fire with meaning. On fire with caring. On fire and exciting dissatisfaction. On fire and ferocious enough to make our fire a clarion call for growth, excellence, and equality. We Belles—and though I am not an alumna, I am, indeed, a Belle—speak out for educational access and affordability. We speak out for social and economic justice. We speak out for the homeless. We speak out for the hungry. We speak out for those who lack health insurance. We speak, requiring that our nation become just, that it makes room for us, for our time, talent, and achievement. We speak out, especially in a global context, where we realize that our sisters around the globe face economic disadvantages that make our challenges look minor.

How do we move from good to great? Exciting dissatisfaction. Answering the clarion call. Excellence and equality. Right here. Right now. 🎗

Photo courtesy of Morehouse College

Martin Luther King, Jr. International Chapel at Morehouse College

SAVED, SEALED, DELIVERED:
Martin Luther King, Jr.'s Papers Are Home

by Shaneesa N. Ashford

It was 9:30 P.M. on June 23, 2006, when the call came in. After much wheeling and dealing, the personal papers of one of the greatest leaders of the twentieth century would have a new home: Morehouse College.

Evidence of the importance of the Morehouse College Martin Luther King, Jr. Collection can be found in the entities that wanted it, and the entities that ultimately got it. Scheduled to be auctioned by Sotheby's on June 30, the collection was coveted by many institutions, including the Smithsonian Institution in Washington, D.C., and Boston University, where King received his doctorate in systematic theology in 1955.

However, it was Mayor Shirley Franklin who, intent on keeping the collection in Atlanta, rallied several public and private entities to produce funding to purchase the collection. In a deal sealed at the proverbial eleventh hour, the papers were saved from the auction block. Morehouse became owner of the 10,000-piece collection. Since that day, the college prepared to house the collection, deemed one of the most important in recent history.

From Average Man to Morehouse Man

King was one of many men in his family to attend Morehouse, including his grandfather, Adam Daniel

"Because of the pivotal role Morehouse played in Dr. King's development, we believe there is no better place in the world for his papers to reside."

—President Walter E. Massey

Williams, class of 1898, father Martin Luther King Sr. '30, brother A.D. Williams King '60, son Martin Luther King III '79, and son Dexter Scott King, who attended from 1979 to 1984.

At Morehouse, King was a normal student, graduating with a "C" average. He enjoyed singing, loved football, and practiced chivalry at every turn. But perhaps what is more interesting is that the man who would come to be known as one of the greatest orators of the twentieth century entered many speech contests on campus but never won.

Yet, said Lawrence Carter, dean of King Chapel, his education and experiences at Morehouse provided King with the tools needed in other phases of his life.

"Those attempts at trying—he built on those and was quite successful, because he was the class speaker when he graduated from Crozier Theological Seminary," Carter said. "So you get the impression of how well he did after he left Morehouse—at Crozier and at Boston— that what he got at Morehouse was cumulative."

During his time at Morehouse, King became exposed to various philosophies on the human condition through sociology courses with department chair Walter Chivers and weekly chapel addresses by his mentor, Benjamin E. Mays, the sixth president of Morehouse.

"We know there was a mindset in the faculty at Morehouse that was determined to produce a generation of graduates who would become the still, small whisper of the mighty wind that would blow down the walls of segregation," Carter said.

Through his education at Morehouse, King was exposed to the teachings of Mahatma Gandhi and Henry David Thoreau, whose "Essay on Civil Disobedience" helped to shape King's ideals. Carter said these ideals, as told through papers in the King Collection, provide a blueprint for a modern America.

"King offered a more noble vision of what is possible that will affirm the dignity of difference, demonstrate more diversity, more maturity, more humanity, even for our oppressors," he said. "What makes these papers and Martin Luther King, Jr. so significant is that he provides us the case for a more peaceful way to conflict resolution between groups, between individuals, between nations."

Under the Cloak of ... Daylight

The collection of significant papers arrived on September 14 amid very little fanfare. Representatives from Morehouse and Woodruff watched as a delivery truck pulled up to the Robert W. Woodruff Library and unloaded seventy-one boxes containing report cards, telegrams, sermon notes, even a briefcase—all of which were unloaded and moved to the archiving area for processing. There, Brenda S. Banks, former deputy director of the Georgia Department of Archives and History and chief archivist for the papers, cataloged the boxes, arranging them for effective sorting.

"This, of course, is a very significant collection of a person who actually changed the way most of us see life, what we do, what we know in terms of our education, our lifestyles as African Americans," Banks said. "It gives me a great deal of joy to even be associated with it."

But what was actually in the boxes? Loretta Parham, Woodruff's CEO and library director, opened the first box, discovering a typed copy of King's "The Montgomery Story," the speech he gave to more than 1,000 delegates at the 47th NAACP convention in San Francisco in 1956.

And then, the group realized what scholars for years to come will discover: this collection, containing thousands of pieces of paper, offers insight into the thoughts of a man who would later lead a revolution of non-violence and command the attention and respect of the world.

Presenting to the World

Twenty-five days later, the Martin Luther King, Jr. Collection was officially presented to the world. During a press conference on October 9, 2006, representatives from the college, the City of Atlanta, Woodruff Library, and the King family were on hand to celebrate the papers' arrival.

A proud President Walter E. Massey, class of '58, said the college was honored to serve as the home of the papers of one of the college's most outstanding alumni.

"It was here that he was introduced to the ideals that would form the basis of his philosophy of non-violent social change—ideals that provided the energy and the inspiration for the civil rights movement in the United States and for similar movements for social justice and equality around the world," Massey said. "Because of the pivotal role Morehouse played in Dr. King's development, we believe there is no better place in the world for his papers to reside."

Mayor Franklin, who began her talk by quoting the civil rights leader, thanked the major players in the deal, including SunTrust, who agreed to provide the $32 million loan to purchase the collection, and the Community Foundation of Greater Atlanta, who created the company that purchased the papers and will transfer the title to Morehouse after the loan is paid off.

Franklin also acknowledged the guarantors and donors of the collection, who include AirTran, Arthur M. Blank, BellSouth, the Coca-Cola Co., the Ludacris Foundation, and Radio One.

Ambassador Andrew Young, who worked directly with King during the civil rights movement, said that Morehouse was always considered the home of the papers.

"This was truly one of Coretta's initial visions—that the papers reside at Morehouse College," Young said. "I think [Martin] knew, and she knew, what was happening at [each point] in history, and we needed to preserve it. This is our history, not black history. It's history; it's Atlanta's history."

"This, of course, is a very significant collection of a person who actually changed the way most of us see life, what we do, what we know in terms of our education, our lifestyles as African Americans."

—Brenda S. Banks, former deputy director of the Georgia Department of Archives

"This is our history, not black history. It's history; it's Atlanta's history."

—Ambassador Andrew Young

The Work Begins

Once the papers arrived, Banks and the archivists at Woodruff had a large task at hand. The standard procedures for processing the collection include receipt, accession, arrangement and description of the collection pieces, and re-housing of the collection into standard archival folders and boxes. The archivists also oversee the repair and conservation of the items and digitize or copy each item to establish a long-term facsimile of the materials.

"To be involved in the care, preservation, and provision of scholarly access to the manuscripts, writings, and books of the Morehouse College Martin Luther King, Jr. Collection is of historical significance and a privilege," said Woodruff's Parham. "The City of Atlanta and the world can rest assured that this collection is in good hands."

While the collection was processed, a national advisory committee, chaired by Lonnie Bunch, director of the Smithsonian Institution's Museum of African-American History and Culture, advised the college on ways to provide scholarly access to the papers. To ensure that the community is able to view the papers and benefit from the experience of seeing King's works, Morehouse partnered with various groups and organizations, including the Atlanta History Center, to sponsor educational events and exhibits. The first exhibit was held at the Atlanta History Center in January 2007, around the civil rights icon's birthday and national King Holiday.

But, according to Phillip Howard, Morehouse's vice president for Institutional Advancement, the group who will truly benefit from the collection is the students.

"[The collection] allows us to provide another academic component to enhance courses and provide additional courses," he said. "But it also gives a 3D view of who King was. You see King in a wholly different way, and the students will be able to have that kind of dimension during a time of their discovery and inquiry." **⊞**

HISTORY

BLACK LEGACY ORGANIZATIONS:
Still Key to the Success of HBCUs

by Meta Williams

During the civil rights movement and in the years since, tens of thousands of community-based organizations have formed that are dedicated to the fight for freedom, access, and equality. But it is the African-American legacy, or affinity, organizations that are still a chief mobilizing force around important issues facing black people. Nowhere is this more apparent than in the role legacy groups play in helping to keep the power, legacy, and value of HBCUs alive and thriving.

The historic reality of Barack Obama's election to the presidency is still unfolding all around the world and is ushering in a perceptible shift in how black people are perceived. People of color around the globe have a new-found of sense of pride and belief in their own possibilities. Yet the pride felt among African-American legacy organizations—that have long been on the frontlines of

the battles for freedom and equality—is beyond what most can imagine.

"I don't want nobody to give me nothing. Open up the door and I'll get it myself. Do you hear me?"

This simple, yet powerful lyric offered by one of the greatest poets of the twentieth century, the incomparable James Brown, illustrates the spirit and mindset of American blacks who have fought for independence and freedom throughout history. Even in the face of laws and systems designed to dehumanize and exclude blacks from mainstream society, we have always had leaders with vision who had the yearning and courage to speak truth to power.

One of the earliest demonstrations of this quest for freedom from white-controlled institutions was the founding of the African Methodist Episcopal (AME) Church by Richard Allen in 1816. The AME church also founded the first black-owned institution of higher learning, Wilberforce University, and was a champion of higher learning for blacks. Today, the AME church boasts more than four million members worldwide and is among the largest and most influential of the network of African American legacy organizations. The National Baptist Convention, founded in1895, is also recognized as one of the largest black organizations, with more than eight million members worldwide.

The first fifty years of the twentieth century marked the humble beginnings of the several national civil rights organizations, founded following black reconstruction in America. The National Association of Colored People (NAACP) was founded in 1909, the National Urban League in 1919, and the National Council of Negro Women in 1935. The United Negro College Fund was founded in 1944 as the only national organization to exist for the purpose of providing scholarships for students attending private HBCUs, and in 1946 the National Alumni Council (NAC) was founded to serve the needs of HBCUs.

The civil rights movement was the genesis for organizations focused specifically on the fight to obtain voting and civil rights, most notably the Southern Christian Leadership Conference, founded by Dr. Martin Luther King, Jr. and others in 1957. As blacks moved into various arenas of American society, other groups, such as the Congressional Black Caucus, the U.S. Conference of Black Mayors, and a litany of professional and trade organizations, such as the National Medical Association, National Bar Association, National Association of Black Journalists, National Society of Black Engineers, and many others were formed to foster the power of collective action around key matters. The Thurgood Marshall Scholarship Fund was formed in 1987 to provide scholarships to students attending the nation's Historically Black Public Colleges and Universities.

The organizing strength of these groups has been fueled mainly through local chapters and through national and regional meetings. Each organization has given hope and dignity to legions of people of color and helped make America better. These groups have different missions and agendas and sometimes different approaches to how they address the problems, but they are unanimous in their belief in promoting higher education and to keeping the doors of opportunity open for future generations. The leadership of many of these organizations are themselves graduates of black colleges, and their members include millions of black college alumni.

The NAC is the most prominent black college alumni organization and has chapters—known as local Inter-Alumni Councils (IAC)—throughout the country. IAC members are probably the most visible ambassadors for black colleges in American cities, and they take their role as alumni very seriously. Black Greek letter organizations are another strong link in the chain of groups that help promote the black college experience. Some estimate the combined members exceed two million, and many maintain a lifetime connection to Greek activities.

Today, black affinity organizations provide millions of dollars in support to HBCUs through the many scholarships they offer and the numerous events they host and attend in support of higher education. A new generation of leaders is emerging among these groups and ushering new strategies and tactics for mobilization and messaging. The new media has revolutionized how these groups market and promote their messages and how they interface with their members. Black legacy groups are vital to the success of the growing culture of black college football classics and battle of the bands events—helping to keep the black college experience current and attractive to young people. Many affinity groups also have chapters on HBCU campuses, giving them access to a pipeline of future members with strong loyalty to the organization.

There is extensive overlap in the membership of many of these organizations, helping to expand outreach when it comes to common interests and goals. When school districts don't include HBCUs in college fairs, legacy organizations step up and fill the gap. Affinity organizations sponsor many of the popular black college tours and provide mentoring programs, rites-of-passage programs, and other activities to help students and their families. These groups can be very valuable resources for obtaining letters of recommendation and can assist with SAT preparation courses and other college planning. Legacy organizations are like the roads, bridges, and transit system of the black community—and Historically Black Colleges need them now more than ever. 🚇

Meta Williams is director of Marketing & Communications for the Los Angeles Urban League and a senior consultant for major special events.

GOING MAINSTREAM:
Black College Culture Getting Wide Exposure—Finally

It has been 20 years in the making, but in the twenty-first century, black college culture and lifestyle is living large, has broken a few barriers, and has carved out a niche across platforms in popular culture, America's biggest export. Certainly there is still much to be done and legions of stories yet to be told.

But let's start with the motion picture industry. During the past twenty-five years, it has presented several movies that depict different elements of this cultural phenomenon that has been more than 100 years in the making. The current period was helped along by innovative filmmaker Spike Lee with *School Daze*, a music-filled, offbeat contemporary comedy that took an unforgettable look at black college life. Amid gala coronations, football, fraternities, parades, and

parties, it was "like, *yeah*" for those who witnessed firsthand the various experiences Lee depicted. For those not familiar with the culture, the film was revealing and maybe even controversial. But whatever the reaction, Lee had people around the country talking about black colleges.

School Daze was released February 12, 1988, and, despite being underfinanced by Columbia Pictures, grossed more than twice its cost. Lee was asked to stop production on the campuses of Morehouse, Spelman, and Clark Atlanta University during filming because the colleges' boards of directors had concerns about how historically black colleges were being portrayed in the film. Lee had to finish filming at the neighboring Morris Brown College. From the time Spike Lee burst onto the scene with *She's Gotta Have It*,

"Attending Howard University had a huge impact on my success, especially when I considered that I was on the same campus that produced Debbie Allen, Phylicia Rashad, Wendy Raquel Robinson, Lynn Whitfield and so many others."

—Actress Taraji Henson

one of the talking points quickly attached to his rising persona was that he was a graduate of Morehouse College. His thesis film at New York University Film School, *Joe's Bedstuy Barbershop—We Cut Heads*, starred his Morehouse classmate Monty Ross, who would also go on to co-produce several of his biggest movies. But with *School Daze*, Spike definitely ignited buzz about black colleges.

"Even twenty years later, reflecting on my *School Daze* experience is still a really big deal for me," said Ross. "I am still overjoyed that it was the first the black college experience brought to the silver screen. The exposure gave society an opportunity to see black American college students struggle with issues, concerns, race relations, political activism, love, commitment, and honesty, and come to grips with these situations in an intelligent manner. I will forever be proud of that fact."

Then think of how the movie *Drumline* helped make a star out of Nick Cannon and showcased black college life through the power of the deep and storied marching-band tradition. In addition to influencing bands in middle and high schools across the country, the strut of this Southern powerhouse genre also found its way into hip-hop recordings and videos for some of the biggest stars in the music industry. Corporate America has also taken notice, and companies like Honda host the Battle of the Bands Invitational Showcase, where all HBCUs are invited to participate each year.

Of course, there are the popular dance movies, like *Stomp the Yard* and *How She Move* that use complicated step dance moves that were originated by black fraternities and soror-

ities. Some are copied to the letter, though it is well known in black fraternal social circles that certain steps and movements are unique to particular organizations.

The first African-American fraternity was founded in December 1906 under the name Alpha Phi Alpha Fraternity, Incorporated. Thereafter, many other African-American fraternity and sororities were established, predicated on the belief that there was more to being a member of a fraternity or sorority than skin tone, class, or social status. There are currently nine black fraternal organizations officially recognized by the National Pan-Hellenic Council, known as the "Divine Nine."

In 2008, the film *The Great Debaters* used pop culture to remind the world again that HBCUs are indeed pillars of pride, progress, and prestige. The common themes of perseverance, determination, and the pursuit of excellence still resonate across decades and generations. This critically acclaimed, award-winning movie goes beyond the more well-known brands among black colleges and focuses on Wiley College in tiny Marshall, Texas. There are many other such stars in the constellation of HBCUs and legions of great stories yet untold. It took the combined clout and resources of Denzel Washington and Oprah Winfrey, herself an HBCU graduate of Tennessee State University, to bring the project to the silver screen.

On the television front, *A Different World* enjoyed a successful run on NBC from 1987 to 1993. The half-hour situation comedy was the first to immerse America in student life at an historically black college. Three members of the *School Daze* cast—Kadeem Hardison, Darryl M. Bell, and Jasmine Guy—became principal cast members for the show. Over the course of its run, the show was also credited with tackling social and political issues rarely explored in television fiction, and opening doors to the television industry for unprecedented numbers of young black actors, writers, producers, and directors. It also introduced Jada Pinkett, years before she married superstar Will Smith. It was Jada who introduced Tupac Shakur to American television households when she snagged him a guest appearance on the show in 1993.

When Bill Cosby introduced this groundbreaking show, America was able to see for the first time that black college student life is just as interesting and sprinkled with the same drama, joy, and learning experiences as other American colleges—yet distinctive, as it reflected the cherished cultural and historical nuances that define and reaffirm us as a people. You might say it was great television with a wonderful cultural twist.

According to the *Hollywood Reporter*, when Debbie Allen became the producer-director of *A Different World* after the first season, she transformed it "from a bland Cosby spin-off into a lively, socially responsible, ensemble situation comedy."

To the dismay of many, since the cancellation of *A Different World*, no one else has taken on the challenge of bringing black college life to network or cable television in a sitcom format. Prominent graduates, such as actress Taraji Henson, are bothered by this fact and recognize a great void. "Attending Howard University had a huge impact on my success, especially when I considered that I was on the same campus that produced Debbie Allen, Phylicia Rashad, Wendy Raquel Robinson, Lynn Whitfield, and so many others," said Henson. "But I haven't seen major representation of the black college experience on TV or film since *School Daze* and *A Different World,* which is sad because they inspired me to not only further my education but also give serious thought to attending a black college."

Jumping in on the reality television wave that swept television, BET launched *College Hill* in January 2004, aiming to give mainstream viewers a look into of HBCU life set on the campus of Southern University in Louisiana. Much like *School Daze*, it sparked criticism among university alumni, who claim the show portrays black colleges in a negative way.

While commitment to excellence, education, and learning are the primary focus and driving forces behind all of these institutions, parties are also a big part of black college culture. Parties on these campuses had a role in the early rise of hip-hop music. Before Sean Combs became Diddy, *et. al*, he was Puffy, college boy at Howard University who drove a black Jetta with New York tags. He gained a reputation as a party promoter, showing an early penchant for marketing and promotions. In a display of his tenacity, he would also travel back and forth between Washington, D.C., and New York, juggling his classes and an internship with Uptown Records. Eventually, he left Howard to focus on the internship with Andre Hurrell at Uptown Records ... left Uptown, formed Bad Boy, Sean John ... and the rest, as they say, is history. But before he really blew up, he put Howard University's homecoming on the map, bringing breakout artists such as Jodeci, Mary J. Blige, and others to perform, inspiring artists to pay tribute to Howard in their lyrics. Back in the 90s you could go to a party and see Puffy walking around with the late Christopher Wallace, a.k.a. Notorious B.I.G.

In February 2008, Combs announced that Harve Pierre had been named president of Bad Boy Records. Harve first met fellow New Yorker Combs at Howard University, where the two students promoted campus parties, both together and separately. When Combs began to shuttle between Washington, D.C. and New York City to intern at Uptown Records, Pierre remained at Howard, earning a degree in business and hospitality management. Following graduation, he worked in hotel management and owned his own restaurant.

Jack the Rapper, a popular music industry conference used to take place annually in Atlanta, with four black colleges as the backdrop. It was named in honor of black radio legend Jack Gibson, best known within modern day hip-hop for his music convention. It was considered to be the first hip-hop music convention, and soon was the template for the numerous others that followed. Everyone who was anyone went to Jack the Rapper during the early '90s. It was a welcome change and a more inclusive scene in terms of embracing hip-hop compared to other music conventions at that time. Go to the Rapper, and you might just see Tupac roving the lobby of the Marriott with his entourage, or go to a party thrown by Michael Bivins and his BVD crew. Always, students from black colleges were deep in the mix.

Certain hip-hop songs are the soundtrack for many who have fond memories of their days on the yard. During the 90s, in cities, towns, and hamlets all across America, Doug E. Fresh' unforgettable "Six minutes with Doug E. Fresh and you're on" was an anthem. Def Jam was the standard, and revolutionary artists like Public Enemy gave youth all over America a new sense of consciousness and fearlessness in challenging the status quo—all the while keepin' it in the pocket, spittin' lyrics over James Brown-inspired funky beats. In the new millennium, artists continue to do black college tours, and these days, homecoming at every school features a major concert, along with the requisite celebrities and beautiful people on parade.

This age of multiple new media platforms—citizen journalists creating their own content through podcasts, blogs, and other creative uses of the Internet—has given rise to a new generation of young activists who use tools that allow them to create communities and transmit messages and images around the country and the world at lightening speed. The national outcry around the legal problems facing the so-called Jena Six in Louisiana resulted in television images of thousands of young people who traveled to Louisiana to support the protest activities. Many of the challenges to hip-hop music and its negative, misogynistic images started on HBCU campuses. Top-selling artist Nelly ran afoul the women of Spelman College, who cancelled a planned appearance and fundraiser in protest of the lyrics in his song "Tip Drill."

The various strands of social life on black college campuses were born over a century ago, and throughout much of American history, it has been a sort of underground culture, known only to those who have either attended a HBCU, had family who attended one of these historic institutions, or lived in a city where the black community kept its finger on the pulse of one of these campuses, which are mainly on the eastern seaboard and in the South.

Today, the appeal of HBCUs goes beyond African-American communities. Though the student body at most of these schools is predominantly black, HBCUs encourage students from different backgrounds and cultures to join their academic communities. Some of these schools report noticeable increases in the enrollment of white and Latino students.

The names of famous graduates of black colleges have long been staples in American history. Yet the reflection and imprint of black-college culture on American popular culture are relatively recent developments, with great potential for helping increase enrollment and visibility for these schools. Many of these schools still fight the battles of historic and chronic underfunding that perpetually threaten their existence and future survival. They still do not enjoy comparable access to the millions of dollars available to majority institutions for endowments or research and development. Yet they still manage to produce the majority of the African-American college graduates and professionals.

The track record of these schools is also affirmed by the many very wealthy black celebrities who make a conscious decision to send their children to HBCUs, from Denzel and Pauletta Washington, to Samuel Jackson and LaTonya Richardson, to Camille and Bill Cosby and others.

A recent *New York Times* article stated that faced with increasing competition from larger and better-known colleges for a shrinking number of black college-bound students, the nation's black colleges and universities have discovered how they market themselves is as vital as other benchmarks, such as the size of their libraries or the prowess of their athletic teams.

In another sign of this growing trend, *VIBE* magazine has partnered with Boost Mobile and Motorola for the *VIBE* Game Club College Tour. The twenty-

stop tour brings popular hip-hop artists and top Xbox and PC video games to historically black colleges and universities. The time-honored ritual of spring break has long been the province of well-to-do white college students with the resources to travel to warm, sunny destinations. Black students looking for a culturally relevant vacation experience will not be left out, with options like the Black Spring Break, Black Beach Week, Black College Reunion, and other similar social events, all of which attract sponsorship, media attention, and large crowds.

Congressman James Clyburn, the Majority Whip and highest-ranking African American in Congress and a graduate of South Carolina State College, put black colleges front and center in the 2008 Democratic primary by driving the decision for the party to hold a debate at his alma mater. In the middle of a hotly contested South Carolina primary, suddenly an HBCU was like the "it girl," with media from around the world at her doorstep angling for the money shot. The Democratic Presidential Candidates' Debate was broadcast live from South Carolina State's Martin Luther King Jr. Auditorium and produced by NBC News. It marked the first presidential primary debate broadcast from an HBCU.

From the Rose Bowl to the Cotton Bowl, and a long list of others, football classics are a major staple in American society. For more than thirty years, the Bayou Classic has been the place to be for graduates of HBCU powerhouses Southern University and Grambling University. But things went to a new level when this perennial favorite appeared on network television. There are now more than 40 black college football classics—lucrative events that generate revenue for the participating schools and major excitement and revenue for the host cities. Most importantly, they continue to promote these schools as options to minority youth.

Though none of the schools are located on the West Coast, even Los Angeles has its own classic with the successful Angel City Classic (ACC). Now in its fourth year, this extravaganza brings the pomp and swagger of black colleges to the City of Angels, with full marching bands as well as academic and campus recruiting personnel. Like most urban centers, Los Angeles is grappling with shockingly high dropout rates among African-American and Latino youth. Young people in the city have the added challenge of not being geographically close to any of these schools, which heightens the critical need for events like the ACC. ▥

HBCUs REACH OUT TO LATINO STUDENTS:
Schools Cite Similar Needs and Goals

by Ronald Roach

It had not occurred to Lorena Sajardo to consider Texas Southern University as a possible college until her high school soccer coach suggested during her senior year that she try out for the newly forming women's soccer team at the Houston-based historically Black university. Despite having grown up in Houston, Sajardo admits to knowing almost nothing about TSU at the time. But she decided to give it a try after the university offered her a soccer scholarship.

"At first, it was hard because there wasn't much cultural outreach and support, but it's gotten a lot better … I don't have any complaints," says Sajardo, a junior accounting major who is now on an academic scholarship.

Freshman Arlene Delgado arrived on the campus of Huston-Tillotson University with some idea of what to expect. Her older brother and a sister-in-law were both graduates of the private historically Black school in Austin, Texas. Delgado, the youngest of seven children in a Mexican American family from Brownsville, Texas, says she's finding the comfort and acceptance she had hoped for.

"I wanted to attend a school with small classes where I could get a lot of attention and get to know my professors," says Delgado, who expects to major in international business like her brother.

Sajardo and Delgado are among a growing cohort of Hispanic students enrolling at historically Black colleges

> **Ohio's Central State University has made diversity recruiting, which is heavily targeted at Hispanic students, a full-time position.**

and universities. The trend has become most apparent at historically Black colleges and universities in Texas, North Carolina and Ohio, where officials have taken proactive steps to recruit and enroll Hispanic students.

"We're in Texas, where there's a large Hispanic population. The needs of Hispanic communities are very similar to African-Americans," says Dr. Larry Earvin, the president of Huston-Tillotson.

At Huston-Tillotson, Hispanic students, most of whom are Mexican Americans, account for 10 percent of the undergraduate student body population, according to school officials. That figure gives Huston-Tillotson one of the highest percentages of Hispanic student enrollment among HBCUs.

"[Hispanics are] one of the fastest growing groups in the country," says academic admissions expert Dr. Robert Massa, the vice president of enrollment at Dickinson College in Pennsylvania.

While the bulk of Black college recruiting appears to be drawing upon populations of Mexican American and Central American descended students to southern and midwestern campuses, experts believe HBCUs are also positioned well to attract Afro Latino students, such as Puerto Ricans, Dominicans and Black Cubans, who generally reside in the northeastern United States.

Overall, Hispanics are expected to grow from 13 percent, roughly 35 million, of the U.S. population to 18 percent, or 59 million, by 2025. African-Americans, who also comprise 13 percent of the population, are projected to grow to nearly 15 percent in that same period, according to U.S. Census population estimates. Today, one-third of those entering the work force are Hispanic. In 2025, that number will jump to one-half. Institutions that are successfully attracting and enrolling Hispanics must demonstrate they are open to diversity, says Massa. "It's not a question solely of critical mass ... [There] has to be an institution-wide commitment."

Growing the Numbers

By and large, HBCU officials say they welcome the challenge of recruiting, enrolling and retaining Hispanic students. In contrast to majority White institutions, which often struggle with diversity, HBCU officials and advocates tout a long history of having diversity in their student and faculty populations. They also contend that enrolling first-generation college-going Hispanic students represents part of their traditional mission of educating the socially disadvantaged. That focus, however, has been complicated by the fact that Hispanics struggle with a higher than average public school dropout rate and attend college at lower percentages than Blacks and Whites.

"[HBCUs have] always been open to diversity," says Lynn Huntley, the president of the Atlanta-based Southern Education Foundation. "They have the most diverse faculties of any group of colleges and universities."

Statistics demonstrate that HBCUs have been relatively open to Hispanic students. According to the National Center for Education Statistics, Hispanic enrollment from 1976 to 2001 almost doubled—from 3,442 to 6,665—at Black colleges. At specific campuses, recent growth figures reveal a more aggressive posture with regard to Hispanic students.

Texas Southern University has put together an aggressive recruitment strategy that includes embracing its 16 or so feeder high schools, a grass roots recruitment campaign, including a "go bus" that will sign students up on-the-spot so to speak and outreach campaigns to local churches. Marketing and promotional efforts, specifically asking Hispanic students to attend TSU have been implemented and the university is expecting an increase for Fall 2009.

Ohio's Central State University has made diversity recruiting, which is heavily targeted at Hispanic students, a full-time position.

In North Carolina, growing and supporting Hispanic college enrollment is a task shared by a host of institutions and agencies, including historically Black colleges and universities. Fayetteville State University, which employs a recruiter who targets the Latino community, has traditionally seen one of the highest percentages of Hispanic enrollment of the 16 public schools in the state. During the 2008 academic year, 4.3 percent of its students were Hispanic.

Huston-Tillotson's Earvin believes that HBCUs are well-positioned to appeal to Hispanic students and their families given that their socioeconomic profiles are similar to the families Black schools have traditionally served. He adds that alumni, students, faculty, administrators and other supporters of Huston-Tillotson have approved of the school's growing ties to the Hispanic community and its enrollment of Latino students. "It hasn't generated a lot of concern," Earvin says.

Building Bridges

After moving to the Bellville, Texas, area near historically Black Prairie View A&M University from New Jersey in the 1980s, Amparo Isaza-Navarrete, a native of Colombia, recognized that there was a need for local schools to reach out to the parents of Mexican American children. As a volunteer, she proved an able and enthusiastic teacher of English as a Second Language to Mexican American adults. As a result, local school officials encouraged her to pursue a master's degree so that she could continue with the school system as a full-time teacher and eventually as an administrator.

Opting to take a different route than full-time teaching, Isaza-Navarrete completed a master's degree in educational counseling at Prairie View. Since the early 1990s, she has held jobs at Prairie View involving university outreach to the Hispanic community. As recruitment program coordinator in the college of arts and sciences, her current responsibilities include teaching Spanish to Prairie View faculty and administrators and developing K-12 programs that help stimulate Hispanic student interest in college.

"When I came here there were not that many Latino students. That was okay. You have to strike out and be a pioneer," Isaza-Navarrete says. "I saw the need for the communities to be aware of one another … I became a bridge."

A number of HBCU officials say their schools are embracing change as they increase ties to the Hispanic community and facilitate cultural changes on their respective campuses. Colleges are participating in local organizations, Hispanic events and coordinating K-12 initiatives to include Hispanic children.

"We're part of the Hispanic Chamber of Commerce," in the Austin area, says Earvin.

For their part, Hispanic students at HBCUs are putting a cultural stamp of their own on their respective campuses. With Hispanic representation growing, student organizations reflecting their interests have sprouted. Edwin Cuc, a senior computer science major

at TSU, was a founding member of the university's chapter of Sigma Lambda Beta, the largest Latino fraternity in the United States. Like TSU's Sajardo, Cuc, who is of Guatemalan descent, is involved with the Hispanic Student Association and a campus chapter of the League of United Latin American Citizens. These organizations and a Hispanic sorority have all sprung up since Cuc and Sajardo have been students at TSU.

"There was real excitement about there being a Latino fraternity bringing something different to the campus," Cuc says. "And all the groups are hosting social events that include everyone."

The Diversity Movement

To the extent that HBCUs develop and pursue a "diversity" agenda in the wake of the 2003 *Grutter v. Bollinger* U.S. Supreme Court decision that affirmed the use of race-conscious affirmative action in higher education, Black college leaders say cultivating and growing Hispanic enrollment represents a critical part of that mandate. Some officials, however, have been cautious about a diversity movement they feel might compromise the mission of historically Black institutions.

Dr. Ray Winbush, the director of the Institute for Urban Research at Morgan State University, says the mandates of public desegregation orders and the economic and educational interests of White civic and business leaders have put the historical missions of HBCUs at risk in the current diversity era. He says the danger comes from those who would turn majority Black HBCUs into majority White institutions.

"I'm very welcoming of Hispanics coming to Black colleges. This is a good movement," he says.

The effort, Winbush says, represents one of the most positive aspects of Black-Latino relations in the United States. While there's been a tendency in the news media to highlight conflicts between Blacks and Hispanics, Winbush says the long-term benefits of Hispanics educated in historically Black institutions will serve to help make for a positive relationship.

"The movement will strengthen ties between the communities. It allows us to get to know one another better," he says. ⬛

CULTURE

BLACK COLLEGE CAMPUS LIFE:
You Think You Know, But You Have No Idea

by Robert W.H. Price

The campus life at Historically Black Colleges and Universities is a multi-dimensional, multi-layered, multi-faceted experience that has produced some of the most prolific, productive, and successful citizens of the world and American society. It is as diverse as the skin tones and hues that define African Americans. It is rooted in centuries of patterns of human activity and shared experiences of the ancestors of slaves. The symbolic structures of HBCU campuses represent the proverbial village that many believe is required to properly raise a child and reaffirm our

ability to overcome oppression and our long-held commitment to excellence of African Americans.

Every year, hundreds of thousands of freshmen leave home to begin a journey that will be exciting, life-changing, and will prepare them for successful futures. Yet, in making the choice to attend an HBCU, you are making a very special choice that has been the launch pad for some of the greatest Americans in history. In the twenty-first century, you are also choosing environments that look more and more like America and its cultural diversity. You are placing yourself in an environment that reflects and constantly reminds you of the history of your people and your own greatness.

Because of the low student-to-teacher ratio at the majority of HBCUs, get ready for professors who know you by name and who actually care whether or not you succeed. Your classmates will include people up and down the economic and social ladder—from those whose parents write tuition checks to those for whom student loans and work-study are the only salvation. Your classmates will include the best and the brightest merit scholars, academic superstars, pampered athletes, campus activist and rabble rousers. They will include students who may need remedial instruction, but who are also diamonds in the rough, whose potential is discovered and nurtured at institutions that build confidence and inspire people to work for greatness.

You can read about it and hear others talk about it, but it won't be until you experience the thrill of freshman orientation, see a group of frat brothers or sorors stepping on their plot, witness your first group of pledges in formation, attend a football or basketball game that is a video shoot and fashion show, or experience homecoming on "the yard" that the "aha" moment will happen for you.

Organic Sense of Community

The HBCU community predates the electronic age, covering many decades of interstate travel by students and alumni to HBCUs for homecoming, concerts, graduation, and other special events. And at HBCUs, it's not the NCAA that reigns. Can you say CIAA, SWAC, MEAC? Our tournaments are more than just basketball or football. They are long-standing traditions that span generations and spawn family reunions, class reunions, and fraternity and sorority gatherings. Homecomings on every campus are always been the beautiful people on parade.

The notion of attending an HBCU ebbs and flows with each generation and some schools have stronger brands and are better-known. The United Negro College Fund has reported an increase in students from the Western states attending these schools. There are parents in states with lower African-American populations who make the argument that they send their children to HBCUs to make certain that they get the "cultural experience."

The creation of HBCU student unions and student organizations on majority college campuses is a

At HBCUs, your identity will be more than just your name and field of study.

major phenomenon in American society, and practically every major college or university has some type of organization designed to foster a sense of community among African-American students. The fact that such organizations are needed for African-American students on major campuses by definition justifies the continued need and relevance of HBCUs.

HBCUs organically offer a sense of community for African-American students, campuses that provide constant reminders of our powerful history of succeeding and overcoming obstacles, and offer an environment where you will challenged. These schools have professors and administrators who will remind you of people from your family and community. There are many untold stories of faculty going the extra mile to ensure a student is reaching their potential, such as the character portrayed by Denzel Washington in the movie, *The Great Debaters*.

If you are like the vast majority of young people who go away to college, this will be your very first time leaving home and the first time you will make adult decisions. Decisions about how you manage your time, honor your commitments, and take active responsibility for your own future during your matriculation will set the course for the rest of your life. The nurturing and supportive spirit of these campuses gives young people the freedom to make choices, but at the same time provides a network of people who will keep track of your successes and failures. At HBCUs, your identity will be more than just your name and field of study, it will also include what state you are from, whether you are an athlete, or a member of a Greek organization, band member, social club, or organization.

No matter where you choose to go to college, it will be a whole new world, with unexpected twists and turns, and with its own rewards as well as challenges. The people and experiences you will encounter will be many and varied.

The following letter, written by a student, captures some of the angst that is felt by students—and seems to especially speak to the experience of young people born in the post-civil rights era. The answer provided offers great insight and advice.

Dear Campus Advisor:

I have made it through my first semester. I am attending a historically black college after having gone to predominantly white schools all of my life. I have never felt so good. College is phat! I have met some of the most interesting and smart black students I have ever encountered.

So what is my problem? The truth is, I feel very intimidated by my ignorance of black history, culture, language, and everything else that I have missed in my previous education. In my courses, everyone seems so much more aware of black life and culture than I am. My family is black, but they have not emphasized being black. In some ways, I feel ashamed of myself and them for not having more black consciousness. I don't feel that everything in life has to be focused on being black—and I have met students who seem to have taken it to the extreme—but I do feel isolated in a way that I didn't feel in white schools. I realize now that I am in an environment where black culture is the norm and that I have truly been deprived of my own culture. I feel like a cultural zombie. I have focused on being a good student all of my life, but I think I missed something—knowing who I am as an African-American male. I try to hide my ignorance, but I have been called "different" once too many times, and I feel like I'm in hiding.

Do you think that joining a fraternity would help me to catch up with my culture? Please answer as soon as possible. I am enclosing my campus address.

"The Invisible Man"

I am in an environment where black culture is the norm and I have truly been deprived of my own culture.

Dear Invisible,

Your reference to a book by a black author (Ralph Ellison) in closing your letter gives me hope for changing your dilemma. Although I have already answered your letter and mailed it to you directly, I wanted to include it in my column so that other students who are facing similar challenges will not feel alone and might be able to benefit from my advice to you.

You are not alone. Many of today's black college students are arriving on our campus with very little knowledge or appreciation of black life and culture. Like you, they have been isolated from their culture by family who escaped to predominantly white schools and neighborhoods, not only in search of a better life, but also—in some cases—to escape what they consider to be the stigma of being black in America. They have lived in environments where they have been encouraged to assimilate and "fit in" with the majority. They have learned quite well how to mimic white behavior. They have assumed white culture and values and, in many cases, have abandoned their own. They are—as you vividly described yourself—cultural zombies. The walking dead. In their effort to fit in, they have stripped themselves of their core identity.

For some, this poses no problem. They like being colorblind and wish others would be like them. These people are cultural aliens who care nothing about and contribute nothing to the advancement of black people.

And then there are others, like you, who have a profound awakening to the value of discovering and functioning within a real, rather than a feigned or fictitious, cultural context. They realize that a person without an appreciation of himself functions with a self-hate that is terrible. You should not feel out of place in the very place where you most belong. You simply need to find your way home, like Alex Haley.

You will be proud of your race and culture, accepting of others, and a better educated person.

What you need to do is to undertake a self-education process that will allow you to reclaim that which is your birthright, your cultural heritage. You might want to do this before you join any organization, where you might be challenged to accelerate your learning!

First and foremost, read, read, read. Read books, magazines, articles, poetry, and song lyrics by black authors that will introduce you to the complexity of black life in America and the beautiful, lyrical quality, passion, and artistry of black language.

Second, develop an Afrocentric frame of reference. In other words, include in your reflections, in your discussions, in your thinking, quotes, phrases, and brilliant insights from great black thinkers.

Third, accept that the journey toward personal acceptance and self- affirmation is a lifelong process. Even though you feel intimidated in this black environment, you cannot change yourself overnight. Do not fast-forward from one pretense to another. While you may feel ashamed of what you have been deprived of, never be ashamed of yourself.

Fourth, volunteer to do community service as often as you can with an agency or church in the poorest black community in your area. Seek to understand the difficult conditions that black people endure who have less fortunate lives than the one you have enjoyed. Identify solutions that do not blame or humiliate the victims. Broaden your education in this way. Write class papers on your findings and experiences.

Fifth, emerge yourself in the black arts. Go to black theater, to movies in black neighborhoods (this is a very different experience!), to concerts. Listen to jazz, gospel music, blues, and reggae until you can distinguish various artists and can appreciate these classical expressions of black life. Buy black art and artifacts, created by black artists (there is a difference).

Finally, take courses that will further ground you in black history and culture. Participate in class discussions. Do constant self-checks, as you have already begun to do. Try to see what has shaped your perspective, how it compares to those of your peers and professors, and what is missing. Do more reading. Experience more. Talk to your professors. Go to campus lecture series that bring in black scholars. I could go on and on, but enough said.

I have devoted my entire column to your concern because I have met students like you both on my campus and elsewhere. They are painfully ignorant of who they are and have been told that race and culture are insignificant. Yet they have found that this kind of thinking does not match their experiences and feel frightened that their ignorance will be exposed and that they will be rejected by their own people. They have found trying to be white a totally unacceptable alternative to being themselves, but they do not know where to begin.

If you follow my advice (and I certainly encourage you to seek out a black counselor on your campus to further assist you), I am certain you will feel considerably better about yourself. In the end, you will be proud of your race and culture, accepting of others, and a better-educated person—capable of not only making a contribution to society as a whole but significantly improving the life of black people in this country and around the world. ⊞

Linda Bates Parker is online campus advisor for The Black Collegian *magazine.*

Reprinted with permission from The Black Collegian *magazine.*

CULTURE

SPORTS AT HBCUs:
Producing the Finest Athletes and Coaches for More Than a Century

by Michael Hurd

Collectively, HBCUs have given us some of *the* most incredible athletes and coaches in the history of sports.

Of course, you may not know that.

Not to worry, it's kind of a well-kept secret—not so much the names of the athletes but the histories of the athletic programs and institutions that trained, mentored, nurtured, and educated them. The money hasn't always been there, the facilities might have been lacking, and so was the notoriety, but none of that has dimmed the human spirit evident in the programs. For more than a century, HBCU athletic programs have given us:

- A coach who retired with the most wins in college football history. (Eddie Robinson, whose entire coaching career—fifty-six years—was spent at Grambling, where he won 408 games.)

- Dozens of Olympic gold medalists, including the "world's fastest human." (The former includes Ed Temple's Tigerbelles, and Tennessee State's storied women's track squad, whose alumni include sprinters Wilma Rudolph and Wyomia Tyus. The latter is Florida A&M's "Bullet" Bob Hayes, who also starred as a game-breaking wide receiver for the Dallas Cowboys.)

- Two of the three African-American quarterbacks to lead teams in the Super Bowl. (Grambling's Doug Williams and Alcorn State's Steve McNair)

- A woman who became both a Wimbledon and U.S. Open tennis champion. (FAMU's Althea Gibson)

- A man who won more games than any other Division II basketball coach. (Clarence "Big House" Gaines, who won 828 games in forty-seven years at Winston-Salem State University.)

And more, so much more.

But, okay, there's just a bit of a catch. We're mostly talking about a time when "people of color" specifically meant "colored people," "Negroes," and anyone of them who had aspirations of participating in collegiate athletics—heck, if they just wanted to get an education!—had to enroll in a school founded, administered, and attended by members of "the race."

You went to an HBCU.

And you probably lived below the Mason-Dixon Line in a region with a wealth of untapped and untouchable—by white coaches—athletic talent. The Deep South was teeming with African-American kids whose development was brought on by toiling on farms and in fields, playing in spirited after-church games, and mentoring from some of sports greatest strategists, motivators, and competitors.

But, you may not know that.

A "Match Game of Ball"

Football is the bellwether for most athletic programs and, at that, HBCUs got a late start. Princeton and Rutgers had kicked off intercollegiate football in 1869 in a wild affair with twenty-five men per side. At the time, there were only a few HBCUs in existence—Lin-

> "There was great pride ... I'd go to Grambling and be so impressed with the overall pride at the school. Everyone was so close, involved and proud of what they were doing. It was a fun thing, great rapport."
>
> —Hank Stram, former head coach of the Dallas Texans/Kansas City Chiefs

coln (Pennsylvania), Cheyney, Wilberforce, Howard, Hampton—and none of them were immediately caught up in the football mania that quickly spread throughout major colleges, mostly in the Ivy Leagues.

HBCU presidents didn't care about athletics and gave little to no thought toward their importance, and you couldn't blame them. We weren't that far from a time when even learning to read could be a deadly act for a slave. So, after emancipation, HBCUs sprouted to quench the educational thirsts of millions of newly freed men and women, and foremost in the minds of educators was, well, education. They weren't about to squander what already meager school funds they had on fun and games.

Athletics were an unaffordable, unimportant frivolity that firmly took a backseat to academics and uplifting a people.

That began to change in 1892, when, on a snowy day in Salisbury, North Carolina, the men of Biddle University met the Livingstone College eleven for a "match game of ball." Biddle won, 4–0. And it was on.

HBCUs began to adapt to the concept of team sports, with football leading the way. However, in 1904, an African-American Harvard physical-education student returned home to Washington, D.C. and introduced the game of basketball to students at Howard. It took less than ten years for HBCUs to start putting together teams that would, over time, produce some of the game's brightest players, including Winston-Salem State's Earl "The Pearl" Monroe and Grambling's Willis Reed, and coaches John McLendon (Tennessee State) and Davy Whitney (Alcorn State).

HBCU teams have won several NAIA national championships, with Tennessee State winning three straight (1957–59) under McLendon during a stretch where an HBCU team won five of the six NAIA titles. (Grambling won it in 1961 and Prairie View in 1962.)

The schools brought some order to it all by forming their own conferences, beginning in 1912 with the organization of the Central Intercollegiate Athletic Association (CIAA), immediately followed in 1913 by the Southern Intercollegiate Athletic Conference (SIAC), and in 1920 by the Southwestern Athletic Conference (SWAC). The newest kid on the block, the Mid-Eastern Athletic Conference (MEAC), wouldn't come along until 1969.

By then, HBCUs were well into making their mark in all sports, but it was football that put most of the schools on the map, and in the next six decades, at least after Biddle-Livingstone, we would see plenty of lively competition after other schools picked up the game and hired "missionary coaches" from Ivy League schools to start programs. The legacies that would be created were rooted in teams coached by such men as Howard's Samuel Archer, Morgan State's Eddie Hurt, and Tuskegee's Cleve Abbott, and were continued by coaches like Southern's Arnett "Ace" Mumford, Florida A&M's Jake Gaither, and Tennessee State's John Merritt.

Tuskegee dominated the 1920s, winning six HBCU national championships from 1924–1930 behind Abbott's leadership, but they also had "Big Ben"

"Football is football. There are good athletes all over, but black colleges are able to relate to the culture a little bit more."

—Stadford Brown, quarterback for North Carolina Central

Stevenson, arguably the greatest all-around player in HBCU football history (with apologies to fans of Jackson State's Walter Payton!). It's hard to argue with Stevenson's success. From 1923–1930, 'Skegee won sixty-nine of seventy-six games (one loss, six ties), and during that time, Stevenson was a unanimous HBCU All-American pick for seven consecutive seasons (before the NCAA initiated a four-year eligibility limit); led the SIAC in rushing, scoring, and interceptions; and was near the top in receiving each year.

Stevenson, who Abbott literally plucked from the fields of a Liberty, Missouri, farm, was the first HBCU superstar.

We knew of players like him because of the black media—newspapers like *The Pittsburgh Courier* and *The Chicago Defender*, and magazines like *Jet* and *Ebony*, who wrote about HBCU sports because the white media would not. In fact, HBCU football players never got their full due until 1996, when the College Football Hall of Fame began inducting players from HBCUs and other small colleges.

Now, there are a combined twenty-four coaches and players enshrined into the Hall and twenty-two players into the Pro Football Hall of Fame. Also, consider this:

- The National Football League's first modern-day black head coach was from Maryland State (Art Shell).

- The league's all-time leading receiver came from Mississippi Valley State (Jerry Rice).

- The league's former all-time leading rusher came from Jackson State (Walter Payton).

How sweet is all that?

The Pros Come a Callin'

In 1960, the Vietnam War was in its early stages, and HBCU athletics were poised for a breakout year. Rudolph gained a lot of attention by becoming the first American woman to win three Olympic gold medals when she dominated the sprints (100 meters, 200 meters, and the anchor leg of the 400-meter relay team) in Rome. And, at North Carolina A&T, a sophomore transfer quarterback from the University of Illinois enrolled to play for the Aggies. A knee injury would end Jesse Jackson's promising football career, but he'd start a pretty good second career as a civil rights activist.

However, a new pro football league was about to put HBCU teams on the map. And, for most of the schools, you really did need a map—or two—to find them. (Itta Bena, Mississippi, anyone?).

The upstart American Football League (AFL) opened for business in 1960 and they not only brought a different kind of game—wide open, with speed—but also introduced, on a very large scale, a different kind of player: the HBCU athlete. The National Football League had a sprinkling of African-American players but wasn't accepting them with open arms. In 1949, Grambling's Tank Younger was the first player from an HBCU to sign an NFL contract, but the AFL would open the floodgates and tap into a source of talent the NFL had largely ignored.

HBCU players were very instrumental in establishing the league, in what would be a win-win situation for all concerned.

"The desire to prove they were worthy of playing in the NFL was always very impressive," said the late Hank Stram, who was head coach of the Dallas Texans/Kansas City Chiefs and whose early rosters were loaded with players from HBCUs (including Morgan State's Willie Lanier, who Stram installed as pro football's first African-American middle linebacker). "There was great pride in the schools they represented. I'd go to Grambling and be so impressed with the overall pride at the school. Everyone was so close, involved, and proud of what they were doing. It was a fun thing, great rapport.

"We were the underdog and they were, too. It was a good mix."

Fast Forward to Today

In 1969, Florida A&M played the University of Tampa in the state's first football game pitting an HBCU against a white school. It was also the penultimate game of Jake Gaither's career, and the Rattlers would win it, 34–28.

The game was also the symbolic end of a golden era for HBCU football when all the top African-American high school talent in the South went to HBCUs by default and the teams were overloaded with talent several layers deep. Integration put an end to that.

"We used to meet these Southern (white) schools at track meets and run them out of the park," Gaither said, describing a time when the recruitment of African-American athletes by white colleges had heated considerably. "They used to say I had a farm system, and I told them they were right. My boys did come off the farm. Right here under their noses was the greatest talent in the world, and they didn't want it. But, now you can't turn around without a scout from every white school down here beating the bushes for black players."

And the white coaches found them, and in the name of integration, sold them on the promises of training in state-of-the-art facilities, playing in huge stadiums before huge crowds, and regularly appearing on national TV. And money. Much more money for the athletic programs. Basically, everything HBCU programs could not offer.

Some observers say HBCUs weren't prepared for the impact of segregation and what it might do to their programs, perhaps banking too much on their deep social histories, and missions to continue attracting the best and the brightest from the African-American community.

It's an era unlikely to repeat.

"We weren't just warriors on the battlefield, we were friends in the home, we called each other in the off-season, we played cards, went out, and had fun, that kind of thing," said Marino Casem, who has seen HBCU athletics as a football player for Xavier University, as a head coach at Alcorn State, and as an athletic director at Southern. He's also a member of the College Football Hall of Fame. "You miss the camaraderie, because there were some special people to rally around. Now, the only time these guys meet up is at conference meetings.

"We had some great times of bonding between coaches and players, sports information directors, and athletic directors from different institutions," Casem said. "We got to know each other a little bit

"It's a great experience. That connection of HBCUs ... you're part of a unique family, and that serves to create a deeper and broader spirit."

—Joe Taylor, former head football coach at Hampton University and current head football coach at Florida A&M University

better. For instance, I got to know Grambling's president [Dr. Ralph Waldo Emerson Jones] real well. I had been to his house, had meetings with him. So at his funeral, when everybody got up to sing the Grambling (school song), I did, too, because I had been on the media tours and gotten to know some of their players, and from knowing him so well, I got up to sing and knew it just as well as they did.

"It shocked them. And I told them, 'I'd expect them to know our [song], too. It was more than just X's and O's and game plan.'"

It was family, but HBCU programs, post-integration, have mostly sang the blues, and everybody knows the words—"no money, no money, no money"—as they have watched the talent drain weaken their programs.

Now, we see the schools in major re-adjustment mode, trying to get back in the game, and they're doing it by stepping up recruiting and marketing efforts, improving facilities, and putting together TV packages. There's a better quality of play, and coaches are doing better at recruiting. There has also been an influx of coaches with experience in the bigger conferences, such as the SEC, Big Ten, and Big Twelve.

Some better players are falling into the hands of HBCU programs after disillusionment with bigger programs, either because of a lack of playing time, or generally getting lost in the shuffle. Stadford Brown, the outstanding young quarterback for North Carolina Central was recruited by big schools and was headed to Oregon State but decided to stay closer to home, Washington, D.C. If he's an indication of the kind of players getting into HBCU programs, the future's pretty bright.

Brown, a redshirt freshman last year, was the Sheridan Broadcast Network's Doug Williams Offensive Player of the Year as he led the Eagles to a Black College National Championship, and a 10–0 record, the program's first perfect season in their eighty-three-year history.

"Football is football," he said. "There are good athletes all over, but black colleges are able to relate to the culture a little bit more. Otherwise, it's like any college. I knew quite a bit about black colleges before I came here, and have learned a lot more since."

Seems a good time to be in a HBCU program.

"The administrations are starting to realize that small window of opportunity you have to showcase your total

Photo courtesy of Hampton University Athletic Department

Joe Taylor, former head football coach at Hampton University and current head football coach at Florida A&M University

campus comes through a very successful athletic program," said Joe Taylor, former Hampton head football coach and current head football coach at Florida A&M University. "In years past, most of the coaches had to coach and teach classes and didn't have the recruiting budgets to recruit needs, and they weren't competitive in terms of salaries. A lot of those were drawbacks that a lot of people didn't understand.

"It really put HBCU coaches at a disadvantage, because if the opponent has it, then you need it. But, if it hadn't been for black colleges, a lot of people wouldn't have had the opportunity to move forward. They've always been necessary and will continue to be very vital and necessary in the fabric of our total society."

For years, Grambling was the prototype for HBCU programs behind the leadership of President Jones ("Prez"), Robinson, and visionary sports information director Collie J. Nicholson.

Hampton is a pretty good model for today's schools. The Pirates have a solid and supportive administration led by President William Harvey and a football program that has been red hot. Taylor, in seventeen years at the helm, has guided the Pirates to four Black College Championships, eight conference titles, a Heritage Bowl Championship, and seven trips to the NCAA playoffs. As overseer of the Pirates, Taylor has compiled a record of 130–44–1. His career mark of 191–73–4 (.713) places him on the national level as the third-winningest active coach in the Division I Football Championship Subdivision when ranked by total victories, and fifth when ranked by winning percentage.

The Pirates had a Grambling-esque nine players to sign NFL contracts for the 2007 season. If nothing else, that further helped to destroy the myth that playing in an HBCU program limits attention from NFL scouts.

"Our success and visibility really helps, and if you help one, you help all," Taylor said. "But you also have to have the ability to win. When you've got that going, it helps to attract a quality student to an HBCU. Our program is designed so that if you put four or five years into it, you're going to be marketable to corporate America. Everybody's interested in recruiting the total campus and if you do have an outstanding athletic program—the schools doing that also get a better overall student. And, what we say about HBCUs is that somebody's going to care about you, beyond the football field.

"It's a great experience. That connection of HBCUs—you're part of a unique family, and that serves to create a deeper and broader spirit."

Image has long been a problem for HBCUs, from both inside and outside the African-American community. Some think the schools have outlived their usefulness, some say they are racist, and others point to poor administration and instability at the top. From an athletic standpoint, recruiters from bigger schools need only point to the comparative lack of everything. However, the HBCU missions are about nurturing, and giving African-American students a chance.

"The kids don't know the history and that's sad," Casem noted. "You've got to know the black school history, and we're not getting that to prospective students and athletes. What's happening at our institutions is we're changing administrators so frequently—presidents, athletic directors, head coaches—and some of our people don't know the history. We've got to educate our own people about who we are, including the coaches. They're not hearing everyday that we had a Tank Younger or a president like Dr. Jones. That's tough.

"They've got to make a glimmering jewel out of the athletic programs, and if they do that, it will mirror, reflect, and shine on the whole school. Athletics is the window through which the world sees your institution. If athletics is shining out there, that light that everybody sees, your institution gets all the publicity, and they see that Rhodes Scholar coming from your institution—they see your great scholars.

"It takes a wise and crafty leader to be able to visualize and see that if he gives enough vision to athletics, then academics will flourish. It takes a secure person and a strong leader to see over the rainbow," Casem concludes. ⊞

Michael Hurd is a former sportswriter for USA Today *and is also the author of* Black College Football, 1892–1992, *and* Collie J., Grambling's Man with the Golden Pen.

MY JOURNEY TO COLLEGE

by Dr. Sharon Knotts Green

As a child, I always knew I was going to college. My parents were educators by profession and academic achievement fell very close behind "accepting Jesus Christ as your personal Lord and Savior" on the list of family values. Mom and Dad never said, "If you go to college…"; it was always, "When you go to college…." To me, college was as natural as going from third grade to fourth grade.

Since my parents were graduates of Prairie View A&M University, the family often attended the school's homecoming games and made frequent trips to the campus and community. My older sister, Marie, attended the Upward Bound program at PV and several faculty members were family friends. Consequently, I could hardly wait to be a college student "on the yard" decked out in purple and gold.

Two events changed my fixation on Prairie View. First, Marie graduated with highest honors from high school and attended Howard University at the suggestion of her second grade teacher, a Howard graduate. Soon we began talking about having an apartment together during the

time that our college times would overlap. Second, I scored well on the college entrance exams and began receiving mail from colleges and universities from all over the country. Until then, I had not really thought about how vast my college options really were. I was excited to be courted by so many institutions, but also overwhelmed.

My parents, sensing my loyalty to PV and possibly to them, encouraged me to consider all of my options. Their primary requirements were that the selected school be fully accredited and have a good program of study in my desired field of study, biology. They helped me to identify campus characteristics that were important to me and to work out a process for selecting a school. Drawing upon my recollection of other college campuses I had visited through high school activities and family vacations, I decided that the criteria that were most important to me were the size of the school, the city in which the college/university was located, and the prevalence of extracurricular activities.

There was a rationale for my preferences. I wanted to go to a large university in an urban setting because I had

Dr. Sharon Knotts Green

been very well-known in high school (Student Council president, Who's Who member, Speech and Drama team member) and desired more anonymity in college. I also loved doing a variety of activities and was not attracted to the idea of being in a rural setting where going to the local Wal-Mart would be the highlight of the week. I had excelled in a high school that was predominately Caucasian, so racial makeup of the school I selected was not a major factor, although I did want the school to have an African-American presence.

Looking back, I realize that initially I was oblivious to the financial side of the college admission process. When I asked my parents about working during the school year, they frankly told me that my "job" was to go to school and make good grades so that I could get a scholarship to go to college. That should have been my cue that financing college was important. I knew that my parents could not (and, even if they could, would not) buy everything I wanted, but I figured college was so critical that it was safe from being cut. It was not until my parents and I started filling out the financial aid forms—which showed their income and the costs for one year of college—that I understood the potential problem. I was particularly alarmed when the financial applications asked how much of the bill I was going to pay (called "Student Contribution")!

During my last semester of high school, I skipped a class one day to attend a special college presentation with a friend. Okay, I admit that it is not the type of activity students typically do when they skip class, but all of my friends and I were in college panic mode. When the speaker, Dr. Marian, said he was from the University of Texas at Austin, I perked up because that had been one of the schools on my list. After the session, I spoke with Dr. Marian about the possibility of getting a scholarship to UT. He indicated that based on my academic standing (I was scheduled to graduate with highest honors) and our conversation that I could receive a scholarship. Sure enough, shortly thereafter, I received a letter congratulating me on being admitted to UT and being eligible for a four-year scholarship.

In the end, I did select the University of Texas at Austin for my undergraduate work. The school met my parents' and my criteria. An extra bonus was that my friend had also received a scholarship and the university's Black Student Union had sent information highlighting the African-American presence there. Perhaps the tipping point was that the school was close. It is not that I was apprehensive about leaving home. When I considered the cost of my sister's education (she was still at Howard) and me both flying home for the holidays, I knew it would be an extra financial burden on my parents.

A few years after graduation, while serving as the education director for my church in Houston, I was offered the opportunity to pursue a graduate degree in electrical engineering at … Prairie View! During my first semester, I met my first professional mentor, Dr. Thomas Fogarty, who also became my thesis advisor. I had barely squeaked out of UT, so I was grateful for the chance to redeem myself academically with a master's degree in engineering. I will always be especially grateful for the rich cultural experience and personal support I received while matriculating at Prairie View. It was there that my confidence in my ability was restored and I gained clarity about what it means to be a professional in any field.

The rest of my academic story is more traditional. After graduating from Prairie View, I secured an electrical engineering position with a large semiconductor company. I participated in the company's prestigious engineering rotation program and, ultimately, worked in a research group for several years. I also spent many hours volunteering with TAME, a collaboration of technical companies that helped minority students pursue careers in science, engineering, and computer science. I later decided that I had a genuine passion for the development of others. I used the company's internal employment system to switch jobs to a training and education role. Then at the beginning of the following semester, I took advantage of the company's education assistance program to return to the University of Texas at Austin for a doctoral degree in educational administration with an emphasis in human resources development.

There are so many paths one can take to obtain a college education. My profile illustrates just a few. If you are committed to the goal and willing to invest a moderate amount of time in working the plan, the College Success Program can show you how. 🚪

Dr. Sharon Green is vice president of development for College Options Foundation, a free college scholarship search and financial aid information resource that connects students and parents with college funding opportunities.

CULTURE

BLACK GREEKS STILL = BLACK COOL:
Greek Organizations at HBCUs

by Meta Williams

College campuses are rooted in the common values and customs of the young people who matriculate, come of age, and shape their personas during what, for most, is their first time away from home. Life on black college campuses is just like campus life at majority institutions—*not*.

Picture a student walking from class on a bright sunny afternoon when suddenly she sees a huge circular gathering of people. As she approaches, she hears smooth rhymes spoken in unison and sees the group's syncopated steps. She immediately knows that one of the frats or the sorors are holding court with a step show.

At Historically Black Colleges and Universities (HBCUs), the step show is a big deal. Being Greek can have a profound impact on the overall experience of any student. The decision to join a Greek letter organization can be an asset for those who choose to take that path. Being Greek is not for every student, but even those who do not join are still somehow connected, either through a roommate or friend who decides to pledge, by attending Greek parties, or even accepting a scholarship offered by a sorority or fraternity. The black Greek culture is a significant part of the HBCU tapestry. National step shows promoted by major corporations have become a cottage industry, drawing legions of fans.

The art of stepping has become like skateboarding—everybody is doing it! It is intergenerational and invokes major feelings of pride among black people. Beyond black Greeks, there are step teams in communities and churches all over the country. Think *Stomp the Yard* or *Drumline* or even go back to Spike Lee's *School Daze*, and you'll find that stepping has found its way into mainstream culture. Films like these are the only visual images that many of today's youth have of what black college life is like. Given the mainstream success of these films, there is reason to believe that young people across races find themselves drawn to black college culture.

The black Greek legacy, which dates back to the turn of the twentieth century, goes deeper than the social and entertainment aspects of fraternities and sororities. It is rooted in a long-standing commitment to service to others, appreciation for history and tradition, self respect, and belief in the personal bonds of sisterhood and brotherhood.

History

There are nine recognized black Greek letter fraternities and sororities, which some refer to as the divine nine:

- Alpha Phi Alpha Fraternity, founded 1906, Cornell University
- Alpha Kappa Alpha Sorority, founded 1908, Howard University
- Kappa Alpha Psi Fraternity, founded 1911, Indiana University
- Omega Psi Phi Fraternity, founded 1911, Howard University
- Delta Sigma Theta Sorority, founded 1913, Howard University
- Phi Beta Sigma Fraternity, founded 1914, Howard University
- Zeta Phi Beta Sorority, founded 1920, Howard University
- Sigma Gamma Rho Sorority, founded 1922, Butler University
- Iota Phi Theta Fraternity, founded 1963, Morgan State University

Each organization has a national headquarters and regional offices and a chapter on most HBCU campuses. Many chapters also exist on majority campuses, as two of the fraternities were actually founded on white campuses. All exist under the umbrella of the National Pan-Hellenic Council, the largest stakeholder in ensuring that the black Greek tradition continues on college campuses.

"While having their own distinct heritages, the nine member organizations of NPHC offer insight and a unique perspective into this understanding and the development of black socioeconomic and cultural life. Each of the nine NPHC organizations evolved during a period when African Americans were being denied essential rights and privileges afforded others. Racial isolation on predominantly white campuses and social barriers of class on all campuses created a need for African Americans to align themselves with other individuals sharing common goals and ideals. With the realization of such a need, the African

American (black) Greek-lettered organization movement took on the personae of a haven and outlet, which could foster brotherhood and sister-hood in the pursuit to bring about social change through the development of social programs that would create positive change for blacks and the country. Today, the need remains the same."

—National Pan-Hellenic Council,
www.naphchq.org

Each organization has undergraduate chapters that are the major entry point for new members, but it is not the only way to join. Each year thousands of new members join graduate or alumni chapters, which exist for those who have completed their undergraduate degrees but still want to be part of the black Greek experience.

Current Trends

Each of the black Greek letter organizations have national and international members and host regional and national events that attract thousands of members and have a substantial economic impact on major cities, as the location for national events rotate each year.

"Today, America's nine black fraternities and sororities are two-and-one-half million members strong and among the most powerful and influential groups in African American society—with chapters at major universities and colleges across the country, including Stanford University, Howard University, and University of Chicago. Many of America's most prominent business leaders, scientists, politicians, entertainers, and athletes took their first steps toward making a difference in the world in a fraternity or sorority."

—Lawrence Ross, Jr., *The Divine Nine:
The History of African American
Fraternities and Sororities*

In 2008, the celebration of the 100-year anniversary of the nation's oldest sorority, Alpha Kappa Alpha, made national headlines and drew thousands of women to Washington, D.C. Mattel, one of the nation's largest toy manufacturers and home to the ubiquitous Barbie, even created the AKA Barbie to mark the celebration. Delta Sigma Theta hosted its 49th national

convention in 2008 and boasts a sisterhood of more than 200,000 predominately black college-educated women. The sorors of Sigma Gamma Rho celebrated their 52nd Boule in Detroit in 2008 and number more than 90,000 women at more than 500 undergraduate and alumnae chapters throughout the United States, Bermuda, the Bahamas, Africa, and Korea.

Omega Psi Phi is an international fraternity and is the first African-American national fraternal organization founded at an historically black college. Today, Omega Psi Phi has more than 700 chapters throughout the United States, Bermuda, Bahamas, Virgin Islands, Korea, Japan, Liberia, Germany, and Kuwait. There are many notable Omega Men recognized as leaders, including NBA basketball players Shaquille O'Neal and Michael Jordan, and corporate and presidential advisor Vernon Jordan. The Ice Cold Brothers of Alpha Phi Alpha see themselves as a primarily a service organization and have provided leadership and service through some of the nation's greatest challenges, following a model of leadership set by their most renowned member, Dr. Martin Luther King, Jr.

New media has taken networking and community building to a whole new level among black Greeks globally. The tradition of staying connected has always been at the core of the black Greek tradition; over decades, these groups created the institutional infrastructure that allows their members to communicate and build their message in ways that the ancestors could never have envisioned. A Google search uncovers 201,000 web sites, blogs, and social networking sites dedicated to black Greek letter organizations. Blogging and micro-blogging allow Greeks to build communities and quickly organize around key issues. The whole range of new media tools, from Facebook and My Space to Twitter and You Tube, has given these groups wider means to distribute information.

Though the black Greek letter organization history is based on proud and inspiring traditions, for many years questions have been raised about the process of pledging on some campuses and issues of hazing. Unfortunate incidents on some campuses have led to the implementation of a new process—called "intake"—as part of pledging. Walter Kimbrough, in his book *Black Greek 101: The Culture, Customs, and Challenges of Black Fraternities and Sororities,* outlines the history of pledging and the recent movements for reform of this practice. There is debate on how effective and authentic the new procedures are, with some who believe that the new pledging procedures have diminished important elements of the process, such as the limits on how long the pledge process can last. In spite of this ongoing debate, the interest level in black Greek life remains strong.

The tradition of giving back is a profound source of pride for most black Greeks, and they have launched many programs and initiatives to promote youth leadership and help address the staggering problems in communities of color. These organizations have invested innumerable hours as volunteers and mentors, have donated millions to countless causes, and are serious about making sure that the doors of opportunity remain open for future generations.

The benefits that one will reap from joining a black Greek letter organization are much like life in general—you will get out of it what you bring to it. Many students credit their relationships with other Greeks as a major part of their overall support system and the reason they were able to finish school. Others have had doors opened for them in their careers because of support from a frat brother or sorority sister. Many have passed on the Greek legacy to their children and grandchildren. Most will tell you that the Greek experience will bring you lifetime memories and bonds of friendship.

Black sororities and fraternities form the center of gravity for most black college campuses. It is sort of like the poise and self-assurance that media pundits attributed to President Barack Obama—something not easily put to words. Either you have it or you don't. You have to see it, you have to feel it—and the only way to truly appreciate it is to live it. ⏣

Meta Williams is director of Marketing & Communications for the Los Angeles Urban League and a senior consultant for major special events. She is also a proud member of Alpha Kappa Alpha sorority.

PROGRAMS

Blue Jazz, 1994
Bill Dallas
Oil on board
49" x 37"

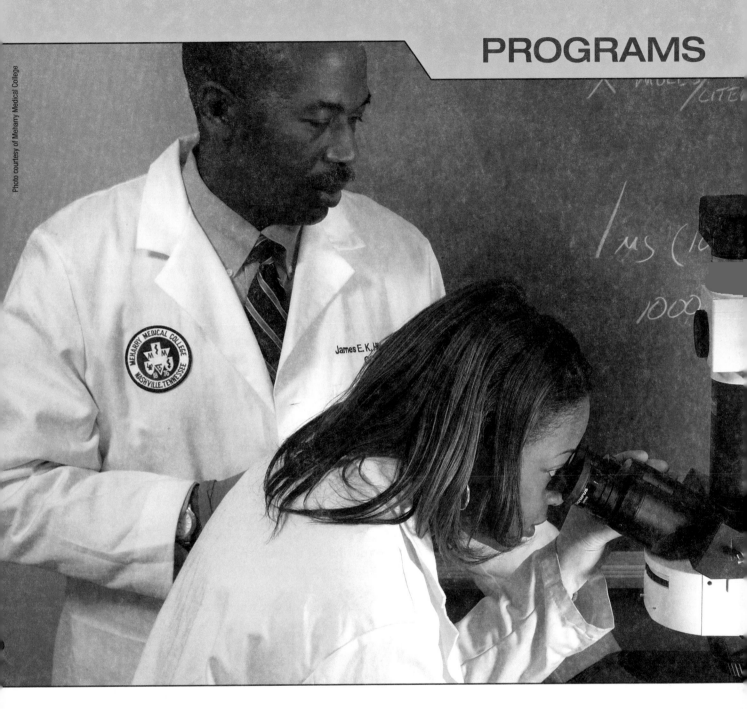

ON A HEALING MISSION:
Meharry Medical College Seeks to Eliminate Health Care Disparities

Access to quality health care for the underserved continues to be a top priority for the nation. Meharry Medical College, located in Nashville, Tennessee, is the nation's largest private, independent, historically black academic health center dedicated solely to educating minority and other health professionals. Committed to its legacy, Meharry's focus is on increasing the number of racial and ethnic minorities among the nation's healthcare workforce so that they may one day return to underserved communities to provide much needed healthcare services. To date, more than 76 percent

More than 76 percent of Meharry's graduates practice in underserved communities and more than 60 percent of the graduates from the School of Medicine enter primary care.

of Meharry's graduates practice in underserved communities and more than 60 percent of the graduates from the School of Medicine enter primary care.

The college's mission is even more vital as industry trends show a decrease in the number of healthcare professionals who choose to practice in areas of greatest need. African Americans face health disparities that threaten their very survival. Whether it is mortality rates, lack of prenatal care, life expectancy, the rise of HIV among minority women, higher death rates from preventable diseases or families without health insurance—studies show that minorities are currently experiencing poorer health status on all fronts. Experts agree that the future health of America as a whole will be influenced substantially by our success in improving the health of minorities.

Meharry exists to improve the health and health care of minority and underserved communities by offering excellent education and training programs in the health sciences; placing special emphasis on providing opportunities to people of color and individuals from disadvantaged backgrounds, regardless of race or ethnicity; delivering high quality health services; and conducting research that fosters the elimination of health status disparities.

History: The Salt Wagon Story

Meharry Medical College exists because two families came together to help one another—they put service above self and overlooked the societal boundaries of race, economics and class to help one another. In the 1820s, a teenage Samuel Meharry was hauling a wagon load of salt through the wilderness of Kentucky. Upon nightfall, his wagon became mired in the mud and he could travel no further. A free black family, whose name remains unknown to this day, helped young Samuel by taking him in for the night. They helped him free his wagon the next morning. Samuel Meharry had nothing to give in return, but he made a promise, saying "when I can, I will repay you ... or members of your race." Fifty years later, when the Methodist Church and its Freedmen's Aid Society were seeking support to establish a medical program to train freed slaves, Samuel Meharry remembered his pledge. He and his four brothers contributed $30,000 in cash and property to establish the Meharry Medical Department of Central Tennessee College, the forerunner of today's Meharry Medical College.

Meharry Medical College originated in 1876. The founding motivation was to train aspiring caregivers to serve not only newly freed African Americans but also all who were deprived of and needed medical attention. The founder and first president of Meharry Medical College was New Hampshire native George Whipple Hubbard (1841-1921), a former Union soldier who had received his medical degree from the University of Nashville. While still in school, Hubbard began the work of building Meharry with himself as sole instructor, religious advisor, and superintendent.

Meharry's dental and pharmaceutical departments were organized in 1886 and 1889, respectively. There was only one member in the first graduating class in 1890; he held the degree of master of arts. In 1910 the School of Nursing of Mercy Hospital was transferred to Meharry. The Hubbard Hospital was built in 1912. On October 13, 1915, Meharry Medical College was granted a charter separate from Central Tennessee College, which had changed its name to Walden University in 1900.

Meharry's Health Disparities Research

According to Diverse Issues in Higher Education, Meharry is one of the top producers of African-American Ph.D.s in biomedical and biological services. Students participate in innovative and cutting-edge research programs with special emphasis in diseases and conditions that disproportionately affect underserved populations.

Research at Meharry focuses on eliminating health status disparities by examining biological, behavioral, molecular, environmental, and other factors that contribute to the disproportionate burden of poor health outcomes borne by minority and underserved populations. The college conducts research in the areas of brain and behavior, cancer, HIV/AIDS, obesity and diabetes, oral health, and women's health.

The Center for AIDS Health Disparities Research (CAHDR) at Meharry's School of Medicine is funded by the National Institutes of Health. The center's principal charge is to conduct research and other scholarly activities designed to identify, understand, and eliminate factors responsible for the profoundly disproportionate burden of AIDS and HIV infection among minority populations in the United States.

Through combining research with community partnerships, the Center for AIDS Health Disparities Research will dramatically reduce the burden of AIDS in the local minority community. Discoveries made and models developed by the center will have permanent national and global impact. Recognizing the need for a multi-discipline approach to both the problem and the research needed to eliminate it, the CAHDR has identified three major areas of focus: biology, behavior, and community outreach.

The mission of the Center for Women's Health Research (CWHR) is to develop culturally sensitive models of health research and intervention that address health disparities in women of color in an integrated and holistic manner. In the twenty-first century, we are faced with incredible challenges in our effort to provide women's health care for an expanding culturally diverse community. The CWHR is dedicated to conducting research on health issues that disproportionately affect women of color by pro-

Photo courtesy of Meharry Medical College

viding a physical and administrative focus where scientists from many disciplines can come together to share insights and methods and deepen the understanding of the cellular, molecular, socio-behavioral, and clinical aspects of women's health.

The Center for Molecular and Behavioral Neuroscience (CMBN) is dedicated to conducting basic, translational, clinical, social, and behavioral research to generate new knowledge that will contribute to the nation's effort to reduce health disparities in the areas of neurological disease, mental health as well as drug abuse, and addiction, including alcoholism, while contributing significantly to the production of the next generation of neuroscientists.

School of Medicine Offers Cutting-Edge Research

The School of Medicine is the oldest and largest of the three schools at Meharry. It receives more than 4,000 applications each year, admitting only 100 medical students and some thirty residents who train in family practice, internal medicine, occupational medicine, preventive medicine, obstetrics and gynecology, or psychiatry.

The school is nationally recognized for its community-based and academic programs. National centers and programs have been established to address sickle cell anemia, hypertension, HIV/AIDS, environmental health, teen pregnancy, cancer, kidney failure, aging, and more.

Meharry's student body reflects the diversity of the nation, with representation from the African American, Caucasian, Hispanic, Asian, and Native American communities.

The school's mission is to deliver quality healthcare primarily to the poor and underserved. It helps students and residents with low resource backgrounds enter and excel the healthcare professions, providing cutting-edge research to help improve healthcare and eliminate disparities. The school aims to become a premier surgical department and national leader in surgical innovations, particularly as they relate to underserved minority populations.

The school is nationally recognized for its community-based and academic programs. National centers and programs have been established to address sickle cell anemia, hypertension, HIV/AIDS, environmental health, teen pregnancy, cancer, kidney failure, aging, and more. The school's faculty, staff, and students actively serve the community in many ways: mentoring for high school and college students; Health Careers Opportunity Programs for elementary, high school, and college students; speakers on health topics ,and more. The school has a program to assist college graduates in preparing to enter health professions schools.

Meharry's primary affiliated clinical training sites include the Veterans Affairs Medical Centers, located in Nashville and Murfreesboro, Tennessee; the Middle Tennessee Mental Health Institute; and the Blanchfield Army Community Hospital at Fort Campbell, Kentucky. Other affiliated clinical facilities include the United Neighborhood Health Services Medical Clinic, the Matthew Walker Comprehensive Health Center, the Centennial Medical Center, and the Baptist Medical Center.

Meharry's student body reflects the diversity of the nation, with representation from the African American, Caucasian, Hispanic, Asian, and Native American communities. The majority of Meharry's graduates keep the commitment of the founding fathers by practicing in underserved urban and rural communities. More than 60 percent of Meharry's School of Medicine graduates have selected generalist fields of family medicine, internal medicine, pediatrics, and obstetrics and gynecology as areas of specialization. Since 1970, Meharry has conferred more than 10 percent of the Ph.D. degrees awarded nationally to African Americans in all of the biomedical sciences. Meharry continues to be proud of its leadership role in helping to ensure diversity in the nation's health professions work force.

In addition to offering the M.D. degree to its medical students, the school trains graduate students for the master of science in public health degree offered through Meharry's School of Graduate Studies and Research. Similarly, the school trains graduate students for the doctor of philosophy degree in biochemistry, microbiology, pharmacology or physiology. Finally, the school provides significant training to students from Meharry's Schools of Dentistry and Allied Health Professions.

School of Dentistry Focuses on Health of Ethnic Minorities

Meharry' s School of Dentistry produces graduates that are recognized nationally and internationally as leaders in all aspects of dental care. Meharry is also among the leaders in providing dental educators for dental schools throughout the nation.

The school receives more than 3,000 applications each year, admitting only 55 dental students annually. It is one of four regional research centers for minority oral health designated by the National Institute of Health. The initiative of these research centers is to improve the oral health of ethnic minorities by expanding research opportunities and strengthening relevant research capacity of minority dental schools.

The School of Dentistry plays a vital role in meeting the needs of the entire social spectrum. It emphasizes comprehensive care that is not contingent on social or economic circumstances, geographical origin, or ethnicity. Graduates have become noted internationally for their achievements, performance, and service. Many have forged into society with vigor and vitality with the mission of the college and adopted a special focus on providing care for the underserved. Meharry graduates also serve on the faculties of many of the United States dental schools.

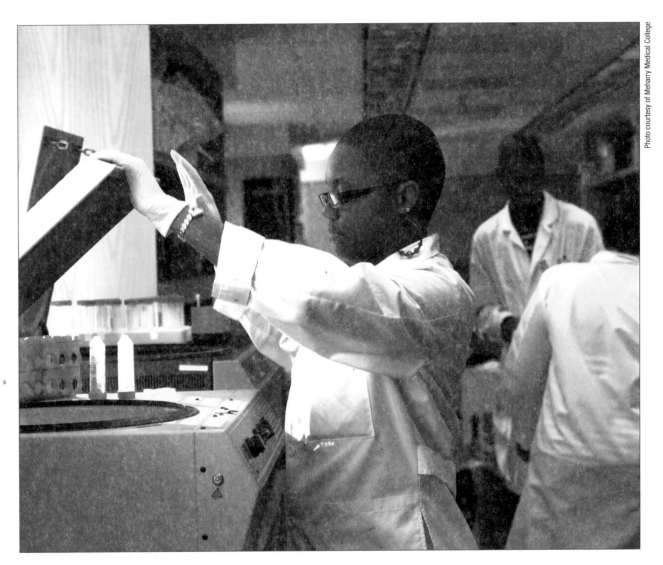

Photo courtesy of Meharry Medical College

Meharry's Health Programs

Meharry Medical College offers the doctor of medicine and joint M.A./Ph. D. degree; the doctor of medicine (M.D.); the doctor of dental surgery (D.D.S.); the doctor of philosophy (Ph.D.); the master of science in public health (M.S.P.H.); and the master of science in clinical investigation (M.S.C.I.).

In addition, the college sponsors two post-doctoral programs: the Oral and Maxillofacial Surgery program and the General Practice Residency program.

The Oral and Maxillofacial Surgery program consists of a four-year residency that is affiliated with the Metropolitan Nashville General Hospital and the Alvin C. York Veterans Administration Medical Center located in Murfreesboro, Tennessee. This program provides ample didactic and clinical educational opportunities to meet the requirements for certification of its graduates by the American Board of Oral and Maxillofacial Surgery. One resident is accepted for admission each year into this program.

The General Practice Residency program offers an opportunity for matriculants to broaden their experiences in all aspects of clinical dentistry with a heightened emphasis on public health service and care for the physically or mentally compromised patient. The resident learns to work efficiently and effectively with other health professionals in a hospital setting.

Since its inception, Meharry Medical College has graduated 3,685 physicians and 1,753 dentists; 286 have received master's degrees and 186 have received doctoral degrees. The college is accredited by the following by the Southern Association of Colleges and Schools (SACS), the Liaison Committee on Medical Education (LCME), and the American Dental Association (ADA). ⊞

Alton B. Pollard III, Ph.D., dean of the School of Divinity

EXPANDING THE VISION OF DIVINITY FOR THE 21ST CENTURY:
Howard University School of Divinity

by Tamara E. Holmes

The School of Divinity sits three miles from Howard's main campus, nestled away from the bustle of nearby traffic. The location "is the bane and the blessing of our existence," says Alton B. Pollard III, Ph.D., the school's dean. "When folks come here from the main campus, it's peaceful,

it's bucolic. But at the same time it's out of sight, out of mind. It's a constant juggling act."

Since taking the helm at the School of Divinity in July 2007, Pollard has been shaping a vision where the school's programs are prominent and more visible. Formerly the director of the Program on Black Church Studies, chair of the American Religious Cultures Program in the Graduate Division of Religion and associate professor of Religion and Culture at Emory University's Candler School of Theology, Pollard arrived at Howard with the intention of moving the School of Divinity to a new level. Today, the school's degree programs include the Master of Divinity, the Master of Arts in Religious Study and the Doctor of Ministry. Pollard is working to create a Doctor of Philosophy program.

"Establishing a Ph.D. program will require considerable investments and resources—human, fiscal and emotional," Pollard says. "It's not a three-year plan; it's not a five-year plan. We're really looking at a good decade's worth of work."

While Pollard is working with faculty to revise the curriculum and to strengthen existing programs—two tasks that he believes to be instrumental in making the Ph.D. program a reality—he is also working feverishly to make sure that the School of Divinity is able to remain relevant in the 21st century. "I think that God has a fresh word for every generation," Pollard says.

In the past, the Black church was not only a place of worship, but it was also a source of political power, with such leaders as Martin Luther King Jr., Jesse Jackson and Ralph David Abernathy using the pulpit to embark on a crusade for civil rights. But with African Americans seeing new levels of success in all areas of life, perhaps best exemplified by the election of President Barack Obama, the role of the Black church is different today, Pollard says.

"It is no longer enough to read the Bible and believe that you can speak a timeless word," Pollard says. "You must also read the newspaper and surf the Internet and advocate on Capitol Hill. You must be engaged in the lives of ordinary people wherever they are in their communities."

Pollard wants students to recognize that there is more than one way to experience religion. While some graduates will choose to preach in traditional churches, others may take their ministries to hospitals, prisons or workplaces.

In a visionary sense, Pollard also sees the Black church as a global phenomenon that extends beyond the borders of the United States. Related yet distinct, the Black church faithful are found on the African continent, and in the Caribbean, South America, Canada, Britain, France, India and elsewhere. He wants the School of Divinity to educate students of African descent everywhere.

Having a more expansive view of religion also means recognizing divinity in different faiths and traditions. While the School of Divinity teaches from a Christian perspective, "I have long understood that God is larger, deeper, broader and vaster than the Christian tradition," Pollard says. "So theological education can also be expansive enough to speak to our sisters and brothers who are interested in the study of religion who are Muslim, Buddhist, agnostic, etc." Most of the School of Divinity students are Christian, though "there's an occasional non-Christian who comes through," Pollard says. "I want to see that grow."

To help students become more comfortable with the idea of divinity being cultivated throughout everyday life rather than from within the four walls of a church, Pollard is also looking to work closely with other schools at Howard. The idea is to give students enough of a knowledge base to be able to minister in a variety of academic and professional fields. "We are working on establishing stronger relationships with the School of Business, the School of Law, the School of Social Work and the School of Medicine," he says. "I fully expect that as time goes on, these relationships will continue to unfold, because we live in a day and age where interdisciplinarity is an everyday event."

Pollard is optimistic about the school's ability to strengthen its role as a leader in theological education despite concerns the Howard community shares with the rest of the country about a troubled economy and an uncertain future. In fact, as Howard has done under the past leadership of such noted theologians as Howard Thurman and Benjamin E. Mays, Pollard says the School of Divinity is well-positioned to groom spiritual leaders who can bring comfort in troubled times.

"When you're the new kid on the block, it takes a while for people to come to know you. It takes longer for people to trust you," he says. "I'm working hard to garner our community's trust, because it's not about how much the dean gets right. It's really all about how much the dean is working to be right. And the rest will take care of itself." 𝕴𝕴

Holmes is a writer based in Maryland. © 2009 This article is reprinted with permission from the summer 2009 issue of Howard Magazine, *Howard University's alumni publication.*

PROGRAMS

SETTING THE STANDARD:
FAMU School of Journalism and Graphic Communication

Since its founding in 1982, Florida A&M University's (FAMU) School of Journalism and Graphic Communication (SJGC) has continually received high marks for the quality of its graduates. Students have earned awards from the Associated Press, CNN, the coveted William Randolph Hearst Medallion, and numerous other honors for their work on multiple media platforms.

This year alone, journalism, graphic, and photography students in SJGC have collected fourteen awards from the Florida Associated Press Broadcast (FAPB) contest and the Florida College Press Association (FCPA) Better Newspaper contest.

Alexis Blackwell, who won a first place AP Award for "Best Radio Newscast" for WANM 90.5, attributed her win to SJGC faculty support. "I don't think I would have received the training, love, and support from any other school than the FAMU SJGC," said Blackwell.

FAMU's WANM-FM radio station, *Journey* Magazine, and four journalism and graphic communication students were named "2008 Best of the South" contest winners by the Southeastern Journalism Conference. The competition included students from thirty-two colleges and universities in Alabama, Arkansas, Florida, Georgia, Louisiana, and Mississippi.

Brent Hatchett, a senior broadcast student from Detroit, Mich., was the first-place winner in the "Best Television Journalist" category. Hatchett served as a FAMU TV 20 news anchor in the fall of 2008 and regularly hosted a gospel program on WANM 90.5. He also won a Hearst Award for one of his TV news packages.

Xion Lester, a senior broadcast student from Tallahassee who also is an anchor for FAMU TV 20 News at Five, won third place in the "Best Radio Journalist" category. Leitoya Snelling, a junior arts education student from Tallahassee, won first place in the "Best Magazine Layout" category. Taylar Barrington, a freshman photography student from Stone Mountain, Ga., received an honorable mention in the Best Press Photographer category.

State-of-the Art Facilities Provide Training for Promising Careers

SJGC is located in a 100,000-square-foot building featuring state-of-the-art technology, including eleven computer labs, digital radio control rooms, two television studios, photography dark rooms, digital photography labs, a convergence newsroom, and numerous lab classrooms for students to learn and develop their skills. The SJGC is home to a variety of award-winning student-run media operations including, *The Famuan* newspaper, *Journey* Magazine, WANM Radio, FAMU-TV20, and Your Capitol Bureau—a news bureau that covers the Florida Legislature.

The school is comprised of two divisions—journalism and graphic communication. Both divisions offer accredited degree programs committed to preparing students for rewarding careers in broadcast (radio and TV) journalism, magazine production, newspaper journalism, public relations, graphic design, photography, and print management. Each program is taught by experienced faculty who are dedicated to teaching students how to enter the workforce as ethically grounded and technologically savvy professionals.

The Division of Journalism was the first journalism program at a historically black university to be nationally accredited by the Accrediting Council on Education in Journalism and Mass Communications (ACEJMC) in 1982. The ACEJMC is the agency responsible for evaluating professional journalism and mass communications programs in colleges and universities.

The Division of Graphic Communication became one of only four graphic communication programs accredited by the Accrediting Council for Collegiate Graphic Communications in 2002.

SJGC students have the opportunity to get involved with several professional student organizations and honor societies, such as the Public Relations Student Society of America; National Association of Black Journalists; Kappa Tau Alpha; Society of Professional Journalists; Epsilon Pi Tau; Graphics Arts Club; and the Association for Women in Communications.

Housed in the SJGC is PRodigy Public Relations Firm, a student-run, campus-based company. The company has a mission to provide real-life, hands-on training and experience for students who are full-time public relations majors by allowing them to manage the company and provide a menu of services to clients.

Today, with a distinguished faculty, nearly 600 undergraduate and graduate students, and several professional organizations, SJGC sets the standard in journalism and graphic communication for the twenty-first century and beyond. **ℍ𝕋**

PROGRAMS

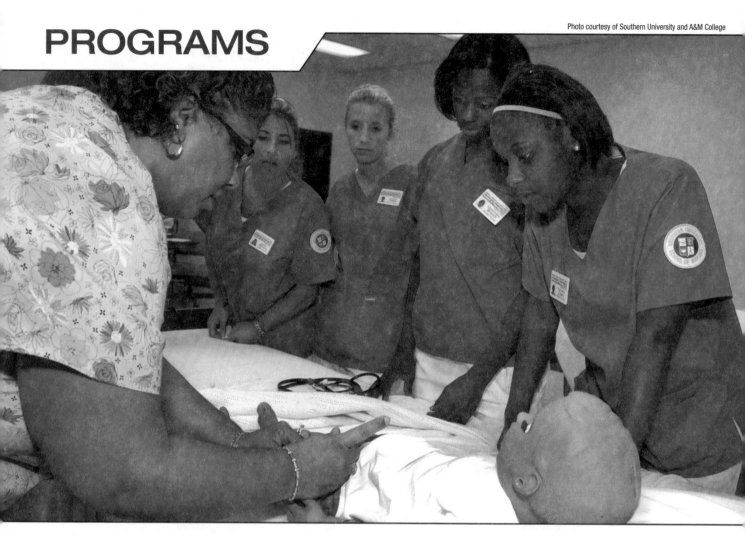

PREPARING TOMORROW'S LEADERS:
Southern University and A&M College

For more than a century, Southern University and A&M College, located in Baton Rouge, Louisiana, has provided a solid foundation for thousands of trailblazing graduates across the globe. With more than forty undergraduate and twenty-five graduate programs, SU has garnered national recognition for outstanding academics, ground breaking research initiatives, and innovative community service programs.

SU School of Nursing:
Visionaries in Critical Care

Understanding the critical issues in health care and the nation's need for quality job-ready nurses, the Southern University School of Nursing has been producing topnotch nursing graduates since 1985. Recognized as one of the largest producers of minority nurses, Southern University's School of Nursing is led by a community of dedicated, award-winning faculty and has received national recognition for its commitment to serving the state of Louisiana and beyond.

In the aftermath of Hurricane Katrina, the SU School of Nursing faculty and students mobilized to provide necessary health care to hurricane evacuees. Katrina was the sixth strongest Atlantic hurricane ever recorded and the third-strongest hurricane on record to make landfall in the United States, devastating much of the north-central Gulf Coast and flooding the levee system in New Orleans.

Heeding the call to serve, the SU School of Nursing led a mobilization of advanced practice nurses, nursing faculty and students, and physician volunteers to provide health care to hurricane evacuees. The school also adopted one of the largest FEMA transitional trailer communities in Baton Rouge. For their work, *Spectrum* and *Nurse Week* magazines awarded the school with the Nurses Hero Award.

The Southern University School of Nursing offers a bachelor's degree in nursing and a masters of nursing (MSN). Students pursuing the MSN can pursue studies in gerontology or complete studies to be a family nurse practitioner. The university also offers a doctor of philosophy in nursing.

SU College of Engineering:
Innovation and Technology on the Bluff

At the forefront of engineering innovation is Southern University's College of Engineering. Lauded as one of the nation's premier engineering programs, SU is one of the top five producers of minority engineers in the nation.

The college is housed in a multi-million dollar facility equipped with a high-tech auditorium, multimedia-ready classrooms, and state-of-the-art mechanical, thermal, materials, fluid mechanics, mechatronics, and computer-integrated manufacturing laboratories and research facilities.

The college offers four-year programs in civil engineering, electrical engineering, mechanical engineering, and electronics engineering technology. Prospective engineering students may also earn a dual degree in chemical engineering through a partnership with Louisiana State University. There are also opportunities for graduate studies through the masters of engineering program. Graduate level programs include environmental engineering, telecommunications and computer network engineering, electronic materials and processing engineering, materials science and engineering, and thermal science and engineering.

Preparing Tomorrow's Business Leaders
for the Global Workforce

The Southern University College of Business is preparing students to be leaders in an increasingly diverse and technologically advanced global workforce. The college's rigorous undergraduate and graduate programs are taking education beyond the four walls of the classroom through study abroad programs and conferences.

Southern University's business majors jet set abroad to countries such as Kampala, Uganda; Johannesburg, South

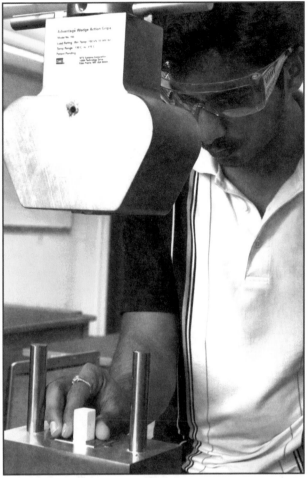

Africa; and Dakar Senegal learning firsthand about international business, finance, and marketing. Students also participate in the Business School Curriculum Development Project in Armenia, the Summer Institute for Future Global Leaders in the Caribbean, and the Mexico Student Exchange and Business Development Program.

College of Business students are also given opportunities to share their work with their peers and national business leaders during conferences such as the National Urban League's Annual Black Executive Exchange Conference. This year, the college placed first in the conference's Case Study Competition.

The SU College of Business offers baccalaureate degrees in accounting, business management, economics, finance, and marketing. The college also maintains a successful master of business education program designed around a two-year schedule of courses including evening studies for working students. The MBA program focuses on e-business, international business, entrepreneurship, and supply-chain management. ᵾ

HBCU FIRST—MARITIME TRANSPORTATION:
Texas Southern University Offers New Program

Texas Southern University is partnering with the Port of Houston Authority (PHA) on a new degree program in Maritime Transportation Management and Security. The program will address three highly prioritized national transportation needs: logistics, security, and environment. This is the first such university degree program related to Maritime Transportation and Security in Houston and the first such program at any Historically Black College and University (HBCU) in the country.

"Preparing graduates in this proposed degree program is not only important to the regional economy but also significant to meeting the workforce needs of the Port of Houston as well as the maritime industry," said Eva Pickens, director of communications at TSU.

PHA has committed $2 million to the program over a two-year period. As outlined in a Memorandum of Understanding, the funds will be primarily allocated to develop, promote, recruit, and graduate students from the Maritime Transportation Management and Security Program at Texas Southern University. Upon approval of the Texas Coordinating Board, classes will begin in the Fall of 2010.

"We are extremely excited about our new Maritime Transportation Management and Security degree program and grateful to the Port of Houston Authority for its commitment to supporting this important initiative," said Dr. John Rudley, president of TSU. "This partnership is a perfect realization of Texas Southern's commitment to providing our students with cutting-edge, relevant academic programs that speak to the real needs of today's and tomorrow's job markets."

PHA Chairman James T. Edmonds, whose organization has a long history of education involvement through the granting of scholarships and an extensive college intern program, calls the new partnership "timely, strategic, and mutually beneficial."

"Recently, there has been a global call for an infusion of prepared workforce into the maritime industry," Edmonds said. "This partnership integrates the resources of two dynamic Houston institutions committed to advancing education, commerce and improving quality of life. The success of this program will reap benefits that will be felt locally, nationally and around the world."

The new program allows the university to partner with the vital public component of the Port of Houston, one of the region's main employers, while creating a program that will not only positively impact Texas Southern students, but also expose area high school students to maritime employment opportunities. It's initiatives like this—the Maritime Transportation Management and Security program—that illustrate Texas Southern's move towards becoming one of the nation's leading, urban-serving educational institutions, TSU officials say.

"Recent studies have pointed to the challenge to continue to grow a well-prepared, diverse workforce to serve the maritime industry," said PHA Commissioner Kase Lawal. "Our partnership announced today is an important step by the port authority and TSU to work together to develop an innovative academic program and research efforts to address this challenge. Aside from developing a strong academic program, we are excited about the opportunity to produce major transportation-related research projects, which will complement the university's newly established National Transportation Security Center of Excellence for Petrochemicals."

Herbert H. Richardson, director emeritus and distinguished professor of engineering, Texas A&M University, said, "This program is important to the maritime industry as it faces challenges of productivity, security, and environmental impact in the decades ahead. Although the economy is down at present, it is certain to recover, producing unprecedented demands on Texas' ports and related marine industries. These demands require workers with new skills and capabilities that are in short supply in the existing workforce."

These programs will be significant steps toward giving better access to maritime careers, by tying into TSU's and PHA's existing partnerships with area high schools, including a high school maritime academy program that PHA is developing with industry partners.

"Since this will be the only university degree maritime transportation program in Houston and the first such program at a Historically Black College or University, the Texas Southern University program is filling a significant need," said Dr. Abelardo Saavedra, HISD Superintendent of Schools. "It completes the educational path from a high school maritime program to a university degree and a career in a field that is rapidly expanding."

C. Michael Walton, Ernest H. Cockrell Centennial Chair in Engineering, University of Texas, said, "The proposed program addresses a growing need in the U.S. and abroad for individuals educated in the aspects of an expanding global trade enterprise via the maritime industry. Houston is a catalyst for such a program because it is a major city in a dynamic country and state, has a world-class port with an established maritime business and is strategically located."

The Maritime Transportation Program, which will be offered at both the undergraduate and graduate level, is intended to produce graduates for a variety of administrative and managerial positions in maritime transportation and port operations;, produce graduates to function effectively in a number of diverse careers in three critical areas of maritime transportation: logistics, security, and environment; provide students with the academic background and preparation for pursuing advanced studies in the field of maritime transportation or affiliated areas; and provide training programs and individual courses to individuals already in the maritime transportation profession.

In the fulfillment of this mission, TSU students will acquire diverse career specialization options in maritime transportation, including but not limited to freight logistics specialist, shipping manager, port manager and operator, port security officer, maritime policy maker, maritime transportation planner, environment compliance coordinator/specialist, and emergency response specialist.

Through the proposed program, students will learn key issues in maritime transportation and port operations, and be prepared for careers in maritime transport and logistics, maritime infrastructure engineering and management, port management and operations, security of port facilities, and environmental protection.

Once approved by the Texas Coordinating Board of Higher Education, TSU will begin offering classes in the fall of 2010. 🎓

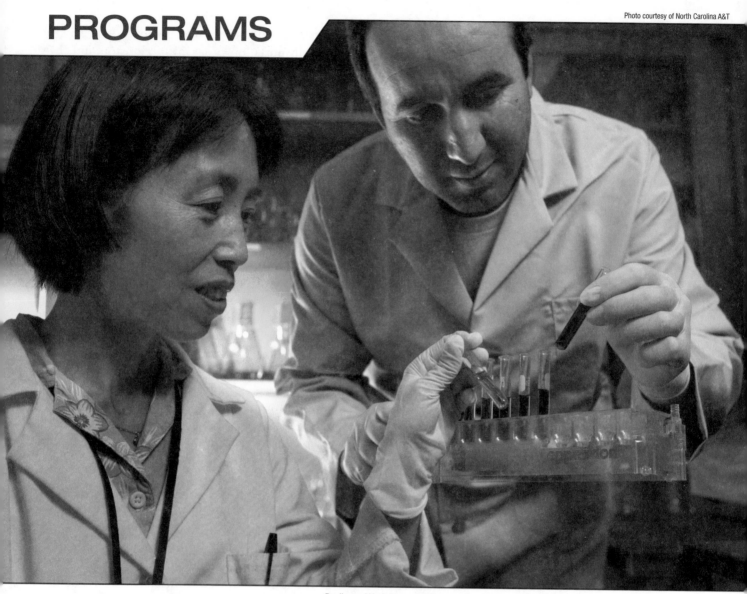

Dr. Jianmei Yu (left), an SAES research scientist, and Djaafar Rehrah, a research associate.

PEANUT BETTER:
NCAT Food Scientist Develops Process to Inactivate Allergens in Peanuts

North Carolina A&T University's Dr. Mohamed Ahmedna would like to see a day when every child—allergic or not—can enjoy a healthy, nutritious peanut butter sandwich. That day might arrive sooner instead of later, thanks to a process that he has perfected to inactivate allergens in peanuts.

The patent-protected process involves treating the whole kernels with a food-grade solution that does not alter the taste, aroma or texture of the kernel. Several food companies are showing interest in the new pro-

cess, according to Doug Speight, associate dean for Outreach and Technology Transfer at N.C. A&T.

The processed peanuts still have to undergo animal and human testing, but laboratory tests using immunoassays have confirmed 100 percent inactivation of the two worst allergens in peanuts, known as Ara h1 and Ara h2.

Peanut allergies are considered to be one of the most dangerous food allergies, afflicting millions of Americans and causing approximately 100–150 deaths and many more hospitalizations each year from anaphylactic shock.

"We are pleased to have developed a method to render this nutritious food safer for allergic individuals," Ahmedna said.

Ahmedna's process is expected to add value to a crop that is already economically and nutritionally important. Peanuts are the 12th largest crop in the United States, with a farm value of close to $1 billion a year, with the Southeast serving as the main peanut-producing region.

Peanuts are important nutritionally, too. Packed with proteins, healthy fats and a broad array of essential vitamins and minerals, they are considered an almost complete food. Their flavor, protein and fat profile make them nearly perfect from a food-processing standpoint, as well. From his lab at Tuskegee University in the early 1900s, the agricultural researcher George Washington Carver discovered approximately 300 food and non-food uses for the versatile legume, including peanut butter. Now, from his lab in a building on the N.C. A&T campus named for the famed food chemist—Carver Hall—Ahmedna is continuing that legacy.

The Challenge

Ahmedna knew he would need to address the allergy issue ever since he began researching alternative, value-added products for peanuts in 2001, with funding from the Collaborative Research Support Programs (CRSP) in the United States Agency for International Development (USAID).

The mission of CRSP is to support university research that improves the economic value of crops that are important in both the United States and a partner nation in the developing world, while at the same time building the agricultural research capacity of that partner. In Ahmedna's case, the selected crop is peanuts, and the partner is the West African nation of Senegal.

Peanuts are regarded by USAID as one of several ideal crops for economic development. Not only are they nutritious, but they are suited to the hot, arid climates and depleted soils that exist in many developing nations. Instead of requiring added fertilizer, they actually build fertility by fixing nitrogen, which makes them suitable for use in crop rotation.

Throughout the project, Ahmedna has developed several products and processes from the legume, including a low-fat, high-protein meat substitute, a nutritious powdered infant formula well-suited for developing nations, and an inexpensive process to remove aflatoxins, which are toxins that come from a mold that is found in virtually all peanuts to varying degrees. His work garnered him the USAID's George Washington Carver Agricultural Excellence Award in 2006, in recognition of his "forward-looking research in peanuts and peanut products to improve the quality of life for West Africans." Early on in the project, he had also started exploring methods for removing allergens.

"Everywhere we went, when we presented our work, inevitably someone would ask, 'But what about allergies?'" Ahmedna said. "We knew that at some point, we would have to address that issue."

To illustrate, he pulled out an article from a local paper that reported in 2005 on his early progress in removing about 70 percent of allergens from defatted peanut flour, and pointed to a section in which a peanut-allergic woman was quoted as saying that she looked forward to the day when she could try a spoonful of peanut butter.

"That was my challenge," Ahmedna said with a smile. "I knew then that I had to continue." In fact, by that time, he had already fully intended to see the project through to completion, and was confident that success was a matter of optimizing the process.

Adding Value to Agriculture

Ahmedna's success has to do with his career-long focus on extracting value-added products from underutilized agricultural byproducts, including procedures to isolate proteins from grains and legumes. Such isolates are used by the food ingredient industry as emulsifiers or functional ingredients in processed foods, or in powdered diet and protein shakes. One process he worked on while pursuing his Ph.D. at Louisiana State University was a protein isolate from wheat, which is now used by a food ingredient company.

At N.C. A&T, Ahmedna brought his expertise in this area to bear on peanuts and peanut byproducts. Originally, he focused on value-added products from defatted peanut flour—a protein-rich byproduct that is left after oil is pressed from the kernels. Ahmedna isolated the proteins from the flour appropriate for use as a food ingredient in convenience foods or shakes for fat-conscious Americans, or as a staple for protein-deficient diets in Senegal and other developing nations.

Because of his success in altering peanut proteins, Ahmedna next wanted to find out what effect his methods would have on allergens in peanuts.

"Allergens are proteins too, so we wanted to see if our protein altering processes had any effect on them as well," he said.

Sure enough, he observed the structure was altered. But more work needed to be done. Was the protein altered enough to make it unrecognizable to the immune system? And would the same process, or one related to it, also work on whole kernels as well as flour?

"We knew that for this to be a viable product, we had to make this work on the whole kernel, so that snack food companies could make use of it," he said.

"We were able to optimize the process until we were able to achieve a 100 percent reduction in allergens on whole kernels, in a relatively short time."

Allergies a Modern Day Issue

Most people are attracted to the rich flavor and aroma of peanuts, but this delicious, nutritious food has increasingly been regarded with a healthy degree of caution, because of the dramatic increases in the number of children with peanut allergies in recent years. Schools, airlines and other institutions that serve the public have increasingly limited their use, due to public health and liability concerns. One study showed that between 1997 and 2002, peanut allergies in children doubled in the United States. Today, experts believe that approximately 1 percent of children in the nation now suffer from an allergy to peanuts, said Dr. Wesley Burks, chief of the pediatric allergy and immunology division at Duke University Medical Center.

"Nobody really knows why," he said.

One possibility, the "hygiene hypothesis," states that children in industrialized nations now live in overly sanitized environments that prevent exposure to the appropriate levels of pathogens that prompt the immune system to develop defenses. The immune system, which develops in the first 12 years of life, evolved over millennia in conjunction with changes in the environment, but nowadays people don't live as close to nature as our ancestors did. However, many scientists acknowledge that testing the hypothesis is difficult to impossible, so it remains speculation. Another theory is that exposure to pesticides or other chemical toxins that are prevalent in industrialized nations interfere with the developing immune system, and are respon-

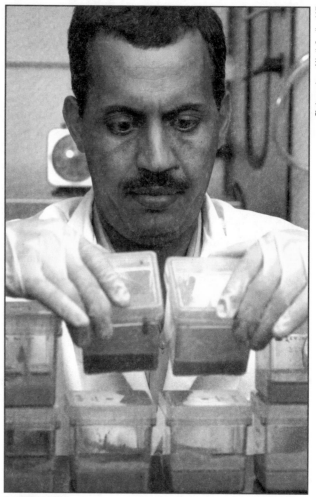

Photo courtesy of North Carolina A&T

Dr. Mohamed Ahmedna

sible for the rise in allergies in general. Still another hypothesis holds that roasting peanuts alters the proteins to make them more allergenic. Cuisine in Asia and elsewhere calls for peanuts to be steamed, boiled or stir-fried, which doesn't seem to affect the proteins the way roasting does. That theory seems plausible to Dr. Jianmei Yu, a research scientist in Ahmedna's lab, and co-inventor of the process.

"In China, we don't see all these allergies," she observed.

Whatever the cause, peanut allergies in the industrialized world appear to be here to stay for the foreseeable future. The process developed through the Agriculture Research Program at N.C. A&T could help reverse that troubling trend. 🚩

COMMITMENT TO BUSINESS AND INDUSTRY:
Drake State Offers Specialized Training

Of the 104 HBCUs currently in existence today, thirteen offer two-year programs that help students prepare for further education or learn needed skills to achieve success in technical, industrial, and vocational careers.

J.F. Drake State Technical College, located in Huntsville, Alabama, is a two-year public institution that provides specialized training for business and industrial communities through its Workforce Development Program. The college provides quality educational opportunities for its students while helping to promote economic growth and enhanced quality of life for the people of Alabama.

Creating Products for Business, Jobs for Graduates

Creating prototypes and services for a local startup business and providing a hands-on education creates quality jobs for recent graduates. This success story is the result of a cooperative partnership between Q-Track and J.F. Drake State Technical College.

The founders of Q-Track patented the "near-field electromagnetic ranging" system, which they call NFER® technology. This technology creates a tracking system that can operate in the harshest of indoor environments by utilizing low frequency electromagnetic waves that diffract around or penetrate through large obstacles that would block traditional GPS-type frequencies. By exploiting near-field properties of electric and magnetic waves, this breakthrough technology provides a unique combination of long-range, high-accuracy tracking at a low cost. The object or subject that has been equipped with a sensor or "tag" is monitored remotely by antennas throughout the covered area. The "tag" can be tracked with accuracy up to one foot in such challenging environments as mine shafts and large urban buildings.

Thanks to a grant from the National Science Foundation and an open house sponsored by the Drake State Amateur Radio Club, students studying for their associate's degree in industrial electronics from Drake State Technical College are gaining hands-on experience and providing valuable services to the local start-up company.

Since nearly all of Q-Track's employees are themselves licensed amateur radio operators, the partnership was easily initiated when Tim Williams, Q-Track's IT manager, visited Drake State to check out the new Ham Club. There he met Karl Henry, the faculty trustee for the club, chairman of the Business and Engineering Technologies Division, and electronics instructor. The two men began discussing the possibility of Henry's students assisting in the development and prototyping of the antenna systems used to detect the "tags" on the subjects being tracked. While the technology sounds more like something from the space program, the applications are very down to earth.

The measurement of electric and magnetic waves being processed in this application allows the military or firefighters to remotely track their counterparts in areas where traditional GPS would fail. The process can also be applied to locating pallets of merchandise in large warehouse facilities much more effectively.

In the past, Q-Track utilized engineering students from area four-year colleges. However, the company has found that Drake students can be utilized to prototype and test the circuitry and provide support without any real additional training.

The students who work on the project are members of the Special Topics–Senior Design Class and are interviewed for selection by both Q-Track and Henry. If selected, a student will receive course credit and payment for their services through a grant from the National Science Foundation.

"It enhances our already rigorous program with new challenges for the students," said Henry of Drake State. "My students are immediately put work in a small, dynamic, and fast-paced engineering design company where the schematics and drawings can change instantly. While this type of technology is based upon the basic principals we teach in our Electronic Communications course, the refinements in application are amazing. It really shows our students the broad spectrum of opportunities available to them once they graduate."

Bob DePierre, Q-Track's Director of Engineering added, "Being a small company with limited resources, it is an exceptional opportunity for us to utilize these students to create prototypes and to provide service to our clients while we are out generating new business. Our regular staff is so limited in size it's helpful to have the students with high level technical abilities here to continue the development processes when we travel."

While still in its infancy, the program has already helped Q-Track grow by one employee. One of the program's first interns will soon become a full-time permanent employee for Q-Track.

"This type of partnership represents the commitment a technical college, like Drake State, has to our community," adds Helen McAlpine, president of Drake State. "We are excited to work with Q-Track and to provide the type of cooperative training to our students that will ultimately allow both our graduates and the company to succeed."

LPN Graduates Exceeding National Average Pass Rate

Drake State's Health Science Technologies Division offers a Licensed Practical Nursing Program in which its graduates consistently exceed the national pass rate.

The testing for nursing students does not end with their last final of the last semester. In fact, the hardest test has yet to come. In order for nurses to practice in their field of study in Alabama, they must first successfully pass the NCLEX Exam to become licensed by the Alabama Board of Nursing (ABN). According to ABN's web site, the national average which passes the NCLEX exam is 86 percent. However, 97.8 percent of the students from Drake State passed the certification exam. The latest results were not a fluke with an average of 97.25 percent for the last two reporting periods.

"We believe the success of our students is due in part to their desire to succeed and to the exceptional staff in the nursing department here at Drake State," commented McAlpine. "It is highly unusual for a college to have an instructor who is selected to assist in writing questions for the NCLEX Exam, but we are privileged to have Thuy Lam and Alice Raymond who have participated in this process. We are also pleased that Alice Raymond has received national recognition for her doctoral dissertation."

According to the 2008-2009 Occupational Outlook Handbook, licensed practical nurses held about 749,000 jobs in 2006. Employment of LPNs is expected to grow 14 percent between 2006 and 2016, faster than the average for all occupations, in response to the long-term care needs of an increasing elderly population and the general increase in demand for health care services.

Drake State has also seen an increase in the demand for this program. While the Licensed Practical Nursing Program is currently near capacity, the student enrollment for Pre-Nursing increased by 75 percent this summer semester, indicating there will be a pipeline of students entering the program for an extended period of time.

"We are doing everything within our means to accommodate those qualified students who desire to enter the field of nursing," stated McAlpine. "Our biggest issue today is the lack of classroom space. Our students are demonstrating a need for additional facilities and our industry partners have requested we add to our Health Science offering of courses. Drake State is prepared to accommodate that request as we are able to move forward with securing additional resources."

Drake State currently offers certificates in License Practical Nursing and Certified Nursing Assistant. Its future goals include expanding the Health Science Program to include an RN degree as well as other medical certificate courses such as Radiological Technician, Phlebotomist, Medical Assisting, Home Health Aide, and Massage Therapy programs.

New Cooperative Educational Program with Army Garrison Command

The Army Garrison Command at Redstone Arsenal and Drake State Technical College have entered into a partnership for a Cooperative Educational Program. The agreement will become effective for the Fall Semester of 2009.

The agreement provides students studying at Drake State the opportunity to participate in STEP–Student Temporary Employment Program at the Army Garrison–Redstone Arsenal. The program allows participating students to work part-time, gaining valuable on-the-job experience while completing their educational requirements.

Joe W. Winston, Director of Human Resources for the Army Garrison, said this is the first agreement the Garrison has signed with a two-year college. "At the current time, we have opportunities for inspectors," stated Winston.

"The Garrison's immediate need for inspectors is a perfect fit for students participating in the Drafting, Electrical and Heating and Air Conditioning Programs of study at Drake," added McAlpine. "The partnership with the Army Garrison is just another opportunity for Drake State to deliver on our motto of: Our Graduates Work."

Winston stated that the student workers of today are truly a conscientious group—contemplating their futures and beginning to see themselves as the decision makers of tomorrow. Co-op agreements provide a valuable workforce development tool for both the student, Garrison Command, and the college.

"The U.S. Army Garrison is vigorously pursuing workforce development and workforce revitalization considering that over half of our current workforce is or will be eligible for retirement within a three- to five-year timeframe, and our workforce is expected to grow due to BRAC/Base Realignment and Closure. In an effort to meet our future manpower requirements, we have established Cooperative Education Agreements with several local four-year colleges and universities which will supplement other recruitment and staffing program," said Winston. "Drake State Technical College is the first two-year college that we have established a Cooperative Education Agreement with as we continue to enhance workforce development and workforce revitalization. These recruitment and staffing tools provide great opportunity and incentives in aiding our manpower requirement."

A student who participates in the Co-op/STEP Program at the Garrison will be considered for permanent placement into an authorized position upon completion of the program, which provides a great opportunity for on-the-job work experience with pay along with pursuing college education.

"Our students are now not only receiving education and hands-on experience on our campus, but the opportunity to put that knowledge to work when participating in a co-op program," said McAlpine. ⧉

Frederick Douglass, 2003
Tina Allen
Bronze
23" x 17.25" x 12"

Part II:
HBCU Profiles

The following profiles are intended to provide an historical, academic, cultural, and athletic overview of our nation's 104 HBCUs. General information includes address and phone number, web site address, year founded, mascot, type (4-year public, 4-year private, 2-year public, 2-year private), staff ratio (student to faculty ratio), and current student enrollment. Additionally, the sections noted below provide detailed information on each HBCU.

We have provided a Notes section in Part III that will allow you to keep notes on the HBCUs that interest you.

HISTORY
HBCUs are an integral part of American history and have rich heritages that show the struggles and victories in the pursuit of higher education. Each profile contains a brief history describing the origins and progression of these institutions.

MISSION
The vision or mission statement for each HBCU is provided.

MOTTO
If applicable, each HBCU's motto is provided.

TRIVIA
Additional information about each HBCU—that is, historical reference, institutional accomplishment, academic achievement, or cultural offering—is provided.

NOTABLES
From Booker T. Washington and Bessie Coleman to Thurgood Marshall and Debbie Allen, graduates from HBCUs have gone on to become world-famous business, educational, and political leaders, adventurers, entertainers, and athletes. This section provides notable graduates from each HBCU.

ACADEMIC PROGRAMS
Academic departments, divisions, schools, and colleges that comprise the institutions are noted. While almost all of the HBCUs also offer master's and doctoral degrees, undergraduate degrees are primarily listed here due to space limitations. If you are interested in post-graduate degrees, please contact the college or university you are interested in, or visit its web site.

STUDENT ORGANIZATIONS
Student clubs and organizations play a large role in the overall experience at HBCUs. Social, cultural, religious, professional, and departmental clubs and organizations are provided as well as an overview of the Greek life represented on each campus.

SPORTS
Team mascots for the HBCUs are noted, as well as information on membership in national and regional associations and intercollegiate sports for men and women.

TUITION
Amounts given are for in-state and out-of-state tuition costs. Please contact the HBCU you are interested in for any additional fees that might apply.

CONTACT INFORMATION
Information for contacting the admissions office for each HBCU is provided.

GEOGRAPHIC LOCATION FINDER

ALABAMA
1. Alabama A&M University
2. Alabama State University
3. Bishop State Community College
4. Concordia College—Selma
5. Gadsden State Community College
6. J. F. Drake State Technical College
7. Lawson State Community College
8. Miles College
9. Oakwood University
10. Selma University
11. Shelton State Community College
12. Stillman College
13. Talladega College
14. Trenholm State Technical College
15. Tuskegee University

ARKANSAS
1. Arkansas Baptist College
2. Philander Smith College
3. University of Arkansas at Pine Bluff

DELAWARE
1. Delaware State University

DISTRICT OF COLUMBIA
1. Howard University
2. University of the District of Columbia

FLORIDA
1. Bethune-Cookman University
2. Edward Waters College
3. Florida A&M University
4. Florida Memorial University

GEORGIA
1. Albany State University
2. Clark Atlanta University
3. Fort Valley State University
4. Interdenominational Theological Center
5. Morehouse College
6. Morehouse School of Medicine
7. Morris Brown College
8. Paine College
9. Savannah State University
10. Spelman College

KENTUCKY
1. Kentucky State University

LOUISIANA
1. Dillard University
2. Grambling State University
3. Southern University and A&M College
4. Southern University at New Orleans
5. Southern University at Shreveport
6. Xavier University of Louisiana

MARYLAND
1. Bowie State University
2. Coppin State University
3. Morgan State University
4. University of Maryland Eastern Shore

MICHIGAN
1. Lewis College of Business

MISSISSIPPI
1. Alcorn State University
2. Coahoma Community College
3. Hinds Community College
4. Jackson State University
5. Mississippi Valley State University
6. Rust College
7. Tougaloo College

MISSOURI
1. Harris-Stowe State University
2. Lincoln University of Missouri

NORTH CAROLINA
1. Barber-Scotia College
2. Bennett College
3. Elizabeth City State University
4. Fayetteville State University
5. Johnson C. Smith University
6. Livingstone College
7. North Carolina A&T State University
8. North Carolina Central University
9. Saint Augustine's College
10. Shaw University
11. Winston-Salem State University

OHIO
1. Central State University
2. Wilberforce University

OKLAHOMA
1. Langston University

PENNSYLVANIA
1. Cheyney University of Pennsylvania
2. Lincoln University of Pennsylvania

SOUTH CAROLINA
1. Allen University
2. Benedict College
3. Claflin University
4. Clinton Junior College
5. Denmark Technical College
6. Morris College
7. South Carolina State University
8. Voorhees College

TENNESSEE
1. Fisk University
2. Knoxville College
3. Lane College
4. LeMoyne-Owen College
5. Meharry Medical College
6. Tennessee State University

TEXAS
1. Huston—Tillotson University
2. Jarvis Christian College
3. Paul Quinn College
4. Prairie View A&M University
5. St. Philip's College
6. Southwestern Christian College
7. Texas College
8. Texas Southern University
9. Wiley College

U.S. VIRGIN ISLANDS
1. University of the Virgin Islands

VIRGINIA
1. Hampton University
2. Norfolk State University
3. Saint Paul's College
4. Virginia State University
5. Virginia Union University
6. Virginia University of Lynchburg

WEST VIRGINIA
1. Bluefield State College
2. West Virginia State University

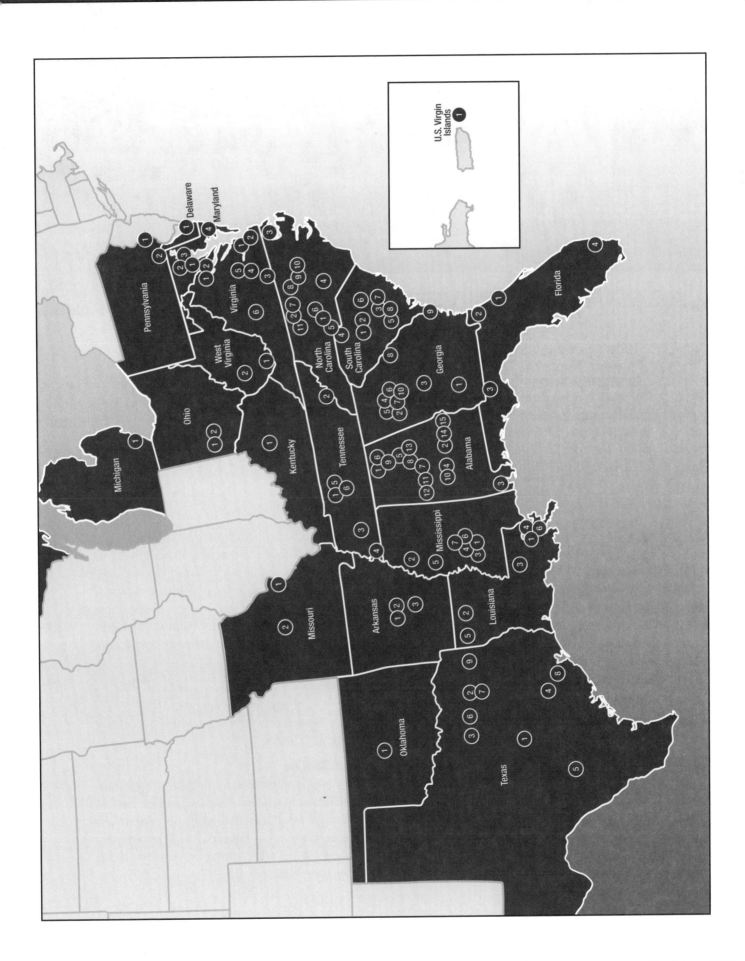

Photo courtesy of Alabama A&M University

ALABAMA A&M UNIVERSITY

ADDRESS: **4900 Meridian Street**
Normal, AL 35762
(256) 372-5000

WEB SITE: **www.aamu.edu**

FOUNDED: **1875**

MASCOT: **Bulldog**

AFFILIATION: **None**

TYPE: **4-Year Public**

RATIO: **14:1**

STUDENT BODY: **5,300**

HISTORY

Alabama A&M University (AAMU) is a land-grant university supported by the State of Alabama and federal funds appropriated by the Morrill Acts of 1862 and 1890. The university opened on May 1, 1875, as the Huntsville Normal School through the efforts of William Hooper Councill, an ex-slave who became its first principal and president.

In 1878, the name changed to the State Normal and Industrial School at Huntsville upon the introduction of industrial education. In 1891, upon receiving the Federal Land-Grant Fund, the school offered training in agriculture and mechanical arts, and thus changed its name again to the State Agricultural and Mechanical College for Negroes.

Upon becoming a junior college in 1919, the name was changed to the State Agricultural

and Mechanical Institute for Negroes. When the State Board of Education allowed the institute to work on the senior college level in 1939, the name was changed to Alabama Agricultural and Mechanical College. In 1969, the Alabama State Board of Education, which is the governing body of the institution, adopted the name of Alabama A&M University.

Alabama A&M University is accredited by the Commission on Colleges of the Southern Association of Colleges and Secondary Schools (SACS).

MISSION

AAMU is committed to providing an environment where scholars, thinkers, and leaders can flourish. The university works in cooperation with businesses, industrial and government agencies, and other institutions to help students put theory into practice.

MOTTO

"Service Is Sovereignty"

TRIVIA

Since 1997, a Nobel Laureate has visited the campus of AAMU every year.

NOTABLES

- Ruben Studdard—American pop, gospel, and R&B singer; winner of American Idol, second season

- John Stallworth—NFL player; selected to Pro Football Hall of Fame

ACADEMIC PROGRAMS

AAMU is comprised of five schools: the School of Agricultural & Environmental Sciences, the School of Arts & Sciences, the School of Business, the School of Education, and the School of Engineering & Technology.

The School of Agricultural & Environmental Sciences awards degrees in Agribusiness, Community Planning and Urban Studies, Food and Animal Sciences, Plant and Soil Sciences, and Family and Consumer Sciences.

The School of Arts & Sciences awards degrees in Biology, Chemistry, English, Mathematics, Military Science, Physics, Political Science, Social Work, Sociology, and Telecommunications.

The School of Business awards degrees in Accounting, Business Administration (with concentrations in Management Information Systems, Logistics and Supply Chain Management, International Business, and Office Systems Management), Business Education, Economics, Finance, Management, and Marketing.

The School of Education awards degrees in Art; Communicative Sciences & Disorders; Curriculum, Teaching & Educational Leadership (Developmental Reading, Ph.D. Reading, Secondary Education, and Educational Leadership); Elementary & Early Childhood Education; Health & Physical Education; Music; Psychology & Counseling (Clinical Psychology, Counseling Psychology, Guidance & Counseling, School Counseling, and Rehabilitation Counseling); and Special Education (Collaborative Teaching).

The School of Engineering & Technology awards degrees in Civil, Electrical, and Mechanical Engineering; Electrical and Mechanical Engineering Technology; Computer Science; Industrial Technology; and Construction Management.

STUDENT ORGANIZATIONS

Alabama A&M University has 115 registered student organizations, including concert, theater, band, choir, Greek societies, and honor societies. Students can join the student-run newspaper or the yearbook. The campus also has a student-run radio station, WJAB.

SPORTS

Alabama A&M University's sports teams, the Bulldogs, are members of the NCAA, Division I and participate in the Southwestern Athletic Conference (SWAC). Currently, there are seven men's varsity programs (baseball, basketball, football, golf, soccer, tennis, track and field) and eight for women (basketball, bowling, cross-country, softball, soccer, tennis, and track and field, and volleyball).

TUITION

$4,500/$9,000

CONTACT INFORMATION

Alabama A&M University
P.O. Box 908
Normal, AL 35762
Phone: (256) 372-5245
Toll-free: (800) 553-0816
Fax: (256) 372-5249
E-mail: admissions@aamu.edu

Photo courtesy of Alabama State University

ALABAMA STATE UNIVERSITY

ADDRESS: 915 S. Jackson Street
Montgomery, AL 36101
(334) 229-4100

WEB SITE: www.alasu.edu

FOUNDED: 1867

MASCOT: Hornet

AFFILIATION: None

TYPE: 4-Year Public

RATIO: 18:1

STUDENT BODY: 5,600

HISTORY

Founded in 1867, Alabama State University (ASU) is the nation's oldest publicly assisted historically black institution. Located in Montgomery, Alabama, ASU attracts a diverse faculty and student body representing all fifty states and thirteen foreign countries.

ASU has a legacy of providing teacher education for African Americans. The school was founded as the first public state institution opened specifically to educate Negro students. Because of its commitment to excellence, the university has been able to expand its mission to include the education of educators of all ethnicities.

Over the past fifteen years, ASU has grown to become a university with a global vision. The university has placed a greater emphasis on science programs at the graduate and undergraduate levels through its College of Health Sci-

ences. The university is also beginning to take the lead in providing research opportunities for students and faculty through its Life Sciences programs, which have received more than $16 million in grants to conduct research in nano-biotechnology and in the development of life-saving vaccines. ASU also boasts a nationally recognized College of Business and an award-winning Theatre Arts program led by actress Dr. Tonea Stewart.

MISSION

Alabama State University is committed to being a student-centered, nurturing, comprehensive, and diverse university through fostering critical thought, artistic creativity, professional competence, and responsible citizenship in its students; by enhancing the quality of life through research and discovery; and by helping to advance the State of Alabama and the nation through thoughtful public service.

MOTTO

"When We Teach Class, the World Takes Note."

NOTABLES

- Rosa Parks—Civil rights pioneer; referred to as the "Mother of the Modern-Day Civil Rights Movement"

- Dr. Ralph D. Abernathy—Civil rights leader and activist; one of the major leaders of the Civil Rights Movement

- Rickey Smiley—Comedian; actor; television host of BET's "ComicView"; radio personality, KBFB in Dallas

- Tarvaris Jackson—NFL quarterback for the Minnesota Vikings

- Fred Gray—Civil rights attorney and activist; represented Rosa Parks during the Montgomery Bus Boycott

ACADEMIC PROGRAMS

Alabama State University consists of eight academic units: the College of Arts & Sciences; the College of Business Administration; the College of Education; the College of Health Sciences; the College of Visual & Performing Arts; the Division of Aerospace Studies; the School of Graduate Studies; and the University College.

Degrees are awarded in Biological Sciences; Business Administration (with concentrations in Accounting, Computer Information Systems, Finance, Management, and Marketing); Business Education; Communications; Early Childhood Education; Educational Leadership, Policy and Law; Elementary Education; General Counseling; Health Education; Health Information Management; Health Sciences; History and Political Science; Languages and Literatures; Library Education Media Administration; Mathematics and Computer Science; Military Science; Music; Occupational Therapy; Physical Education; Physical Sciences; Physical Therapy; Psychology; Recreational Therapy; Secondary Education; Social Work; Sociology and Criminal Justice; Special Education; Theatre Arts; and Visual Arts.

STUDENT ORGANIZATIONS

Alabama State University has more than 70 student organizations. Social and cultural activities include theater, band, chorale, orchestra, musical concerts, and a speakers series, featuring noted artists and professional groups.

Students may get involved in the student-run newspaper, yearbook, or radio station, WVAS 90.7 FM.

Greek fraternities include Alpha Phi Alpha, Kappa Alpha Psi, Omega Psi Phi, Phi Beta Sigma, and Alpha Phi Omega; sororities include Alpha Kappa Alpha, Delta Sigma Theta, Sigma Gamma Rho, and Zeta Phi Beta.

SPORTS

Alabama State University's sports teams, the Hornets, are members of the National Collegiate Athletic Association (NCAA), Division 1 and participate in the Southwestern Athletic Conference (SWAC).

Men's sports include baseball, basketball, cross-country and indoor-outdoor track, football, golf, and tennis. Women's sports include basketball, bowling, cheerleading, cross-country and indoor-outdoor track, golf, soccer, softball, tennis, and volleyball.

TUITION

$4,600/$9,200

CONTACT INFORMATION

Alabama State University
915 S. Jackson Street
Montgomery, AL 36101-0271
Phone: (334) 229-4291
Toll-free: (800) 253-5037

Photo courtesy of Bishop State Community College

BISHOP STATE COMMUNITY COLLEGE

ADDRESS: 351 North Broad Street
Mobile, AL 36603
(251) 405-7000

WEB SITE: www.bishop.edu

FOUNDED: 1927

MASCOT: Wildcat

AFFILIATION: None

TYPE: 2-Year Public

RATIO: 20:1

STUDENT BODY: 3,341

HISTORY

Founded in the summer of 1927, Bishop State Community College was originally the Mobile Branch of Alabama State College (University) in Montgomery, Alabama. It was established as an in-service arm of Alabama State College that offered extension courses to African-American elementary and secondary teachers in Mobile.

Dr. Sanford D. Bishop, Sr. joined the teaching staff of "The Branch" in 1938 as an instructor of English and music. In 1941, he was named dean.

In 1965, the Alabama State Legislature ratified the Alabama State Board of Education's action establishing the Alabama State College–Mobile Center as Mobile State Junior College and severed its relationship with Alabama State College in Montgomery. Dr. Bishop was then appointed president of the new independent junior college.

In 1971, the Alabama State Legislature again changed the name of the college to S. D. Bishop State Junior College. Ten years later, Dr. Yvonne Kennedy was appointed as the second president of the college.

In 1989, the name of the college was changed to Bishop State Community College to reflect its growth in vocational/career offerings, transfer offerings and community service activities.

After 26 years as president, Dr. Kennedy retired on July 30, 2007. Dr. James Lowe, Jr., became the interim president on August 1, 2007, and on May 22, 2008, the Alabama State Board of Education appointed him the third president.

MISSION

Bishop State Community College is committed to providing high-quality educational opportunities and services that are responsive to individual and community needs for the citizenry of Mobile and Washington Counties at an affordable cost.

MOTTO
"Success Starts Here"

TRIVIA
The Bishop State Community College choir and band comprised of students from all academic disciplines, performs throughout Alabama and the Southeast at alumni, social, and governmental events.

ACADEMIC PROGRAMS
Bishop State Community College consists of two programs of study—academic and technical—that include eleven divisions: Division of Social Sciences; Division of Business and Economics; Division of Developmental Education; Division of Education; Division of Health Related Professions; Division of Humanities; Division of Natural Sciences and Mathematics; Division of Workforce Development; Division of Commercial and Industrial Technology; Division of Consumer & Transportation Technology; and Division of Engineering and Construction.

Academic programs are offered in Accounting Technology, American Sign Language, Early Childhood Education, Geographic Information Systems, Interpreter Training Program, Management and Supervision, Office Administration, Associate Degree Nursing, Emergency Medical Services, Funeral Service Education, Health Information Technology, Medical Coding, Medical Transcription, Physical Therapist Assistant, and Practical Nursing.

Technical programs are offered in Air Conditioning and Refrigeration Technology, Automotive Technology, Cabinetmaking, Civil Engineering Technology, Cosmetology, Diesel Technology, Electrical Technology, Electronics Engineering Technology, Graphic Communications Technology, Jewelry Design, Machine Tool Technology, Nail Technology, Process and Maintenance Technology, Truck Driving, Watch Repair, Automotive Body Technology, Barbering and Hair Styling, Commercial Food Service, Masonry, Plumbing, and Welding Technology.

STUDENT ORGANIZATIONS
Bishop State Community College provides organizations for students to participate in a variety of social and educational activities.

Health Occupations Students of America (HOSA) offers leadership opportunities as well as motivation and recognition for students interested in careers in the health industry.

The Students in Free Enterprise is an organization dedicated to educating individuals on concepts of market economics, entrepreneurship, and business ethics through educational outreach projects. Leadership opportunities can be found in the Phi Theta Kappa Society and Student Government Association.

SPORTS
Bishop State Community College's teams, the Wildcats, are members of the National Junior College Athletic Association (NJAA). Men's sports include basketball and baseball; women's sports include basketball, softball, and cheerleading.

TUITION
$2,700/$4,830

CONTACT INFORMATION
Dean of Students
Bishop State Community College
351 North Broad Street
Mobile, AL 36603-5898
Phone: (251) 405-7000
Fax: (251) 438-5403
E-mail: info@bishop.edu

Photo courtesy of Concordia College—Selma

CONCORDIA COLLEGE—SELMA

ADDRESS: **1804 Green Street**
Selma, AL 36701
(334) 874-5700

WEB SITE: www.concordiaselma.edu

FOUNDED: 1922

MASCOT: Hornet

AFFILIATION: Lutheran Church–
Missouri Synod

TYPE: 4-Year Private

RATIO: 18:1

STUDENT BODY: 555

HISTORY

Concordia College–Selma was founded in 1922 as the Alabama Lutheran Academy and Junior College by Lutheran missionaries in Alabama. A plea by Miss Rosa Young to the Lutheran Synodical Conference of North America regarding the spiritual and educational welfare of African Americans led to the founding of more than twenty congregations in her native area.

Three years later, a resolution was adopted for the funding of a school for the purpose of training professional church workers. Selma was selected for the location, and the first classes were conducted in a rented cottage.

In 1925, the college's first campus buildings were dedicated, and the following year Concordia's first class graduated. On July

1, 1981, Alabama Lutheran Academy and Junior College became Concordia College.

Concordia College–Selma is accredited by the Commission on Colleges of the Southern Association of Colleges and Schools (SACS).

MISSION

Concordia College–Selma is committed to preparing students through Christ-centered education for lives of responsible service to the church, community, and the world. To achieve this mission, Concordia engages its students in programs and activities which identify and meet their spiritual, academic, social, and physical needs.

MOTTO

"Opportunitas ad Excellentiam" (Opportunity for Excellence)

TRIVIA

Concordia College–Selma provides an Academic Boot Camp to assist in the development of students, specifically incoming freshman males.

Through the MAN Center and the Rosa J. Young Center for Women activities, students are able to receive resources for making healthy and positive lifestyle choices that facilitate educational and professional career development and wellness. Participants receive encouragement and support to further enhance their spiritual, academic, professional, cultural, and social lives. Students are then able to identify places of service to society and implement programs that make positive contributions to their communities and to the environment.

NOTABLES

- Judge Jo Celeste Pettway—District Judge, Wilcox County (Camden, Alabama)

- Judge Eldora Anderson—Probate Judge, Perry County (Marion, Alabama)

- Joseph Carstarphen—Pharmacist; owner of Interlink Drugs (Selma, Alabama)

- Jamaal Hunter—Mayor of Uniontown, Alabama

ACADEMIC PROGRAMS

Concordia College–Selma consists of the Division of General Education (Math, Physical and Natural Sciences, Physical Education, Humanities and Fine Art); the Division of Business and Computer Information Systems; the Division of Education; the Division of Social Studies, Social/Behavioral Sciences, and Theology; and the Hornets Academy.

An associate degree is awarded in General Studies (with a concentration in Child Development).

A bachelor of science degree is awarded in Education (Early Childhood Education and Elementary Education), Business Administration, and Social Work.

STUDENT ORGANIZATIONS

Concordia College–Selma offers several clubs and organizations for students, including the International Student Union, Concordia Choir, the Magnificent Marching Hornet Band, and the *Hornet Tribune*, the student-run newspaper.

SPORTS

Concordia College–Selma's teams, the Hornets, are members of the United States Christian Athletic Association (USCAA).

Men's sports include basketball, football, soccer, baseball, and track and field; women's sports include basketball, softball, track and field, and volleyball.

TUITION

$6,300

CONTACT INFORMATION

Director of Admissions
Concordia College–Selma
1804 Green Street
Selma, AL 36701
Phone: (334) 874-5700
Fax: (334) 874-3728

GADSDEN STATE COMMUNITY COLLEGE

ADDRESS: **1001 George Wallace Drive**
Gadsden, AL 35903
(256) 549-8200

WEB SITE: **www.gadsdenstate.edu**

FOUNDED: **1925**

MASCOT: **Cardinal**

AFFILIATION: **None**

TYPE: **2-Year Public**

RATIO: **16:1**

STUDENT BODY: **8,225**

HISTORY

Gadsden State Community College is a public community college that was created by the consolidation of Harry M. Ayers State Technical College and Gadsden State Community College in 2003.

The college initially became Gadsden State Community College on February 28, 1985, when the Alabama State Board of Education merged Alabama Technical College, Gadsden State Technical Institute, and Gadsden State Junior College.

Alabama Technical College was founded as the Alabama School of Trades in 1925 and was the first state-operated trade school in the southern United States. In 1973, the name of the school was changed to Alabama Technical College. Gadsden State Technical Institute opened in 1960 as Gadsden Vocational Trade School, a private training facility; in 1972 it was renamed the Gadsden State Technical Institute, and in 1997, it was designated an Historically Black College or University by the U.S. Department of Education. Gadsden State Junior College was established in 1965.

Gadsden State Community College is accredited by Commission on Colleges of the Southern Association of Colleges and Schools (SACS).

MISSION

Gadsden State Community College is committed to meeting the needs of its diverse communities by offering quality educational and cultural experiences that are accessible and affordable and that empower students to become lifelong learners.

MOTTO

"Choose Your Direction"

TRIVIA

Gadsden State Community College's Valley Street Campus was designated an Historically Black College or University (HBCU) in November 1997. This distinction provides the campus eligibility to participate in the Title III, Part B HBCU Program.

NOTABLES

- Jeff Cook—Singer and musician for the award-winning country music group Alabama

- Laura Dodd—Country music singer

- Maurice Dupree—Slot receiver and kick returner for NFL Jacksonville Jaguars

ACADEMIC PROGRAMS

Gadsden State Community College consists of the Academic Division and the Technical Division.

An associate of science degree is awarded in Agribusiness Education; Agriculture; Aquatic Biology; Aquatic Technician; Art; Biology; Business Administration; Chemistry; Computer and Information Science; Computer Science; Computer Science Technology; Computerized Accounting; Criminal Justice; Childhood Development; Early Childhood Education; Elementary Education; Emergency Medical Services; English; Financial Planning and Counseling; General Studies; Health, Physical Education, and Recreation; Health Sciences; History; Human Services; Humanities; Legal Transcriptionists; Liberal Arts; Marketing Management; Mathematics; Mathematics Education; Medical Secretary; Medical Transcriptionist; Music; Office Administration; Paralegal; Pre-Dentistry; Pre-Engineering; Pre-Forestry; Pre-Law; Pre-Medical Technology; Pre-Medicine; Pre-Nursing; Pre-Pharmacy; Pre-Veterinary Medicine; Psychology; Science Education; Science; Speech Communication; Sociology; and Word Processing Specialist.

An associate of applied science degree and certificates are awarded in Air Conditioning and Refrigeration; Automotive Collision Repair; Automotive Manufacturing Technology; Automotive Service; Carpentry; Civil Engineering Technology; Cosmetology; Diesel Technology; Drafting and Design Technology; Electrical Engineering Technology; Electronic Engineering Technology; Industrial Automation Technology; Machine Tool Technology; Mechanical Design Technology; Realtime Reporting; and Welding Technology.

STUDENT ORGANIZATIONS

Gadsden State Community College offers numerous clubs and organizations for students, including Paralegal Club; Residence Hall Council; Circle K (Kiwanis); Gadsden State Singers; Scholars Bowl Team; Information Technology Club; Science, Math, & Engineering Club; International Club; Baptist Campus Ministries; Southern Belles Dance Team; Medical Lab Technology Society; Student Government Association; and Student Nurses Association.

SPORTS

Gadsden State Community College's teams, the Cardinals, are members of the National Junior College Athletic Association (NJCAA). Men's sports include basketball, baseball, and tennis; women's sports include basketball, cross-country, tennis, softball, and volleyball.

TUITION

$2,160/$3,864

CONTACT INFORMATION

Director of Admissions
Gadsden State Community College
1001 George Wallace Drive
Gadsden, AL 35903
Phone: (256) 549-8200

Photo courtesy of J. F. Drake State Technical College

J.F. DRAKE STATE TECHNICAL COLLEGE

ADDRESS: 3421 Meridian Street
North Huntsville, AL 35811
(256) 539-8161

WEB SITE: www.drakestate.edu

FOUNDED: 1961

AFFILIATION: None

TYPE: 2-Year Public

RATIO: 14:1

STUDENT BODY: 1,364

HISTORY

J.F. Drake State Technical College was established in 1961 as the Huntsville State Vocational Technical School. Today it is a two-year, public institution of higher education that provides the citizens of North Alabama with flexible, innovative vocational and technical training at a reasonable cost.

J.F. Drake provides accessible quality educational opportunities while promoting economic growth and enhancing the quality of life for the people of Alabama. It offers career-oriented diploma, certificate, and associate degree programs and courses, as well as comprehensive, specialized training for business and industry.

The college is a member of the Alabama Two Year College System and is accredited by the Commission on Occupational Education.

MISSION

J.F. Drake State Technical College is committed to satisfying the needs and academic pursuits of the community by offering developmental studies, noncredit short-term courses, and continuing education courses on scheduled days, evenings, and weekends.

MOTTO

"Our Graduates Work"

TRIVIA

According to the Alabama Board of Nursing's web site, over 97 percent of Drake State's Nursing Students pass the licensure exam.

Drake State has signed a cooperative educational agreement with the Army Garrison at Redstone Arsenal. This is the first cooperative educational agreement the Army Garrison has signed with a two year college.

NOTABLES

- Bill Curtis—Senior Product Engineer at DRS Test and Energy Management Research and Development Group in Huntsville, Alabama

- Nina Bullock—Instructor in the drafting and design department at Drake State; recognized regionally as a leader in her field

- John Outerbridge, Ph.D.—Defense contractor in Huntsville, Alabama; gives motivational speeches in his home land of Bermuda

ACADEMIC PROGRAMS:

J.F. Drake State Technical College has six divisions: Business and Engineering Technologies; Manufacturing and Applied Technologies; Health Science Technologies; Salon Management Technologies; General Education; and Adult Education.

Programs are offered in Accounting Technology, Culinary Arts/Hospitality Services Management, Industrial Electronics Technology, Information and Communication Technology, Office Systems Technology, Automotive Technology, Electrical Technology, Engineering Graphics Technology, Heating & Air Conditioning Technology, Industrial Systems Technology, Machine Tool Technology, Welding Technology, Practical Nursing, Nursing Assistant, Barbering Technology, Cosmetology Technology, Standard Lists, Area I English, Area II Humanities/Fine Arts, Area III Natural Science/Math/Computer Science, Area IV History/Social/ Behavioral Sciences, Area V Institutional Requirements, and Adult Education.

J.F. Drake State Technical College also provides IT certification programs for CompTia A+ and Net+, Microsoft Certified Systems Engineer, and Cisco Systems CCNA certification training.

STUDENT ORGANIZATIONS

J.F. Drake State Technical College offers opportunities for industry networking and advancement through Phi Beta Lambda Business Fraternity, the International Association of Administrative Professionals and the Amateur Radio Club. Members of Phi Beta Lambda consistently earn the honor of representing the college and the state at the national conference through their professional competencies. Through the IAAP Student Chapter, professional administrative personnel gain access to valuable workshops and participation in the campus wide Career Week. The Amateur Radio Club has served as a valuable outreach program for the Industrial Electronics Program to local high tech industry.

The Student Government Association actively organizes recruiting events, student appreciate activities, and facilitates communication between students and college administrators. The SGA also publishes, *The Blue Pages,* a newsletter distributed on campus.

For students and friends of the campus with musical abilities, Drake State sponsors a choir which performs at campus events and throughout the community.

TUITION

$90 per semester hour

CONTACT INFORMATION

Admissions
J. F. Drake State Technical College
3421 Meridian Street
North Huntsville, AL 35811
Phone: (256) 539-8161

Photo courtesy of Lawson State Community College

LAWSON STATE COMMUNITY COLLEGE

ADDRESS: 3060 Wilson Road SW
Birmingham, AL 35221
(205) 925-2515

WEB SITE: www.lawsonstate.edu

FOUNDED: 1949

MASCOT: Cougar

AFFILIATION: None

TYPE: 2-Year Public

RATIO: 16:1

STUDENT BODY: 3,700

HISTORY

Lawson State Community College was founded in 1949 as the first black trade school in Alabama. Through mergers and campus additions, Lawson State evolved into a community college offering a variety of degrees and certificates to a diversified and growing student population.

Over its sixty-year history, and especially under current president, Dr. Perry W. Ward, Lawson State has significantly increased enrollment, expanded the curriculum, enhanced relations with business and industry, and improved the college's capital outlay. The college now enrolls approximately 7,500 credit and non-credit students on campuses in Birmingham and Bessemer.

Lawson State Community College is accredited by the Commission on Colleges of the Southern Association of Colleges and Schools (SACS).

MISSION

Lawson State Community College is a comprehensive, public, two-year, multi-campus college, which seeks to provide accessible quality educational opportunities, promote economic growth and enhance the quality of life for people in its service area.

MOTTO

"It's All Here!"

TRIVIA

Lawson State Community College is an authorized testing site for Certiport, Drake–KRYTERION, ISO Quality Testing, LaserGrade, PAN Testing and Prometric.

As the leader in automotive education in the state, Lawson State's Alabama Center for Automotive Excellence offers six automotive technology programs, including manufacturer-sponsored Ford ASSET, GM ASEP, and Toyota T-TEN. Lawson State is one of four Snap-on Incorporated Tier One Diagnostic Training and Certification Centers in the nation.

NOTABLES

- Larry Langford—Mayor of Birmingham, Alabama

- Niles Ford—Fire chief of Lincoln, Nebraska

- Leernest Ruffin—Lieutenant colonel, U.S. Air Force

ACADEMIC PROGRAMS

Lawson State Community College has four educational divisions: Business Technologies, Career Technical, Health Professions, and Liberal Arts and Sciences.

The Business Technologies Division, accredited by the Association of Collegiate Business Schools and Programs (ACBSP), awards associate of arts degrees in Business Administration and Business Education; associate in applied science degrees in Accounting Technology, Business Administration & Management, Computer Science (Business), Computer Science (Math), Office Administration (General), Administration (Legal), Administration (Medical); various certificates; and industry certifications for Microsoft, CISCO, CompTIA, IC3, Novell, and Oracle. Every online and web-supported course is on BlackBoard.

The Career Technical Division awards applied science degrees in Air Conditioning/Refrigeration, Automotive Technician, Auto Service Ford Asset, Auto Service GM-ASEP, Auto Service Toyota T-TEN, Building Construction, Commercial Art & Illustration, Drafting/Design Technology, Electronics–Industrial, Graphics and Printing, Horticulture-Ornamental, Medium/Heavy Trucks Technology, and Welding. Certificates are awarded in Air Conditioning/Refrigeration, Automotive

Technician, Barbering Technology, Commercial Art & Illustration, Cosmetology Technology, Drafting/Design Technology, Electronics–Industrial, Graphics and Printing, Medium/Heavy Trucks Technology, and Welding.

The Health Professions Division awards applied science degrees for ADN Program and Mobility Program (LPN-ADN) and certificates in Practical Nursing and Dental Assisting.

The Liberal Arts and Sciences awards degrees in Art; English; Music; Health and Physical Education; Biology; Chemistry; Mathematics; Physics; Child Development/Early Childhood; Criminal Justice; Pre-Law; Political Science; Psychology; Social Science; and Social Work.

STUDENT ORGANIZATIONS

Lawson State Community College offers several organizations, including the Student Government Association, Ambassadors, Association of Information Technology Professionals, International Association for Administrative Professionals, Phi Theta Kappa Honor Society, Phi Beta Lambda, Kappa Beta Delta International Honor Society, American Dental Assistants Association, Society of Manufacturing Engineers, and Students in Free Enterprise.

SPORTS

Men's sports include baseball and basketball; women's sports include basketball and volleyball. The college also offers cheerleading and dance opportunities.

TUITION
$2,210

CONTACT INFORMATION
Director of Admissions
Lawson State Community College
3060 Wilson Road SW
Birmingham, AL 35221
Phone: (205) 929-3416
Fax: (205) 925-3716

Photo courtesy of Miles College

MILES COLLEGE

ADDRESS: **5500 Myron Massey Boulevard**
Birmingham, AL 35064
(205) 929-1000

WEB SITE: www.miles.edu

FOUNDED: 1905

MASCOT: Golden Bear

AFFILIATION: Christian
Methodist
Episcopal
Church

TYPE: 4-Year Private

RATIO: 19:1

STUDENT BODY: 1,800

HISTORY

Miles College was originally founded in 1896 by the Colored Methodist Episcopal Church (now the Christian Methodist Episcopal Church) and named for its first bishop, William H. Miles.

In 1905, the institution, which had operated as a high school in Booker City under the North Alabama Conference in its early years, was chartered by the State of Alabama as Miles Memorial College. In 1941, the college's name was changed to Miles College.

Miles College is accredited by the Commission on Colleges of the Southern Association of Colleges and Schools (SACS).

MISSION

Miles College is committed to motivating and directing its students to seek holistic development that leads to intellectual, ethical, spiritual, and service-oriented lives. Guided by these core values, the Miles College education involves students in rigorous study of the liberal arts as preparation for work and life-long learning; in the acquisition of verbal, technological, and cultural literacy; and in critical community participation—all as a prelude to responsible citizenship in the global society that they will help to shape.

MOTTO

"Knowledge and Peace and Love for All"

TRIVIA

Miles College's marching band, the Purple Marching Machine, was established in 1996. One of its first performances was at a campaign rally for President William Clinton. Since that time, the high-energy band, which combines drills and dance routines into its programs, has performed at the Inaugural Pioneer Bowl in Atlanta, Georgia, as well as the first Historically Black Colleges and Universities Band Extravaganza in 2000 and the Macy's Thanksgiving Day Parade in New York City in 2002.

NOTABLES

Alumni of Miles College include two mayors of Birmingham, judges, physicians, business leaders, legislators, and teachers.

ACADEMIC PROGRAMS

Miles College consists of six academic divisions: the Division of Business & Accounting; the Division of Communications; the Division of Education; the Division of Humanities; the Division of Natural Sciences & Mathematics; and the Division of Social & Behavioral Sciences.

Bachelor of arts degrees are awarded in Communications, English, History, Music, Political Science, and Theater.

Bachelor of science degrees are awarded in Accounting, Biology, Biology Education, Business Administration, Chemistry, Chemistry Education, Child Development, Computer and Information Science, Criminal Justice, Early Childhood/Elementary Education, Elementary Education, English/Language Arts Education, Environmental Science, History/General Social Science, Management, Management Information Systems, Mathematics, Mathematics Education, Music Education, Political Science, and Social Science Education.

Bachelor degrees are also awarded in Social Work and Music Education (choral and instrumental).

Minor programs are offered in Accounting, Biology, Business Administration, Chemistry, Communications, Computer Science, English, Gerontology (certificate program), Mathematics, Music, Political

Science, Public Administration, Religion and Philosophy, and Sociology.

STUDENT ORGANIZATIONS

Miles College offers a wide variety of associations, clubs, and organizations for students, including College Concert/Gospel Choirs, English Club, Health Careers Club, Hospitality Cub, Humanities Club, Institute of Management Accountants, International Students Organization, Mathematics Club, Men of Miles, Pre-Alumni Council of UNCF, Press Club, Student Government Association, Student Library Action Committee, Students in Free Enterprise, Cheerleaders, Purple Marching Machine, Student Center Board, Student Support Services Club, and Varsity Athletics.

Greek fraternities include Alpha Phi Alpha, Kappa Alpha Psi, Omega Psi Phi, and Phi Beta Sigma; sororities include Alpha Kappa Alpha, Delta Sigma Theta, Sigma Gamma Rho, and Zeta Phi Beta.

SPORTS

Miles College's teams, the Golden Bears, participate in the Southern Intercollegiate Athletic Conference (SIAC).

Men's sports include baseball, basketball, cross-country, football, and track. Women's sports include basketball, cross country, softball, volleyball, and track.

TUITION
$8,000

CONTACT INFORMATION

Director of Admissions and Recruitment
Miles College
5500 Myron Massey Boulevard
Fairfield, AL 35064
Phone: (205) 929-1657
Toll-free: (800) 445-0708
Fax: (205) 929-1627

OAKWOOD UNIVERSITY

ADDRESS: **7000 Adventist Blvd. NW**
Huntsville, AL 35896
(256) 726-7000

WEB SITE: www.oakwood.edu

FOUNDED: 1896

AFFILIATION: Seventh-day
Adventist

TYPE: 4-Year Private

RATIO: 13:1

STUDENT BODY: 1,824

HISTORY

Founded by the Seventh-day Adventist Church in 1986 as the Oakwood Industrial School, the institution opened its doors to sixteen students who were taught various trades and skills. The name was changed to Oakwood Manual Training School in 1904, and the school was chartered to grant degrees in 1907. The first postsecondary level courses were offered to more than 100 students at what was then called Oakwood Junior College. Degree curriculum modifications resulted in yet another name change to Oakwood College in 1944, which was accredited by the Southern Association of Colleges and Schools (SACS) to award associate and baccalaureate degrees in 1958. Enrollment first topped 1,000 during the 1974-75 academic year. The most recent reaffirmation of accreditation was voted in June 2001. During the 2008–2009 school year, more than 1,800 students attended. On January 1, 2008, the institution became Oakwood University.

The first graduating class in 1909 numbered five. Nine years later (1918), the first two graduates of Oakwood Junior College received degrees. The first senior college graduating class (Spring 1945) consisted of nine students. Twenty-eight years later, in 1973, the first class in the history of the college to exceed 100 members graduated (124). The first graduating class in excess of 200 finished just nine years later in 1982. The graduating class of 2008 is the first class to graduate under the University status, totaling 315 members.

Oakwood University has a beautiful natural setting on 1,185 acres of prime land and is considered one of the historical landmarks of the city of Huntsville. The university prepares students from across America and from many other nations to serve God and humanity in a variety of positions and careers. Close to 60 percent of the culturally diverse faculty hold doctorate degrees from a wide range of universities and colleges around the nation and world.

MISSION

Oakwood University, an historically black Seventh-day Adventist institution of higher learning, provides quality Christian education that emphasizes academic excellence; promotes harmonious development of mind, body, and spirit; and prepares leaders in service for God and humanity.

MOTTO

"Education. Excellence. Eternity."

TRIVIA

Oakwood is consistently listed among the top 15–20 institutions of higher learning that provide African Americans into medical schools.

NOTABLES

- Barry C. Black—Chaplain of the U.S. Senate

- Angela M. Brown—Soprano; Metropolitan Opera debut in 2004

- Wintley Phipps—Recording artist; minister; founder of the U.S. Dream Academy

ACADEMIC PROGRAMS

Oakwood University offers undergraduate degrees in Biological Sciences, Business & Information Systems, Business Education, Chemistry, Communication, Journalism, Education, English & Foreign Languages, Family & Consumer Sciences, Health & Physical Education, History, Math, Computer Sciences, Music, Nursing, Psychology, Religion, Theology, Social Work, and Organizational Management. A graduate program is offered in Pastoral Studies.

STUDENT ORGANIZATIONS

Oakwood University offers students numerous social and group activities, including religious convocations conducted by distinguished guest speakers and an arts and lecture series.

Leadership opportunities can be found in such groups as the United Student Movement, Adventist Youth Society, Ministerial Forum, residence clubs, or various department clubs that include science, pre-law, business, education, social work, music, home economics, and nursing.

Students can also join the yearbook staff or the student-run newspaper. Communications majors can work at the student-run radio station, WJOU-FM.

TUITION

$10,795 per semester

CONTACT INFORMATION

Director of Enrollment Management
Oakwood University
7000 Adventist Boulevard NW
Huntsville, AL 35896
Phone: 256-726-7354
Toll-free: 800-824-5312
Fax: (256) 726-7154
E-mail: admission@oakwood.edu

Photo courtesy of Selma University

SELMA UNIVERSITY

ADDRESS: 1501 Lapsley Street
Selma, AL 36701
(334) 872-2533

WEB SITE: www.selmauniversity.org

FOUNDED: 1878

MASCOT: Bulldog

AFFILIATION: Baptist

TYPE: 4-Year Private

RATIO: 11:1

STUDENT BODY: 300

HISTORY

Selma University was founded in Mobile, Alabama, in 1878, as the Alabama Baptist Normal and Theological School with the goal of preparing better leaders for the church and schoolroom. The school was relocated to Selma and opened in the Saint Phillips Street Baptist Church.

In 1881, the school was incorporated by an act of the legislature and became the Alabama Baptist Normal and Theological School of Selma. On May 14, 1908, the name was officially changed to Selma University.

Selma University has always had a four-year program in Religion, but in the late 1980s moved all of its programs to the four-year level. In the Fall of 2000, it changed from a Christian liberal arts college to a Bible college.

Selma University is affiliated with the Alabama State Missionary Baptist Convention and has trained several thousand Baptist ministers through its School of Theology, and more than 3,000 graduates in liberal arts, business administration, sciences, mathematics, and computer sciences.

Selma University is accredited by the Commission on Accreditation of the Association for Biblical Higher Education (ABHE) in Canada and the United States.

MISSION

Selma University is committed to preparing men and women for Christian ministry and Christian living in the modern world based on the example of Jesus Christ. As a Christian Bible college, the university seeks to stimulate its students spiritually, intellectually, and socially and to produce graduates who are servant leaders in their churches, communities, and chosen areas of vocation.

MOTTO

"Selma University, training men and women for Christian services."

NOTABLES

- Reverend Nelson Smith, Jr.—Former president of the National Progressive Baptist Convention

ACADEMIC PROGRAMS

Selma University offers an associate of arts degree in Bible and Theology.

A bachelor of arts is awarded in Bible and Pastoral Ministry; General Studies; General Studies (Business Administration Concentration); General Studies (Biology and Physical Education Concentration); and General Studies (Bible, Theology and Christian Education Concentration).

A master of arts degree is awarded in Bible and Pastoral Ministry as well as Bible and Christian Education.

STUDENT ORGANIZATIONS

Selma University offers numerous social and cultural activities for students, including musical concerts and annual events such as Founder's Day and Religious Emphasis Week.

Students can work on the campus quarterly publication, the *Selma University Chronicle,* or seek leadership opportunities in the Student Christian Government Association.

Greek societies include Phi Beta Sigma Fraternity and Zeta Phi Beta Sorority.

SPORTS

Selma University has applied for membership in the United States Collegiate Athletic Association (USCAA). Its teams, the Bulldogs, participate in baseball.

TUITION

$4,150

CONTACT INFORMATION

Director of Admissions
Selma University
1501 Lapsley Street
Selma, AL 36701
Phone: (334) 872-2533
Fax: (334) 872-7746

SHELTON STATE COMMUNITY COLLEGE

ADDRESS: 9500 Old Greensboro Road
Tuscaloosa, AL 35405
(205) 247-SSCC

WEB SITE: www.sheltonstate.edu

FOUNDED: 1979

MASCOT: Buccaneer

AFFILIATION: None

TYPE: 2-Year Public

RATIO: 25:1

STUDENT BODY: 6,700

Shelton State Community College is entering its fourth decade of service as a premier example of Alabama's community colleges.

Shelton State provides a wide range of services and offerings. In 1997, the Alabama Legislature designated Shelton State Community College as the Alabama Community College of the Fine Arts. As its mission, the College is to provide accessible, inclusive educational and cultural opportunities for students and citizens of Alabama through quality instruction and innovative arts programming. As a vital link to the business community, The West Alabama Center for Workforce Development was developed to ensure a coordinated effort between Shelton State Community College, business and industry, and workforce agencies in the West Alabama area. The Center coordinates programs which provide instruction of basic skills to entry level workers as identified by local business and

industry for entry level jobs in their companies.

In the area of Adult Education, the College focuses on assisting adults in its five-county service area in obtaining knowledge and skills for employment and self-sufficiency. GED and Career Readiness Credential preparation, graduation exam help, and skills remediation are also offered at no cost to students.

Shelton State Community College also provides a wide variety of personal interest offerings to all ages through its Community Education and Lifelong Learning programs. Courses include instruction in dance, academic enrichment for children, fencing, computer skills, floral design, carpentry, and exercise classes to name a few.

Shelton State Community College offers financial assistance to eligible students to help pay the cost of their education. Shelton State is approved for Federal Financial Aid, Veterans Benefits, Vocational Rehabilitation Training, and Alabama Prepaid Affordable College Tuition (PACT). The institution also awards state and private scholarships.

HISTORY

Shelton State Community College was established by resolution of the Alabama State Board of Education on January 1, 1979. That resolution combined two existing institutions: Shelton State Technical College, established in 1952, and the Tuscaloosa branch campus of Brewer State Junior College, an institution whose main campus was located in Fayette, Alabama. In 1994, Shelton State Community College consolidated with C. A. Fredd State Technical College, another public two-year college located in Tuscaloosa. Previously, C. A. Fredd State Technical College was recognized as one of the nation's Historically Black Colleges and Universities.

MISSION

Shelton State Community College is a public, open-admission, comprehensive, community college whose primary mission is to provide accessible postsecondary education, training, and community educational opportunities.

TRIVIA

In three of the last four years, Shelton State has been an award winner in the Exemplary Initiatives Competition of the National Council of Instructional Administrators (NCIA). In 2008, a unique collaboration that included Shelton State, entitled "Realizing the Dream: Celebrates the Legacy of Dr. Martin Luther King Jr.," earned Honorable Mention honors.

ACADEMIC PROGRAMS

Accredited by the Commission of Colleges of the Southern Association of Colleges and Schools, Shelton State awards the Associate in Arts Degree, the Associate in Science Degree, and the Associate in Applied Science Degree.

The College also offers two types of certificate programs: certificate programs 30-60 semester hours in length and short-term certificate programs 9-29 semester hours in length. The Associate in Arts Degree and the Associate in Science Degree are designed for students who wish to complete the freshman and sophomore years at Shelton State Community College and transfer to a senior college or university and complete the baccalaureate degree. The Associate in Applied Science Degree and the certificate programs are designed for students who plan to seek employment based upon the competencies and skills attained through those programs of study.

STUDENT ORGANIZATIONS

The College has an athletic department that annually receives state, regional, and national recognition in baseball, softball, men's and women's basketball, and co-ed cheerleading. Other student organizations include Shelton Ambassadors, Phi Theta Kappa Honor Society, Ecology Club, the Courier Student Newspaper, Corsair Fencing Club and the Student Action Team.

SPORTS

Shelton State's teams, the Buccaneers, are members of the National Junior College Athletic Association (NJCAA). Its athletic department annually receives state, regional, and national recognition in baseball, softball, men's and women's basketball, and co-ed cheerleading.

TUITION
$2,700/$4,830

CONTACT INFORMATION
Shelton State Community College
9500 Old Greensboro Road
Tuscaloosa, AL 35405
Phone: (205) 391-2236
Fax: (205) 391-391

Photo courtesy of Stillman College

STILLMAN COLLEGE

ADDRESS: 3601 Stillman Boulevard
Tuscaloosa, AL 35401
(800) 841-5722

WEB SITE: www.stillman.edu

FOUNDED: 1876

MASCOT: Tiger

AFFILIATION: Presbyterian
Church (USA)

TYPE: 4-Year Private

RATIO: 18:1

STUDENT BODY: 1,000

HISTORY

Stillman College's history began in 1874 when the Reverend Doctor Charles Allen Stillman and a group of Presbyterians asked the Presbyterian Church to establish a school in Tuscaloosa for the purpose of training African-American males to be ministers. Authorization was granted by the General Assembly of the Church in 1875, and in 1876, Stillman Institute held its first classes.

In 1898, the school moved to its present location in western Tuscaloosa. Over the next fifty years, the institute organized a junior and senior high school, established a junior college program, and operated a hospital and nursing training school.

In 1948, the name of the institution was changed to Stillman College; a year later, in 1949, it became a four-year liberal arts college.

Primarily a teaching institution, Stillman College is accredited by the Commission on Colleges of the Southern Association of Colleges and Schools (SACS) to award the bachelor of arts and the bachelor of sciences degrees.

MISSION

Stillman College is committed to fostering academic excellence and providing high-quality educational opportunities for diverse populations with disparate levels of academic preparation.

MOTTO

"Tradition—Excellence—Vision"

TRIVIA

Stillman College's William H. Sheppard Library, which houses approximately 117,550 books, journals, and media materials, is named for Dr. William H. Sheppard, who completed his training for the ministry at

Stillman in 1887, and, with Samuel B. Lapsley, founded the missionary work of the Presbyterian Church in the Congo (now Zaire). The library features special collections that include the Martha L. O'Rourke African-American Collection and a microfilm collection of materials from the Schomberg Collection of Negro Life and History.

NOTABLES

- Al Denson—President/CEO of Birmingham-Shuttlesworth International Airport

- Major General Willie Williams—Commanding General of the Marine Corps Logistics Command

- James Lewis—Owner of the *Birmingham Times Newspaper*

ACADEMIC PROGRAMS

Stillman College consists of three academic divisions: the Division of Arts & Sciences; the Division of Business; and the Division of Education.

Bachelor of arts degrees are awarded in Art, Broadcasting, Communications, Computer Science, English, Foreign Languages, History and Government, International Studies, Journalism, Music, Music Education, Philosophy/Religion, Sociology, Speech, and Visual Art.

Bachelor of science degrees are awarded in Biology, Business Administration, Chemistry, Computer Science, Elementary Education, Health, Physical Education and Recreation, Mathematics, Physics, Psychology, Social Work, and Telecommunications Technology.

STUDENT ORGANIZATIONS

Stillman College offers numerous group and cultural activities for students, including theater, band, and chorale, as well as chess, history, and science clubs. Students can work on the student-run newspaper (*The Tiger's Paw*), the yearbook (*The Stillmanite*), or participate in special interest organizations, such as the Tigerettes Dance Team, Blue Pride Marching Band, or Stillman College Choir.

Leadership opportunities can be found in the Student Government Association, the Christian Student Association, or numerous college-wide committees.

Greek sororities include Alpha Kappa Alpha, Delta Sigma Theta, Sigma Gamma Rho, and Zeta Phi Beta; fraternities include Alpha Phi Alpha, Kappa Alpha Psi, Omega Psi Phi, and Phi Beta Sigma. Honor societies represented include Gamma Iota Sigma and Alpha Kappa Mu.

SPORTS

Stillman College's teams, the Tigers, are members of National Collegiate Athletic Association (NCAA), Division II and participate in the Southern Intercollegiate Athletic Conference (SIAC).

Men's sports include baseball, basketball, cross-country, football, tennis, and track and field; women's sports include basketball, cross-country, softball, tennis, track and field, and volleyball.

TUITION

$12,160

CONTACT INFORMATION

Director of Admissions
Stillman College
3601 Stillman Boulevard
Tuscaloosa, AL 35401
Phone: (205) 366-8817
Toll-free: (800) 841-5722

TALLADEGA COLLEGE

ADDRESS: 627 West Battle Street
Talladega, AL 35160
(256) 362-0206

WEB SITE: www.talladega.edu

FOUNDED: 1867

MASCOT: Tornado

AFFILIATION: United Church of Christ

TYPE: 4-Year Private

RATIO: 12:1

STUDENT BODY: 601

HISTORY

Talladega College was founded in 1867 when two freedmen, William Savery and Thomas Tarrant, conceived the idea of building a school for the children of former slaves in Talladega.

Aided by the Freedmen's Bureau, they constructed a one-room schoolhouse that quickly became too small for the increasing number of students. When the Baptist Academy—which Savery and Tarrant had helped build thirteen years earlier—became available, the American Missionary Association helped with the purchase of it. The building was named Swayne School, after General Wager Swayne of the Freedmen's Bureau, and opened in 1867. Two years later, the school was chartered as Talladega College.

The institution first introduced collegiate-level courses in 1890 and graduated the first class with bachelor's degrees in 1895.

Talladega College is accredited by the Commission on Colleges of Southern Association of Colleges and Schools to award degrees at the baccalaureate level.

MISSION

Talladega College is committed to providing academic programs and experiences for students, that among other outcomes, produce graduates who think analytically and strategically, speak effectively and read critically, write with precision and clarity, exhibit competency in their academic discipline, and assume leadership roles in society.

MOTTO

"An Education of Distinction"

TRIVIA

Talladega College's Savery Library is home to the Amistad Murals, artist Hale Aspacio Woodruff's best known works. The collection consists of three panels—*The Revolt, The Court Scene,* and *Back to Africa*—that depict the story of the 1839 revolt by African captives aboard the ship *La Amistad.*

NOTABLES

- Dr. Eunice Walker Johnson—President of Ebony Fashion Fair

- Dr. William Harvey—President of Hampton University

- Dr. Oscar L. Prater—Former president of Talladega College and Fort Valley State University

ACADEMIC PROGRAMS

Talladega College consists of four divisions: the Division of Business and Administration; the Division of Humanities and Fine Arts; the Division of Natural Sciences and Mathematics; and the Division of Social Sciences and Education.

A bachelor of arts degree is awarded in African American Studies, Biology, Business Administration, Chemistry, Computer Science, Education, English, History, Fine Arts, French, History, Mass Media Studies, Mathematics, Music Performance, Physics, Psychology, Public Administration, Social Work, Sociology, and Spanish.

STUDENT ORGANIZATIONS

Talladega College offers numerous social and cultural activities for students that include theater, chorale, choir, and departmental clubs.

Students may work on the *Talladega Student Star* (student-run newspaper) or the *Amistad* (yearbook), or join the Student Government Association, Crimsonnette Dance Team, Pan Hellenic Council, Talladega College Film Club, Talladega College Dance Company, or Faith Outreach Campus Ministry.

Greek fraternities include Alpha Phi Alpha, Kappa Alpha Psi, Omega Psi Phi, and Phi Beta Sigma; sororities include Alpha Kappa Alpha, Delta Sigma Theta, Sigma Gamma Rho, and Zeta Phi Beta.

SPORTS

Talladega College's teams, the Tornadoes, are members of the National Association of Intercollegiate Athletics (NAIA) within the United States Collegiate Athletic Association.

Men's sports include basketball, baseball, golf, and soccer; women's sports include basketball, volleyball, and softball.

TUITION

$6,720

CONTACT INFORMATION

Director of Admissions
Talladega College
627 West Battle Street
Talladega, AL 35160
Phone: (256) 761-6235
Toll-free: (800) 762-2468 (in-state);
(800) 633-2440 (out-of-state)
Fax: (205) 362-0274

Photo courtesy of Trenholm State Technical College

TRENHOLM STATE TECHNICAL COLLEGE

ADDRESS: 1225 Air Base Boulevard
Montgomery, AL 36108
(334) 420-4200

WEB SITE: www.trenholmstate.edu

FOUNDED: 1962

AFFILIATION: None

TYPE: 2-Year Public

RATIO: 10:1

STUDENT BODY: 1,400

HISTORY

H. Councill Trenholm State Technical College was created through the consolidation of John M. Patterson State Technical College and H. Councill Trenholm State Technical College in April 2000. The Trenholm Campus was designated as the main campus.

The John M. Patterson State Technical School was established as a result of the 1947 passage of Regional Vocational and Trade School Act 673 by the Alabama State Legislature. The Montgomery County Board of Revenue and the City of Montgomery purchased forty-three acres of land at the junction of the Southern Bypass and U.S. 231 South in 1961. The school opened on September 4, 1962. Patterson was named a technical college by action of the State Board of Education in 1974.

H. Councill Trenholm State Technical College was authorized by the Alabama State Legislature in May 1963. Construction was completed and classes began in August 1966, with the City of Montgomery and the Montgomery County Board of Revenue contributing to construction costs. The college was named for the late Dr. Harper Councill Trenholm, a past president of Alabama State University.

MISSION

H. Councill Trenholm State Technical College is an associate degree-granting institution with the mission to provide accessible educational opportunities, including credit and non-credit courses and certificates, for career preparation, advancement, and lifelong learning as well as to promote economic growth and enhance the quality of life for residents of central Alabama.

TRIVIA

Trenholm State is the largest technical college in the state.

In February 2009, the Emmy Award-winning reality television series *Extreme Makeover: Home Edition* provided a home renovation to a deserving family in Montgomery. With permission from President Munnerlyn, faculty, staff, and students from the Building Construction, Electrical, and Massage Therapy programs volunteered to be a part of the show using the skills they learned at Trenholm.

TECHNICAL PROGRAMS

H. Councill Trenholm State Technical College is a comprehensive two-year technical college located in Montgomery, Alabama. The college provides technical certificate and degree programs; adult learning opportunities; civic, social, cultural, and personal development opportunities; business and industry training opportunities; and support of economic development for the central Alabama region. The college is part of the Alabama Community College System, a statewide system of postsecondary colleges governed by the Alabama Board of Education.

The Business and Service Division offers programs in Accounting, Automotive Collision Repair, Early Care & Education, Horticulture, and Office Administration.

The Health Services Division offers programs in Dental Assisting, Emergency Medical Services, Medical Assisting, Nursing Assisting/Home Health Aide, Practical Nursing, Radiologic Technology, and Sonography.

The Manufacturing Technology Division offers programs in Air Conditioning & Refrigeration, Automotive Manufacturing, Electrical, Industrial Electronics, Industrial Maintenance, Machine Tool Technology, and Welding.

The Industrial Technology Division offers programs in Automotive Service, Building Construction, Diesel Mechanics, Drafting & Design, and Truck Driver Training.

The Service Occupations Division offers programs in Apparel & Design, Cosmetology, Culinary Arts, and Therapeutic Massage.

The General Studies & Communication Division offers programs in Computer Information Systems, Graphic Communications, and Radio/TV Broadcasting as well as an array of general education courses.

The Adult Education and Skills Training Division offers GED testing, Adult Education classes, and Training for Existing Business and Industry.

The Continuing Education Division offers courses designed to provide professional development and personal enrichment.

STUDENT ORGANIZATIONS

Trenholm State Technical College has an active Student Government Association (SGA) designed to provide students with experiences in governance. Student leaders also participate in the College Student Leadership Academy. Several college programs also participate in SkillsUSA.

TUITION

$2,700/$6,840

CONTACT INFORMATION

Office of Admissions & Records
H. Councill Trenholm State Technical College
P.O. Box 10048
Montgomery, AL 36108
Phone: (334) 420-4300
Toll-free: (866) 753-4544
Fax: (334) 420-4344

Photo courtesy of Tuskegee University

TUSKEGEE UNIVERSITY

ADDRESS: 1200 W. Montgomery Road
Tuskegee, AL 36088
(334) 727-8011

WEB SITE: www.tuskegee.edu

FOUNDED: 1881

MASCOT: Golden Tiger

AFFILIATION: None

TYPE: 4-Year Private

RATIO: 12:1

STUDENT BODY: 2,900

HISTORY

Tuskegee University was founded in 1881 as the Normal School for Colored Teachers. It was the vision of Lewis Adams, a former slave, and George W. Campbell, a former slave owner, who shared the dream of creating a school to teach African Americans.

Booker T. Washington, a graduate of Hampton Institute, became the school's first teacher and principal. During his 35-year tenure, the school grew from a one-room shanty to a campus set on a 100-acre abandoned plantation, and was renamed Tuskegee Normal and Industrial Institute.

Dr. Frederick Patterson, the third president of Tuskegee, started the aviation training program at the institute—which included the famous all-black Tuskegee Airman combat squadron—and helped found the United Negro College Fund.

Tuskegee was granted university status in 1985. It is fully accredited by the Commission on Colleges of the Southern Association of Colleges and Schools (SACS).

MISSION

Tuskegee University is committed to nurturing the development of high-order intellectual and moral qualities among students and stressing the connection between education and the highly trained leadership Americans need in general, especially for the work force of the twenty-first century and beyond.

MOTTO

"Knowledge, Leadership, Service"

TRIVIA

The U.S. Army Air Corps awarded Tuskegee University the contract to help train America's first black military aviators. From 1940–1946, 1,000 black pilots were trained at the university's Moton Field. The success of the Tuskegee Airmen during World War II—not losing a single bomber in more than 200 combat missions—is a record unmatched by any other fighter group in U.S. military history.

NOTABLES

- General Daniel "Chappie" James— First African-American four-star general in the United States Armed Forces

- Tom Joyner—Host of the nationally syndicated Tom Joyner Morning Show and founder of REACH Media Inc., The Tom Joyner Foundation, and Black-AmericaWeb.com

- Claude McKay—Member of the Harlem Renaissance and author of *Home to Harlem*

- Ralph Ellison—Author of the National Book Award winner, *The Invisible Man*

- The Commodores—Soul band that included Grammy Award-winner Lionel Ritchie

- Keenan Ivory Wayans—Actor, comedian, director; creator of *In Living Color*

ACADEMIC PROGRAMS

Tuskegee University consists of five colleges: the College of Agricultural, Environmental, and Natural Sciences; the College of Business and Information Science; the College of Engineering, Architecture, and Physical Sciences; the College of Liberal Arts and Education; and the College of Veterinary Medicine, Nursing, and Allied Health.

Degrees are awarded in Accounting, Aerospace Science, Allied Health, Architecture, Biology, Business Administration, Chemical Engineering, Chemistry, Computer Science and Computer Information Systems, Economics, Electrical Engineering, Elementary Education, English, English Language Arts Education, Environmental Science, Finance, Food and Nutrition, General Science Education, History, Hospitality Management, Management Science, Mathematics, Mathematics Education, Mechanical Engineering, Nursing, Physical Education, Political Science, Psychology, Sales & Marketing, Social Work, Sociology, and Veterinary Medicine.

STUDENT ORGANIZATIONS

Tuskegee University offers students more than 100 organizations and groups, including theater, chorale, debate team, jazz ensemble, marching band, concerts, and lecture series. Students may work on publications such as the yearbook, *Tuskeana,* or the student-run newspaper, *Campus Digest.* Leadership opportunities are found in the Student Government Association.

SPORTS

Tuskegee University's teams, the Golden Tigers, are members of the National Collegiate Athletic Association (NCAA), Division II and participate in the Southern Intercollegiate Athletic Conference (SIAC). Men's sports include baseball, basketball, cross-country, football, tennis, and track and field; women's sports include basketball, cross-country, softball, tennis, track and field, and volleyball.

TUITION

$15,630

CONTACT INFORMATION

Admissions
Tuskegee University
102 Old Administration Building
Tuskegee, AL 36088
Phone: (334) 727-8500
Toll-free: (800) 622-6531

Photo courtesy of Arkansas Baptist College

ARKANSAS BAPTIST COLLEGE

ADDRESS: 1621 Dr. Martin Luther King, Jr. Drive
Little Rock, AR 72202
(501) 370-4000

WEB SITE: www.arkansasbaptist.edu

FOUNDED: 1884

MASCOT: Buffalo

AFFILIATION: Baptist

TYPE: 4-Year Private

RATIO: 22:1

STUDENT BODY: 626

HISTORY

Arkansas Baptist College (ABC), originally known as the Minister's Institute, was founded by both black and white religious leaders in 1884. ABC is a private, historically black, four-year liberal arts college dedicated to the development of graduates who are exceptionally educated, spiritually and culturally aware, and able to meet the demands of our rapidly advancing society. The college's underlying mission is to "serve the underserved." Simply put, ABC seeks to attract and provide educational opportunities to all who wish to better themselves, including those often excluded by traditional college recruitment strategies.

The college is exceptionally proud of its small student-to-teacher ratio. Faculty and staff take a sincere interest in "meeting students where they are" socially, financially, and spiritually to ensure academic success. Arkansas Baptist College is committed to graduating caring, self-actualized learners who are competent researchers, effective communicators, critical thinkers, and contributing members of society. Christian principles are emphasized in the curriculum, as well as in student and administrative activities.

The college has a small, cohesive, student-centered environment with an open-enrollment policy, accepting all eligible students with a high school diploma or GED equivalent. The campus is located in the center of Little Rock near the State Capitol. Arkansas Baptist College is accredited by the Higher Learning Commission of the North Central Association of Colleges and Schools and affiliated with the Consolidated Missionary Baptist State Convention (CMBSC).

MISSION

Arkansas Baptist College is committed to the following purposes: (1) showing personal interest in every student with regard to scholarship and the development of character and personality; (2) providing basic tools, communication skills, global perspectives, and a general education; (3) providing the knowledge and skills necessary to secure employment; and (4) providing a Christian philosophy of life within the framework of proper moral conduct. Arkansas Baptist College is committed to graduating students with an enhanced sense of community awareness and social responsibility.

MOTTO

"It's a GOoD Thing!"

TRIVIA

Arkansas Baptist College was initially funded by the Colored Baptists of the State of Arkansas (now the Consolidated Missionary Baptist State Convention or CMBSC), and is the only historically black Baptist college west of the Mississippi River.

NOTABLES

- Bishop Charles Harrison Mason—Founder of the Church of God in Christ (COGIC)

- Dr. Emeral Crosby—First African-American president of the North Central Association of Colleges and Schools accrediting body

- Charles Price Jones—Founder of the Church of Christ

ACADEMIC PROGRAMS

Arkansas Baptist College consists of three schools: the School of Business & Applied Science Technology; the School of Liberal Arts & General Studies; and the School of Social Science, Religion & Christian Leadership.

The School of Business & Applied Science Technology offers bachelor and associate degrees in Accounting, Business Administration, and Public Administration.

The School of Liberal Arts and General Studies offers bachelor degree in African American Community Leadership, and an associate degree in general studies.

The School of Social Science, Religion & Christian Leadership offers degrees in Criminal Justice, Human Services, and Religious Studies.

STUDENT ORGANIZATIONS

Arkansas Baptist College offers several clubs and organizations that students may join in the areas of academic, international, religious, special interest, and social student organizations. In addition to these clubs and organizations, the college offers the National Pan-Hellenic Council and Student Government Association. The black Greek-letter organizations represented on ABC's campus include Delta Sigma Theta Sorority, Inc., Kappa Alpha Psi Fraternity, Inc., Omega Psi Phi Fraternity, Inc., Phi Beta Sigma Fraternity Inc., and Zeta Phi Beta Sorority, Inc.

SPORTS

The ABC sports teams, the Buffaloes and Lady Buffaloes, participate in the National Junior College Athletic Association (NJCAA). The sports offered include cheerleading, men and women's basketball, men's baseball and football. Men and women's golf, track, and softball will be added during the 2009–10 academic year.

TUITION

$6,400 per year

CONTACT INFORMATION

Arkansas Baptist College
Office of Admissions
1621 Dr. Martin Luther King, Jr. Drive
Little Rock, AR 72202
Phone: (501) 244-5186
Fax: (501) 372-0321

Photo courtesy of Philander Smith College

PHILANDER SMITH COLLEGE

ADDRESS: One Trudie Kibbe Reed Drive
Little Rock, AR 72202
(501) 375-9845

WEB SITE: www.philander.edu

FOUNDED: 1877

MASCOT: Panther

AFFILIATION: United
Methodist
Church

TYPE: 4-Year Private

RATIO: 11:1

STUDENT BODY: 600

HISTORY

Philander Smith College was founded in 1877 as Walden Seminary, named after Dr. J.M. Walden, one of the originators of the Freedmen's Aid Society. Affiliated with the United Methodist Church, the college's primary purpose was to provide educational opportunities for freedmen west of the Mississippi River.

In 1882, the name of the college was changed to Philander Smith College in recognition of a $10,500 donation from Adeline Smith, widow of Philander Smith. The college was chartered as a four-year institution in 1883, and for the next sixty years, expanded its academic programs.

Philander Smith College is accredited by the North Central Association of Colleges and Schools (NCACS).

MISSION

Philander Smith College is committed to graduating academically accomplished students who are grounded as advocates for social justice, determined to intentionally change the world for the better.

MOTTO

"You Shall Know the Truth"

TRIVIA

Former United States Surgeon General Joycelyn Elders, at the age of fifteen, began attending Philander Smith College in Little Rock on a scholarship. She graduated three years later, became a U.S. Army first lieutenant in 1952, and was later appointed by former President William Jefferson Clinton as the first African-American and second female surgeon general.

NOTABLES

- Dr. Joycelyn Elders—Former Surgeon General of the United States

- Geese Ausbie—Basketball player for the Harlem Globetrotters

- Dr. James Cone—Creator of black liberation theology

- Dr. Robert Williams—Considered the father of black psychology

ACADEMIC PROGRAMS

Philander Smith College is a small, four-year liberal arts institution currently offering four degrees including the bachelor of arts, the bachelor of science, the bachelor of business administration and the bachelor of social work. The curricula are offered through six academic divisions: the Division of Business and Economics, the Division of Education, the Division of Humanities, the Division of Natural and Physical Sciences, the Division of Social Sciences and the Philander Smith Management Institute.

Degrees are awarded in Accounting; Biology; Chemistry; Christian Education; Computer Science; Early Childhood Administration; Early Childhood Education; English; General Science; Mathematics; Middle Childhood/Early Adolescence; Music; Organizational Management; Philosophy & Religion; Physical Education; Political Science; Psychology; Social Work; Sociology; and Vocational Education Business Technology.

STUDENT ORGANIZATIONS

Philander Smith College offers its students numerous social and cultural activities, including theater (the Panther Players), the renowned Philander Smith Collegiate Chorale, and the Chosen Generation gospel choir. Annual programs include *Bless the Mic: A Hip-Hop President's Lecture Series*; the Dr. Martin Luther King, Jr. Birthday Celebration; Black History Month activities; Religious Emphasis Week activities; President's Convocation; and International Students Week.

Students may get involved in the Student Government Association, the Bless the Mic Street Team, and the Panther Programming Union as well as our highly touted Black Male Initiative Program and the Platinum by Design program for women. Leadership opportunities avail in various departmental clubs, such as Biology, Business, Language, and Home Economics.

Greek fraternities include Alpha Phi Alpha, Kappa Alpha Psi, and Omega Psi Phi; sororities include Alpha Kappa Alpha, Delta Sigma Theta, Sigma Gamma Rho, and Zeta Phi Beta. Honor societies include Alpha Kappa Mu and Beta Kappa Chi.

SPORTS

Philander Smith College's teams, the Panthers and Lady Panthers, are members of the National Association of Intercollegiate Athletics (NAIA). The college offers men's basketball and women's basketball and volleyball.

TUITION

$8,620

CONTACT INFORMATION

George R. Gray
Director of Recruitment and Admissions
Philander Smith College
One Trudie Kibbe Reed Drive
Little Rock, AR 72202
Phone: (501) 370-5310
Toll-free: (800) 446-6772
Fax: (501) 370-5225
E-mail: admissions@philander.edu
Web site: www.philandersmithadmissions.com

UNIVERSITY OF ARKANSAS AT PINE BLUFF

ADDRESS: 1200 N. University Drive
Pine Bluff, AR 71601
(870) 575-8000

WEB SITE: www.uapb.edu

FOUNDED: 1873

MASCOT: Golden Lion

AFFILIATION: None

TYPE: 4-Year Public

RATIO: 18:1

STUDENT BODY: 3,525

HISTORY

The University of Arkansas at Pine Bluff (UAPB) was founded in 1873 as Branch Normal College, a branch of the Normal Department of the Arkansas Industrial University (now University of Arkansas, Fayetteville) "especially for the convenience of the poorer classes."

Under the 1890 Morrill Act, it was given land-grant status and soon separated from Arkansas Industrial University to become Branch Normal College, operating primarily as a junior college. In 1929, the college changed its name to Arkansas Agriculture, Mechanical, and Normal College. In 1972, it merged with the University of Arkansas System and, after gaining its university status, was renamed University of Arkansas at Pine Bluff.

The University is accredited by the Higher Learning Commission of the North Central Association of Colleges and Schools.

MISSION

The University of Arkansas at Pine Bluff is committed to assisting America in building a new social organism that will accommodate racial, ethnic, and cultural pluralism in a manner that will enhance the quality of lives and patterns of living and weld the nation into one people.

MOTTO

"Quality Education with a Personal Touch"

TRIVIA

The University of Arkansas at Pine Bluff's marching band, Marching Musical Machine of the Mid-South, performed in the inaugural parade for President Barack Obama in January 2009.

NOTABLES

- L.C. Greenwood—Former Pittsburgh Steelers defensive lineman; member of the famous Steel Curtain defense

- Rev. W. R. "Smokie" Norful, Jr.—Gospel singer and pianist; Grammy Award winner

- Dr. Ruth D. Jones–Aerospace Engineer, NASA/Marshall Space Flight Center, Huntsville, AL

- Danny K. Davis–U.S. Representative, State of Illinois

ACADEMIC PROGRAMS

The University of Arkansas at Pine Bluff consists of the School of Agriculture, Fisheries and Human Sciences; School of Arts and Sciences; School of Business and Management; School of Education; Honor's College; University College; Division of Graduate Studies and Continuing Education; and Division of Military Science.

A bachelor of arts degree is awarded in Art; Criminal Justice Studies; English; Gerontology; History; Journalism; Political Science; Social Work; Sociology; and Speech & Drama.

A bachelor of science degree is awarded in Accounting; Agricultural Education; Agriculture; Applied Mathematics; Art; Art (Visual Arts); Biology; Business Administration; Business Education; Chemistry; Computer Science; Early Childhood Education; English Education; Fisheries Biology; General Studies; Health & Physical Education; Home Economics; Human Sciences; Industrial Technology; Mathematics; Mathematics Education; Middle Level Education; Music; Music (Non-education); Nursing; Parks & Community Recreation; Physics; Psychology; Regulatory Science; Rehabilitation Services; Science Education (Biology, Chemistry); Social Science; Special Education (Mildly Handicapped K-12); and Trade & Industrial Education.

STUDENT ORGANIZATIONS

The University of Arkansas at Pine Bluff offers numerous social and cultural activities for students, including theater, jazz ensemble, concert band, wind symphony, and marching band.

Students may join the student-run newspaper, *Arkansawyer*, the *Lion*, an annual student publication, or the student-run radio station, KWAP. Concerts, art exhibits, lectures, and dramatic presentations are offered through the Lyceum Program.

National Pan-Hellenic Council fraternities and sororities represented on campus include Alpha Phi Alpha, Alpha Kappa Alpha, Delta Sigma Theta, Kappa Alpha Psi, Omega Psi Phi, Phi Beta Sigma, Zeta Phi Beta, and Sigma Gamma Rho.

SPORTS

The University of Arkansas at Pine Bluff's teams, the Golden Lions, are members of the NCAA Division I (I-AA for football) and participate in the Southwestern Athletic Conference (SWAC).

Men's sports include baseball, basketball, football, golf, tennis, and track and field; women's sports include basketball, cross-country, soccer, softball, tennis, track and field, and volleyball.

TUITION

$3,450/$8,010

CONTACT INFORMATION

Director of Admissions
University of Arkansas at Pine Bluff
1200 N. University Drive
Pine Bluff, AR 71611
Phone: (870) 575-8462
Toll-free: (800) 264-6585

DELAWARE STATE UNIVERSITY

ADDRESS: 1200 N. DuPont Highway
Dover, DE 19901
(302) 857-6060

WEB SITE: www.desu.edu

FOUNDED: 1891

MASCOT: Hornet

AFFILIATION: None

TYPE: 4-Year Public

RATIO: 20:1

STUDENT BODY: 3,700

HISTORY

On May 15, 1891, the State College for Colored Students, now known as Delaware State University (DSU), was established by the Delaware General Assembly under the provisions of the Morrill Act of 1890, through which land-grant colleges for blacks came into existence. On February 2, 1892, the college launched with its mission of education and public service by offering five courses of study: Agricultural, Chemical, Classical, Engineering, and Scientific.

In 1893, a Preparatory Department was established, and in 1897, a three-year normal course leading to a teacher's certificate was initiated. In the 1916–1917 school year, the Preparatory Department was phased out, a Model Grade School was established, and a high school diploma was granted on completion of a four-year course of study. In 1923, a Junior College Division was added.

On July 1, 1993, the college was renamed Delaware State University.

Delaware State University is accredited by the Middle States Commission on Higher Education in 1944.

MISSION

Delaware State University is committed to providing meaningful and relevant education that emphasizes both the liberal and professional aspects of higher education.

MOTTO

"Making Our Mark on the World"

TRIVIA

DSU has more than 30 formal international partnerships with institutions in countries such as Egypt, Nigeria, Serbia, Mexico, China, and Cuba that facilitate student exchanges and research and conference collaborations.

NOTABLES

- Jamaal Jackson—NFL player for the Philadelphia Eagles

- Dr. Donald A. Blakey—Delaware House of Representatives legislator

- Dr. Clyde Bishop—Former U.S. State Department ambassador

ACADEMIC PROGRAMS

Delaware State University consists of six colleges: the College of Agriculture and Related Sciences; the College of Arts, Humanities and Social Sciences; the College of Business; the College of Education; the College of Health and Public Policy; and the College of Mathematics, Natural Science and Technology.

DSU offers sixty-two diverse undergraduate degree programs through its six colleges. Unique and popular bachelor degree programs include Airway Science, Arts Management, Biotechnology, Community Health, Forensic Biology, Hospitality & Tourism Management, Information Technology, Mass Communications, Nursing, Social Work, Sport Sciences, and many others. Many of the majors offer several different concentration tracks.

The University has twenty-four masters degrees in disciplines such as Agriculture, Applied Optics, Chemistry, Education, Historic Preservation, Molecular & Cellular Neuroscience, Social Work, Sports Administration, and many others, including its newest masters program, English as a Second Language (ESL).

Over the last five years, DSU has established its first doctoral programs in the history of the institution. The doctoral programs include Applied Chemistry; Education Administration, Leadership & Supervision; Interdisciplinary Applied Mathematics, and Mathematical Physics; Neuroscience, as well as Optics.

STUDENT ORGANIZATIONS

DSU offers more than seventy registered organizations, including Greek-lettered groups, honors societies, the DSU Gospel Choir, *The Hornet* newspaper, and WDSU radio station, as well as many academic-related organizations.

DSU students are lead by the Student Government Associations, which include the Executive Council, Men's Council, Women's Senate, class officers, and Pan-Hellenic Council, as well as Mr. and Miss DSU Royal Courts.

SPORTS

Delaware State University's teams, the Hornets, are members of the National Collegiate Athletic Association (NCAA), Division I (I-AA for football). The major sports teams compete in the Mid-Eastern Athletic Conference.

Men's sports include basketball, baseball, cross-country, football, indoor track, outdoor track, and tennis. Women's sports include basketball, bowling, cross-country, equestrian, indoor track, outdoor track, soccer, softball, tennis, and volleyball.

TUITION

$6,481/$13,742

CONTACT INFORMATION

Office of Undergraduate Admission
1200 N. DuPont Highway
Dover, DE 19901
Phone: (302) 857-6351
Toll-free: (800) 845-2544
Fax: (302) 857-6352
E-mail: admissions@desu.edu
Web site: www.desu.edu

HOWARD UNIVERSITY

ADDRESS: **2400 Sixth Street NW**
Washington, DC 20059
(202) 806-6100

WEB SITE: www.howard.edu

FOUNDED: 1867

MASCOT: Bison

AFFILIATION: None

TYPE: 4-Year Private

RATIO: 8:1

STUDENT BODY: 10,100

HISTORY

Founded shortly after the end of the Civil War, Howard University was named for its founder, General Oliver O. Howard, a Civil War hero and commissioner of the Freedman's Bureau.

The university was originally conceived as a theological seminary for the education of African-American clergymen by members of the First Congregational Society of Washington; however, the concept was expanded, and within two years, it included Liberal Arts and Medicine colleges. On March 2, 1867, the university charter was approved by President Andrew Johnson, and Howard University became "a University for the education of youth in the liberal arts and sciences."

Howard University is accredited by the Middle States Association of Colleges and Schools (MSACS).

MISSION

Howard University is committed to producing teachers, administrators, researchers, program evaluators, and human-development professionals for leadership in urban and diverse educational settings, as well as significantly influencing the national education agenda for African-American children.

MOTTO

"Veritas Et Utilitas" or "Truth and Service"

TRIVIA

Howard produces more on-campus African-American Ph.D.s than any other university in the world. Since 1998, it has produced two Rhodes Scholars, two Truman Scholars, 21 Fulbright Scholars, and nine Pickering Fellows.

NOTABLES

- Thurgood Marshall—U.S. Supreme Court Justice

- L. Douglas Wilder—First African-American governor

- Toni Morrison—Nobel Laureate and Pulitzer Prize-winning author

- Dr. LaSalle Leffall—Surgeon; oncologist; educator; first African American to lead the American Cancer Society

ACADEMIC PROGRAMS

Howard University has twelve schools and colleges: Arts and Sciences; Business; Communications; Dentistry; Divinity; Education; Engineering, Architecture & Computer Sciences; Graduate School; Law; Medicine; Pharmacy, Nursing & Allied Health Sciences; and Social Work.

Howard University offers degrees in more than 100 areas, including Accounting; Administration of Justice; African Studies; Afro-American Studies; Anthropology; Architecture; Architecture; Art; Biology; Business Administration; Chemical Engineering; Chemistry; Civil Engineering; Clinical Laboratory Science; Communication Studies; Computer Engineering; Computer-Based Information Systems; Dental Hygiene; Design; Economics; Education; Electrical and Computer Engineering; English; Fashion Merchandising; Finance; Fine Arts; French; German; Greek; Health Management Sciences; Health Sciences; History; Hospitality Management; Human Development; Insurance; Interior Design; International Business; Journalism; Management; Marketing; Mathematics; Mechanical Engineering; Music Education; Music; Nursing; Nutritional Sciences; Occupational Therapy; Pharmacy; Philosophy; Physical Education; Physician Assistant Studies; Physics; Political Science; Psychology; Radiation Therapy; Radio/Television/Film; Recreation; Russian; Science; Sociology; Spanish; Systems and Computer Sciences; Theater Arts; and Visual Arts.

STUDENT ORGANIZATIONS

Howard University has nearly 220 recognized student organizations that are an active part of the Howard community. Organizations and associations include Greek letter organizations, student government bodies, religious organizations, state and departmental clubs, international organizations, sports clubs, and professional and honor societies.

Students can work on the award-winning newspaper, *The Hilltop*, the Bison yearbook, or participate in the Marching Band, the Cheerleaders, and the Campus Pals (who assist new Howard students). Many students involve themselves in volunteer service in the communities of the Washington metropolitan area.

SPORTS

Howard University is a member of the Mid-Eastern Athletic Conference (MEAC). Men's teams include basketball, football (Division IAA), soccer, swimming and diving, tennis, cross-country, and track. Women's teams include basketball, bowling, lacrosse, soccer, swimming and diving, softball, tennis, cross-country, track, and volleyball.

TUITION

$32,480

CONTACT INFORMATION

Enrollment Management/Admission
Howard University
2400 Sixth Street NW
Washington, DC 20059
Phone: (202) 806-2763
Toll-free: (800) 822-6363
E-mail: admission@howard.edu

Photo courtesy of University of the District of Columbia

UNIVERSITY OF THE DISTRICT OF COLUMBIA

ADDRESS: 4200 Connecticut Avenue NW
Washington, DC 20008
(202) 274-5000

WEB SITE: www.udc.edu

FOUNDED: 1977

MASCOT: Firebird

AFFILIATION: None

TYPE: 4-Year Public

RATIO: 13:1

STUDENT BODY: 5,400

HISTORY

The University of the District of Columbia has its origins in two schools. In 1851, a school for black girls, Miner Normal School, was established. In 1873, a similar school for white girls, Washington Normal School, was established and later renamed Wilson Normal School. Both schools became four-year teacher training colleges in 1929, known as Miner Teachers College and Wilson Teachers College, respectively. In 1955, the two united to become the District of Columbia Teachers College.

In the 1960s, Federal City College, governed by the Mayor of the District of Columbia, and Washington Technical Institute, governed by the president of the United States, were established. In 1975, Congress authorized the consolidation of all three schools—District of Columbia

Teachers College, Federal City College, and Washington Technical Institute—into what is now known as the University of the District of Columbia.

The University of the District of Columbia is accredited by the Middle States Association of Colleges and Schools, Commission on Higher Education.

MISSION

The University of the District of Columbia is an urban land-grant institution committed to preparing students for immediate entry into the workforce, for the next level of education, for specialized employment opportunities, and for lifelong learning.

MOTTO

"Pathway to Excellence"

TRIVIA

The University of the District of Columbia will be launching a community college in 2009.

ACADEMIC PROGRAMS

The University of the District of Columbia consists of the College of Arts and Sciences; the School of Business and Public Administration; the School of Engineering and Applied Sciences; the David A. Clarke School of Law; and Community Outreach and Extension Services.

Baccalaureate degrees are awarded in Accounting, Administration of Justice, Architecture, Art, Biology, Business Management, Chemistry, Civil Engineering, Computer Information and Systems Science, Computer Science, Early Childhood Education, Economics, Electrical Engineering, Elementary Education, English, Environmental Science, Finance, Fire Science Administration, French, Graphic Communications, Health Education, History, Information Technology, Marketing, Mass Media, Mathematics, Mechanical Engineering Music, Nursing, Nutrition and Food Science, Office Administration, Physics, Political Science, Procurement and Public Contracting, Psychology, Respiratory Therapy, Social Work, Sociology/Anthropology, Spanish, Special Education, Speech & Language Pathology, Theater Arts, and Urban Studies.

STUDENT ORGANIZATIONS

The University of the District of Columbia offers numerous groups and organizations, including theater, band, jazz ensemble, chorale, art exhibits, orchestra, drum and bugle corps, Firebird Cheerleaders, Literary Club, NAACP, and Drama Club.

Students may work on *The Trilogy* (student-run newspaper), the *Firebird* (yearbook), or at the university's television station, UDC-TV. Leadership opportunities can be found in the Student Government Association and departmental clubs.

National Pan-Hellenic Council organizations include sororities Alpha Kappa Alpha, Delta Sigma Theta, Sigma Gamma Rho, and Zeta Phi Beta; fraternities include Alpha Phi Alpha, Kappa Alpha Psi, Omega Psi Phi, Iota Phi Theta, and Phi Beta Sigma. Other Greek organizations include Delta Mu Delta Honor Society, Omicron Delta Epsilon Honor Society, Pi Sigma Alpha, and Psi Chi.

SPORTS

The University of the District of Columbia's teams, the Firebirds, are members of National Collegiate Athletic Association (NCAA) Division II and participate in the Eastern Collegiate Athletic Conference (ECAC).

Men's sports include basketball, cross-country, soccer, and tennis; women's sports include basketball, cross-country, indoor track, outdoor track and field, tennis, and volleyball.

TUITION

$5,370/$12,300

CONTACT INFORMATION

Director of Admissions
University of the District of Columbia
4200 Connecticut Avenue NW
Washington, DC 20008
Phone: (202) 274-6110
Fax: (202) 274-5553
Web site: www.udc.edu/admissions

Photo courtesy of Bethune-Cookman University

BETHUNE-COOKMAN UNIVERSITY

ADDRESS: 640 Dr. Mary McLeod Bethune Blvd.
Daytona Beach, FL 32114
(386) 481-2000

WEB SITE: www.bethune.cookman.edu

FOUNDED: 1904

MASCOT: Wildcat

AFFILIATION: United Methodist

TYPE: 4-Year Private

RATIO: 17:1

STUDENT BODY: 3,633

HISTORY

Bethune-Cookman University came into being through the sheer will and determination of Mary McLeod Bethune. In 1904, she opened the Daytona Educational and Industrial Training School for Negro Girls.

In 1923, the school merged with Cookman Institute of Jacksonville, Florida, and became a co-ed high school. A year later, the school became affiliated with the United Methodist Church; it evolved into a junior college by 1931 and became known as Bethune-Cookman College.

In 1941, it became a four-year baccalaureate program for liberal arts and teacher education upon approval from the Florida State Department of Education. In 2007, it achieved university status.

Bethune-Cookman University is accredited by the by the Commission on Colleges of the Southern Association of Colleges and Schools (SACS).

MISSION

Founded by Dr. Mary McLeod Bethune in 1904, Bethune-Cookman University is an historically black, United Methodist Church-related university offering baccalaureate and master's degrees. The mission is to serve in the Christian tradition the diverse educational, social, and cultural needs of its students and to develop in them the desire and capacity for continuous intellectual and professional growth, leadership and service to others. The University has deep roots in the history of America and continues to provide services to the broader community through a focus on service learning and civic engagement.

Bethune-Cookman University accomplishes its mission by providing quality instruction in an intellectually stimulating environment that nurtures the mind (intellect), the heart (transformative leadership) and the hand (service learning) according to our founder's motto and the institution's seal.

MOTTO

"Enter to Learn; Depart to Serve"

TRIVIA

Bethune-Cookman University is situated on what was once the city's garbage dump—"Hell's Hole." It now sits on more than seventy acres of prime Daytona Beach, Florida, real estate.

NOTABLES

- John Chaney—Former college basketball coach (Cheyney State, Temple University) and member of Basketball Hall of Fame

- Larry Little—NFL player; member of Pro Football Hall of Fame

- Yvonne Scarlett-Golden—First African-American mayor of Daytona Beach, Florida

ACADEMIC PROGRAMS

Bethune-Cookman University consists of seven schools: School of Arts & Humanities; School of Business; School of Education; School of Nursing; School of Social Sciences; School of Graduate & Professional Studies; and School of Science, Engineering & Math.

A bachelor of arts degree is awarded in English; English Education; History; International Studies; Mass Communications; Music Education; Music Performance; Music Technology; Political Science; Religion and Philosophy; Social Studies Education; Sociology; and Speech Communication.

A bachelor of science degree is awarded in Accounting; Biology; Biology Education; Business Administration; Business Education; Chemistry; Computer Engineering; Computer Information Systems; Computer Science; Criminal Justice; Educational Studies; Elementary Education; Exceptional Student Education (K-12); Gerontology; Hospitality Management; Integrated Environmental Science; International Business; Mathematics; Nursing; Physical Education K-12; Physical Education/Recreation; and Psychology.

A master of science degree is offered in Transformative Leadership.

STUDENT ORGANIZATIONS

Bethune-Cookman University offers more than fifty organizations and clubs, including the Student Government Association, Young Democrats, Black Women's Power Circle, Caribbean Students Association, Criminal Justice Association, FACES Modeling Troupe, Orchesis Dance Ensemble, Radio Club, What's Next Dance Group, and Young Democrats. Greek organizations are represented on campus.

SPORTS

Bethune-Cookman's teams, the Wildcats, are members of the National Collegiate Athletic Association (NCAA), Division I (with the exception of football, which is in Division IAA). Men's sports include baseball, football, cross-country, and basketball; women's sports include basketball, bowling, cross-country, golf, softball, tennis, track and field, and volleyball.

TUITION

$12,936

CONTACT INFORMATION

Bethune-Cookman University
640 Dr. Mary McLeod Bethune Boulevard
Daytona Beach, FL 32114-3099
Phone: (386) 481-2600
Toll-free: (800) 448-0228
Fax: (386) 481-2601

Photo courtesy of Edward Waters College

EDWARD WATERS COLLEGE

ADDRESS: 1658 Kings Road
Jacksonville, FL 32209
(904) 470-8000

WEB SITE: www.ewc.edu

FOUNDED: 1866

MASCOT: Tiger

AFFILIATION: AME Church

TYPE: 4-Year Private

RATIO: 15:1

STUDENT BODY: 850

HISTORY

Following the Civil War, Presiding Bishop Daniel Alexander Payne of the African Methodist Church sent the Reverend Charles H. Pearce, presiding Elder of the AME Church, to Florida (1865) to establish the African Methodist Episcopal Church. Reverend Pearce, observing fast-paced social and political changes of the reconstruction era, immediately observed the need for an educated ministry and recognized that no provisions were made for the public education of newly emancipated blacks. Accordingly, and aided by the Reverend William G. Steward, the first AME pastor in the State of Florida, he began to raise funds to build a school which, established in 1866, eventually evolved into Edward Waters College.

Florida's State Legislature chartered Brown Theological Institute in January 1872. Construction of the first building began in October 1872 on ten acres of land in Live Oak. Further support for this new educational institution came from numerous friends, including railroad magnate General M.S. Littlefield, State Treasurer, Simon Conaber, and Lieutenant-General William Gleason. In 1892, the school's name was changed to Edward Waters College in honor of the third bishop of the AME Church. The city of Jacksonville was destroyed by fire in 1901, and Edward Waters College was reduced to ashes. In 1904, the Board of Trustees purchased the present site of the school on Kings Road with the imperative from Bishop M.B. Salter that Edward Waters College must be rebuilt.

Under the continued visionary leadership and direction of great Bishops of the AME Church and energetic and focused presidents, Edward Waters College continues to experience the triumphs that only a rich history provide. Its past presidents include many academic and religious notables, including one of the founders of the national fraternity, Phi Beta Sigma.

Today, Edward Waters College offers a rigorous, relevant, and cutting-edge liberal arts curriculum. As a co-educational liberal arts college, we value a liberal education that is grounded in the examination of a diversity of ideas, events, and experiences. As we continue to educate young men and women, the goal is to equip graduates with the knowledge, skills, and attitudes necessary to achieve professional and personal success in a twenty-first century global society.

In June of 2007, Claudette H. Williams, Ed.D. began her tenure as the twenty-eighth president of Edward Waters College and the first female president in the college's history.

MISSION

Edward Waters College is a small private, Christian, historically black, urban, liberal arts college that offers quality baccalaureate degree programs. The college strives to prepare students holistically to advance in a global society through the provision of intellectually simulating programs and an environment which emphasizes high moral and spiritual values in keeping with the African Methodist Episcopal Church. Edward Waters College seeks to develop excellence in scholarship, research, and service for the betterment of humanity.

MOTTO

"Sustaining the Principals of Excellence and Ethics through Unity of Purpose, Integrity, and Effectiveness Practices"

NOTABLES

- Nathaniel Glover —First African-American sheriff of Jacksonville, Florida

- John Jordan "Buck" O'Neil—Baseball player in Negro league; first African-American coach in Major League Baseball

ACADEMIC PROGRAMS

Edward Waters College's academic program is designed to prove a high-quality undergraduate education to all students. Degree programs available are a bachelor of arts degree in Communications, Music & Fine Arts, Psychology, and Criminal Justice; a bachelor of science degree in Biology, Elementary Education, and Mathematics; and a bachelor of business administration degree in Organizational Management and Business Administration.

STUDENT ORGANIZATIONS

Edward Waters College offers social and group activities that include band, choir, debating team, and cheerleading. Students can join the newspaper or yearbook staff, or get involved in the student-run radio and television shows.

Leadership opportunities can be found in the Student Government Association, various academic clubs, the student ministerial group, the international club, and many other student organizations on campus. Greek societies and honor societies are also represented on campus.

SPORTS

Edward Waters College's teams, the Tigers, are members of the National Association of Intercollegiate Athletics (NAIA).

Sports offered include basketball, baseball, cross-country, football, golf, softball, track and field, and volleyball.

TUITION

$9,990 (per year)

CONTACT INFORMATION

Edward Waters College
1658 Kings Road
Jacksonville, FL 32209
Phone: (904) 470-8000
Toll-free: (888) 898-3191

FLORIDA A&M UNIVERSITY

ADDRESS: **1500 Wahnish Way**
Tallahassee, FL 32307
(850) 599-3000

WEB SITE: **www.famu.edu**

FOUNDED: **1887**

MASCOT: **Rattler**

AFFILIATION: **None**

TYPE: **4-Year Public**

RATIO: **21:1**

STUDENT BODY: **11,500**

HISTORY

Florida Agricultural and Mechanical University (FAMU) was founded as the State Normal College for Colored Students, and on October 3, 1887, it began classes with fifteen students and two instructors.

In 1992, 1995, and 1997, FAMU enrolled more National Achievement Scholars than Harvard, Yale, and Stanford. In 1999, *Black Issues in Higher Education* cited FAMU for awarding more baccalaureate degrees to African Americans than any other institution in this nation.

During the 110th anniversary celebration, FAMU was selected by the *TIME* magazine-*Princeton Review* as The 1997–1998 College of the Year. FAMU was selected from among some of the most prestigious schools in the country to be the first recipient of this honor.

Today, FAMU is located on 422 acres in Florida's capital city of Tallahassee. The university has thirteen schools and colleges and one institute. FAMU remains the only public historically black university in the State University System of Florida.

Florida A&M University is accredited by the Commission on Colleges of the Southern Association of Colleges and Schools (SACS).

MISSION

The mission of Florida Agricultural and Mechanical University, as an 1890 land-grant institution, is to provide an enlightened and enriched academic, intellectual, moral, cultural, ethical, technological, and student-centered environment conducive to the development of highly qualified individuals who are prepared and capable of serving as leaders and contributors in our ever-evolving society.

NOTABLES

- Althea Gibson—First African American to win Wimbledon women's single crown

- Dr. LaSalle D. Leffall, Jr.—Acclaimed cancer surgeon; first African-American president of the American Cancer Society

- Rob Hardy and Will Packer—Filmmakers (*Stomp the Yard, This Christmas,* and *Obsessed*)

- Anika Noni Rose—Actress; 2004 Tony Award Winner for Best Featured Actress in a musical

- Robert "Bullet Bob" Hayes—Olympic Gold Medalist

ACADEMIC PROGRAMS

Undergraduate degrees are awarded in Accounting, African-American Studies, Agricultural Business, Agricultural Engineering, Agricultural Sciences, Architecture, Art Education, Biological and Agricultural Systems Engineering, Biology, Business Administration, Business Education, Cardiopulmonary Sciences, Chemical Engineering, Chemistry, Civil Engineering, Civil Engineering Technology, Computer Engineering, Computer Information Systems, Construction Engineering Technology, Criminal Justice, Dramatic Arts/Theatre, Economics, Early Childhood Education, Electrical Engineering, Electronic Engineering Technology, Elementary Education, English, English Education, Environmental Sciences, French, Graphic Communication, Graphic Design, Health Information Management, Health Science, History, Industrial Engineering/Technology, International Agriculture and Business, Jazz Studies, Journalism, Landscape Design and Management, Mathematics, Mathematics Education, Mechan-ical Engineering, Music, Music Education, Nursing, Philosophy, Religion, Physical Education, Physics, Political Science, Psychology, Public Relations, Science Education, Social Science, Social Work, Sociology, Spanish, Studio/Fine Art, Teacher Education, and Technology Education.

STUDENT ORGANIZATIONS

FAMU offers more than eighty student organizations including Gospel Choir; Habitat for Humanity; Student Government Association; Art, Band, and Dance Clubs; Student Publications; and NAACP Chapter.

Greek fraternities include Alpha Phi Alpha, Omega Psi Phi, Phi Beta Sigma and Iota Phi Theta. Sororities include Alpha Kappa Alpha, Delta Sigma Theta, Sigma Gamma Rho, and Zeta Phi Beta.

SPORTS

FAMU athletic teams, the Rattlers, are members of the Mid-Eastern Athletic Conference, a NCAA Division I Conference.

Intercollegiate sports include men's football, baseball, basketball, track and field, golf, swimming, and tennis. Women's sports include basketball, bowling, softball, swimming, tennis, track and field, and volleyball.

TUITION
$9,000/$27,000

CONTACT INFORMATION
Florida A&M University
Office of Admissions
1700 Lee Hall Drive
G9 Foote-Hilyer Administration Center
Tallahassee, FL 32307
Phone: (850) 599-3796

FLORIDA MEMORIAL UNIVERSITY

ADDRESS: **15800 NW 42nd Avenue Miami Gardens, FL 33054 (305) 626-3600**

WEB SITE: **www.fmuniv.edu**

FOUNDED: **1879**

MASCOT: **Fighting Lion**

AFFILIATION: **American Baptist Home Mission Society**

TYPE: **4-Year Private**

RATIO: **19:1**

STUDENT BODY: **1,700**

HISTORY

Florida Memorial University has its origins in two institutions—Florida Baptist Institute and Florida Baptist Academy.

Florida Baptist Institute was established in 1879 in Live Oak, Florida, by black Baptists. Florida Baptist Academy was established in 1892 in Jacksonville, Florida, by Reverend Matthew Gilbert, Reverend J. T. Brown, and Sarah Ann Blocker. Support from the Rockefeller General Education Board as well as Baptist organizations, the Bethany Association, and the American Home Mission Society helped keep both institutions financially solvent.

In 1918, Florida Baptist Academy relocated to St. Augustine, Florida. It achieved accreditation by the Southern Association of Colleges and Secondary Schools and the Florida Department of Education in 1931, changed its name to Florida Normal and Industrial Institute, and merged with Florida Baptist Institute in 1941.

In 1963, the institution's name was changed to Florida Memorial College, and, five years later, the college relocated to Miami, Florida. In March 2006, it became Florida Memorial University.

Florida Memorial University is the only Historically Black College or University (HBCU) in Miami, Florida. It is accredited by the Commission on Colleges of the Southern Association of Colleges and Schools (SACS).

MISSION

Florida Memorial University is committed to inculcating in students the importance of lifelong learning, character, and a commitment to leadership through service in the enhancement of their lives and the lives of others.

MOTTO
"Leadership, Character, and Service"

TRIVIA
The famous bell that sits above Florida Memorial University's Susie C. Holley Chapel was originally used at the Old Homes Plantation to gather slaves to issue daily orders. Historians believe that the bell was cast at the same foundry as the Liberty Bell.

NOTABLES
- J. Rosamond Johnson—Faculty member in 1900, who, with his brother, James Weldon Johnson, wrote what has become known as the Negro National Anthem, "Lift Ev'ry Voice and Sing"

- Barrington Irving—Youngest and first African American to fly solo around the world

ACADEMIC PROGRAMS
Florida Memorial University consists of three schools: the School of Arts and Sciences, the School of Business, and the School of Education.

A bachelor of arts degree is awarded in Criminal Justice; International Studies; Political Science & Public Administration; Communications; Communications–Television; English; Religion and Philosophy; Sociology; and Music.

A bachelor of science degree is awarded in Accounting; Biology Education (6-12); Business Administration; Computer Information Systems; Computer Science; Elementary Education/ESOL (K-6); Exceptional Education/ESOL (K-12); Finance; Human Resource Management; Management Information Systems; Marketing; Mathematics; Middle Grades English/ESOL (5-9); Middle Grades Mathematics Education (5-9); Middle Grades Science (5-9); Music Education (K-12); Physical Education (K-12); and Psychology.

A bachelor of Social Work, bachelor of Music in Church Music, and bachelor of Music in Jazz Studies are also awarded.

STUDENT ORGANIZATIONS
Florida Memorial University offers its students numerous clubs and organizations, including the Aviation Club, Ambassador Chorale, Criminal Justice Society, Drama Club–Players Guild, Gospel Choir, Jamaican Student Association, Jazz Band, NAACP, PEP Band, Sapphire & Ice Dancers, and Women of Character.

Students can join the Student Government Association; *The Lion's Tale*, the student-run newspaper; or *The Arch*, the student-run yearbook.

Greek fraternities include Alpha Phi Alpha, Iota Phi Theta, Kappa Alpha Psi, and Phi Beta Sigma; sororities include Alpha Kappa Alpha, Delta Sigma Theta, Mu Sigma Upsilon, Sigma Gamma Rho, and Zeta Phi Beta.

SPORTS
Florida Memorial University's teams, the Fighting Lions, are members of the National Association of Intercollegiate Athletics (NAIA).

Men's sports include baseball, basketball, cross-country, soccer, and track and field; women's sports include basketball, cheerleading, cross-country, soccer, track and field, and volleyball.

TUITION
$13,356

CONTACT INFORMATION
Director of Admissions
Florida Memorial University
15800 NW 42nd Avenue
Miami Gardens, FL 33054
Phone: (305) 626-3147
Toll-free: (800) 822-1362

ALBANY STATE UNIVERSITY

ADDRESS: 504 College Drive
Albany, GA 31705
(229) 430-4600

WEB SITE: www.asurams.edu

FOUNDED: 1903

MASCOT: Golden Ram

AFFILIATION: None

TYPE: 4-Year Public

RATIO: 19:1

STUDENT BODY: 4,000

HISTORY

Albany State University was founded by Joseph Winthrop Holley in 1903 as the Albany Bible and Manual Training Institute. Holley, born in 1874 to former slaves in Winnsboro, South Carolina, had attended Revere Lay College in Massachusetts. While there, he met one of the school's trustees, New England businessman Rowland Hazard, who arranged for him to continue his education at Phillips Academy in Andover, Massachusetts.

Holley, who aspired to be a minister, completed his education at Pennsylvania's Lincoln University. He was inspired to return to the South after reading W.E.B. Du Bois's The Souls of Black Folk, which was on the plight of blacks in Albany, GA. With the help of a $2,600 gift, Holley organized a board of trustees and purchased fifty acres of land for the campus.

The institution provided elementary education and teacher training for the local black population. In 1917, it was financially supported by the state as a two-year agricultural and teacher training college, and its name was changed to the Georgia Normal and Agricultural College. In 1932, it became part of the University System of Georgia; in 1943, it was granted four-year status and renamed Albany State College. It was granted university status in June 1996, and the name of the institution was changed to Albany State University.

In 1994, the university received $153 million in funding, most of it from FEMA, flooding of the adjacent Flint River left most of the campus under water.

Albany State University is accredited by the Commission on College of the Southern Association of Colleges and Schools (SACS).

MISSION

Albany State University is committed to educating students so they can become outstanding contributors to society. It seeks to foster the growth and development of the region, state, and nation through teaching, research, creative expression, and public service.

MOTTO

"A Past to Cherish, A Future to Fulfill"

TRIVIA

Albany State University played a significant role in the American Civil Rights movement in the early 1960s. Students from the school, along with representatives from the Student Nonviolent Coordinating Committee and other black organizations, created the Albany Movement, which brought Martin Luther King, Jr. and other prominent civil rights leaders to the town.

NOTABLES

- Dr. Bernice Johnson Reagon—Civil rights activist; singer who founded the all-women, African-American Sweet Honey in the Rock *a cappella* ensemble

- Caldwell Jones—Former NBA player who spent most of his career with the Philadelphia 76ers

- James Henderson—Powerlifter; won five world bench press titles

ACADEMIC PROGRAMS

Albany State University consists of four colleges: the College of Arts and Humanities; the College of Business; the College of Education; and the College of Sciences and Health Professions.

Degrees are awarded in Accounting; Business Information Systems; Business Management; Computer Science; Counseling & Education Leadership; Criminal Justice; English; Fine Arts; Forensic Science; Health, Physical Education & Recreation; Healthcare Management; History; Logistics Management; Marketing; Mass Communication; Mathematics; Modern Languages; Natural Sciences; Nursing; Political Science; Psychology; Public Administration; Social Work; Sociology; Teacher Education; and Technology Management.

STUDENT ORGANIZATIONS

Albany State University offers numerous groups and organizations for students, including theater group, drama club, concert chorale, and marching band. Students can join the student-run newspaper, Student Government Association, Student Activities Advisory Board, or NAACP.

Greek organizations include Alpha Phi Alpha, Alpha Kappa Alpha, Kappa Alpha Psi, Omega Psi Phi, Delta Sigma Theta, Phi Beta Sigma, Zeta Phi Beta, Sigma Gamma, and Rho Iota Phi Theta.

SPORTS:

Albany State University's teams, the Golden Rams, participate in the National Collegiate Athletic Association (NCAA), Division II.

Men sports include football, basketball, baseball, track and field, and cross-country; women's sports include basketball, cross-country, volleyball, and track and field.

TUITION

$3,500/$12,000

CONTACT INFORMATION

Office of Recruitment and Admissions
Albany State University
504 College Drive
Albany, GA 31705
Phone: (229) 430-4645
Toll-free: (800) 822-RAMS
Fax: (229) 430-3936

Photo courtesy of Clark Atlanta University

CLARK ATLANTA UNIVERSITY

ADDRESS: 223 James P. Brawley Drive SW
Atlanta, GA 30314
(404) 880-8000

WEB SITE: www.cau.edu

FOUNDED: 1988

MASCOT: Panther

AFFILIATION: United Methodist Church

TYPE: 4-Year Private

RATIO: 16:1

STUDENT BODY: 4,100

HISTORY

Clark Atlanta University, a private, co-educational institution located in Atlanta has its origins in two institutions—Atlanta University and Clark College.

Atlanta University was founded in 1865 by the American Missionary Association to educate and supply black teachers and librarians to the public schools of the South.

Clark College was founded in 1869 by the by the Freedmen's Aid Society. Named for Bishop Davis W. Clark, the first president of the Freedmen's Aid Society, its purpose was to provide education to freedmen. Its first class was held in a room in Clark Chapel, a Methodist Episcopal Church. In 1877, the school was chartered as Clark University.

In 1988, Clark College and Atlanta University were consolidated into Clark Atlanta Univer-

sity. The university is accredited by the Commission on Colleges of the Southern Association of Colleges and Schools (SACS).

MISSION

The university is committed to providing a quality education to a student body that is predominantly African-American and also diversified by students from various other racial, ethnic, cultural, and socio-economic backgrounds.

MOTTOS

"I'll Find a Way or Make One" and "Culture for Service"

TRIVIA

Clark Atlanta University's Mighty Marching Panthers Band has appeared in television commercials for McDonald's and were featured in the 2002 hit movie *Drumline,* which filmed the marching band sequences at the campus.

NOTABLES

- Henry O. Flipper—First African-American graduate of West Point

- James Weldon Johnson—Author; statesman; composer of "Lift Ev'ry Voice and Sing"

- Ralph Abernathy—Leader of the Southern Christian Leadership Conference

- W.E.B. Du Bois—Author; educator; scholar; activist

ACADEMIC PROGRAMS

Clark Atlanta University consists of four schools: the School of Arts and Sciences; the School of Business Administration; the School of Education; and the Whitney M. Young, Jr. School of Social Work.

The School of Arts and Sciences awards bachelor's, master's and doctoral degrees. Academic programs include African and African-American Studies, Africana Woman's Studies, Art, Biology, Chemistry, Computer and Information Science, Criminal Justice, English, Fashion Design/Merchandising, French, History, Mass Media Arts, Mathematics, Music, Physics, Political Science, Psychology, Public Administration, Religion and Philosophy, Sociology, Spanish, and Speech Communication and Theater Arts.

The School of Business awards the bachelor of arts degree in Business Administration (with concentrations in Accounting, Finance, Management, Marketing, and Supply Chain Management); an MBA program (with concentrations in Accounting, Finance, Marketing and Operations Research/Supply Chain Management); and an MBA for Working Professionals.

The School of Education offers undergraduate degrees in Early Childhood Education and Educational Studies, and graduate degrees in Educational Leadership, School Counseling, and Community Counseling.

The Whitney M. Young, Jr., School of Social Work offers bachelor's, master's and Ph.D. degrees in Social Work.

STUDENT ORGANIZATIONS

Clark Atlanta University offers students several clubs and organizations, including the African Student Organization, Clark Atlanta University Players, Onyx Dance Team, Panther Diamonds, Thurgood Marshall Legal Society, Young Entrepreneurs Club, the Student Government Association; *The Panther*, the student-run newspaper; *Panther*, the university yearbook; WCLK 91.9, the student radio station; or CAU-TV, the educational public access channel. Greek fraternities include Alpha Phi Alpha, Kappa Alpha Psi, Omega Psi Phi, Phi Beta Sigma, and Iota Phi Theta; sororities include Alpha Kappa Alpha, Delta Sigma Theta, Zeta Phi Beta, and Sigma Gamma Rho.

SPORTS

Clark Atlanta University's teams, the Panthers and Lady Panthers, are members of the National Collegiate Athletic Association (NCAA), Division II and participate in the Southern Intercollegiate Athletic Conference (SIAC). Men's sports include baseball, basketball, football, and cross-country/track and field; women's sports include basketball, softball, tennis, cross-country/track and field, and volleyball.

TUITION
$17,038 (2008–2009)

CONTACT INFORMATION
Office of Admissions
Clark Atlanta University
223 James P. Brawley Drive SW
Atlanta, GA 30314
Phone: (404) 880-6605
Toll-free: (800) 688-3228
Fax: (404) 880-6174

Photo courtesy of Fort Valley State University

FORT VALLEY STATE UNIVERSITY

ADDRESS: 1005 State University Drive
Fort Valley, GA 31030
(478) 825-6211

WEB SITE: www.fvsu.edu

FOUNDED: 1895

MASCOT: Wildcat

AFFILIATION: None

TYPE: 4-Year Public

RATIO: 23:1

STUDENT BODY: 3,100

HISTORY

Fort Valley State University is a four-year, land-grant institution whose history began in 1895 as the Fort Valley High and Industrial School. The school, which offered elementary and secondary education for students of African descent, was supported and supervised by the American Church Institute for Negroes of the Protestant Episcopal Church.

In 1902, the State Teachers and Agricultural College of Forsyth was founded. In 1939, it merged with Fort Valley High and Industrial School and became Fort Valley State College.

In 1947, the land-grant designation that had been previously given to Savannah State College was transferred to Fort Valley State College. The school became Fort Valley State University in June 1996.

Fort Valley State University is accredited by the Commission on Colleges of the Southern Association of Colleges and Schools (SACS) to award associate, baccalaureate, master's, and specialist degrees.

MISSION

Fort Valley State University is committed to providing a learning and living environment that enables its graduates and all who come under its influence to become innovative and critical thinkers, problem-solvers, and responsible citizens.

MOTTO

"Fort Valley State University: A Light for Your Path!"

TRIVIA

The Cooperative Developmental Energy Program (CDEP) at Fort Valley State University is the only one of its kind in the nation. The program, which received start-up funds from the U.S. Department of Energy, is an innovative cooperative between the college, private and government sectors of the nation's energy industry, and other partnering institutions.

NOTABLES

- Catherine Hardy—Gold medalist at 1952 Olympic Games in Helsinki

- Peyton Williams, Jr.—Highest-ranking African-American official in the Georgia Department of Education from 1977–2002

- Rayfield Wright—Former tackle for the Dallas Cowboys; inducted into the Pro Football Hall of Fame in 2006

ACADEMIC PROGRAMS

Fort Valley State University consists of the College of Arts and Sciences, which offers prospective students a wide variety of programs.

Baccalaureate degree programs include Mass Communications, English, Psychology, Criminal Justice, History, Political Science, Sociology, Commercial Design, Economics, General Business, Middle Grades Education, Agricultural Education, Management, Accounting, Marketing, Computer Science, Computer Information Systems, Agricultural Economics, Biology, Mathematics, Chemistry, Veterinary Technology, Agricultural Engineering Technology, Animal Sciences, Plant Science, Ornamental Horticulture, Electronic Engineering Technology, Food and Nutrition, Infant and Child Development, Criminal Justice, Social Work, and Liberal Studies.

Master's degree programs include Environmental Health, Mental Health Counseling, Rehabilitation Counseling, and Animal Science.

Collaborative degree programs include Engineering, Geology, Geophysics, Health Physics, and Hotel Administration (in collaboration with Georgia Tech, University of Oklahoma, University of Texas-Austin, University of Texas-Pan American, Pennsylvania State and the University of Nevada–Las Vegas).

STUDENT ORGANIZATIONS

Fort Valley State University offers numerous departmental, professional, religious, and special interest clubs and organizations for students, including the Criminal Justice Club, Joseph Adkins Players, Sociology Club, Christian Fellowship Society, and FVSU Ambassadors.

Students can join the marching band, concert choir, cheerleading squad, or work at the FVSU radio station (WFVS, 104.3 FM), television station (FVSU-TV), or student-run newspaper, *The Peachite*. Greek fraternities include Alpha Phi Alpha, Iota Phi Theta, Kappa Alpha Psi, Omega Psi Phi, and Phi Beta Sigma; sororities include Alpha Kappa Alpha, Delta Sigma Theta, Sigma Gamma Rho, and Zeta Phi Beta.

SPORTS

Fort Valley State University teams, the Wildcats, are members of the National Collegiate Athletic Association (NCAA), Division II and the Southern Intercollegiate Athletic Conference (SIAC). Men's sports are offered in basketball, cross-country, football, tennis, and track and field; women's sports include basketball, cross-country, softball, tennis, track and field, and volleyball.

TUITION

$7,032/$16,626

CONTACT INFORMATION

Office of Admissions
Fort Valley State University
1005 State University Drive
Fort Valley, GA 31030-4313
Phone: (478) 825-6307
Toll-free: (877) GO-2-FVSU (462-3878)
Fax: (478) 825-6169
E-mail: admissap@fvsu.edu

INTERDENOMINATIONAL THEOLOGICAL CENTER

ADDRESS: **700 MLK, Jr. Drive SW**
Atlanta, GA 30314
(404) 527-7700

WEB SITE: www.itc.edu

FOUNDED: 1958

AFFILIATION: Interdenominational

TYPE: 4-Year Private

RATIO: 13:1

STUDENT BODY: 650

HISTORY

The Interdenominational Theological Center was chartered in 1958 through the mutual efforts of four denominations, which represented four seminaries: the Morehouse School of Religion, the Gammon Theological Seminary, the Turner Theological Seminary, and the Phillips School of Theology.

In February 1867, the Augusta Institute, a school for the training of ministers and other church leaders, was formed. In 1879, it was renamed Atlanta Baptist Seminary, and in 1899, changed to Atlanta Baptist College. The name Morehouse College was adopted in 1913, and, in 1924, the Divinity School of Morehouse College became known as the School of Religion.

Gammon Theological Seminary had its beginning as Gammon School of Theology. It was originally the Department of Reli-

gion and Philosophy at Clark University. It opened as the Gammon School of Theology on October 3, 1883.

Turner Theological Seminary began as a department of Morris Brown College in 1894. It was named in honor of Bishop Henry McNeal Turner, who was the resident bishop of the African Methodist Episcopal Church and senior bishop of the denomination at that time.

Phillips School of Theology is the only seminary of the Christian Methodist Episcopal Church. It was founded on May 30, 1944, and opened its doors on January 2, 1945. In August 1959, Phillips School of Theology became a founding member of the Interdenominational Theological Center.

The four seminaries formed one school of theology in cooperation as an ecumenical cluster and were later joined by the Johnson C. Smith Theological Seminary and the Charles H. Mason Theological Seminary. Today, more than fifteen different denominations are represented, including Disciples of Christ (Christian Church), United Church of Christ, African Methodist Episcopal Zion, Lutheran, Episcopal, and Roman Catholic, as well as students who are non-denominational.

MISSION

The Interdenominational Theological Center is committed to educating Christian leaders for ministry and service in the Church and the global community.

MOTTO

"Students Enter, Leaders Depart"

NOTABLES

Bishop Charles Edward Blake, Sr. serves as the Presiding Bishop and Chief Apostle of the Church of God in Christ (COGIC). Bishop Blake is an alumnus of Charles Harrison Mason Theological Seminary at the ITC.

Dr. Katie Geneva Cannon serves as the Distinguished Annie Scales Rogers Professor of Christian Ethics at Union Theological Seminary. Dr. Cannon is the first African-American woman ordained in the United Presbyterian Church (U.S.A.). She focuses her work in the areas of Christian ethics, womanist theology, and women in religion and society. Dr. Cannon is an alumna of Johnson Crayne Smith Theological Seminary at the ITC.

Bishop Eddie Long is the Senior Pastor of New Birth Missionary Baptist Church in Atlanta, Georgia, is an alumnus of Morehouse School of Religion at the ITC.

ACADEMIC PROGRAMS

The Interdenominational Theological Center offers degree programs for Master of Divinity; Master of Arts in Church Music; and Master of Arts in Christian Education.

Dual degrees are awarded in Master of Divinity/Master of Arts in Church Music and Master of Divinity/Master of Arts in Christian Education.

Doctoral programs include Doctor of Ministry, Doctor of Ministry Specialty, and Doctor of Theology.

TUITION

$8,000/$10,000

CONTACT INFORMATION

Office of Admission
Interdenominational Theological Center
700 Martin Luther King, Jr. Drive SW
Atlanta, GA 30314-4143
Phone: (404) 527-7792
Fax: (404) 527-0901
E-mail: admissions@itc.edu

MOREHOUSE COLLEGE

ADDRESS: 830 Westview Drive SW
Atlanta, GA 30314
(404) 681-2800

WEB SITE: www.morehouse.edu

FOUNDED: 1867

MASCOT: Maroon Tiger

AFFILIATION: None

TYPE: 4-Year Private

RATIO: 15:1

STUDENT BODY: 2,600

HISTORY

Morehouse College is a private, historically black liberal arts college for men. Originally called Augusta Institute, it was established in 1867 in the basement of Springfield Baptist Church in Augusta, Georgia, with the purpose of preparing black men for the ministry and teaching.

In 1879, Augusta Institute moved to the basement of Friendship Baptist Church in Atlanta and changed its name to Atlanta Baptist Seminary. In 1885, it relocated to its current site, which was a gift from John D. Rockefeller. In 1897, the seminary's name was changed to Atlanta Baptist College. In 1913, the college was named Morehouse College in honor of Henry L. Morehouse, the secretary of the Northern Baptist Home Mission Society.

In the early 1900s, during the presidency of Dr. John Hope, the institution's first African-American president, the college expanded its curriculum beyond teaching and ministry.

In 1981, Dr. Hugh Morris Gloster, the first alumnus to serve as president of the college, founded the Morehouse School of Medicine, which became an independent institution.

Morehouse is accredited by the Commission on Colleges of the Southern Association of Colleges and Schools (SACS). Morehouse is one of five Historically Black Colleges and Universities, and one of four undergraduate institutions in Georgia with a Phi Beta Kappa National Honor Society chapter. The college also is one of only four liberal arts colleges in the nation with accreditation from both the International Association for Management Education and a Phi Beta Kappa chapter.

Morehouse College is a member of the United Negro College Fund.

MISSION

Morehouse College is committed to providing a comprehensive academic, social, and spiritual experience that prepares its students for leadership and success in the larger society.

MOTTO

"And There Was Light"

TRIVIA

Morehouse College's campus sits on an historic Civil War site, where Confederate soldiers fought Union forces during General William Tecumseh Sherman's famous siege of Atlanta in 1864.

In 1994, a member of the graduating class, Nima A. Warfield, was named a Rhodes Scholar, the first from an historically black college.

NOTABLES

- Dr. Martin Luther King, Jr.—Civil rights leader; clergyman, Nobel Peace Prize winner

- Julian Bond—Chairman of NAACP; social activist; Civil Rights leader

- Edwin Moses—Track and field athlete; 2-time Olympic gold medalist

- Spike Lee—Film director, producer, writer, and actor

- Samuel L. Jackson—Academy Award-nominated actor

ACADEMIC PROGRAMS

Morehouse College has three divisions: Business Administration and Economics; Humanities and Social Sciences; and Science and Mathematics. The college also offers a dual-degree program in engineering with the Georgia Institute of Technology.

Bachelor of arts and bachelor of science degrees are offered in Business Administration; Economics; African-American Studies; English; Kinesiology, Sports Studies & Physical Education; History; Modern Foreign Language; Philosophy & Religion; Political Science; Sociology; Visual Arts; Biology; Chemistry; Computer Science; Mathematics; Engineering; and Psychology.

STUDENT ORGANIZATIONS

Morehouse College offers its students the opportunity to participate in numerous associations and organizations, such as concert band, jazz ensemble, glee club, marching band, and Student Government Association.

Honor societies include Phi Beta Kappa, Beta Kappa Chi Scientific Society, Golden Key International Honor Society, Pi Delta Phi, Sigma Tau Delta, Alpha Kappa Delta, Phi Alpha Theta, Psi Chi National Honor Society, and Sigma Delta Pi.

The college houses the Morehouse Research Institute, the Andrew Young Center for International Affairs, the Leadership Center At Morehouse College, and the Journal of Negro History.

SPORTS

Morehouse College is a member of the National Collegiate Athletic Association (NCAA), Division II and competes in the Southern Intercollegiate Athletic Conference (SIAC). Its teams, the Maroon Tigers, compete in football, baseball, basketball, cross-country, tennis, and track and field.

TUITION

$20,358

CONTACT INFORMATION

Morehouse College
830 Westview Drive SW
Atlanta, GA 30314
Phone: (404) 215-2632
Toll-free: (800) 851-1254
Fax: (404) 524-5635

Photo courtesy of Morehouse School of Medicine

MOREHOUSE SCHOOL OF MEDICINE

ADDRESS: 720 Westview Drive SW
Atlanta, GA 30310
(404) 752-1500

WEB SITE: www.msm.edu

FOUNDED: 1975

AFFILIATION: None

TYPE: 4-Year Private

STUDENT BODY: 314

HISTORY

Established in 1975 at Morehouse College as a two-year medical education program with clinical training affiliations with several established medical schools for the awarding of the M.D. degree, Morehouse School of Medicine (MSM) separated from the College in 1981 as an independently charted institution. Over the ensuing years, MSM has evolved into one of the nation's leading community-based, primary care-oriented health services institutions.

The School is accredited by the Liaison Committee on Medical Education and the Commission on Colleges of the Southern Association of Colleges and Schools to award the Doctor of Medicine (M.D.), Doctor of Philosophy (Ph.D.) in Biomedical Sciences, Master of Public Health (M.P.H.), the Master of Science in Clinical Research

(M.S.C.R.), the Master of Science in Biomedical Research, and the Master of Science in Biomedical Technology degrees.

MISSION

Morehouse School of Medicine is committed to improving the health and well-being of individuals and communities; increasing the diversity of the health professional and scientific workforce; and addressing primary health-care needs through programs in education, research, and service, with emphasis on people of color and the underserved urban and rural populations in Georgia and the nation.

MOTTO

"A Legacy of Serving the Underserved"

TRIVIA

MSM's research stature and reputation have grown exponentially over the past decade. In 2008, MSM ranked number three among the nation's community-based medical schools in research funding from the National Institutes of Health, and among Georgia's four medical schools, MSM ranks number two. Moreover, MSM ranks in the top five of U.S. medical schools with five or more Institute of Medicine (IOM) members, based on the ratio of IOM members to faculty size.

NOTABLES

- Dr. Rhonda Medows—Commissioner of the Georgia Department of Community Health

- Dr. Wayne Riley—President of Meharry Medical College in Nashville, Tennessee

- Dr. Regina Benjamin—Founder and CEO of the Bayou Clinic, Inc. in Bayou LaBatre, Alabama, was selected as a 2008 John D. and Catherine T. MacArthur Foundation Fellow

ACADEMIC PROGRAMS

Morehouse School of Medicine has twelve academic departments: Community Health and Preventive Medicine; Family Medicine; Medicine; Microbiology, Biochemistry and Immunology; Neurobiology; Obstetrics and Gynecology; Pathology and Anatomy; Pediatrics; Pharmacology and Toxicology; Physiology; Psychiatry and Behavioral Sciences; and Surgery.

Educational degree programs include a Doctor of Medicine Program, Graduate Education in Biomedical Sciences, Master of Public Health Program, and a Master of Science in Clinical Research Program.

MSM has seven residency programs: Family Medicine, Public Health and Preventive Medicine, Internal Medicine, Obstetrics and Gynecology, Psychiatry, Surgery, and Pediatrics. The majority of MSM patient care and clinical training occurs at Grady Memorial Hospital, one of the largest public hospitals in the Southeast.

STUDENT ORGANIZATIONS

Morehouse School of Medicine offers students the opportunity to participate in several organizations, such as the Student National Medical Association, the American Medical Student Association, and the Medical Student Section of the American Medical Association. The Alpha Omega Alpha Honor Society also is represented on campus.

TUITION

$29,484: M.D. program only

CONTACT INFORMATION

Director of Admissions
Morehouse School of Medicine
720 Westview Drive SW
Atlanta, GA 30310
Phone: (404) 752-1650

MORRIS BROWN COLLEGE

ADDRESS: 643 MLK, Jr. Drive NW
Atlanta, GA 30314
(404) 739-1010

WEB SITE: www.morrisbrown.edu

FOUNDED: 1881

MASCOT: Wolverine

AFFILIATION: AME Church

TYPE: 4-Year Private

RATIO: 7:1

STUDENT BODY: 200

HISTORY

Eighteen years after the signing of the Emancipation Proclamation that declared freedom from human bondage for enslaved Negroes in the United States, the Ministers of the African Methodist Episcopal Church of the State of Georgia, fully realizing the necessity of an institution for the preparation of young men and women for every department of Christian work, as well as industrial training, convened in Big Bethel AME Church on Auburn Avenue in Atlanta, Georgia. In their deliberations at this session, on January 5, 1881, they decided "to establish an institution of higher learning for Negro boys and girls" in the city of Atlanta.

The initial resolution by Reverend W.J. Gaines and subsequent submissions acknowledged "the change of times" as well as "the need for improvement of the people we represent" and "further appealed to all good citizens and friends to assist with their efforts through offerings of prayer and money." In May 1885, the State of Georgia granted a charter to Morris Brown College, the first educational Institution in the State of Georgia solely under African-American Patronage. The College is named for Morris Brown, the second consecrated Bishop of the African Methodist Episcopal Church.

The school was opened in 1885, and the first class graduated in 1890. For more than 128 years, Morris Brown College has received and nurtured students from around the world. The institution's commitment to a profound purpose, its diligence in effort, and its perseverance is the continuous response to the founders' clarion call for support of their discernment of the need for improvement of themselves and others through access to the opportunity for educational development in a nurturing environment.

MISSION

Morris Brown College is committed to academic excellence through advancing knowledge. The college seeks to provide higher-education opportunities based on Christian principles at the undergraduate level that will enable students to become dynamic leaders, managers, and entrepreneurs in a global, culturally diverse, and technologically advanced world, characterized by rapid change and complex interdependence.

MOTTO

"For God and Truth"

TRIVIA

The Morris Brown College Alonzo F. Stadium was the field hockey venue for the 1996 Summer Olympics held in Atlanta, GA.

The 25th National Historical Landmark is Fountain Hall on the college's campus.

Morris Brown College is the first educational institution in the State of Georgia solely under African-American patronage.

Movies filmed on the MBC Campus include *Stomp the Yard* and *We Are Marshall*.

NOTABLES

- Albert J. Edmonds—Lt. general, United States Air Force (Retired)

- Dr. Charles L. Harper—Principal, B.T. Washington High School, the first high school for African Americans in the State of Georgia

- Alberta Williams King—Mother of Dr. Martin Luther King, Jr.

- James A. McPherson—Winner of the Pulitzer Prize

- Angelo Taylor—Olympic gold medalist

ACADEMIC PROGRAMS

Morris Brown College academic programs offered are Business Administration; General Studies; General Education; Organizational Management and Leadership. Each student receives a general education core program that provides exposure to the humanities, social and behavioral sciences, natural sciences, and mathematics.

The Morris Brown College Online Program offers an undergraduate degree completion program, the bachelor of arts degree in Organizational Management and Leadership (OML). This bachelor degree completion program provides professionally relevant course work in an accelerated learning environment (18–24 months) that provides the skills and knowledge base to meet the challenges of the twenty-first century workplace.

STUDENT ORGANIZATIONS

Extracurricular organizations and related activities to support healthy development of the "whole" student include the Cheerleading Squad; Dance Teams; Choir & Choral Ensemble; Concert & Marching Bands; Honors Day; Intellectual Forums, New Student Orientation; Religious Emphasis Week; and the Student Government Association.

SPORTS

Club teams include basketball (men and women).

TUITION

On-campus: $17,155 per year, Off-campus: $8,655 per year

CONTACT INFORMATION

Admissions and Records
Morris Brown College
643 Martin Luther King, Jr. Drive NW
Atlanta, Georgia 30314
Phone (404) 739-1010

Photo courtesy of Paine College

PAINE COLLEGE

ADDRESS: **1235 Fifteenth Street**
Augusta, GA 30901
(706) 821-8200

WEB SITE: www.paine.edu

FOUNDED: 1882

MASCOT: Lion

AFFILIATION: United Methodist Church & Christian Methodist Episcopal Church

TYPE: 4-Year Private

RATIO: 11:1

STUDENT BODY: 850+

HISTORY

Paine College was founded in 1882 as Paine Institute through the efforts of leaders from the Methodist Episcopal Church South and the Colored (now Christian) Methodist Episcopal (CME) Church. The institute's goal was to train preachers and teachers to educate the newly freed slaves following the Civil War.

Paine's was chartered in 1883, and its first classes were held in January 1884. In 1903, the institute was rechartered and became Paine College.

Paine College is accredited by the Commission on Colleges of the Southern Association of Colleges and Schools (SACS) to award baccalaureate degrees. The Division of Business Administration is accredited by the Association of Collegiate Business Schools and Programs (ACBSP). The Division of Education is accredited by the National Council for the Accreditation of Teacher Education (NCATE).

MISSION

The mission of Paine College, a church-related private institution, is to provide a liberal arts education of the highest quality that emphasizes academic excellence, ethical and spiritual values, social responsibility, and personal development to prepare men and women for positions of leadership and service in the African-American community, the nation, and the world.

TRIVIA

Initial gifts to fund Paine College included $16, collected penny by penny, from former slaves.

NOTABLES

- Dr. Mack Gipson, Jr.—Founder of the National Association of Black Geologists and Geophysicists; NASA consultant

- Frank Yerby—Internationally acclaimed author of *The Foxes of Harrow* and first African American to write a best-selling novel and to have a book purchased by a Hollywood studio for a film adaptation

- Shirley McBay—Mathematician; first African-American dean at Massachusetts Institute of Technology

- Nathaniel Linsey—Senior bishop of Christian Methodist Episcopal Church

ACADEMIC PROGRAMS

Paine college consists of five divisions: Division of Business Administration; Division of Education; Division of Natural Science & Mathematics; Division of Social Sciences; and Division of Humanities.

A bachelor of arts degree is awarded in English; English Education; History; History Education; Mass Communication; Philosophy and Religion; Psychology; Sociology; and Social Psychology.

A bachelor of science degree is awarded in Biology, Biology Education, Business Administration, Chemistry, Criminology, Early Childhood Education, Mathematics, Mathematics Education, Middle Grades Education, and Secondary Education. Pre-professional degrees are offered in Allied Health, Dentistry, Medicine, Pharmacy, Nursing, and Veterinary Medicine.

STUDENT ORGANIZATIONS

Paine College offers more than forty student-run organizations, including choir, theater, concerts, band, jazz ensemble, chorale, dance, student publications, Student Government Association, and NAACP.

Greek fraternities include members of the National Pan-Hellenic Council, such as Alpha Phi Alpha, Kappa Alpha Psi, Omega Psi Phi, and Phi Beta Sigma; sororities include Alpha Kappa Alpha, Delta Sigma Theta, Sigma Gamma Rho, and Zeta Phi Beta. Honor societies include Alpha Kappa Mu.

SPORTS

Paine college teams, the Lions, are members of the Southern Intercollegiate Athletic Conference (SIAC), which is affiliated with the National Collegiate Athletic Association (NCAA), Division II.

Intercollegiate sports include men's baseball, basketball, cross-country, golf, and track and field; and women's basketball, cross-country, softball, track and field, and volleyball.

TUITION

$15,000–$20,000

CONTACT INFORMATION

Director of Admissions
Paine College
1235 Fifteenth Street
Augusta, GA 30901-3182
Phone: (706) 821-8320
Toll-free: (800) 476-7703
Fax: (706) 821-8691

SAVANNAH STATE UNIVERSITY

ADDRESS: 3219 College Street
Savannah, GA 31404
(912) 356-2181

WEB SITE: www.savannahstate.edu

FOUNDED: 1890

MASCOT: Tiger

AFFILIATION: None

TYPE: 4-Year Public

RATIO: 21:1

STUDENT BODY: 3,450

HISTORY

Savannah State University was originally founded as the Georgia State Industrial College for Colored Youth as a result of the Second Morrill Land Grant Act of August 1890.

The first baccalaureate degree was awarded in 1898. In 1928, the college became a full four-year, degree-granting institution. Four years later, when it became a full member institution of the University System of Georgia, its name was changed to Georgia State College.

In January 1950, after its land grant status was transferred to Fort Valley State, the school became Savannah State College. With continued growth within the college's graduate and research programs, the school was elevated to the status of state university by the University System of Georgia and its name changed to Savannah State University.

Savannah State University is accredited by the Commission on Colleges of the Southern Association of Colleges and Schools (SACS).

MISSION

Savannah State University's mission is to graduate students prepared to perform at higher levels of economic productivity, social responsibility, and excellence in their chosen fields of endeavor in a changing global community.

MOTTO

"You can get anywhere from here"

TRIVIA

The Marine Biology Department at Savannah State University operates two research vessels: the R/V *Sea Otter* and the R/V *Tiger*.

NOTABLES

- Shannon Sharpe—NFL player; selected to eight Pro Bowls; won three Super Bowl rings; CBS Sports commentator

- Donnie L. Cochran—United States Navy Captain (Retired); the first African-American pilot to fly with and later command the U.S. Navy Flight Demonstration Squadron, *The Blue Angels*

- Virginia A. Edwards—First African-American female to be named superintendent of Savannah-Chatham County Public Schools in Savannah, Georgia

- Percy A. Mack—Superintendent of Richland County School District One in Columbia, South Carolina; previously superintendent of Dayton, Ohio Public Schools

ACADEMIC PROGRAMS

Savannah State University has three colleges: the College of Business Administration; the College of Liberal Arts and Social Sciences; and the College of Sciences and Technology.

Degrees are awarded in Accounting; Africana Studies; Behavior Analysis; Biology; Business; Chemistry; Civil Engineering Technology; Computer Information Systems; Criminal Justice; Computer Science Technology; Electronics Engineering Technology; English Language & Literature; Environmental Studies; Homeland Security and Emergency Management; History; Management; Marketing; Mathematics; Marine Sciences; Mass Communication; Political Science; Public Administration; Urban Studies; Social Work; Sociology; and Visual and Performing Arts.

STUDENT ORGANIZATIONS

Savannah State University has more than seventy-five clubs and organizations, including concert choir, band, or Wesleyan gospel choir. Students can join the student newspaper, *Tiger's Roar,* or the college radio station (WHCJ-FM). Leadership opportunities can be found in the Student Government Association, as well as service and departmental clubs.

Greek fraternities include Alpha Phi Alpha, Kappa Alpha Psi, Omega Psi Phi, and Phi Beta Sigma; sororities include Alpha Kappa Alpha, Delta Sigma Theta, Sigma Gamma Rho, and Zeta Phi Beta.

Honor societies include Alpha Kappa Mu, Beta Beta Beta, Beta Kappa Chi, Kappa Delta Pi, Phi Beta Lambda, Phi Mu Delta, Pi Gamma Mu, Sigma Delta Chi, Sigma Tau Delta, and Tau Alpha Pi.

SPORTS

Savannah State University's teams, the Tigers, are members of the NCAA, Division IAA.

Men's sports include football, basketball, baseball, cross-country, track and field, and golf. Women's sports include basketball, softball, tennis, cross country, track and field, volleyball and golf.

TUITION

$3,726/$13,018

CONTACT INFORMATION

Director of Admissions
Savannah State University
P.O. Box 20209
Savannah, GA 31404
Phone: (912) 356-2181
Toll-free: (800) 788-0478
Fax: (912) 356-2256

SPELMAN COLLEGE

ADDRESS: 350 Spelman Lane SW
Atlanta, GA 30314
(404) 681-3643

WEB SITE: www.spelman.edu

FOUNDED: 1881

MASCOT: Jaguar

AFFILIATION: Baptist

TYPE: 4-Year Private

RATIO: 12:1

STUDENT BODY: 2,100

HISTORY

Spelman College, a four-year, private, female liberal arts institution, was founded in 1881 as Atlanta Baptist Female Seminary by Sophia B. Packard and Harriet E. Giles, two women commissioned by the Baptist church to provide educational lessons for newly freed black women.

The first class, which consisted of eleven African-American women, was held in the basement of the Friendship Baptist Church. In 1883, the seminary relocated to a nine-acre site in Atlanta after receiving financial support and gifts from the local black community. However, the greatest financial benefactor would be John D. Rockefeller, who paid off the seminary's property debts in 1884. Soon after, the seminary's name was changed to Spelman Seminary in honor of Rockefeller's wife, Laura Spelman, and her parents, Harvey Buel and Lucy Henry Spelman, who were longtime activists in the anti-slavery movement.

In 1887, the first diplomas were handed out to graduates. The first college degrees were awarded in 1901. In 1924, the name of the school was changed to Spelman College, and five years later, the college signed an agreement of affiliation with Morehouse College and Atlanta University.

Spelman College is accredited by the Commission on College of the Southern Association of Colleges and Schools (SACS).

MISSION

Spelman College is committed to promoting academic excellence in the liberal arts, and developing the intellectual, ethical, and leadership potential of its students. Spelman seeks to empower the total person, who appreciates the many cultures of the world and commits to positive social change.

MOTTO

"Our Whole School for Christ"

TRIVIA

Spelman College's endowment is the richest of all Historically Black Colleges and Universities, growing 86 percent since 1995, from about $123 million to $258 million in 2006.

Spelman boasts the first all-black, all-female, and only undergraduate robotics team, SpelBots, to compete in national and international robotics competitions.

Spelman, which is the only HBCU consistently ranked in the top seventy-five of *U.S. News & World Report's* Best Liberal Arts Colleges, was the first HBCU to build a "green" residence hall.

NOTABLES

- Marian Wright Edelman—Founder and president of Children's Defense Fund
- Bernice Johnson Reagon—Founder of Sweet Honey in the Rock
- Jerri DeVard—Marketing/communications powerbroker
- Keshia Knight Pulliam—Actress; known for role of Rudy on *The Cosby Show*

ACADEMIC PROGRAMS

Spelman College offers twenty-six majors and twenty-five minors in fields such as the social sciences, mathematics, the arts, and the natural sciences.

A bachelor of arts degree is awarded in Anthropology, Art, Child Development, Comparative Women's Studies, Drama, Economics, English, French, History, Human Services, Music, Philosophy, Political Science, Psychology, Religion, Sociology, and Spanish.

A bachelor of science degree is awarded in Biochemistry, Biology, Chemistry, Computer and Information Sciences, Mathematics, Environmental Science, and Physics.

STUDENT ORGANIZATIONS

Spelman College offers eighty-two clubs and organizations, including choral groups, music ensembles, dance groups, drama/theater groups, and jazz band. Students can participate in the literary magazine, the student newspaper (*Spelman Spotlight*), film society, Student Government Association, or in recognized chapters of the NAACP and Sister Steps.

Religious organizations include Baha'i Club, Al-Nissa, Alabaster Box, Atlanta Adventist Collegiate Society, Campus Crusade for Christ, Crossfire International Campus Ministry, Happiness In Praise for His Overflowing Presence, Inter Varsity Christian Fellowship, Movements of Praise Dance Team, The Newman Organization, The Outlet, and The Pre-Theology Society Minority.

Greek sororities include Alpha Kappa Alpha, Delta Sigma Theta, Gamma Sigma Sigma, Zeta Phi Beta, and Sigma Gamma Rho.

SPORTS

Spelman College's teams, the Jaguars, compete in the National Collegiate Athletic Association (NCAA), Division III and participate in the Great South Athletic Conference. Sports include basketball, golf, cross-country, soccer, softball, tennis, and volleyball.

TUITION

$30,988 on campus/$20,926 off campus

CONTACT INFORMATION

Admissions Office
Spelman College
350 Spelman Lane SW
Atlanta, GA 30314-4399
Phone: (404) 681-3643
Toll-free: (800) 982-2411
Fax: (404) 270-5201

KENTUCKY STATE UNIVERSITY

ADDRESS: 400 East Main Street
Frankfort, KY 40601
(502) 597-6000

WEB SITE: www.kysu.edu

FOUNDED: 1886

MASCOT: Thorobred

AFFILIATION: None

TYPE: 4-Year Public

RATIO: 15:1

STUDENT BODY: 2,700

HISTORY

Kentucky State University is distinguished by the cultural, ethnic, racial and gender diversity of its faculty, staff, and students. It is committed to student-centered learning, free scholarly inquiry and academic excellence.

The university was chartered in May 1886 as the State Normal School for Colored Persons. The new school opened on October 11 with three teachers and fifty-five students. Three years later, the school became a land grant college.

In 1902, the school's name was changed to Kentucky Normal and Industrial Institute for Colored Persons. In 1926, it became Kentucky State Industrial College for Colored Persons. In 1938, the school was again renamed, this time to Kentucky State College for Negroes; however, the term "for Negroes" was discontinued in 1952.

Kentucky State College became a university in 1972. Today, Kentucky State University has 914 acres, including a 296-acre Research and Demonstration Farm and a 306-acre Environmental Education Center.

KSU is accredited by the Commission on Colleges of the Southern Association of Colleges and Schools (SACS).

MISSION

Kentucky State University, building on its legacy of achievement as an historically black, liberal arts, and 1890 land-grant university, affords access to and prepares a diverse student population of traditional and non-traditional students to compete in a multifaceted, ever-changing global society by providing student-centered learning while integrating teaching, research, and service through high-quality undergraduate and select graduate programs. Kentucky State University is committed to keeping relevant its legacy of service by proactively engaging the community in partnerships on civic projects driven by the objective of positively impacting the quality of life of the citizens of the Commonwealth.

MOTTO

"Kentucky State University ... Inspiring Innovation. Growing Leaders. Advancing Kentucky."

NOTABLES

- Anna Mac Clarke—Member of the Women's Army Corps during WWII; first African-American officer of an all-white company

- Tom Colbert—First African-American Oklahoma Supreme Court Justice

- Elmore Smith—NBA player with Buffalo Braves, Los Angeles Lakers, Milwaukee Bucks, and Cleveland Cavaliers

- Whitney M. Young, Jr.—Executive director of the National Urban League from 1961 until his death in 1971

ACADEMIC PROGRAMS:

Kentucky State University consists of three colleges: the College of Arts, Social Sciences, and Interdisciplinary Studies; the College of Mathematics, Sciences, Technology, and Health; and the College of Professional Studies.

A bachelor of arts degree is offered in Art, Business Administration, Child Development and Family Relations, Criminal Justice, Elementary Education, English, General Social Sciences, Liberal Studies, Mass Communication and Journalism, Mathematics, Music, Physical Education, Political Science, Psychology, Public Administration, and Social Work.

A bachelor of science degree is offered in Applied Information Technology, Biology, Chemistry, Computer Science, Nursing, and Physical Education and Health.

Master's degrees are offered in Special Education, Business Administration, Public Administration, Aquaculture/Aquatic Sciences, and Computer Science Technology.

STUDENT ORGANIZATIONS

Kentucky State University has more than sixty recognized student-run organizations and associations on campus. Cultural and group activities include theater, band, choral, and dance. Students can work on the student-run newspaper, *The Thorobred News*. There is also a student-run radio station. Leadership activities can be found in the Student Government Association. Greek fraternities include Alpha Phi Alpha, Iota Phi Theta, Kappa Alpha Psi, Phi Beta Sigma, and Omega Psi Phi. Sororities include Alpha Kappa Alpha, Delta Sigma Theta, Sigma Gamma Rho, and Zeta Phi Beta. The band fraternity and sorority are Kappa Kappa Psi and Tau Beta Sigma, respectively.

SPORTS

Kentucky State University's teams, the Thorobreds, are members of the National Collegiate Athletic Association (NCAA), Division II and participate in the Southern Intercollegiate Athletic Conference (SIAC). Men's varsity teams include baseball, basketball, track and field, football, and golf. Women's teams include basketball, softball, track and field, and volleyball.

TUITION

$5,920/$14,208

CONTACT INFORMATION

Kentucky State University
400 East Main Street
Frankfort, KY 40601-2334
Phone: (502) 597-6813
Toll-free: (877) 367-5978
Fax: (502) 597-5814

DILLARD UNIVERSITY

ADDRESS: 2601 Gentilly Boulevard
New Orleans, LA 70122
(504) 283-8822

WEB SITE: www.dillard.edu

FOUNDED: 1869

MASCOT: Blue Devil

AFFILIATION: United Church of
Christ and United
Methodist Church

TYPE: 4-Year Private

RATIO: 8:1

STUDENT BODY: 851

HISTORY

The University's historical origins date back to 1869 with the founding of Straight University by the American Missionary Association of the Congregational Church and of the Union Normal School by the Freedmen's Aid Society of the Methodist Episcopal Church. Later named Straight College and New Orleans University, respectively, these two institutions merged in 1930 to form Dillard University, which has always been committed to producing African-American men and women dedicated to public service throughout the world.

With 140 years of academic excellence, Dillard University continues its historical commitment to excellence in education and strives to position itself as one of the nation's premier centers for undergraduate research. Dillard is currently ranked among the top HBCUs in the country by *U.S. News & World Report*.

Dillard University is accredited by the Commission on Colleges of the Southern Association of Colleges and Schools (SACS).

MISSION

True to its heritage, Dillard University's mission is to produce graduates who excel, become world leaders, and are broadly educated, culturally aware, and concerned with improving the human condition. Through a highly personalized and learning-centered approach, Dillard's students are able to meet the competitive demands of a diverse, global, and technologically advanced society.

MOTTO

"Ex Fide Fortis" (Out of Faith, Strength)

TRIVIA

Emmy Award-winning and Oscar-nominated actor Beah Richards graduated from Dillard University in 1948 and embarked on a 50-year career on stage, in movies, and on television. She appeared in the 1967 version of *Guess Who's Coming to Dinner* with Spencer Tracy and Katharine Hepburn, and in the original Broadway productions of *Purlie Victorious*, *The Miracle Worker*, and *A Raisin in the Sun*.

NOTABLES

- Dr. Ruth Simmons—President, Brown University, Providence, RI

- Cynthia M. A. Butler-McIntyre—24th National President, Delta Sigma Theta Sorority, Inc.

- Ellis Marsalis—Internationally known jazz artist and educator

- Dr. Sheila Tlou—Member of Parliament in Botswana, Africa; former Minister of Health of Botswana

ACADEMIC PROGRAMS

Dillard University consists of six academic divisions: the Division of Business; the Division of Education and Psychology; the Division of Humanities; the Division of Natural Sciences and Public Health; the Division of Nursing; and the Division of Social Sciences.

Degrees are offered in Accounting, Business Management, Marketing, Economics, International Business, Early Childhood, Elementary Education, Educational Studies, Secondary Education, Special Education, Psychology, Visual Art, English, Mass Communications, Music, Philosophy and Religion, Theatre Arts, World Languages (French, Spanish), Biology, Chemistry, Computer Science, Mathematics, Physics, Public Health, Nursing, African World Studies, History, Political Science, Sociology/Criminal Justice, Sociology/Social Work, and Urban Studies, and Public Policy.

STUDENT ORGANIZATIONS

Dillard University offers nearly fifty clubs and organizations in which students can participate.

Organizations include the Student Government Association (SGA), Pre-Alumni Council, National Pan-Hellenic Council (NPHC), Student-Trustee Liaison Committee, Soul of a Poet, International Student Association, Conquered the Grave Religious Club, Students for Environmental Justice Club, and many more.

Greek sororities include Alpha Kappa Alpha Sorority, Inc., Delta Sigma Theta Sorority, Inc., Sigma Gamma Rho Sorority, Inc., and Zeta Phi Beta Sorority, Inc.; Fraternities include Phi Beta Sigma Fraternity, Inc., Omega Psi Phi Fraternity, Inc., and Kappa Alpha Psi Fraternity, Inc.

Service fraternities and sororities include Phi Gamma Nu National Business Fraternity, Gamma Sigma Sigma National Service Sorority, and Alpha Phi Omega National Service Fraternity.

SPORTS

Dillard University's teams, the Blue Devils are members of the National Association of Intercollegiate Athletics (NAIA) and participate in the Gulf Coast Athletic Conference (GCAC). Men's sports include basketball, cross-country, and track and field; women's include basketball, cross-country, track and field, and volleyball.

TUITION

$13,000

CONTACT INFORMATION

Dillard University
2601 Gentilly Boulevard
New Orleans, LA 70122
Phone: (504) 816-4670
Toll-free: (800) 216-6637
Fax: (504) 816-4895
E-mail: admissions@dillard.edu

Photo courtesy of Grambling State University

GRAMBLING STATE UNIVERSITY

ADDRESS: 403 Main Street
Grambling, LA 71245
(800) 569-4714

WEB SITE: www.gram.edu

FOUNDED: 1901

MASCOT: Tiger

AFFILIATION: None

TYPE: 4-Year Public

RATIO: 20:1

STUDENT BODY: 5,100

HISTORY

Grambling State University was founded in 1901 as the Colored Industrial and Agricultural School of Lincoln Parish by Charles Phillip Adams, who was sent to the area from Tuskegee Institute in Alabama at the request of the Farmer's Relief Bureau of Ruston, Louisiana. The original mission was to improve the quality of life for poor farmers of Lincoln Parish. Families were taught how to maximize crop production, prepare food for long-term storage, secure land, and build homes.

From this very basic beginning, Grambling has truly expanded academically and progressed from a small agricultural school into a university offering varied degree programs. The university evolved from a two-year institution in 1936 to a four-year school in 1944, and achieved university status in the mid-1970s.

Grambling State University is accredited by the Southern Association of Colleges and Schools (SACS), and is a member of the University of Louisiana System.

MISSION

Grambling State University is committed to preparing its graduates to compete and succeed in careers related to its programs of study, to contribute to the advancement of knowledge, and to lead productive lives as informed citizens in a democratic society.

MOTTO

"The Place Where Everybody Is Somebody"

TRIVIA

Grambling was the home of football coach Eddie Robinson, who after fifty-seven years leading the Tigers, retired in 1997 with the NCAA record for the most career wins as a head coach.

NOTABLES

- Erykah Badu—Grammy-winning soul singer and songwriter

- Ronnie Coleman—Professional bodybuilder; eight-time Mr. Olympia

- Doug Williams—First and only African-American quarterback to win Super Bowl; selected MVP of Super Bowl XXII

- Judy Mason—Playwright, actress, and motivational speaker

- Willie Rockward, Ph.D.—Scientist and lecturer

ACADEMIC PROGRAMS

Grambling State University consists of four colleges: Arts and Sciences, Business, Education, and Professional Studies. The three schools at the university are Nursing, Graduate Studies and Research, and Social Work.

Degrees are awarded in Accounting; Applied Music–Performance; Art; Art Education (Grade K–12); Biology; Biology Education (Grades 6–12); Chemistry; Child Development; Computer Information Systems; Computer Science; Criminal Justice; Curriculum and Instruction; Developmental Education; Drafting Design Technology; Early Childhood Education (Grades PK–3); Economics; Educational Leadership; Electronics Engineering Technology; Elementary Education (Grades 1–5); Elementary/Early Childhood Education; English Education (Grades 6–12); English; Family Science Education (Grades 6–12); Family Nurse Practitioner; Family Nurse; French; French Education (Grades 6–12); History; Kinesiology; Leisure Studies; Liberal Arts; Management; Marketing; Mass Communication; Mathematics; Mathematics Education (Grades 6–12); Music Education–Instrumental (Grades K–12); Music Education–Vocal (Grades K–12); Nursing; Nursing–Family Nurse Practitioner; Nursing–Nurse Educator; Paralegal Studies; Physics; Physics Education (Grades 6–12); Political Science; Psychology; Public Administration; Social Studies Education (Grades 6–12); Social Sciences; Social Work; Sociology; Spanish; Spanish Education; Special Education; Sports Administration; and Theatre.

STUDENT ORGANIZATIONS

Grambling State University offers numerous academic, social, religious, international, and sports clubs and organizations for students, including the Art Guild, Economics Club, Grambling Council of Black Engineers & Scientists, S.W.A.T. Ministry in Motion, Tiger Marching Band, GSU Choir, African Student Connection, Student Government Association, and Orchesis Dance Company. Greek fraternities and sororities are represented on campus.

SPORTS

Grambling State University teams, the Tigers, are members of the National Collegiate Athletic Association (NCAA), Division I (football Division I-AA) and participate in the Southwestern Athletic Conference (SWAC). Men's sports include baseball, basketball, cross-country, football, golf, tennis, and track and field; women's basketball, bowling, golf, soccer, softball, tennis, track and field, cross-country, and volleyball.

TUITION

$4,800/$7,500

CONTACT INFORMATION

Director of Admissions
Grambling State University
P.O. Drawer 1165
100 Main Street
Grambling, LA 71245
Phone: (318) 274-6183
Web site: www.gram.edu (Click Admissions)

SOUTHERN UNIVERSITY AND A&M COLLEGE

ADDRESS: P.O. Box 9374
Baton Rouge, LA 70813
(225) 771-4500

WEB SITE: http://web.subr.edu

FOUNDED: 1880

MASCOT: Jaguar

AFFILIATION: None

TYPE: 4-Year Public

RATIO: 17:1

STUDENT BODY: 7,500

HISTORY

Southern University and A&M College grew out of a movement in Louisiana to establish an equal-opportunity institution of higher learning for persons of color in New Orleans. This movement resulted in the establishment in 1880 of Southern University in New Orleans. Southern opened with twelve students and a $10,000 appropriation and was later granted land-grant status with the passage of the 1890 Morrill Act.

In 1912, Legislative Act 118 authorized the closing of Southern University in New Orleans and the reestablishment of the University on a new site. In 1914, Southern University opened in Scotlandville, Louisiana, receiving a portion of a $50,000 national land-grant appropriation. Southern University in New Orleans and Southern University in Shreveport were authorized by Legislative Acts 28 and 42 in 1956 and 1964, respectively. In 1974, the

Southern University Board of Supervisors, was created to govern the Baton Rouge, New Orleans, and Shreveport campuses. In 1985, the A.A. Lenoir Law School was designated the Southern University Law School. Dedicated in January 2002, Ashford O. Williams Hall is home to the fifth SU System campus, the Agricultural Research and Extension Center, which is located in Baton Rouge.

MISSION

The mission of Southern University and A&M College, an historically black, 1890 land-grant institution, is to provide opportunities for a diverse student population to achieve a high-quality, global educational experience, to engage in scholarly research and creative activities, and to give meaningful public service to the community, the state, the nation, and the world so that Southern University graduates are competent, informed, and productive citizens. (Adopted by Board of Supervisors October 25, 2007.)

MOTTO

"A People's Institution Serving the State, the Nation, and the World"

TRIVIA

The legendary Southern University Human Jukebox has performed at several Super Bowls and collegiate bowls, in Yankee Stadium and foreign countries, and at presidential inaugurations and Radio City Music Hall.

NOTABLES

- Randy Jackson—Judge on *American Idol*

- Avery Johnson—Former coach of the Dallas Mavericks, and ESPN basketball analyst

- Aeneas Williams—Former NFL football cornerback and free safety

ACADEMIC PROGRAMS

Southern University and A&M College consists of the Dolores Margaret Richard Spikes Honors College, University College, College of Agricultural, Family, and Consumer Sciences; College of Arts and Humanities; College of Business; College of Education; College of Engineering; College of Sciences; School of Architecture; School of Nursing; and the Nelson Mandela School of Public Policy and Urban Affairs.

A bachelor of arts degree is awarded in Elementary Education, English, Visual Arts, French, History, Mass Communications, Music, Music Education, Psychology, Spanish, Rehabilitation Services, Sociology, Speech Communications, Theater Arts, Therapeutic Recreation, and Leisure Studies.

A bachelor of science degree is awarded in Accounting, Agricultural Science, Agricultural Economics, Biological Sciences, Chemical/Chemical Engineering Technology, Chemistry, Civil Engineering, Economics, Computer Science, Electrical Engineering, Electronic Engineering Technology, Family and Consumer Sciences, Management, Marketing, Mathematics, Mechanical Engineering, Physics, Secondary Education, Social Work, Speech Pathology and Audiology, and Urban Forestry.

STUDENT ORGANIZATIONS

Southern University and A&M College offers activities that include theater, jazz band, marching band, chorale, and dance. Students may get involved in the *Southern University Digest* (student-run newspaper) or the *Jaguar* (yearbook). Communication majors may work at the student-run radio or television station. Leadership opportunities are found in the Student Government Association. Religious groups include the Newman Club and clubs representing Baptist, Interdenominational, United Methodist, and Church of God in Christ. Greek sororities and fraternities are represented on campus.

SPORTS

Southern University and A&M College's teams, the Jaguars, are members of the National Collegiate Athletic Association (NCAA) and participate in the Southwestern Athletic Conference (SWAC). Men's sports include baseball, basketball, cross-country, football, golf, and track and field; women's sports include basketball, bowling, cross-country, soccer, softball, tennis, track and field, and volleyball.

TUITION

$3,706/$9,498

CONTACT INFORMATION:

Director of Admissions
Southern University and A&M College
P.O. Box 9901
Baton Rouge, LA 70813
Phone: (225) 771-2430
Toll-free: (800) 256-1531
Fax: (225) 771-2500
E-mail: admit@subr.edu

SOUTHERN UNIVERSITY AT NEW ORLEANS

ADDRESS: 6400 Press Drive
New Orleans, LA 70126
(504) 286-5000

WEB SITE: www.suno.edu

FOUNDED: 1956

MASCOT: Knight

AFFILIATION: None

TYPE: 4-Year Public

RATIO: 30:1

STUDENT BODY: 3,105

HISTORY

Southern University at New Orleans was founded in 1956 as a branch of Southern University and Agricultural & Mechanical College in Baton Rouge. It opened its doors on September 21, 1959, and has become a primary destination for those seeking careers in social work, criminal justice, and education.

Although the university's original campus was devastated by Hurricanes Katrina and Rita, Southern University at New Orleans has flourished into a two-campus university as recovery continues on the Park Campus (the original site) and new construction has begun on the Lake Campus (adjacent to Lake Pontchartrain). The new construction includes a 700-bed student housing complex, set for a January 2010 opening.

Southern University at New Orleans is accredited by the Commission on Colleges of the Southern Association of Colleges and Schools (SACS) to award associate, bachelor, and masters degrees.

MISSION

Southern University at New Orleans is dedicated to creating and maintaining an environment conducive to learning and growth, to promoting the upward mobility of diverse populations by preparing them to enter into new as well as traditional careers, and to equipping them to function optimally in the mainstream of the global society.

MOTTO

"Where Preparation for Tomorrow Begins Today"

TRIVIA

Southern University at New Orleans has the largest, most significant authenticated collection of African and African-American art in the southern United States. Artifacts from the collection have been borrowed for study and display by major museums in Louisiana and other states.

The university's athletics program boasts seven national championships, the most among NAIA institutions in Louisiana.

NOTABLES

- Dr. Louis J. Westerfield, JD—First African-American dean of both the Loyola University (New Orleans) College of Law and the University of Mississippi Law School

- Warren J. Riley—Superintendent, New Orleans Police Department

- Avery C. Alexander—Civil rights activist and former Louisiana State Representative

- Timolynn Sams—Executive director, Neighborhoods Partnership Network (New Orleans) and selection for "50 Visionaries Who Are Changing Your World" by *Utne Reader*

ACADEMIC PROGRAMS

Southern University at New Orleans consists of five colleges: the College of Arts & Sciences, the College of Business & Public Administration, the College of Education, the School of Social Work and the School of Graduate Studies.

The university offers undergraduate degrees in Biology, Business Entrepreneurship, Child Development & Family Studies, Criminal Justice, Early Childhood Education, Elementary Education, English, General Studies, Health Information Management, History, Management Information Systems, Mathematics, Psychology, Public Administration, Social Work, Sociology, and Substance Abuse Counseling.

STUDENT ORGANIZATIONS

Southern University at New Orleans offers more than thirty social and cultural activities that include class organizations, student publications, honor societies, academic and professional groups, political clubs, and cultural arts and religious groups.

Leadership opportunities are found in the Student Government Association (SGA) or the various other departmental, social, and service organizations.

Greek sororities include Alpha Kappa Alpha, Delta Sigma Theta, Sigma Gamma Rho, and Zeta Phi Beta; fraternities include Alpha Phi Alpha, Kappa Alpha Psi, Omega Psi Phi, and Phi Beta Sigma.

SPORTS

Southern University at New Orleans's teams, the Knights, are members of the National Association of Intercollegiate Athletics (NAIA) and participate in the Gulf Coast Athletic Conference (GCAC).

Men's sports include basketball, cross-country, and track and field; women's sports include basketball, track and field, cross-country, and volleyball.

TUITION

$2,970/$6,708

CONTACT INFORMATION

Admissions Director
Southern University at New Orleans
6400 Press Drive
New Orleans, LA 70126-1009
Phone: (504) 286-5314
Toll-free: (866) 641-0295

Photo courtesy of Southern University at Shreveport

SOUTHERN UNIVERSITY AT SHREVEPORT

ADDRESS: 3050 Martin Luther King, Jr. Drive
Shreveport, Louisiana 71107
(318) 670-6000

WEB SITE: http://web.susla.edu

FOUNDED: 1967

MASCOT: Jaguar

AFFILIATION: None

TYPE: 2-Year Public

RATIO: 16:1

STUDENT BODY: 2,300

HISTORY

Southern University at Shreveport (SUSLA) is the third unit of the Southern University System, which includes sister institutions Southern University and A&M College and Southern University at New Orleans.

Originally intended as an extension of the main Baton Rouge campus, SUSLA opened in September 1967 as a two-year commuter college offering basic college courses for the Shreveport–Bossier City area. In 1974, SUSLA was designated as a "unit" of the Southern University System and granted approval to award associate's degree in six fields; in ensuing years, more academic programs were added, helping it develop into a comprehensive college.

SUSLA is accredited by the Commission on Colleges of the Southern Association of Colleges and Schools (SACS).

MISSION

Southern University at Shreveport is committed to providing education to students with diverse abilities and varying academic backgrounds, and to preparing students for technical and semiprofessional careers.

MOTTO

"Opportunity Starts Here"

ACADEMIC PROGRAMS

Southern University at Shreveport has seven academic divisions: Division of Academic Outreach, Division of Allied Health, Behavioral Sciences and Education Division, Division of Business Studies, Humanities Division, Division of Science and Technology, and the School of Nursing.

Associate degrees are awarded in Accounting, Aviation Maintenance Technology, Biology, Business Management, Chemistry,

Computer Science, Criminal Justice Administration, Dental Hygiene, Early Childhood Education, Electronics Technology, Event Management, Funeral Services Administration, Health Information Technology, Human Services, Mathematics, Medical Laboratory Technician, Nursing, Radiologic Technology, Respiratory Therapy, Safety and Hazardous Materials Technology, and Surgical Technology.

Certificates for technical studies programs are awarded in Childhood Development, Day Care Administration, Dialysis Technician, Emergency Medical Technician, Event Management, Food and Beverage Management, Histotechnology, Hospitality Operations, Paralegal Studies, Phlebotomy, Polysomnography. Certificates are also awarded for Airframe and Powerplant Maintenance and for Computer Network Technology.

STUDENT ORGANIZATIONS

Southern University at Shreveport offers several student clubs and organizations. Students may join the student-run newspaper *(The Jaguar Speaks)*, Student Government Association, International Club, the Jazzy Jags Dancers, NAACP, University Ambassadors, International Club, Business Club, Dental Hygienic Club, Engineering Club, Electronics Technology Club, Health Information Technology Association, and the Radiologic Technology Club.

Two Greek organizations are represented on campus: Alpha Sigma Epsilon and Phi Theta Kappa.

SPORTS

Southern University at Shreveport teams are called the Port City Jags and Lady Jags. The athletic program consists of men's and women's basketball and golf teams.

The Port City Jags men's basketball team competes at the Division I level and is a member of the MISS-LOU Conference. The Lady Jags women's basketball team competes at the Division I Level.

TUITION

$2,252/$3,382

CONTACT INFORMATION

Southern University at Shreveport
3050 Martin Luther King, Jr. Drive
Shreveport, LA 71107
Phone: (318) 670-6000
Toll-free: (800) 458-1472

XAVIER UNIVERSITY OF LOUISIANA

ADDRESS: One Drexel Drive
New Orleans, LA 70125
(504) 486-7411

WEB SITE: www.xula.edu

FOUNDED: 1915

MASCOT: Gold Rush/Gold Nugget

AFFILIATION: Roman Catholic

TYPE: 4-Year Private

RATIO: 13:1

STUDENT BODY: 3,100

HISTORY

Philadelphia-born Katharine Drexel, later canonized a saint in the Roman Catholic Church, and her Sisters of the Blessed Sacrament religious community established Xavier University initially as a high school for African-American students in 1915. A normal school was added in 1917, the four-year college program in 1925, the College of Pharmacy in 1927, and the Graduate School in 1933. Years later, in 1970, the Sisters transferred control to a joint lay/religious Board of Trustees. With improved opportunities for students after the passage of anti-discrimination laws in the 1960s, enrollment in Xavier's arts and sciences and professional curricula accelerated during the next several decades. Today, Xavier produces graduates well educated to serve the community, state, and nation.

Xavier University is accredited by the Southern Association of Colleges and Schools, the American Council of Pharmaceutical Education, the National Association of Schools of Music, the American Chemical Society, the Association of Collegiate Business Schools and Programs, the Louisiana Department of Education, and the National Council for Accreditation of Teacher Education (NCATE). Xavier is the only private school in Louisiana accredited by NCATE.

MISSION

Xavier University of Louisiana, founded by Saint Katharine Drexel and the Sisters of the Blessed Sacrament, is Catholic and historically black. The ultimate purpose of the university is to contribute to the promotion of a more just and humane society by preparing its students to assume roles of leadership and service in a global society. This preparation takes place in a diverse learning and teaching environment that incorporates all relevant educational means, including research and community service.

MOTTO

"With God as our helper we have nothing to fear."

TRIVIA

Xavier is the only historically black, Catholic university in the Western Hemisphere. The university ranks first in the nation in placing African-American students into medical schools, where it has been ranked for the past fifteen years. Xavier ranks first nationally in the number of African-American students earning undergraduate degrees in both the biological/life sciences and the physical sciences. The College of Pharmacy is among the nation's top three producers of African-American Doctor of Pharmacy degree recipients.

NOTABLES

- Regina Benjamin—Physician; named a 2008 MacArthur Fellow "Genius Grant" winner and awarded the 1997 Nelson Mandela Award for Health and Human Rights

- Alexis Herman—First African-American U.S. Secretary of Labor

- Marie McDemmond—First female president of Norfolk State University

- Annabelle Bernard—First African American to perform as a principal player with the Deutsche Opera in Berlin, Germany

ACADEMIC PROGRAMS

Xavier University's academic units consist of the College of Arts and Sciences, which awards baccalaureate degrees; the College of Pharmacy, which awards the doctor of pharmacy degree; and a graduate program, which awards master's degrees in Education and Theology.

Undergraduate degrees are awarded in Accounting, Art, Art Education, Biochemistry, Biology, Biology Education, Business, Chemistry ACS, Chemistry Pre-Pharmacy, Chemistry Pre-Professional, Chemistry, Chemistry Education, Computer Information Systems, Computer Science, Elementary Education, Engineering Dual Degree, English, English Education, French, History, Language Education, Mass Communications, Mathematics, Mathematics Education, Microbiology, Middle School Education, Music, Music Education, Music Performance, Philosophy, Physics, Political Science, Psychology, Social studies Education, Sociology, Spanish, Speech Pathology, Statistics, and Theology.

STUDENT ORGANIZATIONS

Xavier University offers many services, resources, and programs that enhance student life experiences, including athletics and recreational sports, campus activities and student organizations, campus ministry, residence life, the Center for Student Leadership and Services, Health Services, and Career Services.

SPORTS

Xavier University offers men's and women's intercollegiate sports in basketball, tennis, and cross-country. The Gold Rush (men) and Gold Nuggets (women) are members of the National Association of Intercollegiate Athletics (NAIA), Division I and compete in the Gulf Coast Athletic Conference (GCAC).

TUITION

Arts and Sciences: $14,500 annually

College of Pharmacy: $19,600 annually

CONTACT INFORMATION

Dean of Admissions
Xavier University of Louisiana
One Drexel Drive
New Orleans, LA 70125
Phone: (504) 520-7388
Toll-free: (877) XAVIERU
Fax: (504) 520-7941

BOWIE STATE UNIVERSITY

ADDRESS: 14000 Jericho Park Road
Bowie, MD 20715-9465
(301) 860-4000

WEB SITE: www.bowiestate.edu

FOUNDED: 1865

MASCOT: Bulldog

AFFILIATION: None

TYPE: 4-Year Public

RATIO: 17:1

STUDENT BODY: 5,500

HISTORY

Bowie State University was founded in 1865 through the efforts of the Baltimore Association for the Moral and Educational Improvement of Colored People. Originally an outgrowth of the first school opened in Baltimore, its first classes were held in the African Baptist Church. In 1868, a grant from the Freedmen's Bureau allowed the Baltimore Association to purchase a building from the Society of Friends and relocate the school, which was then reorganized as a normal school to train Negro teachers.

In 1935, the school was renamed Maryland State Teachers College at Bowie and the curriculum, previously a two-year and then three-year program, was expanded to a four-year program for the training of elementary school teachers. In 1951, the program was expanded to train teachers for junior high schools, and in 1961, expanded once again for a teacher-train-ing program for secondary education. In 1963, the college became Bowie State College. University status was awarded in 1988. The university is accredited by the Middle States Association of Colleges and Schools and the Maryland State Department of Education.

MISSION

Bowie State University, through the effective and efficient management of its resources, provides high-quality and affordable educational opportunities at the bachelor's, master's, and doctoral levels for a diverse student population of Maryland citizens and the global community. The educational programs are designed to broaden the knowledge base and skill set of students across disciplines and to enable students to think critically, value diversity, become effective leaders, function competently in a highly technical world, and pursue advanced graduate study.

MOTTO

"Prepare for Life"

TRIVIA

In 2003, the Bowie Satellite Operations Control Center (BSOCC), where students can participate in satellite operations and earn mission controller certification, went fully operational. The program is a joint venture between the university, the Honeywell Corporation, and NASA's Goddard Space Flight Center.

NOTABLES

- Gwendolyn Britt—Member of the Maryland State Senate

- Christa McAuliffe—First teacher selected for NASA Teacher in Space Program; died in 1986 Space Shuttle *Challenger* disaster

- William Teel—President & CEO of 1 Source, Inc., ranked as one of the nation's fastest-growing companies

ACADEMIC PROGRAMS

Bowie State University consists of four colleges: the College of Arts and Sciences, the College of Business, the College of Education, and the College of Professional Studies.

The College of Arts and Sciences awards degrees in Communications, Computer Science, English and Modern Languages, Fine and Performing Arts, History and Government, Mathematics, Military Science, and Natural Sciences.

The College of Business awards degrees in Accounting, Economics, Finance, Information Systems, Management, Marketing, and Public Administration.

The College of Education awards degrees in Counseling, Educational Leadership, and Teaching, Learning, and Professional Development.

The College of Professional Studies awards degrees in Behavioral Sciences, Human Services, Nursing, Psychology, and Social Work.

STUDENT ORGANIZATIONS

Bowie State University offers students numerous clubs and organizations, including the African Student Association, Apostolic Campus Ministry, Bowie State University Cheerleaders, International Student Association, Latino/Hispanic Student Association, Lighthouse Campus Ministries, National Council of Negro Women, Student Government Association, Students in Free Enterprise, Student Nurses Association, Symphony of Soul Marching Band, and Women's Studies Club. Greek fraternities include Alpha Phi Alpha, Iota Phi Theta, Kappa Alpha Psi, Omega Psi Phi, and Phi Beta Sigma; sororities include Alpha Kappa Alpha, Alpha Nu Omega, Chi Eta Phi, Delta Sigma Theta, Sigma Gamma Rho, and Zeta Phi Beta.

SPORTS

Bowie State University's teams, the Bulldogs and Lady Bulldogs, are members of the National Collegiate Athletic Association (NCAA), Division II and participate in the Central Intercollegiate Athletic Association (CIAA). Men's sports include football, basketball, cross-country, indoor track and field, and outdoor track and field; women's sports include basketball, softball, tennis, volleyball, cross-country, indoor track and field, outdoor track and field, and bowling.

TUITION

$3,019 (undergraduate)/$4,759 (graduate)

CONTACT INFORMATION

Director of Admissions
Bowie State University
14000 Jericho Park Road
Bowie, MD 20715-9465
Phone: (301) 860-3415
Toll-free: (877) 772-6943
Fax: (301) 860-3438

Photo courtesy of Coppin State University

COPPIN STATE UNIVERSITY

ADDRESS: 2500 W North Avenue
Baltimore, MD 21216
(410) 951-3000

WEB SITE: www.coppin.edu

FOUNDED: 1900

MASCOT: Eagle

AFFILIATION: None

TYPE: 4-Year Public

RATIO: 22:1

STUDENT BODY: 4,050

HISTORY

Coppin State University was founded in 1900 as the Colored High School (later named Douglass High School), a one-year training course for the preparation of African-American elementary school teachers. By 1909, it had developed into a normal school and become a separate entity from the high school.

In 1926, the school was renamed Fanny Jackson Coppin Normal School in honor of the African-American educator who was a pioneer in teacher education. In 1938, the name of the normal school was changed to Coppin Teachers College, the curriculum was expanded to four years, and the college was authorized to give the bachelor of science degree.

In a 1950, Coppin was renamed Coppin State Teachers College. In 1963, it was officially renamed Coppin State College.

Coppin State University is accredited by the Middle States Association of Colleges and Schools (MSACS).

MISSION

Coppin State University is committed to excellence in teaching, research, and continuing service to its community. It provides educational access and diverse opportunities for students with a high potential for success and for students whose promise may have been hindered by a lack of social, personal, or financial opportunity. High-quality academic programs offer innovative curricula and the latest advancements in technology to prepare students for new workforce careers in a global economy.

MOTTO

"Nurturing Potential. Transforming Lives."

TRIVIA

Coppin State University is named after Fanny

Jackson Coppin, a former servant in the Newport, Rhode Island, household of author George Henry Calvert. Coppin was one of the first black women to earn a bachelor's degree from a major American college. She later became a teacher and principal of the Institute for Colored Youth in Philadelphia.

NOTABLES

- Bishop Robinson—First African-American police commissioner of Baltimore

- Stephanie Ready—First female coach of a men's professional league (Greenville Groove of the National Basketball Development League)

- Raheem DeVaughn—R&B singer and songwriter; received Grammy nomination for Best Male R&B Vocal Performance

ACADEMIC PROGRAMS

Coppin State University consists of the School of Arts and Sciences; the School of Education; the School of Professional Studies; the Helene Fuld School of Nursing; the School of Graduate Studies; the School of Management Science and Economics; and the Honors College.

Degrees are awarded in Biology; Chemistry; Computer Science; Criminal Justice; Early Childhood Education; Elementary Education; English; Entertainment Management; General Science (Biology Emphasis); General Science (Chemistry Emphasis); Global Studies; Health Information Management; History; Interdisciplinary Studies; Management Science; Mathematics; Nursing; Psychology (Alcoholism and Drug Abuse Counseling or Psychological Services Concentrations); Rehabilitation Services; Social Sciences (General, Political Science, and Sociology); Social Work; Special Education; Sports Management (Sports Medicine, Sports Business, Sports Journalism, Sports Marketing); and Urban Arts.

STUDENT ORGANIZATIONS

Coppin State University offers numerous clubs and organizations for students, including the African Student Association, Akira Anime & Video Game Club, American Humanics Student Association, Coppin Dance Ensemble, Coppin Models, Coppin Players, Coppin Top Model Organization, CSU Cheerleaders, CSU Marching Band, Dancing Diva's, Eagle's Nest Poetry & Spoken Word Society, Honda Campus All-Star Team, Psychology Club, Social Work Association, STEM Club (Science, Technology, Engineering, Mathematics), Student Alumni Ambassador Club, Student Senate, and The Talented Tenth Social Sciences Club.

Greek fraternities include Alpha Phi Alpha, Kappa Alpha Psi, Omega Psi Phi, Phi Beta Sigma, and Iota Phi Theta; sororities include Alpha Kappa Alpha, Alpha Nu Omega, Chi Eta Phi Nursing Sorority, Delta Sigma Theta, Zeta Phi Beta, and Sigma Gamma Rho.

SPORTS

Coppin State University's teams, the Eagles, are members of the National Collegiate Athletic Association (NCAA), Division I and participate in the Mid-Eastern Athletic Conference (MEAC).

Men's sports include baseball, basketball, cross country, tennis, and track. Women's sports include basketball, bowling, cross country, softball, tennis, track, and volleyball.

TUITION
$4,910/$11,934

CONTACT INFORMATION
Director of Admissions
Coppin State University
2500 W North Avenue
Baltimore, MD 21216
Phone: (410) 951-3600
Toll-free: (800) 635-3674

Photo courtesy of Morgan State University

MORGAN STATE UNIVERSITY

ADDRESS: 1700 East Cold Spring Lane
Baltimore, MD 21251
(443) 885-3333

WEB SITE: www.morgan.edu

FOUNDED: 1867

MASCOT: Bear

AFFILIATION: None

TYPE: 4-Year Public

RATIO: 18:1

STUDENT BODY: 7,700

HISTORY

Morgan State University, founded in 1867 as a private institute for the training of young men in ministry, was originally known as the Centenary Biblical Institute. Established by the Baltimore Conference of the Methodist Episcopal Church, the institute later expanded to a teaching college for both men and women.

In 1890, the school was renamed Morgan College in honor of the Reverend Lyttleton Morgan, who had donated land for the college and had served as the first chairman of institute's Board of Trustees.

In 1917, after receiving a $50,000 grant from Andrew Carnegie, the college moved to its present site in northeast Baltimore. In 1939, the college officially transferred to the State of Maryland, becoming Morgan State College. The name was changed to Morgan State University in 1975. The Carnegie Foundation for the Advancement of Teaching has classified Morgan State University as a Doctoral Research Institution.

Morgan State University is accredited by the Middle States Association of Colleges and Schools (MSACS).

MISSION

Morgan State University is designated as Maryland's public urban university. The university serves an ethnically and culturally diverse student body. Similarly, the student body reflects the traditional college-going cohort as well as part-time and adult learners.

MOTTO

"Stairway to excellence, gateway to opportunity!"

TRIVIA

Morgan State University is the nation's leading HBCU in the production of Fulbright Scholars.

Morgan State University consistently ranks in the top echelon of universities in the State of Maryland as well as nationally awarding bachelor's and doctorate degrees to African Americans in science and engineering.

NOTABLES

- General William "Kip" Ward—Commander of U.S. African Command

- Earl Graves—Publisher of *Black Enterprise Magazine*

- Kweisi Mfume—Former U.S. Congressman from Maryland and former president and CEO of the NAACP

ACADEMIC PROGRAMS

Morgan State University consists of the College of Liberal Arts; School of Education and Urban Studies; School of Business and Management; School of Computer, Mathematical, and Natural Sciences; School of Engineering; School of Community Health and Policy; School of Graduate Studies; and School of Architecture and Planning.

Morgan State University offers bachelor's degrees in Accounting; Architecture and Environmental Design; Biology; Business Administration; Chemistry; Computer Science; Economics ; Elementary Education; English; Civil Engineering; Electrical and Computer Engineering; Industrial Engineering; Family Consumer Sciences; Finance; Fine Arts; Foreign Languages; Health Education; History and Geography; Hotel, Restaurant, and Hospitality Management; Information Systems; Management; Marketing; Mathematics; Medical Technology; Mental Health Technology; Military Science; Music; Nursing; Nutritional Science/Dietetic; Philosophy and Religious Studies; Physical Education; Physics and Engineering Physics; Political Science; Psychology; Social Work; Sociology and Anthropology; Speech Communications; Telecommunications; Theater Arts; and Transportation Systems.

STUDENT ORGANIZATIONS

Morgan State University offers many social and cultural activities for its students, including theater, band, chorale, dance, and jazz ensemble.

Students may get involved in the student-run newspaper, *Spokesman,* or the yearbook, *Promethean.* There is also a student-run radio station, WEAA-FM, and television production studio. Leadership opportunities are found in the Student Government Association.

Greek fraternities include Alpha Phi Alpha, Kappa Alpha Psi, Omega Psi Phi, and Phi Beta Sigma; sororities include Alpha Kappa Alpha, Delta Sigma Theta, Sigma Gamma Rho, Zeta Phi Beta, and Iota Phi Lambda.

SPORTS

The university's mascot is the bear. Morgan State enjoys membership in the National Collegiate Athletic Association (NCAA), Division I-AA and the Mid-Eastern Athletic Conference (MEAC). Men's sports include basketball, cross-country, football, tennis, and track and field. Women's sports include basketball, bowling, cheerleading, cross-country, softball, tennis, track and field, and volleyball.

TUITION

$6,318/$14,438

CONTACT INFORMATION

Director of Admissions and Recruitment
Morgan State University
1700 East Cold Spring Lane
Baltimore, MD 21251
Phone: (443) 885-3000
Toll-free: (800) 332-6674

Photo courtesy of University of Maryland Eastern Shore

UNIVERSITY OF MARYLAND EASTERN SHORE

ADDRESS: University of MD Eastern Shore
Princess Anne, MD 21853
(410) 651-2200

WEB SITE: www.umes.edu

FOUNDED: 1886

MASCOT: Hawk

AFFILIATION: Methodist
Episcopal

TYPE: 4-Year Public

RATIO: 17:1

STUDENT BODY: 4,290

HISTORY

The University of Maryland Eastern Shore was founded in 1886 by the Delaware Conference of the Methodist Episcopal Church. Originally called the Delaware Conference Academy, it became the industrial branch of Morgan State College and was renamed Princess Anne Academy.

In 1919, the State of Maryland gained control of the academy, and its name was changed to Eastern Shore Branch of the Maryland Agricultural College. In 1926, it became Maryland State College. In 1970, it became the University of Maryland Eastern Shore and expanded its academic programs. Today, the university offers thirty-two bachelor's degree programs, ten master's degree programs, and seven doctoral degree programs.

The University of Maryland Eastern Shore is accredited by the Middle States Association of Colleges and Schools.

MISSION

The University of Maryland Eastern Shore is committed to providing access to a high-quality, values-based educational experience, especially to individuals who are first-generation college students of all races, while emphasizing multicultural diversity and international perspectives.

MOTTO

"Learning and Leadership"

TRIVIA

In Super Bowl III, held in 1968, the University of Maryland Eastern Shore was represented by five alumni—Earl Christy, Johnny Sample, Emerson Boozer, Charles Stukes, and James Duncan.

NOTABLES

- Dr. Earl Richardson—President, Morgan State University

- Art Shell—Former NFL player and coach of the Oakland Raiders, Hall of Fame Class of '89

- Starletta DuPois—Actress

ACADEMIC PROGRAMS

The University of Maryland Eastern Shore consists of five schools: the School of Agricultural and Natural Sciences; the School of Arts and Professions; the School of Business and Technology; the School of Graduate Studies; and the School of Pharmacy and Health Professions.

Undergraduate degrees are awarded in Accounting, African and African-American Studies, Agribusiness and General Agriculture, Applied Design, Art Education, Aviation, Biology, Business Administration, Business Education, Chemistry, Computer Science, Construction Management, Criminal Justice, Education, Engineering Technology, Engineering, English, Environmental Sciences, History, Hotel and Restaurant Management, Human Ecology, Mathematics, Modern Languages, Music Education, Professional Golf Management, Social Studies Teacher Education, Sociology, Sociology/Social Work, Teacher Education, and Technology Education.

STUDENT ORGANIZATIONS

The University of Maryland Eastern Shore offers numerous organizations and clubs, including the Caribbean International Club, Centennial Club, Collegiate Chapter of Future Farmers of America, Engineering Technology Society, Eta Rho Mu, Groove Phi Groove Social Fellowship, Human Ecology Club, Miaka Club, NAACP, National Student Business League, Pan-Hellenic Council, Students for Progressive Action, Accounting Club, Student Construction Association, and Wicomico Hall Men's Association.

Students may get involved in the student-run newspaper and yearbook. Communication majors or volunteers can work on the student-run radio station. Leadership opportunities can be found in the Student Government Association, international student groups, or the undergraduate student council.

Greek sororities include Alpha Kappa Alpha; fraternities include Alpha Phi Alpha, Kappa Alpha Psi, Omega Psi Phi, Phi Beta Sigma, and Iota Phi Theta.

SPORTS

The University of Maryland Eastern Shore's teams, the Hawks, are members of the National Collegiate Athletic Association (NCAA), Division I and participate in the Mid-Eastern Athletic Conference.

Men's sports include baseball, basketball, cross-country, golf, indoor track, outdoor track, and tennis; women's sports include basketball, bowling, cross-country, softball, tennis, indoor track, outdoor track, and volleyball.

TUITION

$5,988/$12,555

CONTACT INFORMATION

Director of Admissions and Recruitment
University of Maryland Eastern Shore
Princess Anne, MD 21853-1299
Phone: (410) 651-8410
Fax: (410) 651-7922
E-mail: umesadmissions@mail.umes.edu

LEWIS COLLEGE OF BUSINESS

ADDRESS: 17370 Meyers
Detroit, MI 48235
(313) 862-6300

WEB SITE: www.lewiscollege.edu

FOUNDED: 1929

AFFILIATION: None

TYPE: 2-Year Private

RATIO: 13:1

STUDENT BODY: 400

HISTORY

Lewis College of Business was originally founded as the Lewis Business College in 1928 by Violet T. Lewis, an African-American woman who dreamed of providing African-American young adults with post-secondary education in Indianapolis, Indiana. When Indiana's segregation laws prevented the enrollment of African Americans in any post-secondary schools, Lewis traveled to Detroit and opened the college there.

Lewis Business College was incorporated in 1941 as the Lewis Association for the Study and Practical Application of Business and Commercial Science. It was later renamed the Lewis College of Business. In 1987, the college was designated an Historically Black College and University (HBCU) by the U.S. Department of Education and is the only HBCU in the State of Michigan.

Lewis College of Business is accredited by North Central Association of Colleges and Schools (NCACS).

MISSION

Lewis College of Business is committed to supporting students to stretch their mental capacity and open the unexplored horizons of their learning capabilities, equipping them to pursue further academic studies, to enter the world of work, or to become entrepreneurs upon graduation.

MOTTO

"Learn, Conquer, Become"

TRIVIA

The State of Michigan, recognizing the historical significance of Lewis College, erected a Michigan historical marker at the first permanent site of the college at John R. and Ferry streets in Detroit in September 1988.

ACADEMIC PROGRAMS

Lewis College of Business consists of four divisions: the Division of Business Administration, the Division of Liberal Arts, the Division of Allied Health, and the Division of Computer Information Technologies.

The Business Administration Division awards associate degrees in Business Administration with concentrations in Marketing, Management, Hospitality Management, and Accounting.

The Liberal Arts degree consists of coursework in English, History, Philosophy, Psychology, and Sociology.

The Allied Health Division offers an Office Information Systems Degree Program for Executive Administrative Assistant, Medical Administrative Assistant, Legal Administrative Assistant, Medical Office Assistant, and Medical Billing.

The Computer Information Technologies Degree Program consists of Computer Information Systems, Computer Programming, and CIS Certification.

TUITION
$5,900

CONTACT INFORMATION:
Admissions Secretary
Lewis College of Business
17370 Meyers Road
Detroit, MI 48235-1423
Phone: (313) 862-6300

ALCORN STATE UNIVERSITY

ADDRESS: 1000 ASU Drive
Alcorn State, MS 39096
(800) 222-6790

WEB SITE: www.alcorn.edu

FOUNDED: 1871

MASCOT: Braves

AFFILIATION: None

TYPE: 4-Year Public

RATIO: 16:1

STUDENT BODY: 3,700

HISTORY

Alcorn State University is situated on the site originally occupied by Oakland College, a school established by the Presbyterian Church for whites. The college closed at the beginning of the Civil War, and when it failed to reopen at the war's end, the property was sold in 1871 to the State of Mississippi and renamed Alcorn University in honor of then governor James L. Alcorn.

In 1878, its name was changed from Alcorn University to Alcorn Agricultural and Mechanical College. For the first two decades of its history, the school was exclusively for black males; however, in 1895, women were admitted—and today outnumber men at the university. While early graduates had limited horizons, more recent alumni are successful doctors, lawyers, dentists, teachers, principals, administrators, managers, and entrepreneurs.

In 1974, the college received university status and was renamed Alcorn State University. It is fully accredited by the Commission on Colleges of the Southern Association of Colleges and Schools (SACS).

MISSION

Alcorn State University is committed to providing outreach programs and services that are geared toward assisting and meeting the educational, economic, recreational, and cultural needs of the immediate community, the region, and the state.

TRIVIA

Alcorn State University has three campuses—one in Lorman, one in Natchez, and one in Vicksburg.

NOTABLES:

- Medgar Evers—NAACP's first field secretary

- Alex Haley—author of *Roots*

- Donald Driver—NFL wide receiver for the Green Bay Packers

- Steve McNair—Former NFL quarterback for the Baltimore Ravens

- Kimberly Morgan—Miss Mississippi

- J.J. Williamson—Comedian; actor

- Alexander O'Neal—R&B and soul singer

ACADEMIC PROGRAMS

Alcorn State University consists of seven schools: the School of Arts and Sciences; the School of Agriculture and Applied Sciences; the School of Education and Psychology; the School of Business; the School of Nursing; the School of Graduate Studies; and the College for Excellence.

Degrees are awarded in Accounting; Advanced Technologies; Agribusiness Management; Agricultural Economics; Animal Science; Art; Biochemistry; Biology Education; Business Administration; Chemical Physics; Chemistry; Chemistry Education; Child Development; Computer and Information Science; Computer Science; Computer Science and Applied Mathematics; Criminal Justice; Economics; Elementary Education; English Education; Environmental Biology/Ecology; General Agriculture; General Studies; Health and Physical Education; History; History Education; Literature; Mass Communication; Mathematics; Mathematics Education; Military Science; Music; Nursing; Nutrition and Dietetics; Plant and Soil Science; Political Science; Professional Writing; Psychology; Recreation; Social Work; Sociology; Special Education; Speech; Sports Medicine; and Theatre.

STUDENT ORGANIZATIONS

Alcorn State University offers numerous social activities for students, including glee club, drama, choir, band and drill team, and jazz ensemble.

Students can join the NAACP Chapter, Black History Month Society, Campus Union Board, Cheering Squad, Beaté Noire Modeling Squad, Student Government Association, or work on the *Alcornite* yearbook, the *Greater Alcorn Herald* newspaper, or at the university's public broadcasting radio station, WPRL.

Greek sororities include Alpha Kappa Alpha, Delta Sigma Theta, Sigma Gamma Rho, and Zeta Phi Beta; fraternities include Alpha Phi Alpha, Kappa Alpha Psi, Omega Psi Phi, and Phi Beta Sigma. Honorary societies are also represented on campus.

SPORTS

Alcorn State University's teams, the Braves, are members of the National Collegiate Athletic Association (NCAA), Division I and participate in the Southwest Athletic Conference (SWAC).

Men's sports include baseball, basketball, cross-country running, football, and golf; women's sports include soccer, softball, tennis, track and field, and volleyball.

TUITION

$4,500/$10,700

CONTACT INFORMATION

Alcorn State University
1000 ASU Drive, #300
Alcorn State, MS 39096-7500
Phone: (601) 877-6147
Toll-free: (800) 222-6790
Fax: (601) 877-6347

Allied Health Center
Photo courtesy of Coahoma Community College

COAHOMA COMMUNITY COLLEGE

ADDRESS: 3240 Friars Point Road
Clarksdale, MS 38614
(662) 627-2571

WEB SITE: www.coahomacc.edu

FOUNDED: 1949

MASCOT: Tiger

AFFILIATION: None

TYPE: 2-Year Public

RATIO: 26:1

STUDENT BODY: 2,200

HISTORY

Coahoma Community College has its origins in the Coahoma County Agricultural High School, which was established in 1924 under the then existing "separate but equal" doctrine for the education of African Americans. In 1949, a junior college curriculum was added and the high school became Coahoma Junior College and Agricultural High School.

In 1949, its first full year in operation, the college was supported entirely by county funds. The following year, however, it was included in the State of Mississippi's system of public junior colleges and became eligible for state funding.

In 1965, the college opened its doors to all students and, in 1989, with the approval of the Board of Trustees of Coahoma Junior College and the State Board for Community and Junior Colleges, the college became Coahoma Community College.

Coahoma Community College is accredited by the Commission on Colleges of the Southern Association of Colleges and Schools (SACS).

MISSION

Coahoma Community College is committed to serving Bolivar, Coahoma, Quitman, Tallahatchie, and Tunica counties and beyond. Serving as a catalyst for economic and community development, Coahoma Community College provides accessible, affordable, diverse, and quality educational opportunities and services that foster a nurturing teaching and learning environment, promote intellectual and work readiness skills, support personal and professional growth, and prepare students to enter the job market or transfer to a college or university.

MOTTO

"The College that Cares"

TRIVIA

Coahoma ranks in the Top 50 of America's fastest-growing two-year colleges.

ACADEMIC PROGRAMS

Coahoma Community College consists of the College of Liberal Arts, the College of Mathematics & Science, and the College of Business & Technology.

The College of Liberal Arts offers programs of study in Art Appreciation, Art History II, Child Development, Communicative Disorders, Criminal Justice, Drawing II, Design II, Early Childhood Education, Elementary Education, English, General Education, Painting I, Political Science, Pre-Law, Psychology, Radio & Television Broadcasting, Secondary Education, Special Education, Social Science, Social Science Education, Social Work, Spanish/Foreign Languages, and Speech Pathology/Audiology.

The College of Mathematics & Science offers programs of study in Administration, Administration/Health Records, Biology, Chemistry, Mathematics, Mathematics Education, Medical Records, Pre-Clinical Library Science, Pre-Dental Hygiene, Pre-Medical, Pre-Nursing, Pre-Occupational Therapy, Pre-Optometry, Pre-Pharmacy, and Pre-Physical Therapy.

The College of Business & Technology offers programs of study in Accounting, Business, Computer Information, and Systems Management Information.

In addition, the Career and Technical Education Division offers programs in Accounting Technology, Barbering Instructor Training, Barber/Stylist, Child Development Technology, Collision Repair, Computer Servicing, Cosmetology, Hotel and Restaurant Management, Industrial Maintenance Mechanics, Medical Office Technology, Office Systems Technology, Practical Nursing, Residential Carpentry, and Welding and Cutting.

The Health Sciences offers programs in Associate Degree Nursing (ADN), Licensed Practical Nursing (LPN), Certified Nursing Assistant (CNA), Respiratory Care, Polysomnography (Sleep Technology), Emergency Medical Technologist (EMT-B), and Phlebotomy.

The college's Educational Outreach and Distance Learning includes online courses and evening classes. The Workforce Development Center offers specialized training for business and industry, special needs of the workforce, and GED training programs.

STUDENT ORGANIZATIONS

Coahoma Community College offers students numerous clubs and organizations, including the Education Club, English Club, Phi Beta Lambda, Students in Free Enterprise, Science & Math Symposium, El Circulo Español (Spanish Club), Choir, Band, Student Government Association, Social Science Forum, Black Literary Society, Residence Hall Council, Phi Theta Kappa (Alpha Omicron Pi Chapter), *The Coahoma Tribune* (student newspaper), and *The Coahoman* (campus-wide project offering a pictorial history of the college).

SPORTS

Coahoma Community College's teams, the Tigers, are members of the National Junior College Athletic Association (NJCAA). Men's sports include baseball, basketball, and football; women's sports include basketball and softball.

TUITION

$1,700

CONTACT INFORMATION

Director of Admissions and Records
Coahoma Community College
3240 Friars Point Road
Clarksdale, MS 38614
Phone: (662) 621-4205

HINDS COMMUNITY COLLEGE

ADDRESS: 501 E Main Street
Raymond, MS 39154
(601) 857-5261

WEB SITE: www.hindscc.edu

FOUNDED: 1917

MASCOT: Eagle/Bulldog

AFFILIATION: None

TYPE: 2-Year Public

RATIO: 17:1

STUDENT BODY: 19,500

HISTORY

Hinds Community College was founded in September 1917 as Hinds County Agricultural High School, a small agricultural school whose purpose was to serve as a "Poor Man's College" for children from the nearby farming communities.

In 1922, the school began offering college-level academic courses. Over the next fifty years, its curriculum expanded to include vocational and technical training, and the school came to be known as Hinds Junior College. In 1982, it merged with Utica Junior College—an historically black junior college that was founded in 1903—under Federal court order as part of a class action racial discrimination lawsuit. In 1987, the name was changed to Hinds Community College.

Hinds Community College, which has six locations, is accredited by the Commission on Colleges of the Southern Association of Colleges and Schools (SACS).

MISSION

Hinds Community College is committed to offering pertinent and diverse educational programs and services for persons with various interests.

MOTTO

"The College for All People"

TRIVIA

The previous owner of the forty-five acres of land on which Hinds Community College's Raymond campus now sits was John R. Eggleston, a lieutenant aboard the Confederate ironclad C.S.S. *Virginia* (also known as the *Merrimac*) that battled the U.S.S. *Monitor* in the famous naval battle of 1862.

NOTABLES

- Chad Bradford—Major league baseball player

- Brad Banks—Football player for National Football League and Canadian Football League; Heisman Trophy finalist

ACADEMIC PROGRAMS

Hinds Community College awards associate in arts degrees or allows students to transfer coursework to a four-year college in pursuit of a baccalaureate degree.

Instruction is given in Accounting Technology; Agriculture; Art; Automotive & Trucking Career Programs; Aviation; Banking & Finance Technology; Biology; Business Administration; Business Office Technology; Career Tech Center (Secondary); Child Development Technology; Communication & Journalism; Computer Network Support Technology; Computer Programming Technology; Computer Servicing Technology; Court Reporting; Culinary Arts Technology; Dance; Drafting & Design Technology; eLearning; Electrical Technology; Electronics Technology; English & Modern Foreign Languages; Geographic Information Systems Technology; Graphic Design Technology; Health-Related Professions; History, Political Science and Philosophy; Honors Program; Hospitality & Tourism Management; Hotel & Restaurant Management Technology; International Programs; Interpreter Training Technology; Landscape Management; Machine Tool Technology; Marketing Management Technology; Medical Billing & Coding Technology; Medical Office Technology; Microcomputer Technology; Music; Nutrition & Food Science; Office Systems Technology; Paralegal Technology; Pharmacy Technology; Plumbing & Construction Technology; Psychology; Reading & Education; Speech, Theatre & Dance; Telecommunications Technology; and Travel & Tourism Management Technology.

STUDENT ORGANIZATIONS

Hinds Community College offers more than ninety religious, social, service, academic, and special interest clubs and organizations. Students can join the Eagles Marching Band, jazz ensemble, chamber orchestra, choir, cheerleading squad, or precision dance team. Leadership opportunities can be found in Diamond Darlings and Associated Student Government. Honor societies include Phi Theta Kappa.

SPORTS

Hinds Community College's teams are members of the National Junior College Athletic Association (NJCAA) and participate in the Mississippi Junior College Athletic Association (MJCAA). Men's and women's basketball teams, the Bulldogs, are in Utica. Other men's sports (Eagles) include baseball, football, golf, soccer, tennis, and track and field. Women's sports (Eagles) include soccer, softball, tennis, and track and field. The Eagles are in Raymond.

TUITION

$1,700/$3,906

CONTACT INFORMATION

District Office of Admissions and Records
Hinds Community College
Raymond, MS 39154
Phone: (601) 857-3212
E-mail: records@hindscc.edu

JACKSON STATE UNIVERSITY

ADDRESS: 1400 Lynch Street
Jackson, MS 39217
(800) 848-6817

WEB SITE: www.jsums.edu

FOUNDED: 1877

MASCOT: Tiger

AFFILIATION: American Baptist
Home Mission Society

TYPE: 4-Year Public

RATIO: 18:1

STUDENT BODY: 8,375

HISTORY

Founded in 1877, Jackson State University (JSU) is a comprehensive university located in Mississippi's largest metropolitan area. The fourth-largest institution of higher learning in the state and the only four-year public institution in the central Mississippi area, JSU provides its approximately 8,400 students from more than fifty foreign countries and nearly all of Mississippi's eighty-two counties with opportunities to develop knowledge and skills that empower them to succeed in an increasingly complex world.

Designated as Mississippi's "Urban University," JSU is one of the top educators of African-Americans with graduate and doctoral degrees in the nation and consistently ranks among the top two producers of African Americans with baccalaureates in education. As a "high research activity" university, JSU generates more than

$66 million in federal and other sponsored program awards.

In 1956, the name was changed to Jackson State College. In 1974, it received university status. Jackson State University is accredited by the Commission on Colleges of the Southern Association of Colleges and Schools (SACS).

MISSION

Jackson State University is committed to providing public service programs designed to enhance the quality of life and seek solutions to urban problems in the physical, social, intellectual, and economic environments.

MOTTO

"Challenging Minds, Changing Lives"

TRIVIA

Among historically black colleges and universities, JSU was the first to have a College of Public Health and an undergraduate program in meteorology. The university has been ranked among the top two producers of African Americans with bachelor degrees in education. In addition to academics, JSU emphasizes research and public service programs designed to enhance the quality of life and seek solutions to urban problems.

NOTABLES

- Walter Payton—NFL running back with Chicago Bears; Sports Hall of Fame member; JSU and Mississippi's Sports Halls of Fame member

- Vivian Brown Swain—Meteorologist, The Weather Channel

- Cassandra Wilson—Grammy award-winning jazz artist

ACADEMIC PROGRAMS

Jackson State University consists of six colleges and three divisions: the College of Education and Human Development; the College of Business; the College of Public Service; the College of Science, Engineering, and Technical Arts; the College of Liberal Arts; the College of Lifelong Learning; and the Divisions of Graduate Studies, International Studies, and Undergraduate Studies.

Bachelor's degrees are awarded in Accounting; Entrepreneurship; Economics; Finance; General Business Entrepreneurship; Special Education; Elementary Education & Early Childhood; Health, Physical Education & Recreation; Social and Cultural Studies; Educational Leadership; Educational Technology & Support Services; School, Community & Rehabilitative Counseling; Art; Music; History & Philosophy; Military Science; Political Science; Psychology; Criminal Justice & Sociology; Criminal Justice; English & Modern Foreign Language; Mass Communications; Speech Communications;

Behavioral & Environmental Health; Epidemiology & Bio-Statistics; Communicative Disorders; Health Policy & Management; Public Policy & Administration; Urban & Regional Planning; Air ROTC Biology; Chemistry; Physics, Atmospheric Science & General Sciences; Mathematics; Technology; Civil Engineering; Computer Engineering; Computer Science; Telecommunications Engineering; Graduate Engineering Programs; and Professional Interdisciplinary Studies.

STUDENT ORGANIZATIONS

Jackson State University offers several student organizations, including the Student Government Association, Campus Ministries, Spirit Team, Orchestra Club, Dunbar Drama Guild, as well as student-run publications such as its weekly newspaper and yearbook. Greek sororities and fraternities are represented on campus.

SPORTS

JSU, a Division 1 school (Division I-AA in football), is affiliated with the National Collegiate Athletic Association (NCAA) and offers men's sports programs in football, basketball, baseball, golf, tennis, cross-country track, and indoor and outdoor track; and women's sports programs in basketball, volleyball, golf, tennis, softball, soccer, bowling, cross-country track, and indoor and outdoor track.

TUITION

$4,634/$10,978

CONTACT INFORMATION

Director of Undergraduate Admissions
Jackson State University
P.O. Box 17330
Jackson, MS 39217
Phone: (601) 979-2100
Toll-free: (800) 848-6817
Fax: (601) 979-3445
Web site: www.jsums.edu

Photo courtesy of Mississippi Valley State University

MISSISSIPPI VALLEY STATE UNIVERSITY

ADDRESS: 14000 Highway 82 West
Itta Bena, MS 38941
(662) 254-9041

WEB SITE: www.mvsu.edu

FOUNDED: 1950

MASCOT: Delta Devil

AFFILIATION: None

TYPE: 4-Year Public

RATIO: 20:1

STUDENT BODY: 3,000

HISTORY

Mississippi Valley State University was founded in 1950 as Mississippi Vocational College. In 1946, the Mississippi Legislature had authorized the establishment of an institution for the training of teachers for rural and elementary schools. The college officially opened in the summer of 1950 with fourteen students and seven faculty members.

In 1964, the name of the college was changed to Mississippi Valley State College. University status was granted on March 15, 1974, and the institution's name was again changed, this time to Mississippi Valley State University.

Mississippi Valley State University is accredited by the Commission on Colleges of the Southern Association of Colleges and Schools (SACS).

MISSION

Mississippi Valley State University is com-
mitted to providing accessible, relevant, and quality academic and public service programs, and endeavors to provide additional programs that are vital and unique to the needs of the population it serves.

MOTTO

"Live for Service"

TRIVIA

Mississippi Valley State University's Delta Research and Cultural Institute allows students and faculty to engage in research on the cultural, social, economic, and political concerns of the Mississippi Delta, one of the poorest regions in the United States.

NOTABLES

- David "Deacon" Jones—NFL player; twice named defensive player of the year; elected to Pro Football Hall of Fame in 1980

- Jerry Rice—NFL player; considered greatest wide receiver of all time; MVP of Super Bowl XXIII with San Francisco 49ers

ACADEMIC PROGRAMS

Mississippi Valley State University consists the College of Arts & Sciences, the College of Education, the College of Professional Studies, and the Graduate School.

Degrees are awarded in Accounting; Biology; Applied Management Technology; Architectural Construction Management; Automated Identification Technology; Broadcasting; Business Administration; Chemistry; Communications; Early Childhood Education; Electronic Technology; Elementary Education; English; English Education; Environmental Health; Computer Aided Drafting & Design; Computer Science; Criminal Justice; General Art; Health, Physical Education & Recreation (Teaching); Health, Physical Education & Recreation (Non-Teaching); History; Industrial Management Technology; Information Science; Instrumental Music Education; Journalism; Keyboard Music Education; Mathematics; Mathematics Education; Music Composition; Music Performance; Office Administration; Painting; Political Science; Public Administration; Public Relations; Recording Industry; Science Education; Secondary Education; Social Science Education; Social Work; Sociology; Speech; Two-Dimensional Design; Visual Communication; and Vocal Music Education.

STUDENT ORGANIZATIONS

Mississippi Valley State University offers numerous clubs and organizations for students, including Baptist Collegiate Ministry; Campus Diversity Program Student Advisory Board; Cheerleading Squad; Cliché Fashion & Modeling Squad; *Delvian* Yearbook; League of BEEP Associates; Mass Communication Club; Mathematics, Computer & Information Science Club; National Association for the Advancement of Colored People (NAACP); National Pan Hellenic Council; Political Science Club; Pre-Alumni Club; Pre-Law Club; Social Work Club; Southern Christian Leadership Conference; Student Government Association; Student Programming Board; Student Supporting Students Coalition; Xtreme' Modeling Squad; and University Choir.

Greek fraternities include Alpha Phi Alpha, Gamma Phi Theta, Kappa Alpha Psi, Omega Psi Phi, and Phi Beta Sigma; sororities include Alpha Kappa Alpha, Gamma Sigma Sigma, and Zeta Phi Beta. Honor societies include Alpha Chi, Alpha Delta, Alpha Phi Sigma National Criminal Justice Honor Society, Lambda Pi Eta, and Pi Sigma Alpha National Political Science Honor Society.

SPORTS

The Mississippi Valley State University's teams, the Delta Devils and Devilettes, are members of the National Collegiate Athletic Association (NCAA), Division I (football is Division I-AA) and participate in the Southwestern Athletic Conference (SWAC).

Men's sports include basketball, baseball, cross-country, track and field, golf, tennis, and football; women's sports include volleyball, basketball, bowling, tennis, track and field, cross-county, golf, softball, and soccer.

TUITION
$4,686/$7,956

CONTACT INFORMATION
Director of Admissions and Recruitment
Mississippi Valley State University
14000 Highway 82 West
Itta Bena, MS 38941-1400
Phone: (662) 254-3344
Toll-free: (800) GO2MVSU
Fax: (662) 254-7900

Photo courtesy of Rust College

RUST COLLEGE

ADDRESS: 150 Rust Avenue
Holly Springs, MS 38635
(662) 252-8000

WEB SITE: www.rustcollege.edu

FOUNDED: 1866

MASCOT: Bearcat

AFFILIATION: United Methodist
Church

TYPE: 4-Year Private

RATIO: 19:1

STUDENT BODY: 980

HISTORY

Rust College is a private, four-year, co-ed college founded in 1866 by the Freedman's Aid Society of the Methodist Episcopal Church. It began as Shaw School and was chartered in 1870, in honor of Reverend S. O. Shaw, a major donor to the school.

The college's name was changed from Shaw School to Rust University in honor of Richard S. Rust, the secretary of the Freedmen's Aid Society. In 1915, the name was again changed to Rust College.

Rust College is the oldest of the eleven Historically Black Colleges and Universities related to the United Methodist Church, the second oldest private college in Mississippi, and one of the remaining five historically black colleges in America founded before 1867.

Rust College is accredited by the Commission on Colleges of the Southern Association of Colleges and Schools (SACS) to award associate and bachelor degrees.

MISSION

Rust College is committed to serving students with a variety of academic preparations through a well-rounded program designed to acquaint students with cultural, moral, and spiritual values, both in theory and in practice.

MOTTO

"By Their Fruits Ye Shall Know Them"

TRIVIA

Rust College was the location of General Ulysses S. Grant's army camp during the Civil War.

Rust College houses six special collections valuable for viewing and for research. They include the Roy L. Wilkins Collection, the Ronald Trojcak African Tribal Art Collection, the Pre-Columbian Collection, the Inuit Indian Collection, the United Methodist Collection, and the International Collection.

Rust College recently completed construction on the new Hamilton Science Center, a $4.7 million, two-story, 18,000-square-foot state-of-the-art facility.

Natalie Doxey, the founding director of the world-renowned Rust College A'Cappella Choir, was an accompanist for opera singer Marian Anderson as well as Patti Brown and the Patti Brown Concert Singers.

NOTABLES

- Ida B. Wells Barnett—Co-founder of the NAACP

- Ruby Elzy—1930s opera and film star; best known for her role as Serena in George Gershwin's *Porgy and Bess*

- Cowan "Bubba" Hyde—Negro League player

- Alvin Childress—Actor; portrayed Amos in the *Amos and Andy Show* and later Mr. Jacobs in *Sister, Sister*

- Anita Ward—Disco singer; had top hit with "Ring My Bell"

ACADEMIC PROGRAMS

Rust College is organized under five divisions: the Division of Business; the Division of Education; the Division of Humanities; the Division of Science and Mathematics; and the Division of Social Science.

The college offers degrees in Biology Education; Biology; Business Administration; Business Education; Chemistry; Child Care Management; Computer Science; Early Childhood Education; Elementary Education; English Education; English/Liberal Arts; Mass Communication/Broadcast Journalism; Mass Communication/Print Journalism; Mathematics Education; Mathematics; Medical Terminology (in collaboration with Meharry Medical College/Tennessee State University); Music; Political Science; Social Science Education; Social Science; Social Work; and Sociology.

STUDENT ORGANIZATIONS

Rust College offers several social and group activities for students, including theater, band, chorale, dance, music, book reviews, plays, and lectures. Students may get involved with the student newspaper, the *Rustorian*, or join the *Bearcat* yearbook staff. Communication majors may work in the campus public radio station (WURC-FM) or the television station (RC-TV2). Leadership opportunities may be found in the Student Government Association. Greek fraternities and sororities are represented on campus.

SPORTS

Rust College's teams, the Bearcats, are members of National Collegiate Athletic Association (NCAA), Division III. Men's sports include basketball, tennis, baseball, cross-country, soccer, and track and field; women's sports include basketball, tennis, cross-country, volleyball, track and field, and softball.

TUITION

$7,000

CONTACT INFORMATION

Director of Enrollment Services
Rust College
150 Rust Avenue
Holly Springs, MS 38635-2328
Phone: (601) 252-8000
Toll-free: (888) 886-8492
Fax: (662) 252-8895
E-mail: admissions@rustcollege.edu

Photo courtesy of Tougaloo College

TOUGALOO COLLEGE

ADDRESS: 500 West County Line Road
Tougaloo, MS 39174
(601) 977-7700

WEB SITE: www.tougaloo.edu

FOUNDED: 1869

MASCOT: Bulldog

AFFILIATION: American Missionary Association

TYPE: 4-Year Private

RATIO: 15:1

STUDENT BODY: 850

HISTORY

Tougaloo College was founded in 1869 when the American Missionary Association of New York purchased 500 acres of land that was formerly the Boddie Plantation to establish a school for the training of young people. In 1871, the college was chartered under the name Tougaloo University; its name was changed to Tougaloo College in 1916.

In 1875, six years after Tougaloo College's founding, the Home Missionary Society of the Disciples of Christ chartered Southern Christian Institute in Edwards, Mississippi. As Tougaloo and Southern Christian had similar missions and goals, the supporting churches of the two institutions decided to merge the two; thus, in 1954, Tougaloo Southern Christian College was created. In 1962, the name was changed again to Tougaloo College.

During the turbulent 1960s, Tougaloo College was at the forefront of the Civil Rights Movement in Mississippi, opening its campus to the Freedom Riders and other Civil Rights workers and leaders who helped change the economic, political, and social fabric of the State of Mississippi and the nation.

Tougaloo College is accredited by the Commission on Colleges of the Southern Association of Colleges and Schools (SACS) to award the associate of arts, bachelor of arts, and bachelor of science degrees.

MISSION

Tougaloo College is committed to teaching students to become self-directed learners and self-reliant persons capable of dealing with people, challenges, and issues.

MOTTO

"Where History Meets the Future"

TRIVIA

Tougaloo College has a rich civil rights history and holds an impressive archival collection of papers and photographs. A parcel of land adjacent to the college's campus was recently selected as the site for the National Civil Rights Museum in Mississippi.

NOTABLES

- Walter J. Turnbull—Founder of the Boys Choir of Harlem

- Deborah Hyde, M.D.—One of four African-American female neurosurgeons in the country

- Bennie G. Thompson—U.S. Representative, Second Congressional District, Chair, Homeland Security Committee

- Eugene M. DeLoatch, Ph.D.—Dean and founder, School of Engineering, Morgan State University

ACADEMIC PROGRAMS

Tougaloo College consists of four divisions: Division of Education Supervision and Instruction; Division of Humanities; Division of Natural Science; and Division of Social Science.

Associate degrees are awarded in Child Development, Early Childhood Education, Hotel and Hospitality Management, and Religious Studies.

Bachelor degrees are awarded in Art, Art Secondary Education, Biology, Chemistry, Computer Science, Economics, English Secondary Education, English, Health Education, History, Interdisciplinary Career Oriented Humanities, Mass Communication, Mathematics, Music Education, Music, Physical Education, Physics, Political Science, Psychology, Sociology, and Special Education.

STUDENT ORGANIZATIONS

Tougaloo College offers students several organizations and activities, including the Reuben V. Anderson Pre-Law Society, Amnesty International, Ministry in Motion, NAACP, Anointed Voices of G.R.A.C.E. Gospel Choir, Tougaloo Dance Ensemble, as well as departmental clubs, weekly assembly programs, and religious groups.

Students may join the student newspaper, *Harambee,* or the Student Government Association.

Greek-letter fraternities include Alpha Phi Alpha, Kappa Alpha Psi, Omega Psi Phi, and Phi Beta Sigma; sororities include Alpha Kappa Alpha, Delta Sigma Theta, Sigma Gamma Rho, and Zeta Phi Beta. Honor societies and service organizations include Alpha Kappa Delta, Alpha Kappa Mu Honor Society, Alpha Lambda Delta Honor Society, and Alpha Phi Omega National Service Fraternity.

SPORTS

Tougaloo College's athletic teams, the Bulldogs and Lady Bulldogs, are members of the National Association of Intercollegiate Athletics (NAIA), Division I and participates in the Gulf Coast Athletic Conference (GCAC).

Men's sports include baseball, basketball, cross-country, tennis, and golf; women's sports include basketball, cross-country, and tennis.

TUITION

$10,000-15,000

CONTACT INFORMATION

Student Enrollment Management Center
Tougaloo College
500 West County Line Road
Tougaloo, MS 39174
Phone: (601) 977-7768
Toll-free: (888) 42GALOO

Photo courtesy of Harris-Stowe State University

HARRIS-STOWE STATE UNIVERSITY

ADDRESS: **3026 Laclede Avenue**
St. Louis, MO 63103
(314) 340-3366

WEB SITE: **www.hssu.edu**

FOUNDED: **1857**

MASCOT: **Hornet**

AFFILIATION: **None**

TYPE: **4-Year Public**

RATIO: **30:1**

STUDENT BODY: **2,000**

HISTORY

Harris-Stowe State University's history began in 1857 when Harris Teachers College was founded by the St. Louis Public School System as a normal school for white students. Named for William Torrey Harris, a superintendent in the St. Louis public school system and a former United States Commissioner of Education, it became a teaching institution for whites.

Stowe Teachers College, which was named in honor of the abolitionist and novelist Harriet Beecher Stowe, began in 1890 as a normal school for future black teachers of elementary schools in the city of St. Louis. Originally an extension of Sumner High School—called the Sumner Normal School—it became a four-year institution in 1924. In 1929, it became Stowe Teachers College.

In 1954, Harris Teachers College and Stowe Teachers College were merged by the Board of Education of the St. Louis Public Schools. The name Harris Teachers College was retained until requests from alumni of Stowe Teachers College and members of the Greater St. Louis community made the Board of Education agree to restore to the college's name the word "Stowe" and to drop the word "Teachers." The institution's name was again changed with the addition of the word "State" and it became officially known as Harris-Stowe State College.

In August 2005, Harris-Stowe State College obtained university status. Today the university hosts collaborative graduate degree programs with Maryville University, the University of Missouri-St. Louis, and Webster University.

Harris-Stowe University is accredited by the North Central Association of Colleges and Schools (NCACS).

MISSION

Harris-Stowe State University is committed to providing a high-quality higher education experience that is both affordable and accessible to the diverse populations within and beyond the metropolitan St. Louis region.

MOTTO

"Affordable, Accessible, Diverse"

TRIVIA

From its two predecessor institutions, Harris Teachers College and Stowe Teachers College, Harris-Stowe State University has evolved into Harris Junior College, Stowe Junior College, Harris-Stowe College, Harris-Stowe State College, and into its current title and university status.

U.S. News ranked Harris-Stowe as one of America's Best Colleges in the Midwest.

NOTABLES

- Julius Hunter—Former anchorman, KMOV Channel 4

- The Honorable Charles Shaw—Federal judge

ACADEMIC PROGRAMS

Harris-Stowe State University has four academic departments: Department of Business Administration, Department of Teacher Education, Department of Urban Specializations, and Department of Arts and Sciences.

The university awards bachelor of science degrees in Accounting, Business Administration, Criminal Justice, Education, Health Care Administration, Hospitality and Tourism Management, Information Systems and Computer Technology, Secondary Teacher Education, and Urban Education.

STUDENT ORGANIZATIONS

Harris-Stowe State University offers students numerous social and cultural activities, including HSSU Drumline, Concert Chorale, Gospel Choir, HSSU Honeycomb Majorettes Dance Team, Harris-Stowe Players Theater Group, African-American Studies Society, Collegiate 100, and Student Government Association.

Greek fraternities include Alpha Phi Alpha, Kappa Alpha Psi, Omega Phi Phi, Phi Beta Sigma, Sigma Tau Gamma, and Iota Phi Theta; sororities include Alpha Kappa Alpha, Delta Sigma Theta, Sigma Gamma Rho, and Zeta Phi Beta.

SPORTS

Harris-Stowe State University's teams, the Hornets, are members of the National Association of Intercollegiate Athletics (NAIA).

Men's sports include baseball, basketball and soccer; women's sports include basketball, soccer, softball, and volleyball.

TUITION

5,130/$9,550

CONTACT INFORMATION

Director of Enrollment Management
Harris-Stowe State University
3026 Laclede Avenue
St. Louis, MO 63103
Phone: (314) 340-3301
Fax: (314) 340-3555
E-mail: admissions@hssu.edu

LINCOLN UNIVERSITY OF MISSOURI

ADDRESS: 820 Chestnut Street
Jefferson City, MO 65101
(573) 681-5000

WEB SITE: www.lincolnu.edu

FOUNDED: 1866

MASCOT: Blue Tiger

AFFILIATION: None

TYPE: 4-Year Public

RATIO: 17:1

STUDENT BODY: 3,200

HISTORY

Lincoln University was founded in 1866 by the enlisted men of the 62nd and 65th Colored Infantry Regiments. It is the only institution of higher learning to be established by members of the military. Opened under the name Lincoln Institute, the school began receiving state aid for its teacher training program four years after its inception in 1870. State support for Lincoln Institute was implemented in 1879. In 1890, Lincoln became a land-grant institution with the passage of the Second Morrill Act. State legislation changed the name to Lincoln University in 1921.

Originally established to provide education to freed African Americans, Lincoln University began serving a more diverse population in 1954, following the U.S. Supreme Court's *Brown v. Board of Education* ruling. Today, the Lincoln University student population consists primarily of students from Missouri, Arkansas, Illinois, Iowa, Kansas, Kentucky, Nebraska, Oklahoma, and Tennessee. A total of 35 countries are represented in the international student population, with the highest enrollment from Jamaica, Ghana, and Nigeria.

MISSION

Lincoln University is an historically black, 1890 land-grant, public, comprehensive institution that provides excellent educational opportunities, including theoretical and applied learning experiences to a diverse population within a nurturing, student-centered environment.

MOTTO

"Laborare et Studere" ("To Labor and Study")

TRIVIA

The Lincoln University Women's Track Team holds a total of nine NCAA Division II Track and Field Championship Titles. In 2009, the team won both the Indoor and Outdoor titles. The team also won the indoor championships in 2004 and 2006. They hold the record for most consecutive outdoor titles—five—with their first win in 2003 and continuing through 2007.

NOTABLES

- Jesse Hill—Entrepreneur, civil rights activist
- Leo Lewis—Professional football player (CFL/NFL)
- Dr. Edward Anthony Rankin—President of the American Academy of Orthopaedic Surgeons
- Romona Robinson—News anchor (Cleveland, OH)
- Joe Torry—Actor, comedian

ACADEMIC PROGRAMS

Lincoln University offers six undergraduate degrees in more than fifty programs of study, with the most selected majors in the areas of Nursing Science, Business Administration, Criminal Justice, Elementary Education, Environmental Science, and Computer Information Systems.

Lincoln University is the only institution in the State of Missouri with an undergraduate program in Environmental Science, from which the first student graduated in May 2009. Lincoln University also offers master's level and specialist degrees.

In addition to regular coursework, Lincoln University students have the unique opportunity to participate in research projects, many of which are funded through a partnership with the Department of Defense. Current projects include suicide prevention among soldiers in the United States Army, land mine detection, and the use of non-lethal weapons in crowd control.

STUDENT ORGANIZATIONS

Lincoln University provides a true college experience with student involvement in athletics, academic competitions, and performance arts, including dance, instrumental, and vocal music and theatrical productions. Students may choose from more than fifty student organizations, including social and scholastic clubs, as well as Greek-letter organizations. Those interested in the media have the option of working at the campus radio or television stations, or the student newspaper.

SPORTS

Lincoln University is an NCAA Division II school and is a member of the Heartland Conference, with the exception of football, which is a member of the Great Lakes Conference. Men's sports include baseball, basketball, golf, and track and field. Women's sports offerings include basketball, softball, track and field, tennis, and, beginning in the fall of 2009, golf.

TUITION

$5,685/$10,395

CONTACT INFORMATION

Lincoln University of Missouri
820 Chestnut Street
Jefferson City, MO 65101
Phone: (573) 681-5000
Toll-free: (800) 521-5052
Web site: www.lincolnu.edu

Photo courtesy of Barber–Scotia College

BARBER-SCOTIA COLLEGE

ADDRESS: 145 Cabarrus Avenue West
Concord, NC 28025
(704) 789-2900

WEB SITE: www.b-sc.edu

FOUNDED: 1867

MASCOT: Mighty Saber

AFFILIATION: Presbyterian
Church

TYPE: 4-Year Private

STUDENT BODY: 20

HISTORY

Barber-Scotia College was founded by Reverend Luke Dorland in 1867 as the Scotia Seminary. Dorland was commissioned by the Presbyterian Church to establish an institution in the South for the training of Negro women as social workers and teachers. The seminary's original curriculum consisted of elementary, secondary, and normal school work.

In 1916, the name of the institution was changed to Scotia Women's College. Fourteen years later, the college merged with Barber-Scotia Memorial College of Anniston, Alabama, and the school was renamed Barber-Scotia College.

The college granted its first bachelor's degree in 1945. In 1954, the school became a co-educational institution.

On January 18, 2009 (Dr. Martin Luther King, Jr. Day), Barber-Scotia College submitted its application for accreditation candidacy with the Transnational Association of Christian Colleges and Schools (www.tracs.org), a U.S. Department of Education-sanctioned national accrediting agency. The campus received a two-member pre-accreditation visiting team for an institutional review in Spring 2009. The results of the visit will be presented to the college through the formal TRACS Staff Report in the coming months. For further information regarding campus accreditation please contact the Office of President at 704-789-2900.

MISSION

Barber-Scotia College is committed to providing an opportunity for all students to realize their capabilities. It provides this opportunity through a liberal arts education in a community concerned with the interaction of cultures, Christian heritage, scholarship, citizenship, and leadership. The college continually seeks to provide an atmosphere and environment in which learning will always be adventurous for the total community of scholars.

MOTTO

"Lumen Veritas et Utilitas" (Knowledge, Truth and Service)

TRIVIA

The Barber-Scotia College Energy Institute offers a comprehensive bio-energy training program to meet the demands of the renewable energy industry. The institute, in cooperation with the private sector, seeks environmentally conscious clean technologies and renewable energy products, including renewable energy, fuel cells, transportation efficiency, water quality, water conservation, waste energy reclamation, advanced materials, energy efficiency, and clean distributed energy generation.

NOTABLES

- Mary McLeod Bethune—Educator and civil rights leader; founder of Bethune-Cookman University

- Katie Cannon—First African-American female ordained as minister by the Presbyterian Church

ACADEMIC PROGRAMS

Barber-Scotia College offers a bachelor of arts degree in Religion.

A bachelor of science degree is awarded in Bio-Energy and Business Entrepreneurship.

STUDENT ORGANIZATIONS

Barber-Scotia College has a very active Pre-Alumni Club.

SPORTS

Barber-Scotia College's teams are the Mighty Sabers. Men's sports include basketball; women's sports include basketball.

TUITION

$14,400

CONTACT INFORMATION

Dr. David Olah, President
Barber-Scotia College
145 Cabarrus Avenue West
Concord, NC 28025
Phone: (704) 789-2900

BENNETT COLLEGE

ADDRESS: 900 East Washington Street
Greensboro, NC 27401
(336) 273-4431

WEB SITE: www.bennett.edu

FOUNDED: 1873

MASCOT: Belle

AFFILIATION: United
Methodist
Church

TYPE: 4-Year Private

RATIO: 11:1

STUDENT BODY: 689

HISTORY

Bennett College is a small, private, historically black, liberal arts college for women. Founded in 1873, it had its beginning in the basement of the Warnersville Methodist Episcopal Church. Within five years, a group of emancipated slaves purchased the present site for the school, and college-level courses and permanent facilities were added.

In 1926, the Women's Home Missionary Society joined with the Board of Education of the church to make Bennett a college for women. Since that time, women from around the country have found Bennett to be an institution offering an education conducive to excellence in scholarly pursuits; preparation for leadership roles in the workplace, society, and the world; and life-long learning in a technologically advanced, complex global society.

Since 1930, more than 5,000 women have graduated from Bennett College. Known as Bennett Belles, they continue to be among contributing women of achievement in all walks of life.

As a United Methodist Church-related institution, Bennett College promotes morally-grounded maturation, intellectual honesty, purposeful public service, and responsible civic action.

Bennett College is accredited by the Commission on Colleges of the Southern Association of Colleges and Schools (SACS).

MISSION

Under the leadership of its fifteenth president, Dr. Julianne Malveaux, Bennett College is committed to focusing on the intellectual, spiritual, and cultural growth of young women.

MOTTO

"Educate. Celebrate. Oasis."

TRIVIA

In October 2006, Bennett College raised thousands of dollars at a benefit gala featuring media mogul Oprah Winfrey. Bennett board member Maya Angelou also attended and introduced Oprah Winfrey as speaker for the event. Winfrey spent part of the afternoon speaking with Bennett students, faculty, and staff in a private seminar on campus.

NOTABLES

- Helen Newberry McDowell—Oldest living Bennett alumna

- Carolyn R. Payton—First woman and first African American to hold the position of Director of the United States Peace Corps

- Beverly Buchanan—Artist who explores Southern vernacular architecture in her art

- Neda Brown—Vice Consul in the Non-Immigrant Visa Unit, United States Embassy–Bogota

ACADEMIC PROGRAMS

Bennett College consists of three divisions: the Division of Humanities, the Division of Social Sciences and Education, and the Division of Natural and Behavioral Sciences/Mathematics.

Majors are offered in Arts Management (Music and Visual Arts Track), Biology, Business Administration, Chemistry, Computer Science, Elementary Education (K-6), English (Teaching and Non-teaching Tracks), Interdisciplinary Studies, Journalism & Media Studies (Four Tracks), Mathematics (Teaching and Non-teaching Tracks), Middle Grades Education (6-9), Political Science, Psychology, Social Work, Special Education, Visual and Performing Arts (Three Tracks: Theatre, Music, and Visual Arts).

Unique programs include Womanist Religious Studies, Global Studies, and Africana Women's Studies. Dual-degree programs with North Carolina A&T State University include Chemistry/Chemical Engineering, Electrical Engineering, and Mechanical Engineering. Bennett also has a Collaborative Degree Program with Howard University for Nursing.

STUDENT ORGANIZATIONS

Bennett College offers a variety of recreational, social, cultural, and educational clubs and organizations for students, including the drama/theater group, student-run newspaper, choral group, Christian Fellowship, Pre-Alumnae Council, Belles of Harmony, NAACP Chapter, National Council of Negro Women, and Christian Fellowship.

National Greek sororities are represented on campus.

SPORTS

Bennett College has an active basketball program and students can also participate in intramural sports that include golf and soccer.

TUITION

$22,195 per year

CONTACT INFORMATION

Bennett College
900 East Washington Street
Greensboro, NC 27401
Phone: (800) 413-5323
Web site: www.bennett.edu

Photo courtesy of Elizabeth City State University

ELIZABETH CITY STATE UNIVERSITY

ADDRESS: 1704 Weeksville Road
Elizabeth City, NC 27909
(252) 335-3400

WEB SITE: www.ecsu.edu

FOUNDED: 1891

MASCOT: Viking

AFFILIATION: None

TYPE: 4-Year Public

RATIO: 14:1

STUDENT BODY: 3,021

HISTORY

Elizabeth City State University (ECSU) is a 117-year-old public institution in the University of North Carolina system. It was founded on March 3, 1891, when House Bill 383 was enacted by the North Carolina General Assembly, establishing a normal school for the specific purpose of "teaching and training teachers of the colored race to teach in the common schools of North Carolina." The bill was sponsored by Hugh Cale, an African-American representative from Pasquotank County. Between 1891 and 1928, curricula and resources were expanded under the leadership of Peter Wedderick Moore. Enrollment increased from 23 to 355 and the faculty from two to fifteen members by the time Dr. Moore retired as President-Emeritus on July 1, 1928.

Under the leadership its second president John Henry Bias, who served from July 1, 1928,

until his death on July 15, 1939, the institution was elevated from a two-year normal school to a four-year teachers college in 1937. The institution's name was officially changed to Elizabeth City State Teachers College on March 30, 1939, and the mission was expanded to include the training of elementary school principals for rural and city schools. The first bachelor of science degrees in Elementary Education were awarded in May 1939.

The number of majors increased between 1959 and 1963 from a single elementary education major to twelve additional academic majors. The name changed from Elizabeth City State Teachers College to Elizabeth City State College by the General Assembly in 1963. Effective July 1, 1969, the college became Elizabeth City State University. In 1971, the General Assembly redefined The University of North Carolina system with sixteen public institutions.

Between 1999 and 2008, *American's Best Colleges (U.S. News and World Report* magazine) ranked ECSU among its top five in the category of "Top Public Comprehensive Colleges" in the south. In 2008, ECSU ranked No. 3 in that category and 12th among Historically Black Colleges and Universities.

Elizabeth City State University is accredited by the Southern Association of Colleges and Schools (SACS).

MOTTO

"To Live Is To Learn"

MISSION

Through teaching, research, and community outreach, the university is a valuable resource for developing the intellectual capital of the state and nation and addressing the economic needs of northeastern North Carolina.

TRIVIA

Since 2005, student athletes have won five Central Intercollegiate Athletic Association championship trophies: the softball and baseball teams (2005); basketball (Vikings 2007); volleyball (2008) and bowling (Lady Vikings 2009). ECSU teams also won three CIAA Eastern Division titles: football (2006 and 2008); basketball (Lady Vikings 2007); volleyball (2007).

NOTABLES

- Dr. Willie J. Gilchrist—Chancellor of Elizabeth City State University and the university's ninth chief executive officer. He was installed on March 15, 2007.

ACADEMIC PROGRAMS

Elizabeth City State University offers 37 baccalaureate degree programs, four master's degree programs and a doctor of pharmacy in collaboration with the Eshelman School of Pharmacy at UNC-Chapel Hill. ECSU has earned national acclaim for its advances in academics: In 2007, *Diverse Issues in Higher Education* ranked the ECSU No. 1 among Historically Black Colleges and Universities for their black male student-athlete graduation rate.

STUDENT ORGANIZATIONS

Elizabeth City State University offers numerous academic and social clubs for its students. Students can join associations and organizations such as the Student Activity Council, the Student Government Association, the Essence of Praise Gospel Choir, the Kuumba Art Society, the Library Club, the NAACP Chapter, the New Generation Campus Ministries, the Pep Squad, the University Players, and the Vike Nu Models. Greek societies include Alpha Kappa Alpha Sorority, Delta Sigma Theta Sorority, Kappa Alpha Psi Fraternity, Nu Gamma Psi Fraternity, Omega Psi Phi Fraternity, Phi Beta Sigma, Sigma Gamma Rho, and Zeta Phi Beta.

SPORTS

Elizabeth City State University teams compete in the Central Intercollegiate Athletic Association (CIAA). Men's sports include basketball, baseball, cross-country, football, golf, and track and field; women's sports include basketball, bowling, cheerleading, cross-country, softball, tennis, track and field, and volleyball.

TUITION

$3,354/$12,235

CONTACT INFORMATION

Elizabeth City State University
Campus Box 901
Elizabeth City, NC 27909-7806
Phone: (252) 335-3305
Toll-free: (800) 347-3278
Fax: (252) 335-3537
E-mail: admissions@mail.ecsu.edu

FAYETTEVILLE STATE UNIVERSITY

ADDRESS: **1200 Murchison Road**
Fayetteville, NC 28301
(910) 672-1111

WEB SITE: **www.uncfsu.edu**

FOUNDED: **1867**

MASCOT: **Bronco**

AFFILIATION: **None**

TYPE: **4-Year Public**

RATIO: **18:1**

STUDENT BODY: **6,271**

HISTORY

Fayetteville State University was founded in 1867 when seven black men paid $136 for two lots on Gillespie Street and established them as a site for the education of black children in Fayetteville. General O. Howard of the Freedman's Bureau, a proponent of black education, erected a building on the site, and the institution became known as the Howard School.

In 1877, the North Carolina General Assembly decided upon the establishment of a normal school for the education of black teachers, and Howard was selected as the most promising school for this endeavor. It was thus designated a teacher training institution, and its name was changed to the State Colored Normal School.

In 1939, the school became Fayetteville State Teachers College. The college received both state and regional accreditation in 1947. Over the

years, the curriculum was expanded to include majors in secondary education, as well as programs for degrees other than teaching. In 1963, the name of the school was changed again, this time to Fayetteville State College.

In 1969, the institution acquired its present name, Fayetteville State University. In 1972, the university became a constituent institution of the University of North Carolina System, and its curriculum was expanded to include a variety of both baccalaureate and master's level programs. The Fort Bragg-Pope AFB Extension Center, as well as the Weekend and Evening College, was established in order to provide military personnel and other persons employed full-time with the opportunity to further their education. In 1985, the university became a Comprehensive Level 1 Institution.

Fayetteville State University is accredited by the

Commission on College of the Southern Association of Colleges and Schools (SACS).

MOTTO

"Res Non Verba" ("Deeds Not Words")

TRIVIA

The seven founders of Fayetteville State University were visionary black citizens of Fayetteville: David A. Bryant, Nelson Carter, Andrew J. Chesnutt, George Grainger, Matthew Leary, Thomas Lomax, and Robert Simmons.

NOTABLES

- Darrell Armstrong—NBA player for the New Jersey Nets

- Sylvester Ritter—Professional wrestler known as "The Junkyard Dog"

ACADEMIC PROGRAMS

Fayetteville State University consists of the College of Arts & Sciences, the School of Business & Economics, and the School of Education.

The College of Arts and Sciences offers bachelor of arts and bachelor of science degrees in Criminal Justice, Biology, Biology-Medical Technology, Biotechnology, Chemistry, Fire Science, Forensic Science, English, Spanish, Geography, History, Political Science, Police Science, Public Administration, Art Education, Communication, Music, Music Education, Speech and Theater, Visual Arts, Computer Science, Mathematics, Mathematics Secondary Education, Psychology, and Sociology.

The School of Business & Economics offers bachelor of science degrees in Accounting, Banking & Finance, Business Administration, Health Care Management, Management Information Systems, Entrepreneurship, Marketing, and an award-winning MBA Program.

The School of Education officers degrees in elementary, secondary, middle grades education, and special education as well as physical education, Master of School Administration, and a doctorate in educational leadership.

STUDENT ORGANIZATIONS

Fayetteville State University has more than seventy registered student organizations, including the Arnold Air Society, Art Guild, Association of Women in Mathematics, Student Nurses' Association, Cadet Officers Association, Civil Air Patrol, Criminal Justice Club, Political Science Club, Psychology Club, Social Work Club, Spanish Club, and Student Government Association. Students can join the newspaper or yearbook staffs, or work at the student-run radio station, WFSB.

Greek sororities include Alpha Kappa Alpha, Delta, Sigma Theta, Sigma Gamma Rho, and Zeta Phi Beta. Fraternities include Alpha Phi Alpha, Kappa Alpha Psi, Omega Psi Phi and Phi Beta Sigma. Honor societies include Alpha Kappa Mu, Phi Beta Sigma, Alpha Kappa Delta, Beta Kappa Chi, Delta Mu Delta, Kappa Delta Pi, Pi Gamma Mu, Pi Omega Pi and Sigma Tau Delta.

SPORTS

Fayetteville State University's teams, the Broncos, are members of the Central Intercollegiate Athletic Association (CIAA).

Men's sports include football, basketball, cross-country, and golf. Women's sports include basketball, volleyball, softball, cross-country, tennis, and bowling.

TUITION

$3,834/$14,178

CONTACT INFORMATION

Fayetteville State University
Office of Admissions
1200 Murchison Road
Fayetteville, NC 28301
Phone: (910) 672-1371
Toll-free: (800) 222-2594

JOHNSON C. SMITH UNIVERSITY

ADDRESS: **100 Beatties Ford Road
Charlotte, NC 28216
(704) 378-1000**

WEB SITE: www.jcsu.edu

FOUNDED: 1867

MASCOT: Golden Bull

**AFFILIATION: Presbyterian
Church**

TYPE: 4-Year Private

STUDENT BODY: 1,400

HISTORY

Johnson C. Smith University was founded in 1867 when two ministers—the Rev. S.C. Alexander and the Rev. W. L. Miller—established the institution and were elected by the Catawba Presbytery to serve as its first teachers.

From 1867 to 1876, the school was called the Biddle Memorial Institute, named in honor of the late Major Henry Biddle, whose wife, Mary D. Biddle, had contributed funds to assist with running the institute. In 1876, the institute became Biddle University.

In 1922, another benefactor of the university, Jane Berry Smith of Pittsburgh, Pennsylvania, donated money so the school could build a theological dormitory, science hall, teachers' cottage, and memorial gate. She also provided a handsome endowment in memory of her late husband, Johnson C. Smith. In recognition of these gifts, the university's Board of Trustees voted to change the name of the institution to Johnson C. Smith University.

In 1924, the university was recognized as a four-year college by the North Carolina State Board of Education. Eight years later, in 1932, its charter was amended, and the institution, which had been for men only, became partially co-educational. By 1942, the university was a fully co-educational institution.

Johnson C. Smith University is fully accredited by the Commission on College of the Southern Association of Colleges and Schools (SACS).

MISSION

Johnson C. Smith University is committed to providing an outstanding education for a diverse group of talented and highly-motivated students from various ethnic, socio-economic, and geographical backgrounds.

MOTTO

"Surround Yourself with Success"

TRIVIA

In Fall 2000, Johnson C. Smith University launched the IBM Laptop Initiative, which provided an IBM laptop computer to every student.

NOTABLES

- Freddie "Curly" Neal—Harlem Globetrotter

- Eva Clayton—Former congresswoman from North Carolina

ACADEMIC PROGRAMS

Johnson C. Smith University consists of the College of Arts and Letters, the College of Professional Studies, and the College of Science, Technology, Engineering, and Mathematics.

A bachelor of arts degree is awarded in Art, Economics, English, English Education, Drama and Film, History, Liberal Arts, Music, Philosophy and Religion, Political Science, Psychology, Social Sciences, Social Studies, Social Studies Education, Sociology, and Speech.

A bachelor of science degree is awarded in Applied Banking and Finance, Biology, Business Administration, Chemistry, Computer Science, Criminal Justice, Education (Early Childhood and Intermediate), Engineering, Mathematics, Mathematics Education, Mathematics/Physics, Physics, and Science.

STUDENT ORGANIZATIONS

Johnson C. Smith University offers organizations for students in seven areas: academic; fraternity, sorority and social fellowship; honor society; religious; service; special interest; and sports and recreation.

Service organizations include Student Government Association, NAACP, and Habitat for Humanity. Religious organizations include the Ronald Walter Johnson Gospel Choir and Student Christian Association. Special interest organizations include Debate Society, Golden Rule Dance Troupe, Student with a Realistic Mission–Peer Educators, and Toastmasters.

Fraternities, sororities, and fellowships include Alpha Phi Alpha Fraternity, Delta Sigma Theta Sorority, Groove Phi Groove Social Fellowship, Kappa Alpha Psi Fraternity, National Pan-Hellenic Council, Omega Psi Phi Fraternity, Phi Beta Sigma Fraternity, Sigma Gamma Rho Sorority, and Zeta Phi Beta Sorority.

SPORTS

Johnson C. Smith University's teams, the Golden Bulls, are members of the Central Intercollegiate Athletic Association (CIAA).

Men's sports include basketball, football, golf, tennis, track and field, and cross-country. Women's sports include volleyball, bowling, basketball, cross country, soccer, tennis, and track and field.

TUITION

$21,886 (Does not include optional room and board charges)

CONTACT INFORMATION

Isabel DiSciullo, Director of Admissions
Office of Admissions
Johnson C. Smith University
Biddle Hall, 1st Floor
Charlotte, NC 28216
Phone: (704) 378-3500
Toll-free: (800) 782-7303
Fax: (704) 378-1242

Photo courtesy of Livingstone College

LIVINGSTONE COLLEGE

ADDRESS: 701 West Monroe Street
Salisbury, NC 28144
(800) 835-3435

WEB SITE: www.livingstone.edu

FOUNDED: 1879

MASCOT: Blue Bear

AFFILIATION: AME Zion Church

TYPE: 4-Year Private

RATIO: 17:1

STUDENT BODY: 990

HISTORY

Livingstone College was originally founded in 1879 as part of the Zion Wesley Institute—which also included the Hood Theological Seminary—by a group of African Methodist Episcopal Zion ministers. The purpose of the institution was to train ministers in the town of Concord, North Carolina, but after only three sessions the institute was closed.

In 1881, Dr. Joseph Charles Price and Bishop J. W. Hood attempted to re-establish Zion Wesley Institute. A donation of $1,000, as well as the invitation to relocate the institute, was given by the town of Salisbury. Both the gift and offer were accepted, and in 1882 the institute reopened on Delta Grove, a 40-acre farm.

In 1887, the name of the institute was changed to Livingstone College in honor of David Livingstone, the Scottish missionary and explorer.

Livingstone College is fully accredited by the Commission on Colleges of the Southern Association of Colleges and Schools (SACS).

MISSION

Livingstone College is a private historically black institution that is secured by a strong commitment to quality instruction. Through a Christian-based environment suitable for learning, it provides excellent liberal arts and religious education programs for students from all ethnic backgrounds designed to develop their potential for leadership and service to a global community.

MOTTO

"A Call to Commitment … Taking Livingstone College to the Next Level"

TRIVIA

In December 1892, the very first black collegiate football game in America was played on the campus of Livingstone College in Salisbury, against Biddle Institute (now known as Johnson C. Smith University). The Commemorative Classic football game celebrates this historic legacy that gave birth to the black college football traditions and competition 117 years ago.

NOTABLES

- James R. Gavin III, M.D., Ph.D.—President and CEO of Microislet, Inc.; chief executive officer and chief medical officer of Healing Our Village, Inc.

- Brigadier General Velma L. Richardson—One of five African-American women who have earned the rank of brigadier general in the United States Army; has received numerous awards, including the Legion of Merit

- Ben Coates—Former NFL player; selected to five Pro Bowls, NFL Hall of Fame

ACADEMIC PROGRAMS

Livingstone College consists of four academic divisions: the Division of Business; the Division of Education, Social Work, and Psychology; the Division of Liberal Arts; and the Division of Mathematics and Sciences.

The Division of Business offers a bachelor of science in Accounting, Business Administration, and Computer Information Systems.

The Division of Education, Social Work, and Psychology offers a bachelor of arts degree in Elementary Education; a bachelor of science in Physical Education, Sports Management, and Psychology; and a bachelor of social work degree in Social Work.

The Division of Liberal Arts offers degrees in Criminal Justice, English Liberal Arts, History, Liberal Studies, Music Secondary Education, Political Science, Religious Studies, Sociology, and Theater Arts.

The Division of Mathematics and Sciences offers a bachelor of science degree in Biology, Chemistry, Mathematics Liberal Arts, Mathematics Secondary Education, and SEED Ecology.

STUDENT ORGANIZATIONS

Livingstone College offers a wide variety of student clubs, organizations, and associations for students, including the Blue Bear Buddy Program, History/Political Science Club, Intercollegiate Music Association, International Students Organization, Lions Club, Psychology Club, Science Journal Club, Students for a Free Enterprise, Campus Ministry, AME Zion Student Fellowship, Entourage Modeling Troupe, Evolution Dance Troupe, Livingstone Gospel Choir, NAACP Chapter, OutKast Step Team, Optimist Club, Rotary Club, SEEDS Ecology, Student Ambassadors, and Student Government Association. Greek sororities and fraternities are represented on campus.

SPORTS

Livingstone College's teams, the Blue Bears, are members of the National Collegiate Athletic Association (NCAA) and participate in the Central Intercollegiate Athletic Association (CIAA). Men's sports include basketball, football, cross-country, and track and field; women's sports include basketball, bowling, cheerleading, cross-country, softball, tennis, track and field, and volleyball.

TUITION

$18,115

CONTACT INFORMATION

Admissions
Livingstone College
701 West Monroe Street
Salisbury, NC 28144
Phone: (704) 216-6001
Toll-free: (800) 835-3435
Fax: (704) 216-6215

NORTH CAROLINA A&T STATE UNIVERSITY

ADDRESS: **1601 East Market Street**
Greensboro, NC 27411
(336) 334-7500

WEB SITE: **www.ncat.edu**

FOUNDED: **1891**

MASCOT: **Aggie**

AFFILIATION: **None**

TYPE: **4-Year Public**

RATIO: **24:1**

STUDENT BODY: **10,385**

HISTORY

North Carolina Agricultural and Technical State University is a public, comprehensive, land-grant university that is classified as a high research intensive, doctoral institution. Established in 1891, N.C. A&T, a constituent member of the University of North Carolina System, offers degree programs at the baccalaureate, masters, and doctoral levels with emphasis on engineering, business, science, technology, agriculture, education, and nursing. A&T graduates the largest number of African-American engineers at the undergraduate, masters, and doctoral levels and psychology undergraduates in the nation. Through its nationally accredited AACSB School of Business and Economics, the institution is one of the top producers of African-American certified public accountants. True to its heritage, North Carolina A&T is home to the largest agricultural school among HBCUs and the second-largest producer of minority agricultural graduates. The institution was recently awarded a prestigious National Science Foundation's Engineering Research Center (ERC) grant for biomedical engineering and nano-bio applications research.

MISSION

North Carolina A&T State University is committed to offering exemplary undergraduate and graduate instruction, scholarly and creative research, and effective public service.

MOTTO

"Mens et Manus" (Minds and Hands)

TRIVIA

On February 1, 1960, four North Carolina A&T State University freshmen, Jibreel Khazan (formerly known as Ezell Blair), Joseph McNeil, Franklin McCain and David Richmond staged a sit-in at Woolworth's, an all-white establishment in Greensboro, N.C., to demand equal service at the lunch counter. Their non-violent civil rights protest ignited the Sit-in Movement and enhanced the quality of life for minorities in this country.

NOTABLES

- Rev. Jesse Jackson, Sr.—Civil rights activist and founder of the Rainbow Coalition

- Jesse Jackson, Jr.—Congressman, Second Congressional District of Illinois

- Edolphus Towns—U.S. House of Representatives, 10th District

- Ronald McNair—Astronaut; died in Space Shuttle *Challenger* explosion in 1986

ACADEMIC PROGRAMS

North Carolina A&T State University is comprised of seven schools—School of Agriculture and Environmental Sciences; School of Business & Economics; School of Education; School of Technology; School of Nursing; School of Graduate Studies; and Joint School of Nanoscience and Nanoengineering—and two colleges—College of Arts & Sciences and College of Engineering.

Undergraduate degrees are awarded in Accounting; Agricultural Economics; Agricultural Science; Bioengineering; Biological Engineering; Biology; Chemistry; Child Development and Family Studies; Child Development Early Education and Family Studies; Civil Engineering; Computer Science; Computer Technology; Construction Management & Safety; Earth and Environmental Science; Economics; Electrical and Computer Engineering; Electronics, Computer & Information Technology; English; Family and Consumer Sciences; Foods and Nutritional Science; Foreign Languages; Graphic Communications Systems; History; Human Development & Services; Industrial and Systems Engineering; Journalism & Mass Communication; Laboratory Animal Science; Landscape Architecture; Marketing; Mathematics; Mechanical and Chemical Engineering; Nursing; Physics; Political Science & Criminal Justice; Psychology; Sociology & Social Work; Theatre; and Visual and Performing Arts.

STUDENT ORGANIZATIONS

Registered and approved student organizations do not discriminate on the basis of race, creed, color, religious affiliation, sex, national origin, age or disability in any aspect of their functions and operations. The university provides a well-balanced program of activities for moral, spiritual, cultural, and physical development of the students. Various committees, departments, and organizations of the university sponsor religious, cultural, social, and recreational activities. Outstanding artists, lectures, and dramatic productions are brought to the campus through programs and projects sponsored by student organizations. There are approximately 150 organizations.

SPORTS

The North Carolina A&T State University Aggies are NCAA Division I members who compete in the Mid-Eastern Athletic Conference. Men's sports include football, basketball, baseball, cross country, indoor track and field, and outdoor track and field; women's sports include basketball, volleyball, bowling, softball, tennis, swimming, cross country, indoor track and field, and outdoor track and field.

TUITION (PER SEMESTER)

$997/$5,718

CONTACT INFORMATION

North Carolina A&T State University
1601 East Market Street, Webb Hall
Greensboro, NC 27411
Phone: (336) 334-7946
Toll-free: (800) 443-8964
Fax: (336) 954-5551

Photo courtesy of North Carolina Central University

NORTH CAROLINA CENTRAL UNIVERSITY

ADDRESS: 1801 Fayetteville Street
Durham, NC 27707
(919) 530-6100

WEB SITE: www.nccu.edu

FOUNDED: 1910

MASCOT: Eagle

AFFILIATION: None

TYPE: 4-Year Public

RATIO: 16:1

STUDENT BODY: 8,400

HISTORY

North Carolina Central University was founded by Dr. James E. Shepard in 1909 as a private institution. It opened to students in 1910 as the National Religious Training School and Chautauqua.

In 1915, the school was sold and became the National Training School. In 1923, the General Assembly of North Carolina purchased the school and it was renamed Durham State Normal School. In 1925, it was renamed the North Carolina College for Negroes, with the purpose of offering of liberal arts education and preparing teachers and principals of secondary schools. It was the nation's first state-supported liberal arts college for African-American students.

In 1947, the General Assembly changed the name of the institution to North Carolina College at Durham. It then became North Carolina Central University in 1969.

North Carolina Central University is accredited by the Southern Association of Colleges and Secondary Schools (SACS).

MISSION

NCCU is committed to preparing students academically and professionally to become leaders prepared to advance the consciousness of social responsibility in a diverse, global society.

MOTTO

"Truth and Service"

TRIVIA

NCCU has a state-of-the-art biotechnology research institute that collaborates with some of the largest pharmaceutical companies in the world, including GlaxoSmithKline and Merck.

NOTABLES

- Mike Easley—Former governor of North Carolina

- Ivan Dixon—Actor; played Ivan Kinchloe in *Hogan's Heroes*

- Herman Boone—Football coach; featured in *Remember the Titans*

ACADEMIC PROGRAMS

North Carolina Central University has three colleges—Behavioral & Social Sciences; Liberal Arts; and Science & Technology—and five schools—Nursing, Business, Education, Law, and Library & Information Services.

The College of Behavioral & Social Sciences awards degrees in Criminal Justice; Human Sciences; Physical Education & Recreation; Political Science; Psychology; Public Administration; Public Health Education; Social Work; and Sociology.

The College of Liberal Arts awards degrees in Aerospace Studies; Art; Drama; English; Global Studies; History; Mass Communications; Military Science; Modern Foreign Languages; Music; and Theatre.

The College of Science and Technology awards degrees in Biology; Chemistry; Computer Science; Environmental, Earth and Geospatial Sciences; Mathematics; Pharmaceutical Sciences; and Physics.

The School of Business awards degrees in Accounting; Business Information Technology; Computer Information Systems; Finance; Hospitality and Tourism; Management; and Marketing.

The School of Education awards degrees in Elementary Education; Middle Grades Education; and Secondary Education. The School of Law awards the Juris Doctor degree. The School of Nursing awards a bachelor of science in Nursing. The School of Library and Information Services awards a master's degrees in Information Science and Library Science.

STUDENT ORGANIZATIONS

North Carolina Central University offers many clubs and organizations that students may join in the areas of academic, ethnic, multicultural, international, political, religious, special interest, social, and student media.

In addition to departmental clubs, the university offers National Pan-Hellenic Council, Student Government Association, 100 Black Women, 100 Black Men, NAACP, College Life Ministry, NCCU Dance Group, Women Center's Alliance, and a student-run radio station.

Greek fraternities include Alpha Phi Alpha, Kappa Alpha Psi, Omega Psi Phi, and Phi Beta Sigma; sororities include Alpha Kappa Alpha, Delta Sigma Theta, and Zeta Phi Beta.

SPORTS

North Carolina Central University's teams, the Eagles, participate in National Collegiate Athletic Association (NCAA) at the Division I level.

Men's sports include baseball, basketball, football, golf, tennis, and track and field; women's sports include basketball, bowling, softball, tennis, track and field, and volleyball.

TUITION

$4,661/$14,707

CONTACT INFORMATION

North Carolina Central University
P.O. Box 19717
Durham, NC 27707
Phone: (919) 530-6298
Toll-free: (877) 667-7533
Fax: (919) 530-7625

SAINT AUGUSTINE'S COLLEGE

ADDRESS: **1315 Oakwood Avenue**
Raleigh, NC 27610
(919) 516-4000

WEB SITE: www.st-aug.edu

FOUNDED: 1867

MASCOT: Falcon

AFFILIATION: Protestant
Episcopal

TYPE: 4-Year Private

RATIO: 17:1

STUDENT BODY: 1,400

HISTORY

In 1867, Saint Augustine's College was founded in Raleigh, North Carolina, by Episcopal clergy and laymen for the education of freed slaves. From the beginning, the college's focus was not only to transform the lives of its students, but the world at large. Saint Augustine's College, along with other historically black colleges of the time, was a crucial stepping-stone to progress at the turn of the century. The first faculty and students built the original structures of the college by hand and raised produce and livestock to support the college community and form a strong self-supporting learning environment. Their strength, initiative, and leadership are the cornerstones of the college's legacy.

Today, Saint Augustine's College is recognized as one of the leading accredited, undergraduate, co-educational institutions in the nation. The college has a main campus accommodating 38 facilities, three of which are registered landmarks—College Chapel, St. Agnes Hospital, and Taylor Hall.

Saint Augustine's College is accredited by the Southern Association of Colleges and Secondary Schools (SACS).

MISSION

The mission of Saint Augustine's College is to sustain a learning community in which students can prepare academically, socially, and spiritually for leadership in a complex, diverse, and rapidly changing world.

MOTTO

"The Truth Will Set You Free"

TRIVIA

Saint Augustine's College was the nation's first historically black college to have its own on-campus commercial radio and television stations (WAUG-AM 750, WAUG-TV 68, and Time Warner cable channel 102).

NOTABLES

- Ralph Campbell, Jr.—Former North Carolina State Auditor; first African American elected to that position in North Carolina

- Anna Julia Cooper—Writer; educator; one of the first African-American women to receive a Ph.D.

- George Williams—Internationally acclaimed track and field coach

- Alex Hall—NFL player for the Cleveland Browns

- Bessie and Sadie Delany—African Americans who published their best-selling memoir, *Having Our Say,* at the ages of 102 and 104, respectively

- Luther Barnes—Gospel music recording artist

ACADEMIC PROGRAMS

Saint Augustine's College has placed major emphasis on the highest development of each student offering exceptional opportunities to both traditional and non-traditional students. Undergraduate degrees are offered through five divisions: the Division of Business and Computer Science; the Division of Liberal Arts and Education; the Division of Military Science; the Division of Natural Sciences and Mathematics; and the Division of Social Sciences.

Saint Augustine's College awards bachelor of arts degrees in Communication; Elementary Education; English; History; Music; Political Science; Psychology; Religion & Community Service; Sociology; Theater & Film; and Visual Arts.

Bachelor of science degrees are awarded in Accounting; Biology; Biomedical & Scientific Communication; Business Administration; Chemistry; Computer Information Systems; Computer Science; Criminal Justice; Forensic Science; History; International Business; Psychology; Religious Studies; and Sociology.

STUDENT ORGANIZATIONS

Saint Augustine's Colleges offers numerous clubs and organizations, including the Student Leaders Organization; Student Government Association; CAB (Campus Activities Board); CFO (Christian Fellowship Organization); New Beginnings Gospel Choir; BlueChip Cheerleading Squad; Collegiate 100 of the 100 Black Men; Phi Beta Lambda (National Business Association); Nubiance Modeling Troupe; Belle J'Adore Modeling Troupe; Marching/Jazz/Pep Band; Falcon Battalion/Army ROTC; Falcons 4 Obama; National Association for the Advancement of Colored People; Residence Halls Association; Foreign Language Club; Falcons for the Cause; and Falcon Fanatikz Pep Squad.

SPORTS

The Saint Augustine's College Falcons are members of the Central Intercollegiate Athletic Association (CIAA).

Men's sports include baseball, basketball, cross-country, football, golf, tennis, indoor track, and outdoor track. Women's sports include basketball, bowling, cross-country, softball, tennis, indoor track, outdoor track, and volleyball.

TUITION

$15,689

CONTACT INFORMATION

Admissions Office
Saint Augustine's College
1315 Oakwood Avenue
Raleigh, NC 27610-2298
Phone: (919) 516-4012
Toll-free: (800) 948-1126
Fax: (919) 516-5805

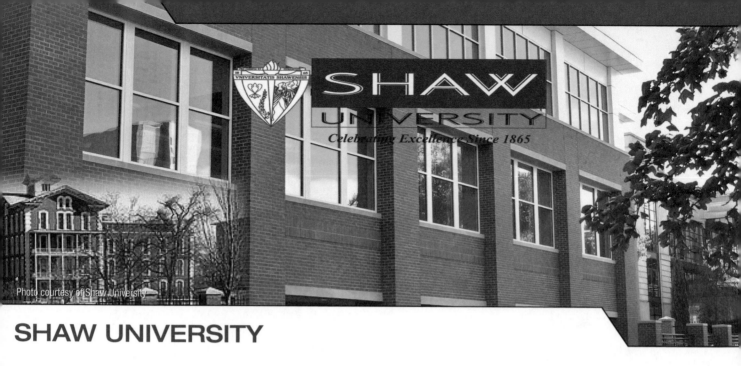

Photo courtesy of Shaw University

SHAW UNIVERSITY

ADDRESS: 118 East South Street
Raleigh, NC 27601
(919) 546-8200

WEB SITE: www.shawuniversity.edu

FOUNDED: 1865

MASCOT: Bear

AFFILIATION: National Baptist Convention

TYPE: 4-Year Private

RATIO: 15:1

STUDENT BODY: 2,750

HISTORY

Shaw University was founded in 1865 by Rev. Dr. Henry Martin Tupper as a means of teaching freedmen to read and interpret the Bible. Originally named the Raleigh Institute, it became the Shaw Collegiate Institute in 1870.

In 1875, the institute was incorporated and became known as Shaw University in honor of Elijah Shaw, the benefactor who provided funds for the first building, Shaw Hall, which was erected in 1871. The first women's dormitory on a co-educational campus in the United States, Estey Hall, was erected in 1873. The building, listed in the National Register of Historic Places, remained a residence hall for women until 1968.

Shaw University is accredited by the Commission on Colleges of the Southern Association of Colleges and Schools (SACS).

MISSION

Shaw University is committed to maintaining excellence in research and academic programs that foster intellectual enhancement and technological skills.

MOTTO

"Pro Christo et Humanitate" (For Christ and Humanity)

TRIVIA

Shaw University has been affectionately referred to as the "mother" of African-American colleges in North Carolina due to the fact that the founding presidents of North Carolina Central University, Elizabeth City State University, and Fayetteville State University were Shaw University graduates. In addition, the founder of Livingstone College spent his first two college years at Shaw before transferring to Lincoln

University, and North Carolina A&T was originally located on Shaw's campus during its first year of operation.

NOTABLES

- Eleanor Dunn, Ph.D.—Co-founder of Student Nonviolent Coordinating Committee (SNCC); civil rights activist; educator

- Ella Baker—Leader of SNCC

- Willie E. Gary—Attorney and founder of Black Family Channel

- Shirley Caesar—Pastor and gospel music artist

ACADEMIC PROGRAMS

Shaw University consists of the College of Arts and Sciences, the College of Graduate and Professional Studies, and the Shaw University Divinity School.

The College of Arts and Sciences awards degrees in English, Liberal Studies, Spanish, Mass Communications, Military Science, Biology, Chemistry, Environmental Science, Mathematics, Physics, Religion and Philosophy, African Studies, International Relations, Political Science, Psychology, Sociology, Social Work, and Visual and Performing Arts.

The College of Graduate and Professional Studies awards degrees in Athletic Training; Adapted Physical Education (Kinesiotherapy Concentration); Recreation; Speech Pathology and Audiology; Therapeutic Recreation; Business Administration (with concentration in Accounting); Business Administration (with concentration in Management); Public Administration; Public Administration (with concentration in Emergency Management); Birth-Kindergarten Education; English Education; Elementary Education; Mathematics Education; Computer Information Systems; and Computer Science.

STUDENT ORGANIZATIONS

Shaw University offers students several organizations and clubs, including The Shaw Players and Company, the Student Government Association, cheerleading, intramural sports, choir, jazz, pep, marching, and concert bands.

Students can work with the university's radio station, WSHA; participate in the Honda Quiz Bowl team, the mock trial team, or in any number of scholastic honors societies. Students can also take part in any of a number of modeling troupes, entertainment groups, student government, and public service organizations.

Greek societies include Alpha Phi Alpha, Omega Psi Phi, and Phi Beta Sigma; sororities include Alpha Kappa Alpha, Delta Sigma Theta, Sigma Gamma Rho, and Zeta Phi Beta.

SPORTS

Shaw University's teams, the Bears, are members of National Collegiate Athletic Association (NCAA), Division II and the Central Intercollegiate Athletic Association (CIAA).

Men's sports include baseball, basketball, cross-country, football, tennis, and outdoor track. Women's sports include basketball, bowling, cross-country, softball, tennis, outdoor track, and volleyball.

TUITION

$11,696

CONTACT INFORMATION:

Shaw University
118 East South Street
Raleigh, NC 27601
Admissions: (919) 546-8275; (800) 214-6683
Fax: (919) 546-8271
Marketing and Public Relations: (919) 546-8269

WINSTON-SALEM STATE UNIVERSITY

ADDRESS: 601 Martin Luther King, Jr. Drive
Winston-Salem, NC 27110
(336) 750-2000

WEB SITE: www.wssu.edu

FOUNDED: 1892

MASCOT: Ram

AFFILIATION: None

TYPE:4-Year Public

RATIO: 16:1

STUDENT BODY: 6,400

HISTORY

Winston-Salem State University was founded in 1892 as the Slater Industrial Academy. In 1897, it was recognized by the State of North Carolina and granted a charter as the Slater Industrial and State Normal School with the purpose of educating teachers.

In 1925, the name of the school was changed to Winston-Salem Teachers College and the institution was granted authorization to award degrees for elementary education. In 1957, was changed once again, this time to Winston-Salem State College.

In 1969, the college, with its expanded curricula that included a nursing school, became Winston-Salem State University.

Winston-Salem State University is accredited by the Commission on Colleges of the Southern Association of Colleges and Schools (SACS).

MISSION

Winston-Salem State University is committed to offering high-quality educational programs at the baccalaureate and graduate level for diverse and motivated students. While the primary focus is on teaching and learning, the university encourages scholarship and creative relationships with the community in ways which complement its educational mission.

MOTTO

"Enter to Learn, Depart to Serve."

TRIVIA

Coach Clarence "Bighouse" Gaines was a faculty member of Winston-Salem State University for forty-seven years. During his tenure as coach and athletic director, the men's basketball team compiled a record of 828–447. Gaines was inducted into the Naismith Memorial Basketball Hall of Fame in 1982.

NOTABLES

- Louis Farrakhan—Leader of the Nation of Islam

- Earl "The Pearl" Monroe—NBA player for the Baltimore Bullets (now Washington Wizards) and New York Knicks

- Stephen A. Smith—Sportswriter and media personality

ACADEMIC PROGRAMS

Winston-Salem State University consists of the College of Arts and Sciences; the School of Business and Economics; the School of Education and Human Performance; and the School of Health Sciences.

Degrees are awarded in Accounting, Art, Art Education, Biology, Business Administration and Management, Chemistry, Clinical Laboratory Science, Computer Programming, Computer Science, Computer and Information Sciences, Economics, Education, Elementary Education and Teaching, English, English Literature, Family Practice Nursing, Gerontology, History, Information Technology, Junior High/Intermediate/Middle School Education and Teaching, Kindergarten/Preschool Education and Teaching, Kinesiology and Exercise Science, Mass Communication, Media Studies, Mathematics, Mathematics Teacher Education, Molecular Biology, Music Business and Merchandising, Music Teacher Education, Nursing, Occupational Therapy, Physical Education, Physical Therapy, Political Science and Government, Psychology, Public Administration, Social Studies Teacher Education, Social Work, Sociology, Spanish Language and Literature, Spanish Language Teacher Education, Exercise Science, Therapeutic Recreation/Recreational Therapy, and Vocational Rehabilitation Counseling/Counselor.

STUDENT ORGANIZATIONS

Winston-Salem State University offers more than 90 student organizations, including social, departmental, business, and religious clubs.

Students can join the Association of Black Journalists, Black Men for Change, Drama Guild Players, Epiphany Modeling Troupe, Fellowship of Christian Athletes, Honda Quiz Bowl All Stars, Pre-Law Society, Sociology Club, Student Government Association, Sound University Music Group, Student International Association, and Students In Free Enterprise.

Greek fraternities include Alpha Phi Alpha, Kappa Alpha Psi, Kappa Kappa Psi, Omega Psi Phi, and Phi Beta Sigma; sororities include Alpha Kappa Alpha, Delta Sigma Theta, Sigma Gamma Rho, and Zeta Phi Beta.

SPORTS

Winston-Salem State University's teams, the Rams, are members of the National Collegiate Athletic Association (NCAA), Division I and participate in the Mid-Eastern Athletic Conference (MEAC).

Men's sports include basketball, cross-country, football, golf, tennis and track and field; women's sports include bowling, basketball, cheerleading, cross-country, softball, tennis, track and field, and volleyball.

TUITION
$4,278/13,111

CONTACT INFORMATION

Director of Admissions
Winston-Salem State University
601 Martin Luther King, Jr. Drive
Winston-Salem, NC 27110-0003
Phone: (336) 750-2070
Toll-free: (800) 257-4052
Fax: (336) 750-2079

Photo courtesy of Central State University

CENTRAL STATE UNIVERSITY

ADDRESS: 1400 Brush Row Road
Wilberforce, OH 45384
(937) 376-6011

WEB SITE: www.centralstate.edu

FOUNDED: 1887

MASCOT: Marauder

AFFILIATION: None

TYPE: 4-Year Public

RATIO: 13:1

STUDENT BODY: 2,200

HISTORY

Central State University is a nationally-recognized, academic institution located in the heart of Ohio. The University has leading-edge programs in urban education, engineering and science, and fine and performing arts.

The Ohio General Assembly in an act that created a Combined Normal and Industrial Department at Wilberforce University established Central State University on March 19, 1887.

The older institution was founded by the African Methodist Episcopal Church in 1856 and named in honor of the great abolitionist William Wilberforce. In 1941, the General Assembly expanded the new Department, which was considered as a separate school with its own Board of

Trustees, into a College of Education and Industrial Arts offering four-year college programs. In 1947, the College began independent operations continuing its programs in teacher education, industrial arts, and business, and adding a four-year liberal arts college under the name Wilberforce State College. In 1951, the legislature provided the name Central State College, and in 1965, Central State was granted university status.

Central State is Ohio's only predominantly African-American public institution of higher education, but remains true to the dictum of the enacting legislation that the University "be open to all persons of good moral character." Central State actively promotes ethnic diversity in its student body, faculty, and staff and maintains an unwavering commitment to affordably educate students for success, leadership, and service to the state, the country, and the world.

MOTTO

"Change Is Central"

TRIVIA

Central State University's Paul Robeson Center for Music and the Performing Arts pays tribute to Paul Robeson, a scholar, gifted athlete, attorney, acclaimed actor, and one of the finest bass-baritone singers the nation has ever known. Robeson could speak, write, and sing in twenty different languages, and he used his talents to speak out against racism and economic injustice.

NOTABLES

- Dr. Hastings Kamuzu Banda—Led the country of Nyasaland (now Malawi) out from under British rule; appointed prime minister; became president of Malawi

- Leontyne Price—World-renowned opera singer

- Teddy Seymour—First African American to sail solo around the world

ACADEMIC PROGRAMS

Central State University consists of three colleges: the College of Arts and Sciences, the College of Business and Industry, and the College of Education.

Degrees are awarded in Accounting; Advertising Graphics; Art Education; Biology; Chemistry; Computer Science; Criminal Justice; Earth Science; Economics; English; Finance; Gerontology; History; Hospitality Management; Industrial Technology; International Business; International Languages and Literatures; Jazz Studies; Journalism and Mass Communication; Management; Management Information Systems; Manufacturing Engineering; Marketing; Mathematics; Military Science; Music Education; Music Performance; Philosophy and Religion; Physics; Political Science; Psychology; Social Work; Sociology; Studio Art; Theatre; Water Resources Management.

STUDENT ORGANIZATIONS

Students can join more than thirty organizations on campus; business, religions, honorary, and Greek-letter. Students can join the Pre-Law Society, The Black Oak Project, CSU Marching and Concert Band the CSU Chorus, Interfaith Campus Ministry, Gold Torch Newspaper, and Student Government Association. Greek organizations are represented on campus and governed by the National Pan-Hellenic Council.

SPORTS

Central State University's teams, the Marauders, are members of the National Collegiate Athletic Association (NCAA), Division II. Men's sports include basketball, football, cross-country, track and field, tennis, and golf. Women's sports include basketball, cross-country, track and field, volleyball, tennis, and cheerleading.

TUITION

$5,294/$11,806

CONTACT INFORMATION

Central State University
1400 Brush Row Road
P.O. Box 1004
Wilberforce, OH 45384
Phone: (937) 376-6348
Toll-Free: (800) 388-CSU1
E-mail: admissions@centralstate.edu
or tour@centralstate.edu

WILBERFORCE UNIVERSITY

ADDRESS: 1055 N. Bickett Road
Wilberforce, OH 45384
(937) 376-2911

WEB SITE: www.wilberforce.edu

FOUNDED: 1856

MASCOT: Bulldog

AFFILIATION: African Methodist
Episcopal Church

TYPE: 4-Year Private

RATIO: 20:1

STUDENT BODY: 850

HISTORY

Wilberforce University, founded in 1856, is the nation's first private, black university. Named for eighteenth-century British abolitionist, William Wilberforce, the university was a stop on the Underground Railroad, which helped enslaved African Americans escape to freedom in the North. In 1862, ravages of the Civil War caused the Methodist Episcopal Church to close the university. The following year, one of the original 1856 incorporators, Daniel A. Payne, Bishop of the African Methodist Episcopal (AME) Church, purchased Wilberforce on behalf of the AME Church. The AME Church re-incorporated Wilberforce on July 10, 1853, and reopened it.

Two other educational institutions—Payne Theological Seminary and Central State University—grew out of Wilberforce University.

Wilberforce University is accredited by the Commission on Colleges of the North Central Association of Colleges and Schools (NCACS).

MISSION

Wilberforce University's mission is to help our students identify and prepare for their respective purposes in life as global citizens by imparting knowledge, instilling discipline, and inspiring lifelong learning through critical inquiry, personal and spiritual development, and practical application.

MOTTO

"Suo Marte" (By One's Own Strength)

TRIVIA

Wilberforce University graduated 75 percent of the African-American engineering students in the state of Ohio in 2008.

Wilberforce students come from thirty-eight states and six countries.

Wilberforce's renowned choir was established in 1878.

Wilberforce engages in sponsored research with the Department of Energy, NASA, and the UNCF-Special Programs.

NOTABLES

Daniel Payne was the first black president of an American university. Its early teachers included Hallie Q. Brown, the famous nineteenth-century elocutionist; Mary Church Terrell, the political activist; W.E.B. Du Bois; W.S. Scarborough, the Greek scholar whose Greek grammar text was used at Harvard; and B.O. Davis, Sr., professor of Military Science and Tactics.

Its prominent graduates and former students include Reverdy C. Ransom, whose oratory at a meeting of the Niagara Movement led to the founding of the NAACP; William Grant Still, the world-famous composer; Bayard Rustin, the civil rights activist and an architect of the 1963 March on Washington; Leonidas Berry, Chicago physician and pioneer gastrointestinal endoscopy; Leontyne Price, the opera diva; William Julius Wilson, the present Malcolm Wiener Professor of Social Policy at Harvard; Glenn T. Johnson, former Judge, Appellate Court in Chicago; Charity Adams Early, highest-ranking African-American woman in the Women's Auxiliary Corps and author; and Floyd H. Flake, former congressman from New York and president of WU (2002–2008).

ACADEMIC PROGRAMS

Wilberforce University, a liberal arts university, complements its major programs with practical, workplace application through its leading-edge Co-operative Education Program, established in 1964, where students experience two professional internships before graduation.

The university awards bachelor's degrees in Accounting, Biology, Computer Engineering, Computer Information Systems, Computer Science, Electrical Engineering with a minor in Nuclear Engineering, English, English Literature, Health Services Administration, Management, Marketing, Mass Media Communications, Music, Political Science, Psychology, Rehabilitation Services, Sociology, and Social Work.

STUDENT ORGANIZATIONS

Wilberforce University offers students numerous campus organizations as well as academic clubs, professional organizations, and religious groups, including a renowned concert choir, gospel chorus, campus newspaper, literary magazine, yearbook staff, and radio station (WURS). Greek fraternities and sororities include Alpha Phi Alpha, Kappa Alpha Psi, Omega Psi Phi, Alpha Kappa Alpha, Delta Sigma Theta, Zeta Phi Beta Sigma Gamma Rho, and Iota Phi Theta.

SPORTS

Wilberforce University's teams, the Bulldogs, are members of the National Association of Intercollegiate Athletics (NAIA) and participate in the American Mideast Conference. Sports teams include men's and women's' basketball, cross-country, and golf. The university also has intramural sports.

TUITION

$11,240

CONTACT INFORMATION

Dean of Admission
Wilberforce University
P.O. Box 1001
Wilberforce, OH 45384-1001
Phone: (937) 708-5789
Toll-free: (800) 367-8568
Fax: (937) 376-4751

LANGSTON UNIVERSITY

ADDRESS: P.O. Box 1500
Langston, OK 73050
(877) 466-2231

WEB SITE: www.lunet.edu

FOUNDED: 1897

MASCOT: Lion

AFFILIATION: None

TYPE: 4-Year Public

RATIO: 17:1

STUDENT BODY: 2,900

HISTORY

Langston University, Oklahoma's only historically black college, was founded in 1897 as the Colored Agricultural and Normal University. It was established by Oklahoma's territorial legislature in response to the requests of black settlers—who provided money for the land—to provide agricultural, mechanical, and industrial arts education to their children. The institution opened on September 3, 1898, in a Presbyterian church.

In 1941, the university was renamed Langston University in honor of John Mercer Langston, an abolitionist and educator who helped runaway slaves escape through the Underground Railroad. Langston, an attorney who once served as inspector general for the Freedman's Bureau, had a distinguished career as the dean of Howard University's law school, U.S. minister to Haiti during the Hayes administration, and as a member of the U.S. House of Representatives.

Langston University is accredited by the North Central Association of Colleges and Schools (NCACS).

MISSION

Langston University is committed to providing excellent postsecondary education to individuals seeking knowledge, skills, and attitudes that will enhance the human condition and promote a world that is peaceful, intellectual, technologically advanced, and one that fulfills the needs of nations and individuals alike.

MOTTO

"Education for Service"

TRIVIA

Langston's current president, Dr. JoAnn W. Haysbert, is the university's fifteenth and first female president. She is also the first African-American woman to be president of any university in the state of Oklahoma.

NOTABLES

- Bessie Coleman—First African-American woman to earn a pilot's license

- Nathan Hare—Publisher of *The Black Scholar* and author of *The Black Anglo Saxons*

- Thomas "Hollywood" Henderson—NFL player for Dallas Cowboys; elected to Pro Bowl

ACADEMIC PROGRAMS

Langston University consists of six schools: the School of Arts & Sciences; the School of Business; the School of Agriculture & Applied Sciences; the School of Education & Behavioral Sciences; the School of Nursing & Health Professions; and the School of Physical Therapy.

Degrees are awarded in Accounting; Agribusiness–Urban; Agricultural Science; Animal Science–Urban; Biology; Biology Education; Broadcast Journalism; Chemistry; Chemistry Education; Childhood Development; Computer & Information Sciences; Corrections; Crop and Soil Science–Urban; Early Childhood Education; Economics; Elementary Education; English; English Education; Family and Consumer Sciences Education; Finance; Financial Economics; Gerontology; Health Administration; Health, Physical Education, and Recreation; Management Information Systems; Mathematics; Mathematics Education; Music Education; Natural Resources Management; Nursing; Nutrition and Dietetics; Organization Management; Organization Management–Supply Chain Management; Physical Therapy; Psychology; Sociology; Special Education; Technology; Technology Education; and Theatre Arts.

STUDENT ORGANIZATIONS

Langston University offers numerous organizations for students, including the Dust Bowl Players (theatre group), choir, marching band, jazz band, symphonic band, as well as departmental, social, special interest, and religious clubs.

Students can join the Student Government Association; the *Langston Gazette,* the university newspaper; the *Langston Lion,* the university yearbook; or the radio station, KALU 89.3 FM, that serves the students at Langston University as well as the surrounding communities of Guthrie, Coyle, Stillwater, Perkins, and Meridian.

Greek sororities include Alpha Kappa Alpha, Delta Sigma Theta, Sigma Gamma Rho, and Zeta Phi Beta; fraternities include Alpha Phi Alpha, Kappa Alpha Psi, Omega Psi Phi, and Phi Beta Kappa.

SPORTS

Langston University's teams, the Lions and Lady Lions, are members of the National Association of Intercollegiate Athletics (NAIA).

Men's sports include basketball, football, and track and field; women's sports include basketball, cross-country, track and field, and softball.

TUITION
$3,595/$8,710

CONTACT INFORMATION
Director of Admissions
Langston University
P.O. Box 728
Langston, OK 73120
Phone: (405) 466-2984
Toll-free: (877) 466-2231
Fax: (405) 466-3391

CHEYNEY UNIVERSITY OF PENNSYLVANIA

ADDRESS: 1837 University Circle
Cheyney, PA 19319
1-800-CHEYNEY

WEB SITE: www.cheyney.edu

FOUNDED: 1837

MASCOT: Wolf

AFFILIATION: None

TYPE: 4-Year Public

RATIO: 17:1

STUDENT BODY: 1,490

HISTORY

Cheyney University was founded as the Institute for Colored Youth in 1837, making it the oldest institute of higher learning for African Americans and the first of the Historically Black Colleges and Universities in the United States.

The institute came to be when Richard Humphreys, a Quaker philanthropist, bequeathed $10,000 for the establishment of a school to educate African Americans. Humphreys, who had been born in the West Indies and later settled in Philadelphia in 1764, asked his fellow Quakers "... to instruct the descendents of the African Race in school learning, in the various branches of the mechanic arts, trades and agriculture."

The institute opened in Philadelphia, but in 1902 moved 25 miles west of Philadelphia to a farm owned by George Cheyney. The name of the institute has changed several times over the years: it was renamed Cheyney State Teachers College in 1913; the State Normal School at Cheyney in 1921; and Cheyney State College in 1959.

In 1983, Cheyney was awarded university status and became known as Cheyney University of Pennsylvania.

Cheyney University of Pennsylvania is accredited by the Commission on Higher Education of the Middle States Association of Colleges and Schools (MSACS).

MISSION

Cheyney University of Pennsylvania is committed to preparing confident, competent, reflective, visionary leaders and responsible citizens.

MOTTO

"America's Oldest Black Institution of Higher Education"

TRIVIA

Cheyney University of Pennsylvania has an extensive collection of rare books, manuscripts, and photographs housed at its Leslie Pinckney Hill Library. Collections include paintings and artwork by Henry O. Tanner, Laura Wheeler Waring, and Reba Dickerson Hill; letters of Booker T. Washington; and records of the Society of Friends.

NOTABLES

- Octavius Catto—Educator and civil rights activist; founder of Philadelphia Pythians of the Negro Baseball League

- Robert Bogle—Publisher of *The Philadelphia Tribune,* the oldest black newspaper in circulation today

- Ed Bradley—Award-winning journalist; regular contributor to the CBS program *60 Minutes*

ACADEMIC PROGRAMS

Cheyney University of Pennsylvania consists of two schools: the School of Arts and Sciences and the School of Education.

The School of Arts and Sciences awards degrees in Art; Biology; Biology–Secondary Education; Biology/Chemistry Dual Degree; Business Administration (with concentrations in Accounting, Management, and Marketing); Chemistry; Chemistry–Secondary Education; Communications; English; Fashion Merchandising and Management; General Science; General Science–Secondary Education; Geographic Information Science; Graphic Design; Hotel, Restaurant and Tourism Management; Mathematics; Mathematics Education; Music; Political Science; Psychology; Social Relations; Social Science; and Theater Arts.

The School of Education offers degrees in Education (with majors in early childhood education, elementary education, special education, and family and consumer sciences education), and Recreation.

Cheyney's graduate campus, located in Philadelphia, offers a master of education in Educational Administration, Elementary Education, and Special Education; a master of science in Adult & Continuing Education and Special Education; a master of arts in Teaching (Elementary and Secondary); and a masters in Public Administration.

STUDENT ORGANIZATIONS

Cheyney University of Pennsylvania offers students the opportunity to participate in several clubs and organizations, including Ambassadors for Christ, Cheerleaders, Honda All Stars, National Society of Minorities in Hospitality, Recreation Leisure and Management Club, Student Government Association, University Band, University Choir, and WCUB, the campus radio station. Greek fraternities, sororities, and honor societies are represented on campus.

SPORTS

Cheyney University of Pennsylvania's teams, the Wolves, are members of the National Collegiate Athletic Association (NCAA), Division II.

Men's sports include football, basketball, and cross-country, and track and field; women's sports include basketball, bowling, volleyball, tennis, cross-country, and track and field.

TUITION

$5,358/$13,396

CONTACT INFORMATION

Director of Admissions
Cheyney University of Pennsylvania
1837 University Circle
Cheyney, PA 19319
Phone: (610) 399-2275
Toll-free: (800) CHEYNEY
Fax: (610) 399-2099

Photo courtesy of Lincoln University of Pennsylvania

LINCOLN UNIVERSITY OF PENNSYLVANIA

ADDRESS: 1570 Baltimore Pike
Lincoln University, PA 19352
(484) 365-8000

WEB SITE: www.lincoln.edu

FOUNDED: 1854

MASCOT: Lion

AFFILIATION: None

TYPE: 4-Year Public

RATIO: 17:1

STUDENT BODY: 2,500

HISTORY

Lincoln University of the Commonwealth of Pennsylvania was founded in 1854 by John Miller Dickey, a Presbyterian minister, and his wife, Sarah Emlen Cresson. It was originally called the Ashmun Institute, named for Jehudi Ashmun, a social reformer who led the repatriation efforts of slaves to Liberia.

The institute was chartered in April 1854 as "the first institution found anywhere in the world to provide a higher education in the arts and sciences for male youth of African descent." In 1866, the institute was renamed Lincoln University in honor of President Abraham Lincoln. In 1972, it became a state-run institution of the Commonwealth of Pennsylvania.

Lincoln University of Pennsylvania is accredited by the Middle States Association of Colleges and Schools and offers academic programs in undergraduate study in the arts and sciences as well as graduate programs in human services, reading, education, mathematics, and administration.

MISSION

Lincoln University of Pennsylvania is committed to infusing its curricula with modules of instruction that require its students to recognize an international community of people and to understand moral and ethical issues, human dimensions, and leadership challenges posed by technology.

MOTTO

"If the Son shall make you free, ye shall be free indeed."

TRIVIA

Lincoln University of Pennsylvania's Office of International Programs and Services offers students the opportunity to study abroad through its university exchange programs. Countries included in the program include Argentina, Australia, Belgium, Botswana, Chile, China, Costa Rica, Czech Republic, Egypt, England, Ethiopia, France, Gambia, Germany, Ghana, Italy, Japan, Kenya, Mexico, Morocco, Poland, Russia, Senegal, Spain, Switzerland, and Taiwan.

NOTABLES

- Christian Fleetwood—Civil war soldier; awarded Medal of Honor

- Thurgood Marshall—First African-American Supreme Court Justice

- Benjamin Nnamdi Azikiwex—First president of Nigeria

- Kwame Nkrumah—First president of modern Ghana

- Langston Hughes—Acclaimed poet; member of the Harlem Renaissance

- Lillian Fishburne—Rear Admiral, U.S. Navy; first African-American female to hold the rank of rear admiral

ACADEMIC PROGRAMS

Lincoln University offers 50 majors, 22 minors, and five pre-professional programs. The university consists of four schools: the School of Humanities; the School of Natural Sciences & Mathematics; the School of Social Sciences & Behavioral Studies; and the School of Graduate Studies.

Students can study under the newly implemented, rigorous Five Centers of Excellence: Lincoln Barnes Visual Arts; Grand Research Educational Awareness and Training (GREAT) for Minority Health; Mass Communications; Teacher Education and Urban Pedagogy; and Business and Information Technology.

Degrees are awarded in Anthropology; Biology; Business & Information Technology; Chem-istry; Computer Science; Criminal Justice; Education; English; Environmental Sciences; Fine Arts; Foreign Languages & Literatures; Health, Physical Education & Recreation; History; Mass Communications; Human Services; Mathematics; Music; Philosophy; Political Science; Physics; Pre-Law; Psychology; Religion; Sociology; and Visual & Performing Arts.

STUDENT ORGANIZATIONS

Lincoln University of Pennsylvania offers students numerous clubs and organizations in which to participate, including Deuce Deuce Drill Team; International Club; Dance Troupe; Gospel Choir; Jazz Ensemble; National Coalition of 100 Black Women; Student Government Association; the campus newspaper, *The Lincolnian;* the yearbook, *The Lion;* the campus radio station, WWLU 88.7 FM; or LUC-TV. Greek fraternities include Alpha Phi Alpha, Omega Psi Phi, Kappa Alpha Psi, Phi Beta Sigma, and Iota Phi Theta; sororities include Alpha Kappa Alpha, Delta Sigma Theta, Sigma Gamma Rho, and Zeta Phi Beta.

SPORTS

Lincoln University's teams, the Lions, are members of the National Collegiate Athletic Association. Men's sports include baseball, basketball, cross-country, football, soccer, tennis, and track and field; women's sports include basketball, bowling, cross-country, soccer, softball, tennis, track and field, and volleyball.

TUITION

$8,324/$12,930

CONTACT INFORMATION

Director of Admissions
Lincoln University of Pennsylvania
P.O. Box 179, MSC 147
Lincoln University, PA 19352-0999
Phone: (484) 365-7206
Toll-free: (800) 790-0191
Fax: (610) 932-1209

ALLEN UNIVERSITY

ADDRESS: 1530 Harden Street
Columbia, SC 29204
(803) 376-5700

WEB SITE: www.allenuniversity.edu

FOUNDED: 1870

MASCOT: Fighting Yellow Jacket

AFFILIATION: AME Church

TYPE: 4-Year Private

RATIO: 12:1

STUDENT BODY: 720

HISTORY

Allen University, founded in 1870 by the African Methodist Episcopal (AME) Church, was originally called Payne Institute, named in honor of Daniel Alexander Payne, an apostle of black education in the United States. It opened during the Reconstruction period in South Carolina, one of the most troubling times in history for African Americans.

In 1880, the institution was renamed Allen University in honor of Bishop Richard Allen, founder of the African Methodist Episcopal Church. During its early years, the university offered elementary and high-school education as well as collegiate level studies. In fact, a student could have entered Allen as a child in the first grade and graduated with a degree in teaching, theology, or law. The grammar school was

discontinued in the 1920s, and the high school was closed in 1933.

Allen was able to keep afloat during the economic hardships of the Depression, and following World War II it experienced higher enrollment rates due to an influx of veterans seeking college studies. The campus underwent major physical expansion during the 1940s and 1950s.

Allen University is accredited by the Commission of Colleges of the Southern Association of Colleges and Schools (SACS).

MISSION

Allen University is a Christian liberal arts institution committed to preparing its students as leaders skilled in communication and critical thinking, and who demonstrate high moral character. The university's goal is to provide an environment of academic excellence that will heighten its students' chances of succeeding in a culturally diverse and economically global world.

MOTTO

"We Teach the Mind to Think, the Hands to Work, and the Heart to Love"

TRIVIA

Allen University is the first institution of higher education in South Carolina founded by African Americans for the express purpose of educating African Americans.

NOTABLES

- Ralph Anderson—Senator, South Carolina
- Kay Patterson—Former state senator
- Margaret Dixon—Former president of AARP
- Mildred W. McDuffie—Former summary court judge

ACADEMIC PROGRAMS

Allen University is an academic community that provides students an opportunity to obtain a baccalaureate degree in liberal arts and professional programs. It offers the bachelor of arts or the bachelor of science degree in Biology, Business Administration, Chemistry, English, Mathematics, Music, Religion, and Social Science.

The General Education Core, consisting of classes in the humanities, the social sciences, the laboratory sciences, and basic communications, are required for all students.

STUDENT ORGANIZATIONS

Allen University's student activities include the Student Government Association as well as co-curricular clubs, honor societies, and civic and religious, leadership and development, special interest organizations.

Departmental clubs are offered in Biology, Speech and Debate, Spanish, Mathematics, French, Social Science, Music, Business, Drama, and English.

Greek fraternities include Alpha Phi Alpha, Omega Psi Phi, and Phi Beta Sigma; sororities include Alpha Kappa Alpha, Delta Sigma Theta, Sigma Gamma Rho, and Zeta Phi Beta.

Honor societies include Sigma Tau Delta, Sigma Phi Omega, and Phi Beta Lambda.

SPORTS

Allen University's teams, the Fighting Yellow Jackets, are members of the National Association of Intercollegiate Athletics (NAIA) and participate in the Eastern Intercollegiate Athletic Conference (EIAC).

Men's sports include basketball, golf, and track and field; women's sports include basketball, track and field, and volleyball.

TUITION

$16,124

CONTACT INFORMATION

Office of Admissions
Allen University
Chappelle Administration Building
1530 Harden Street
Columbia, SC 29204
Phone: (803) 376-5735
Fax: (803) 376-5733

BENEDICT COLLEGE

ADDRESS: **1600 Harden Street**
Columbia, SC 29204
(803) 253-5000

WEB SITE: **www.benedict.edu**

FOUNDED: **1870**

MASCOT: **Tiger**

AFFILIATION: **American Baptist**
Home Mission
Society

TYPE: **4-Year Private**

RATIO: **19:1**

STUDENT BODY: **2,885**

HISTORY

Benedict College is a 139-year-old historically black liberal arts college located on 110 acres in the heart of the Columbia, South Carolina, the State's capital city. The private institution is positioned to be the best open enrollment college in the country. Benedict College offers degrees throughout the bachelor's level in the arts, sciences, and social work.

Nationally, Benedict has the fourth-largest undergraduate population within UNCF network. Of the twenty independent colleges in South Carolina, Benedict has one of the largest undergraduate student bodies in the state and is the sixth largest overall with an undergraduate population of 2,885 students.

Benedict is committed to establishing and maintaining high-quality programs of teaching, research, and public service. Of 4,000 colleges across the nation, Benedict has been ranked 13th in granting degrees in Physical Sciences, 41st in granting degrees in Computer and Information Sciences, and 42nd in granting degrees in Biology Biomedical Sciences by *Diverse* magazine.

The college's pioneering Service Learning Program is a national model program and serves more than 114 non-profit organizations around the South Carolina Midlands area. The Service Learning Program recently won The 6th Annual Commission on Higher Education's Service Learning Competition.

Recently, Benedict was named one of the top 100 institutions in the nation for graduating African-American students by *Diverse Magazine*. Benedict is distinguished by its continued commitment to facilitate the empowerment, enhancement, and full participation of African Africans in the American society.

MISSION

Benedict College is committed to establishing and maintaining high quality programs of teaching, research, and public service.

MOTTO

"A Power for Good in the 21st Century"

TRIVIA

Under the auspices of the American Baptist Home Mission Society, Mrs. Bathsheba A. Benedict of Pawtucket, Rhode Island, provided the amount of $13,000 to purchase the land to open Benedict Institute (now Benedict College) on December 12, 1870.

ACADEMIC PROGRAMS

Benedict College consists of five schools: the School of Business and Economics; the School of Education; the School of Humanities, Arts, and Social Sciences; the School of Science, Technology, Engineering and Mathematics; and the School of Continuing Education.

The School of Business and Economics awards degrees in Business Administration, Accounting, and Economics.

The School of Education awards degrees in Early Childhood Education, Elementary Education, Child and Family Development, Recreation and Leisure, Public Health, and Social Work.

The School of Humanities, Arts and Social Sciences awards degrees in English, Mass Communications, Studio Art, Art Education, Music, Criminal Justice, History, Political Science, Psychology, Sociology, Religion and Philosophy.

The School of Science, Technology, Engineering and Mathematics awards degrees in Biology, Chemistry, Environmental Health Science, Computer Engineering, Electrical Engineering, Physics, Mathematics, Computer Science, and Computer Information Science.

The School of Continuing Education awards a degree in Interdisciplinary Studies. Additional continuing education programs "Call Me Mister"–Male Teacher Education; Minority Access to Teacher Education (MATE); Minority Biomedical Research (MBRS); and NASA Research Support Infrastructure at Minority Institutions (RIMI).

STUDENT ORGANIZATIONS

Benedict College offers students social and cultural activities that include theater, band, dance, and concert and gospel choir. Students may work on student-run publications or join the writer's club. Communication majors or student volunteers may get involved in the student-run radio station. Leadership opportunities are found in the many organizations on campus, such as the NAACP Chapter, the International Council, and the Foreign Language Club. Greek sororities and fraternities are represented on campus.

SPORTS

Benedict College's teams, the Tigers, are members of the National Collegiate Athletic Association (NCAA), Division II and participate in the Southern Intercollegiate Athletic Conference (SIAC). Men's sports include baseball, basketball, football, golf, track, and tennis; women's sports include basketball, golf, track, volleyball, and tennis.

TUITION

$14,570

CONTACT INFORMATION

Mrs. Phyllis Thompson
Director of Admissions and Student Marketing
Benedict College
1600 Harden Street
Columbia, SC 29204-1058
Phone: (803) 705-4491
E-mail: thompsonp@benedict.edu

Photo courtesy of Claflin University

CLAFLIN UNIVERSITY

ADDRESS: 400 Magnolia Street
Orangeburg, SC 29115
(803) 535-5000

WEB SITE: www.claflin.edu

FOUNDED: 1869

MASCOT: Panther

AFFILIATION: United Methodist
Church

TYPE: 4-Year Private

RATIO: 12:1

STUDENT BODY: 1,750

HISTORY

Claflin University, the oldest Historically Black College and University in South Carolina, was founded by Methodist missionaries in 1869 and named for the two Methodist churchmen—Boston philanthropist Lee Claflin and his son, Massachusetts Governor William Claflin—who provided funds to purchase the land.

The university was chartered in 1869 as an institution to prepare freed slaves to take their rightful place in American society. The following year, the Baker Biblical Institute merged with Claflin. Two years later, in 1872, the South Carolina State Agricultural and Mechanical Institute also merged with the university; however, in 1896, the South Carolina General Assembly authorized the separation the Agricultural and Mechanical Institute from Claflin, and it subsequently became South Carolina State University.

Claflin University is a liberal arts university affiliated with the United Methodist Church. It is accredited by the Commission on Colleges of the Southern Association of Colleges and Schools (SACS).

MISSION

Claflin University is dedicated to educational excellence and to preparing students without regard to gender, race, religion, or ethnic origin. It is committed to offering quality undergraduate programs, select graduate programs, and viable continuing education opportunities.

MOTTO

"The World Needs Visionaries"

TRIVIA

Three of Claflin University's historic buildings—Tingley Memorial Hall, the Arthur Rose Museum (formerly the Lee Library) and

Ministers' Hall—are included in the Council of Independent Colleges' Historic Campus Architecture Project.

NOTABLES

- Ernest Finney—Former chief justice of the Supreme Court of South Carolina

- Daniel Howard—Sundance Festival and Emmy Award-winning filmmaker

- Cecil Williams—Author and civil rights photographer

ACADEMIC PROGRAMS

Claflin University consists of four schools: the School of Business; the School of Education; the School of Humanities and Social Sciences; and the School of Natural Sciences and Mathematics.

The School of Business offers a bachelor of science in Business Administration (with concentrations in Accounting and Finance), Business Administration (with non-business minor), Marketing, Management, and Organizational Management.

The School of Education offers degrees in Early Childhood Education, Elementary Education, Middle Level Education, Sport Management, and Human Performance & Recreation.

The School of Humanities and Social Sciences offers a bachelor of arts degree in African and African American Studies, American Studies, Art, Art Education, English, English Education, History, Mass Communication (with single or dual concentration in Broadcast Journalism, Music, Music Education, Philosophy and Religion, Print Journalism, Public Relations, Radio Production, Sound Recording, and Television Production), and Sociology.

The School of Natural Sciences and Mathematics offers a bachelor of science degree in Biochemistry, Bioinformatics, Biology, Biotechnology, Chemistry, Computer Science, Computer Engineering, Environmental Science, Management Information Systems, Mathematics, and Mathematics Education.

STUDENT ORGANIZATIONS

Claflin University offers students numerous opportunities to participate in campus clubs and organizations, including the University Theatre Ensemble, University Literary Arts and Film Society, Spanish Club, French Club, University Concert Choir, University Gospel Choir, University Chamber Chorus, University Lyric Theater (Opera), Claflin Wind Ensemble, University Jazz Ensemble, University Jazz Combo, University Woodwind Ensemble, and University Brass Ensemble.

Student can join the Student Government Association or *The Panther*, the university's award-winning student newspaper.

Greek sororities and fraternities are represented on campus.

SPORTS

Claflin University's teams, the Panthers and Lady Panthers, are members of the National Collegiate Athletic Association (NCAA), Division II and participate in the Southern Intercollegiate Athletic Conference (SIAC). Men's sports include basketball, cross-country, and track and field; women's sports include basketball, softball, and volleyball.

TUITION

$12,500

CONTACT INFORMATION

Director of Admissions
Claflin University
400 Magnolia Street
Orangeburg, SC 29115
Phone: (803) 535-5719
Toll-free: (800) 922-1276
Fax: (803) 535-5387

Photo courtesy of Clinton Junior College

CLINTON JUNIOR COLLEGE

ADDRESS: 1029 Crawford Road
Rock Hill, SC 29730
(803) 327-7402

WEB SITE: www.clintonjuniorcollege.edu

FOUNDED: 1894

MASCOT: Golden Bear

AFFILIATION: AME Zion Church

TYPE: 2-Year Private

RATIO: 17:1

STUDENT BODY: 120

HISTORY

Clinton Junior College was founded in 1894 by the African Methodist Episcopal Zion Church to provide higher education for newly freed African Americans. The presiding elder of the church at that time, the Rev. Nero A Crockett, along with the assistance of Rev. W.M. Robinson, established the institution and named it for Bishop Caleb Isom Clinton, the presiding bishop of the AME Zion Church.

Originally called the Clinton Normal and Industrial Institute, the college was instrumental in helping to eradicate illiteracy among freedmen. The vision to "design and implement an educational program that will help all students lead moral, spiritual, and productive lives" came to reality in June 1909 when the school was incorporated and authorized to grant state teacher certificates.

By the late 1940s, the college had grown to approximately nineteen acres in area, and had attracted hundreds of students. The school charter was later amended and the institution was renamed Clinton Junior College.

Clinton Junior College is accredited by the Transnational Association of Christian Colleges and Schools (TRACS).

MISSION

Clinton Junior College is committed to providing a learning milieu for students to promote academic achievement and positive moral and spiritual development. This environment fosters leadership qualities and encourages students to be good citizens who can contribute to a global society.

MOTTO

"A Beacon of Light for Tomorrow's Leaders"

TRIVIA

Clinton Junior College is the only historically black college in the upper part of South Carolina and the oldest existing college in the Rock Hill area (population 71,000).

NOTABLES

- Bishop George W.C. Walker—Elected Bishop by the 43rd General Conference as 81st Bishop in the AME Zion Church

- Bishop S. Chuka Ekemam—Elected Bishop at the 43rd General Conference as the 83rd Bishop in the AME Zion Church

- Bishop George E. Battle, Jr.—Elected Bishop by the 44th General Conference as 84th Bishop in the AME Zion Church

ACADEMIC PROGRAMS

Clinton Junior College offers associate degrees in Liberal Arts, Business, Science (with concentration in Biology, Chemistry, and Mathematics), Religious Studies, and Early Childhood/Elementary Education.

STUDENT ORGANIZATIONS

Clinton Junior College offers several student activities as an integral part of the educational program and academic support services. Activities and programs are conducted to assist students in adjusting to and enjoying the Clinton community and making college life a meaningful growth experience.

SPORTS

Clinton Junior College's teams, the Golden Bears, are members of the National Junior College Athletic Association (NJCAA), Division I.

Men's sports include basketball; women's sports include basketball.

TUITION

$3,600

CONTACT INFORMATION

Clinton Junior College
1029 Crawford Road
Rock Hill, SC 29730
Phone: (803) 327-7402

Photo courtesy of Denmark Technical College

DENMARK TECHNICAL COLLEGE

ADDRESS: 500 Soloman Blatt Avenue
Denmark, SC 29042
(803) 793-5100

WEB SITE: www.denmarktech.edu

FOUNDED: 1948

MASCOT: Panther

AFFILIATION: None

TYPE: 2-Year Public

RATIO: 19:1

STUDENT BODY: 1,600

HISTORY

In 1947, the General Assembly of the State of South Carolina authorized the establishment of Denmark Technical College. The college began operation on March 1, 1948, as the Denmark Branch of the South Carolina Trade School System, functioning under the authority of the South Carolina Department of Education.

In 1969, the control of the college was transferred to the South Carolina Advisory Committee for Technical Training, and that same year the name of the college was changed to Denmark Technical Education Center. In 1979, the name was changed to Denmark Technical College.

Denmark Technical College is accredited by the Commission on Colleges of the Southern Association of Colleges and Schools (SACS).

MISSION

Denmark Technical College is committed to providing students the knowledge and skills necessary for employment and maintenance of employment as technical, semi-professional, and skilled workers in engineering and industrial technologies, business, computer technologies, and public service; to preparing students for transfer to senior institutions; to providing graduates with competency in written and oral communication, computer literacy, information processing, mathematics, problem-solving and interpersonal skills necessary for life-long learning; and to enhancing the economic development and growth of the service area and the state.

MOTTO

"Where Great Things Are Happening"

TRIVIA

Denmark Technical College is the only technical college in the South Carolina state system that maintains residence halls and dining facilities for resident students.

ACADEMIC PROGRAMS

Denmark Technical College offers associate degree programs in Computer Technology, Criminal Justice Technology, Early Care and Education, Electromechanical Engineering Technology, Electronics Technology, General Business, General Technology, Human Services, and Administrative Office Technology.

One-year diploma programs are offered in Automated Office, Barbering, Cosmetology, Pharmacy Technician, and Practical Nursing.

Technical certificate programs are offered in Accounting, Basic Tailoring/Alterations, Building Construction Fundamentals, Computer Servicing and Repair, Criminal Justice, Customer Service, Early Childhood Development, Food Services, General Automotive Technology, Industrial Processing Technology, Laptop Computer Presentations, Legal Research Assistant, Machine Tool, Medical Record Coder, Multi-Skilled Maintenance Technology, Nail Technology, Nurse Aide, Plumbing, Pre-Medical, Professional Secretary, Shorthand, Welding, and Word Processing.

STUDENT ORGANIZATIONS

Denmark Technical College's Student Government Association (SGA) is one of the principal organizations through which students share in the administration of the College. The SGA assists college personnel in coordination of student organizations and activities, including athletic events, awards night, Homecoming, Miss Denmark Technical College Pageant, Miss DTC Coronation and Ball, Family Day, Spring Ball, and Spring Picnic.

Two national Greek fraternities and sororities are active on campus, as well as three local fraternities and sororities. Honor societies include the Kappa Chapter of Alpha Delta Omega National Honor Society.

TUITION

$2,288/$4,376

CONTACT INFORMATION

Admissions
Denmark Technical College
Solomon Blatt Boulevard, Box 327
Denmark, SC 29042-0327
Phone: (803) 793-5176

MORRIS COLLEGE

ADDRESS: 100 West College Street
Sumter, SC 29150
(803) 934-3200

WEB SITE: www.morris.edu

FOUNDED: 1908

MASCOT: Hornet

AFFILIATION: None

TYPE: 4-Year Private

RATIO: 15:1

STUDENT BODY: 875

HISTORY

Morris College was established in 1908 for "the Christian and Intellectual Training of Negro youth," and received a certificate of incorporation from the state of South Carolina on April 12, 1911. It was founded as a center for training ministers and teachers, and in its early years provided schooling on the elementary, high school, and college levels.

The college's original curriculum included programs in liberal arts, theology, and "normal" education for the certification of teachers. The "normal" program was discontinued in 1929, and its elementary school in 1930. For three years—1930–1932—the school operated as a junior college. It resumed its full four-year program in 1933. Its high school was discontinued in 1946.

In 1961, Morris eliminated the word "Negro" from its original certificate of incorporation and opened its doors to students of all ethnic groups.

Morris College is accredited by the Southern Association of Colleges and Schools Commission on Colleges to award baccalaureate degrees.

MISSION

Morris College is committed to equipping its students for careers and professions by providing both the theoretical and practical experiences necessary to function effectively in the larger society; challenging students to strive for academic proficiency; promoting positive mental, physical, social and spiritual health; and encouraging students to devote a part of their lives to the service of others.

MOTTO

"Enter to Learn; Depart to Serve"

NOTABLES

- Captain Leroy Bowman—U.S. Army (Retired); Tuskegee airman
- Tatsha Robertson—Senior news editor, *ESSENCE Magazine*
- The Honorable J. David Weeks—South Carolina House of Representatives

ACADEMIC PROGRAMS

Morris College consists of seven divisions: Division of General Studies; Division of Business Administration; Division of Education; Division of Religion and Humanities; Division of Natural Sciences and Mathematics; Division of Social Sciences; and the MCMI Advance Program.

Morris College offers a bachelor of arts degree in Christian Education, Criminal Justice, English, History, Liberal Studies, Pastoral Ministry, Political Science, and Sociology. Teacher preparation for certification in English and Social Studies is also offered. A bachelor of fine arts degree is awarded in Mass Communication.

A bachelor of science degree is awarded in Biology, Business Administration, Health Science, Mathematics, Organizational Management, and Recreation Administration. Teacher preparation for certification in Biology and Mathematics is also offered.

A bachelor of science in education with majors in Early Childhood Education and Elementary Education is also offered.

STUDENT ORGANIZATIONS

Morris College students can participate in a variety of academic clubs and organizations, including the Literary Society, Media Production Club, Morris College Chorale, Investment Club, Fencing Club, Durham Ministerial Union, Astronomy Club, and Art Club.

Greek fraternities and sororities include Nu Gamma Chapter of Alpha Kappa Alpha Sorority, Xi Epsilon Chapter of Alpha Phi Alpha Fraternity, Xi Rho Chapter of Delta Sigma Theta Sorority, Lambda Epsilon Chapter of Kappa Alpha Psi Fraternity, Iota Zeta Chapter of Phi Beta Sigma Fraternity, Epsilon Lambda Chapter of Omega Psi Phi Fraternity, Iota Eta Chapter of Sigma Gamma Rho Sorority, and Pi Theta Chapter of Zeta Phi Beta Sorority.

SPORTS

Morris College's teams, the Hornets, participate in the National Association for Intercollegiate Athletics (NAIA).

Its men's sports teams include baseball, basketball, cross-country, golf, tennis, and track and field; its women's teams include basketball, cross-country, softball, tennis, track and field, and volleyball.

TUITION

$14,287

CONTACT INFORMATION

Director of Admissions and Records
Morris College
100 West College Street
Sumter, SC 29150-3599
Phone: (803) 934-3225
Toll-free: (866) 853-1345
Fax: (803) 773-8241

SOUTH CAROLINA STATE UNIVERSITY

ADDRESS: 300 College Street NE
Orangeburg, SC 29117
(803) 536-7000

WEB SITE: www.scsu.edu

FOUNDED: 1896

MASCOT: Bulldog

AFFILIATION: None

TYPE: 4-Year Public

RATIO: 17:1

STUDENT BODY: 4,900

HISTORY

South Carolina State University was founded in 1896 as the sole public institution for black youth. Originally called the Colored, Normal, Industrial, Agricultural and Mechanical College of South Carolina, it is a land-grant institution that in its early years provided agricultural and mechanical training to black youth and helped educate impoverished black families.

After World War II, a graduate program and law school were created. In 1954, the name of the institution was changed to South Carolina State College by the South Carolina General Assembly. In February 1992, the college gained university status and appropriately changed its name to South Carolina State University.

Now referred to as SC State University, the school is accredited by the Commission on Colleges of the Southern Association of Colleges and Schools (SACS).

MISSION

SC State University is committed to providing life-long learning opportunities for the citizens of the state and qualified students of varied talents and backgrounds in a caring and nurturing learning environment.

MOTTO

"Scientia, Officium, Honos" (Knowledge, Duty, Honor)

TRIVIA

During the 1950s and 1960s, several hundred SC State University students participated in local civil rights demonstrations. In 1968, twenty-eight students were injured and three killed during what came to be known as the Orangeburg Massacre.

NOTABLES

- Harry Carson—NFL player; inducted into the Pro Football Hall of Fame in 2006

- James E. Clyburn—Majority Whip for the 111th Congress

ACADEMIC PROGRAMS

SC State University consists of three colleges and one school: the College of Business and Applied Professional Sciences; the College of Education, Humanities, and Social Sciences; the College of Science, Mathematics, and Engineering Technology; and the School of Graduate Studies.

Bachelor of arts degrees are awarded in Agribusiness; Art; Art Education; Art: Printmaking; Biology Education; Business Economics; Business Education; Chemistry; Civil Engineering Technology; Computer Science; Criminal Justice; Drama; Early Childhood Education; Electrical Engineering Technology; Elementary Education; English; French; Food and Nutrition; Health Education; History; Industrial Engineering Technology; Music Performance; Music Technology; Political Psychology; Science; Sociology; Speech Pathology and Audiology; Theater; and Visual Arts.

Bachelor of science degrees are awarded in Accounting; Aerospace; Biology; Business Administration; Computer Science; Economics; Family and Consumer Services; Home Economics; Human Services; Industrial Technology Education; Management; Marketing; Mathematics; Mathematics Education; Mechanical Engineering Technology; Music Education; Music Merchandising; Nursing; Office Management and Administration; Physical Education; Physics; Psychology; Secondary Education; Sociology; Social Studies; Social Work; Spanish; Special Education; Speech Pathology; and Audiology.

STUDENT ORGANIZATIONS

SC State University's social and cultural activities include theater, concerts, art exhibits, and band. Students may work on *The Collegian* (student-run newspaper) or *The Bulldog* (yearbook). Communication majors may work at the radio station WSSB-FM. Leadership opportunities are found in the Student Government Association.

Greek sororities include Alpha Kappa Alpha, Delta Sigma Theta, Sigma Gamma Rho, and Zeta Phi Beta; fraternities include Alpha Phi Alpha, Kappa Alpha Psi, Omega Psi Phi, and Phi Beta Sigma.

Honor societies include Alpha Kappa Psi Professional Business Fraternity, Kappa Kappa Psi National Honorary Band Fraternity, Tau Beta Sigma National Honorary Band Sorority, and Phi Mu Alpha Sinfonia Fraternity of America.

SPORTS

The SC State University Bulldogs are a charter member of the Mid-Eastern Athletic Conference (MEAC) and participates in NCAA Division I (I-AA for college football).

Men's sports include basketball, cross-country, football, golf, indoor track and field, outdoor track and field, and tennis. Women's sports include basketball, bowling, cross-country, golf, indoor track and field, outdoor track and field, soccer, softball, tennis, and volleyball.

TUITION

$4,231/$8,313 per semester

CONTACT INFORMATION

Director of Admissions
SC State University
300 College Street NE
Orangeburg, SC 29117-0001
Phone: (803) 536-8408
Toll-free: (800) 260-5956
Fax: (803) 536-8990
E-mail: admissions@scsu.edu

VOORHEES COLLEGE

ADDRESS: 430 Porter Road
Denmark, SC 29042
(803) 780-1030

WEB SITE: www.voorhees.edu

FOUNDED: 1897

MASCOT: Tiger

AFFILIATION: Episcopal Church

TYPE: 4-Year Private

RATIO: 13:1

STUDENT BODY: 520

HISTORY

Voorhees College, founded in 1897 by Elizabeth Evelyn Wright-Menafee, is an independent, four-year, co-educational, residential, career-oriented liberal arts college affiliated with the Episcopal Church. From Voorhees' inception in 1897, its mission has been to offer all students a quality, comprehensive general educational experience, coupled with professional education in a value-centered liberal arts tradition.

Voorhees excels in instruction in liberal studies, arts and sciences, and professional disciplines. In addition, Voorhees seeks to produce highly qualified graduates who combine intellect and faith in their preparation for strong professional performance in a global society.

In 1924, the school became one of the institutions supported by the American Church Insti-

tutes for Negroes, a component of the Episcopal Church. Episcopal bishops from both the Upper Diocese of South Carolina and Diocese of South Carolina assumed leadership of the Board of Trustees.

Today, Voorhees College remains true to Wright-Menafee's vision of educating young people under the leadership of Dr. Cleveland L. Sellers, Jr., a 1962 graduate of Voorhees High School and well-known advocate during the civil rights movement. Dr. Sellers' goals for Voorhees over the next five to ten years include strengthening the liberal arts curriculum, enhancing faculty development, building new facilities, and adding more student activities, particularly in the area of athletics.

Voorhees is fully accredited by the Commission on Colleges of the Southern Association of Colleges and Schools (SACS).

MISSION

The college seeks to produce highly qualified graduates who combine intellect and faith in their preparation for strong professional performance in a global society, pursuit of life-long learning, healthy living, betterment of society, and an abiding faith in God.

MOTTO

"We are Voorhees: A Community of Scholars"

TRIVIA

Voorhees has been recognized nationally for its debate team. The first-ever debate team at Voorhees College made history by being one of only two Historically Black Colleges and Universities selected to participate in the first Inauguration Debate Series, which was held January 19, 2009, at the National Museum of Natural History in Washington, D.C. The Inauguration Debate Series was one of the many events surrounding the historic inauguration of President Barack Obama.

NOTABLES

- Dr. Prezell Robinson—President emeritus of Saint Augustine's College

- Dr. George Bell Thomas—Former president of Voorhees College; founder of the George B. Thomas Sr. Learning Academy, Inc., Bethesda, MD

- Dr. Rita Robinson—Physician, Department of Veterans Affairs, Sumter, S.C.

ACADEMIC PROGRAMS

Voorhees offers degrees in accounting, biology, business administration, criminal justice, English, health and recreation, mathematics, mass communication, and organizational management.

Voorhees offers a certification program in cyber security education and has a special partnership with the National Nuclear Security Administration, which allows students to participate in summer internships in cyber security at various locations across the United States.

In addition, Voorhees is the only historically black college in South Carolina with a Center of Excellence in Rural and Minority Health designed to investigate and combat health disparities in Bamberg County and has a research, education, and clinical component.

STUDENT ORGANIZATIONS

Voorhees College offers numerous clubs and organizations, including the Student Government Association, the E.E. Wright Theatre Guild, the International Student Association, the Pre-Alumni Council, and concert choir. Greek sororities and fraternities include Alpha Phi Alpha Fraternity, Inc., Alpha Kappa Alpha Sorority, Inc., Kappa Alpha Psi Fraternity, Inc., Omega Psi Phi Fraternity, Inc., Delta Sigma Theta, Sorority, Inc., Phi Beta Sigma Fraternity, Inc., Zeta Phi Beta Sorority, Inc., and Sigma Gamma Rho Sorority, Inc. Honor societies include Alpha Sigma Lambda, Alpha Kappa Mu, and Delta Mu Delta Business Honor Society.

SPORTS

The Voorhees College Tigers are in the Association of Independent Institutions of the National Association of Intercollegiate Athletics Division I. The Tigers compete in various sports, including men's baseball, women's softball and volleyball, men and women's basketball, track and field, and cross-country.

TUITION (PER YEAR)

$16,478 (on campus)/$10,164 (off campus)

CONTACT INFORMATION

Voorhees College
Office of Admissions
P.O. Box 678
Denmark, SC 29042
Phone: (803) 780-1030
Toll-free: (866) 237-4570

Photo courtesy of Fisk University

FISK UNIVERSITY

ADDRESS: **1000 17th Avenue North**
Nashville, TN 37208
(615) 329-8500

WEB SITE: **www.fisk.edu**

FOUNDED: **1866**

MASCOT: **Bulldog**

AFFILIATION: **Church of Christ**

TYPE: **4-Year Private**

RATIO: **13:1**

STUDENT BODY: **800**

HISTORY

Fisk University was originally known as the Fisk School. In 1866, two years after the Emancipation Proclamation and six months after the end of the Civil War, John Ogden, the Reverend Erastus Milo Cravath, and the Reverend Edward P. Smith established the Fisk School in Nashville. It was named in honor of General Clinton B. Fisk of the Tennessee Freedmens Bureau, who had provided the school with facilities in former Union Army barracks near the present site of Nashville's Union Station.

Fisk opened its doors on January 9, 1866, to students ranging in age from seven to seventy. The school was sponsored by the American Missionary Association, later part of the United Church of Christ with which Fisk retains an affiliation today.

The university's founders, as well as others in their movement, dreamed of an educational institution that would be open to all, regardless of race, and that would measure itself by the highest standards of American education. Their dream was incorporated as Fisk University on August 22, 1867.

Fisk University is accredited by the Commission on Colleges of the Southern Association of Colleges and Schools (SACS).

MOTTO

"Her Sons and Daughters Ever on the Altar"

MISSION

Fisk University produces graduates from diverse backgrounds with the integrity and intellect required for substantive contributions to society. Our curriculum is grounded in the liberal arts, and our faculty and administrators emphasize the discovery and advancement of knowledge through research in the natural and social sciences, business, and the humanities. We are committed to the success of scholars and leaders with global perspective.

TRIVIA

Fisk is ranked fifth among the 81 schools listed in *U.S. News and World Report's* "Historically Black Colleges and Universities: Top Schools."

Fisk ranks in the top 23 percent of all institutions in the United States receiving federal science and engineering research funds.

A recent National Science Foundation study revealed that Fisk alumni earned more doctorate degrees in the natural sciences than African-American graduates from any other college or university in the nation.

NOTABLES

- Hazel R. O'Leary—Former Secretary of Energy

- W.E.B. Du Bois—NAACP co-founder and scholar

- Matthew Knowles—Music producer and manager; father of Beyoncé Knowles

ACADEMIC PROGRAMS

Fisk University offers degrees in Art; Biology; Business Administration; Chemistry; Computer Science; English; History; Mathematics; Music/Music Education; Nursing; Physics; Political Science; Psychology; Sociology; Spanish; and Special Education.

Pre-Professional Programs include Pre-Medicine, Pre-Dental, Nursing, Pre-Pharmacy, Dual-Degree Engineering, M.B.A., and Teacher Certification.

STUDENT ORGANIZATIONS

Fisk University offers numerous student organizations, including African Students Association, Big Sistas', Caribbean Student Association, Campus Ministry, Exclusive Dance Troupe, Fisk Forum, Fisk-Pearl Cohn Mentoring Program, Gay/Straight Alliance, International Students Association, Ladies of R.A.G.E. Dance Team, NAACP Chapter, Pan-Hellenic Council, Race Relations Student Organization, Student Government Association, Students in Free Enterprise, Tanner Art Club, Target Hope, University Choir, W.E.B. Du Bois Honors Program, and Women of Perfection.

Greek organizations include Alpha Phi Alpha Fraternity, Alpha Phi Omega, Delta Mu Delta, Omega Psi Phi Fraternity, Phi Beta Sigma Fraternity, Phi Mu Alpha Sinfonia, Pi Sigma Alpha, Sigma Eta Chapter, and Zeta Phi Beta Sorority.

SPORTS

Fisk University's teams, the Bulldogs and Lady Bulldogs, are members of the National Collegiate Athletic Association (NCAA), Division II and participate in the Great South Athletic (GSAC).

Sports include men's and women's basketball and women's softball.

TUITION
$15,620

CONTACT INFORMATION

Director of Admissions
Fisk University
1000 17th Avenue North
Nashville, TN 37208-3051
Phone: (615) 329-8665
Toll-free: (800) 443-FISK
Fax: (615) 329-8774

KNOXVILLE COLLEGE

ADDRESS: **901 Knoxville College Drive**
Knoxville, TN 37921
(865) 524-6525

WEB SITE: www.knoxvillecollege.edu

FOUNDED: 1875

MASCOT: Bulldog

AFFILIATION: Presbyterian
Church (USA)

TYPE: 4-Year Private

HISTORY

Knoxville College was founded in 1875 as part of the missionary effort of the United Presbyterian Church of North America to promote religious, moral, and educational leadership among freed men and women. Its mission today is a direct outgrowth of its founding.

Since there were so few blacks in the early days who were prepared for higher education, Knoxville College initially offered classes from first grade through college level. The elementary department was discontinued during the 1926–27 school year; and the high school, or academy, was dropped in 1931.

Between 1902 and 1912, the State of Tennessee contributed to the financial support of the college's agricultural, industrial, and mechanical departments. This arrangement lasted until the State established Tennessee

Agricultural and Industrial College in Nashville. Gradually, other areas of general and specialized training were discontinued, until by 1931, Knoxville College had become a liberal arts institution.

As a work college, Knoxville College guarantees financial resources for all students, while preparing them for responsible roles in society. Knoxville College is authorized to operate by the Tennessee Higher Education Commission.

MISSION

Knoxville College is a private, church-related, four-year coeducational, liberal arts institution. The college is open to students of diverse backgrounds and cultures, who seek a quality liberal arts education. The college provides a challenging and stimulating educational experience for students of demonstrated academic ability and for students of potential who have been afforded little advantage within society. Knoxville College provides various public services for the improvement of the community and promotes concerned citizenship among its constituents.

MOTTO
"Let There Be Light"

TRIVIA
Robert (Bob) J. Booker, Knoxville College historian, is an author and public servant. Currently, Booker is a city councilman, and previously served as state representative, administrative assistant to the mayor of Knoxville, Tennessee, and executive director of the Beck Cultural Exchange Center. Booker has published three books: *Two-Hundred Years of Black Culture in Knoxville, Tennessee, 1791–1991; And There Was Light! The 120-Year History of Knoxville College, 1875–1995;* and *The Heat of a Red Summer.*

NOTABLES
- George Curry—Chairman, Knoxville College Board of Trustees. Journalist and media coach. President and CEO of George Curry Media. Former editor-in-chief of *Emerge Magazine,* which won more than 40 national awards. Served as editor-in-chief of the National Publishers Association Newspaper Service in Washington, D.C. from 2001 to 2007.

- Alonzo Smith "Jake" Gaither—Legendary head football coach who won more than 85 percent of his games at Florida A&M University, and never had a losing season. Gaither introduced the Split-T formation in 1963, and it was soon adopted at other colleges. The Jake Gaither Trophy has been awarded to the best black collegiate football player each year since 1978. The Jake Gaither Gymnasium is located on the campus of Florida A&M University.

- Edith Irby Jones, M.D.—Board member, Knoxville College Board of Trustees. First African American admitted to a white medical school in the South (University of Arkansas School of Medicine in 1948). First female president of the National Medical Association. In 1991, Dr. Edith Irby Jones sponsored the establishment of a medical clinic in Haiti; and has led several health care initiatives in China, Africa, and Russia.

ACADEMIC PROGRAMS
Knoxville College has four academic departments: Humanities, Business and Computer Science, Social and Behavioral Sciences, and Natural Sciences and Mathematics. A Center for Public Health is under development. The college awards a bachelor's degree in Liberal Studies in the four concentrations aforementioned. An associate degree in Science is also offered.

STUDENT ORGANIZATIONS
Several social and cultural activities are available for student participation, including choral ensemble, Honda Bowl, etiquette sessions, job skills workshops, taebo, dances, talent shows, bowling, ice cream socials, and leadership development sessions. Leadership opportunities are available in the Student Government Association (SGA).

SPORTS
The Bulldogs and the Lady Bulldogs participate in basketball and other sports.

TUITION
$11, 528 (includes room and board)

CONTACT INFORMATION
Admissions Office
Knoxville College
901 Knoxville College Drive
Knoxville, TN 37921
Phone: (865) 524-6525

Photo courtesy of Ernest Mitchell

LANE COLLEGE

ADDRESS: 545 Lane Avenue
Jackson, TN 38301
(731) 426-7500

WEB SITE: www.lanecollege.edu

FOUNDED: 1882

MASCOT: Dragon

AFFILIATION: Christian Methodist
Episcopal Church

TYPE: 4-Year Private

RATIO: 24:1

STUDENT BODY: 2,100

HISTORY

Lane College was founded in 1882 by Bishop Isaac Lane and had its beginning through the Colored Methodist Episcopal Church in America to assure that newly-freed slaves would be able to "read, write, and speak correctly." It was built on its founder's beliefs that all men and women increase their usefulness by learning; that mere learning without spiritual experience is incomplete; and that the college must keep pace with changing times and needs of people.

Lane College is accredited by the Commission on Colleges of the Southern Association of Colleges and Schools (SACS) to award bachelor of arts and bachelor of science degrees. Lane is a member of the Tennessee Independent Colleges and Universities Association, the National Association for Equal Opportunity in Higher Education, and the United Negro College Fund, Inc.

MISSION

The college is unabatedly invested in transforming ordinary students into extraordinary scholars, by providing them with the highest quality education. The mission of the college is to pilot students through programs of intellectual and spiritual experiences that will prepare them to assume meaningful positions in their chosen occupations and professions, and pursue graduate studies.

MOTTO

"The Power of Potential®"…that one's potential is not necessarily predicted by one's past performance. This belief is the major factor that separates Lane from all other colleges and universities.

TRIVIA

The founder of Lane College, Isaac Lane, was the fourth bishop of the Christian Methodist

Episcopal (CME) Church who had been born a slave in Jackson, Tennessee.

The Lane College portrait collection is catalogued at the National Society of Colonial Dames of America in Tennessee (NSCDA-TN), a collaboration of the Tennessee State Museum and the State Museum Foundation.

The Lane College Library houses special collections including the Teacher Education Curriculum Center and the Negro Heritage Collection.

Begun in spring of 2007, the Lane Evening Accelerated Program (LEAP) is a degree-track program designed for the working adult.

NOTABLES

- Senior Bishop William H. Graves—Presiding bishop of the CME Church; Chair of the Lane College Board of Trustees, first African-American director to sit on the board of the Tennessee Valley Authority

- The Honorable Angie Blackshear Dalton—First elected African-American female judge in Nashville, Tennessee

- Dr. Louis E. Cunningham—Practicing board-certified cardiologist who founded the Mid-South Heart Center in 1993 in Jackson, Tennessee

- Captain Voressa Croom Booker—United States Navy captain; holds the noteworthy distinction of being one of only twenty-four female African-American captains serving among the 335,000 sailors enlisted in the U.S. Navy

ACADEMIC PROGRAMS

Lane College consists of three divisions: the Division of Business and Social and Behavioral Science; the Division of Liberal Studies and Education; and the Division of Natural and Physical Sciences.

The Division of Business and Social and Behavioral Sciences awards degrees in Business, Criminal Justice, History, and Sociology.

The Division of Liberal Studies and Education awards degrees in English, French, Interdisciplinary Studies, Mass Communications, Music, Physical Education, and Religion.

The Division of Natural and Physical Sciences awards degrees in Biology, Chemistry, Computer Science, Engineering, Mathematics, and Physics.

STUDENT ORGANIZATIONS

Lane College offers a variety of organizations and associations, giving students the opportunity to participate in social, cultural, recreational, and athletic activities. Leadership opportunities are found in the various departmental clubs and the Annual Black Executive Exchange Program sponsored nationally by the National Urban League.

SPORTS

Lane College's teams, the Dragons and Lady Dragons, participate in the Southern Intercollegiate Athletic Conference (SIAC). Men's sports include football, basketball, baseball, tennis, cross-country, and track and field. Women's sports include basketball, softball, tennis, volleyball, cross-county, and track and field.

TUITION

$7,330

CONTACT INFORMATION

Lane College
545 Lane Avenue
Jackson, TN 38301-4598
Phone: (731) 426-7533
Toll-free: (800) 960-7533
Fax: (731) 426-7559
E-mail: admissions@lanecollege.edu

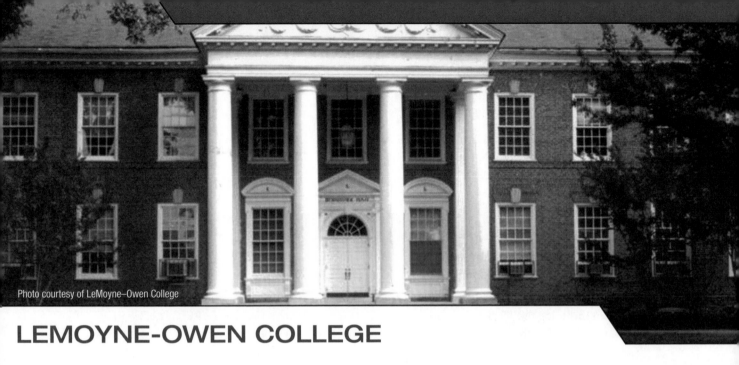

Photo courtesy of LeMoyne–Owen College

LEMOYNE-OWEN COLLEGE

ADDRESS: 807 Walker Avenue
Memphis, TN 38126
(901) 435-1000

WEB SITE: www.loc.edu

FOUNDED: 1862

MASCOT: Magician

AFFILIATION: United Church of Christ

TYPE: 4-Year Private

RATIO: 18:1

STUDENT BODY: 600

HISTORY

The merger of LeMoyne College and Owen College in 1968 joined two institutions, which had rich traditions as private, church-related colleges that have historically served black students, founded and developed to provide higher education to students in the Mid-South area.

LeMoyne Normal and Commercial School opened officially in 1871, but it actually began in 1862 when the American Missionary Association sent Lucinda Humphrey to open an elementary school for freedmen and runaway slaves to Camp Shiloh soon after the occupation of Memphis by federal troops under General Ulysses S. Grant. The School was moved to Memphis in 1863, but was destroyed by fire in the race riots, which followed the withdrawal of federal troops in 1866. Lincoln Chapel, as the school was then known, was rebuilt and reopened in 1867 with 150 students and

six teachers, but the small school was beset by financial problems.

In 1870, Dr. Francis J. LeMoyne, a Pennsylvania doctor and abolitionist, donated $20,000 to the American Missionary Association to build an elementary and secondary school for prospective teachers. The first years were difficult ones, primarily, because of the toll that the yellow fever epidemic took on school personnel, but under the leadership of the third principal, Andrew J. Steele, the institution experienced three decades of growth and development.

In 1914, the school was moved from Orleans Street to its present site on Walker Avenue. In that same year, the first building, Steele Hall, was erected on the new campus. LeMoyne developed rapidly; it became a junior college in 1924 and a four-year college in 1930, chartered by the State of Tennessee just four years later.

Owen College began in 1947, when the Tennessee Baptist Missionary and Educational Convention bought property on Vance Avenue to build a junior college. The merger of Owen and LeMoyne Colleges in 1968 joined two religious traditions at the same time that it reinforced the institutions' shared purpose of combining a liberal arts education with career training in a Christian setting.

MISSION

LeMoyne-Owen College is committed to providing a transformative experience educating students for urban-focused leadership, scholarship, service, and professional careers.

MOTTO

"Leadership. Opportunity. Change."

NOTABLES

- Pastor Benjamin Lawson Hooks—Civil rights leader

- Willie W. Herenton—Mayor, City of Memphis

- Lois DeBerry—Speaker Pro Tempore, State of Tennessee Legislature

ACADEMIC PROGRAMS

LeMoyne-Owen College consists of five divisions: the Division of Business and Economic Development; the Division of Education; the Division of Fine Arts and Humanities; the Division of Natural & Mathematical Sciences; and the Division of Social and Behavioral Sciences.

Degrees are awarded in Art, Biology, Business Administration, Chemistry, Computer Science, Criminal Justice, Early Childhood Education, English, General Mathematics, General Science, History, Humanities, Language Arts, Mathematics, Music, Political Science, Social Science, Social Studies, Social Work, Sociology, and Special Education.

STUDENT ORGANIZATIONS

LeMoyne-Owen College offers students numerous organizations in which to participate. Academic and professionals organizations include Business Students Association, Mathematics and Computer Science Club, National Association of Black Accountants, and Political Science Club.

Performing arts organizations include Cheerleading, Concert Choir, Debut Kashmir Modeling Society, Drama Club, Gospel Choir, Magic Gold Dance Team, and Poetry Society.

Greek fraternities include Alpha Phi Alpha, Kappa Alpha Psi, Omega Psi Phi, and Phi Beta Sigma; sororities include Alpha Kappa Alpha, Delta Sigma Theta, Sigma Gamma Rho, and Zeta Phi Beta. Honor societies include Alpha Kappa Mu Honor Society and W. E. B. Dubois Honor Program.

SPORTS

LeMoyne-Owen College's teams, the Magicians, are members of the Southern Intercollegiate Athletic Conference (SIAC).

Men's sports include cross country, baseball, basketball, tennis and golf. Women's sports include cross country, basketball, softball, tennis, and volleyball.

The LeMoyne-Owen Magicians (men's basketball) were the 2009 winners of the SIAC Championship.

TUITION

$10,318

CONTACT INFORMATION

Admissions Director
LeMoyne-Owen College
807 Walker Avenue
Memphis, TN 38126
Phone: (901) 435-1550
E-mail: admissions@loc.edu

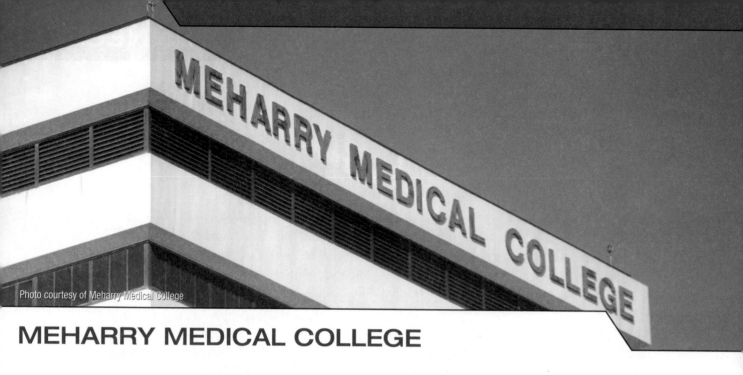

Photo courtesy of Meharry Medical College

MEHARRY MEDICAL COLLEGE

ADDRESS: 1005 Dr. D.B. Todd, Jr. Boulevard
Nashville, TN 37208
(615) 327-6000

WEB SITE: www.mmc.edu

FOUNDED: 1876

AFFILIATION: United
Methodist
Church

TYPE: 4-Year Private

RATIO: 7:1

STUDENT BODY: 740

HISTORY

Legend has it that Meharry Medical College came to be when a black family in Kentucky opened its home to a white stranger needing help. The grateful traveler promised to "do something for your race when I can." Fifty years later, Samuel Meharry and his brothers donated $30,000 in cash and property for a medical education program at Central Tennessee College, which later became Meharry Medical College.

The medical department of Central Tennessee College of Nashville had been founded in 1876 by the Freedman's Aid Society of the Methodist Episcopal Church. In 1900, Central Tennessee College became Walden University, and by 1915 the medical department became a separate entity from the university.

Meharry Medical College is fully accredited by the Commission on Colleges of the Southern Association of Colleges and Schools (SACS).

MISSION

Meharry Medical College is committed to improving the health and health care of minority and underserved communities by offering excellent education and training programs in the health sciences; placing special emphasis on providing opportunities to people of color and individuals from disadvantaged backgrounds, regardless of race or ethnicity; delivering high-quality health services; and conducting research that foster the elimination of health disparities.

MOTTO

"Worship of God through Service to Mankind"

TRIVIA

Meharry Medical College, which is dedicated to examining the biological, behavioral, and other factors that contribute to the poor health of minority and underserved populations, focuses its research on areas that represent the health disparities for people of color—specifically, African Americans—such as cancer, HIV/AIDS, obesity, diabetes, and sickle cell anemia.

NOTABLES

- Dr. Hastings Kamuzu Banda—Led the country of Nyasaland (now Malawi) out from under British rule; appointed prime minister; became president of Malawi

- Dr. Edward S. Cooper—President of the American Heart Association

- Dr. Audrey Manley—Deputy Surgeon General of the United States

- Dr. John E. Maupin—President of Morehouse School of Medicine

- Louis Pendelton—Dentist; civil rights leader who was appointed by President Lyndon B. Johnson to the Louisiana State Advisory Committee to the United States Commission on Civil Rights

- Dr. E. Anthony Rankin—Founder of Rankin Orthopaedics and Sports Medicine; member of the Board of Directors of the American Academy of Orthopaedic Surgeons

- Dr. Charles H. Wright—Founder of the Charles H. Wright Museum of African American History

ACADEMIC PROGRAMS

Meharry Medical College consists of three schools: the School of Medicine, the School of Dentistry, and the School of Graduate Studies and Research.

The School of Medicine provides residency training in Family Medicine, Internal Medicine, Occupational Medicine, Preventative Medicine, and Psychiatry.

The School of Dentistry sponsors two post-doctoral programs: Oral and Maxillofacial Surgery and General Practice Dentistry.

The School of Graduate Studies and Research awards a master of science in Public Health and Clinical Investigation, and a Ph.D. degree in Biomedical Sciences (with concentration areas of Cancer Biology, Microbiology and Immunology, Neurosciences, and Pharmacology).

STUDENT ORGANIZATIONS

Meharry Medical College offers students several organization in which to participate, including the American Association of Women Dentists, American Latino Medical Association, American Medical Student Association, American Student Dental Association, Emergency Medicine Interest Group, Ewell Neil Dental Research Society, Physicians for Human Rights, Student National Dental Association, and Meharry–Vanderbilt Student Alliance.

Greek-letter fraternities and sororities are represented on campus.

SPORTS

None

TUITION

$16,200

CONTACT INFORMATION

Director of Admissions
Meharry Medical College
1005 Dr. D.B. Todd, Jr. Boulevard
Nashville, TN 37208-3599
Phone: (615) 327-6223
Fax: (615) 327-6228

TENNESSEE STATE UNIVERSITY

ADDRESS: **3500 John A Merritt Boulevard**
Nashville, TN 37209
(615) 963-5000

WEB SITE: www.tnstate.edu

FOUNDED: 1912

MASCOT: Tiger

AFFILIATION: None

TYPE: 4-Year Public

RATIO: 17:1

STUDENT BODY: 8,265

HISTORY

Tennessee State University was founded in 1912 as the Agricultural and Industrial State Normal School and began teaching students on June 19 of that same year. The school became a four-year teacher's college in 1922.

In 1924, the name of the school was changed to the Agricultural and Industrial State Normal College. Three years later "Normal" was dropped from the name. During the 1950s, the school expanded its programs and came to be called Tennessee Agricultural & Industrial State University; ten years later, "Agricultural & Industrial" was dropped from the name.

In July 1979, Tennessee State University and the former University of Tennessee at Nashville merged into what is known as the university today.

Tennessee State University is accredited by the Commission on Colleges of the Southern Association of Colleges and Schools (SACS).

MISSION

Tennessee State University, an Historically Black College/University (HBCU), fosters scholarly inquiry and research, life-long learning, and a commitment to service.

MOTTO

"Think. Work. Serve."

TRIVIA

In 1961, Tennessee State University's marching band, the Aristocrat of Bands, became the first HBCU band invited to march in an inaugural parade—that of President John F. Kennedy. The band also marched in the inaugural parades of President Bill Clinton (1993 and 1997).

NOTABLES

- Wilma Rudolph—Olympic gold medalist in track and field

- Ralph Boston—Olympic gold medalist in long jump

- Oprah Winfrey—Talk show host, magazine publisher, and Academy Award-nominated actress

ACADEMIC PROGRAMS

Tennessee State University consists of six colleges and three schools: the College of Arts and Sciences; the College of Business; the College of Education; the College of Engineering, Technology, and Computer Science; the College of Health Sciences; the College of Public Service and Urban Affairs; the School of Agriculture and Consumer Sciences; the School of Graduate Studies and Research; and the School of Nursing.

Bachelor of arts degrees are awarded in English; History; and Speech, Communication and Theatre.

Bachelor of science degrees are awarded in Aeronautical and Industrial Technology; Africana Studies; Agricultural Sciences; Architectural Engineering; Art; Arts & Sciences; Arts & Sciences with Certification in Elementary Education; Biology; Cardiorespiratory Care Sciences; Chemistry; Civil Engineering; Computer Science; Criminal Justice; Dental Hygiene; Early Childhood Education; Electrical Engineering; Family and Consumer Sciences; Health Care Administration and Planning; Health Information Management; Health Sciences; Human Performance and Sport Sciences; Liberal Arts; Mathematics; Music Education; Nursing; Physics; Political Science; Psychology; Speech, Communication and Theatre; Social Work; Sociology; and Urban Affairs.

A Bachelor of business administration degree is awarded in Accounting; Business Information Systems; and Economics and Finance.

STUDENT ORGANIZATIONS

Tennessee State University offers numerous clubs, organizations, and activities for students, including departmental clubs, student publications, and literary and international student organizations. Students can join the gospel and concert choirs; NAACP; National Association of Colored Women's Clubs; B.L.A.C.K., Inc.; National Pan-Hellenic Council; Fellowship of Christian Athletes; Aristocrat of Bands Marching Band, and Student Government Association.

Greek-letter fraternities include Alpha Phi Alpha, Kappa Alpha Psi and Phi Beta Sigma; sororities include Alpha Kappa Alpha, Delta Sigma Theta and Sigma Gamma Rho. Honor societies include Alpha Kappa Mu and Phi Kappa Phi.

SPORTS

Tennessee State University's teams, the Tigers, compete in Division I of the NCAA with the exception of men's football (I-AA) within the Ohio Valley Conference.

Men's sports include basketball, football, golf, tennis, and track/cross-country. Women's sports include basketball, golf, softball, tennis, track/cross-country, and volleyball.

TUITION

$2,566/$8,012

CONTACT INFORMATION

Admissions Coordinator
Tennessee State University
3500 John A Merritt Boulevard
Nashville, TN 37209-1561
Phone: (615) 963-5101
Fax: (615) 963-5108

HUSTON–TILLOTSON UNIVERSITY

ADDRESS: 900 Chicon Street
Austin, TX 78702
(512) 505-3028

WEB SITE: www.htu.edu

FOUNDED: 1875

MASCOT: Ram

AFFILIATION: United Church of Christ/
The United Methodist
Church

TYPE: 4-Year Private

RATIO: 16:1

STUDENT BODY: 768

HISTORY

Huston-Tillotson (HT) University was established through the merger of its two predecessor institutions, Samuel Huston College and Tillotson College, with the promise of educational opportunity for minority students, in a spiritual and nurturing environment.

Tillotson College (founded in 1875) and Samuel Huston College (founded 1876) thrived as separate institutions but enjoyed progress and success when they merged in 1952 and became Huston-Tillotson College. The college officially became a university in 2005.

The university continues its 134-year-old affiliation with its founding religious denominations, now The United Methodist Church and the United Church of Christ. It is a charter member of the United Negro College Fund.

MISSION

The mission of the university is to provide its increasingly diverse student body with an exemplary education that is grounded in the liberal arts and sciences, balanced with professional development, and directed to public service and leadership. The university prepares students with the integrity and civility to thrive in a diverse society, fosters spiritual development, preserves and promotes interest in the accomplishments and experiences of the university's historic constituents and evolving population, and creates and sustains supportive relationships which advance the Huston-Tillotson University community.

MOTTO

"Learn More"

TRIVIA

The former Administration Building was named the Anthony and Louise Viaer-Alumni Hall in honor of Anthony Viaer, who donated $1 million to the university. The building is listed on the National Register of Historic Places.

NOTABLES

- The Honorable Azie Taylor Morton—Served as treasurer of the United States in 1977

- James Polk—Joined the Ray Charles Orchestra first as an organist/pianist, and later as a writer, arranger, and conductor

- Walter M. Batts—Notably one of HT's highest-ranking government officials; currently deputy director, Office of International Programs, Office of the Commissioner, U.S. Food and Drug Administration

- Latricia M. Thompson, M.D.—Practicing obstetrician and gynecologist; completed her residency at Lyndon B. Johnson Hospital

ACADEMIC PROGRAMS

The university offers bachelor of arts and bachelor of science degrees from the College of Arts and Sciences and the College of Business and Technology. The academic offerings include 15 major areas: Biology, Chemistry, Computer Science, Criminal Justice, English, History, Interdisciplinary Studies (Teaching), Kinesiology, Mathematics, Music, Music Education, Political Science, Psychology, Sociology, and Business Administration.

STUDENT ORGANIZATIONS

Huston-Tillotson University offers many associations and organizations for its students. Honor societies include Beta Kappa Chi, Kappa Delta Pi, Phi Beta Lambda, Pi Gamma Mu, Alpha Kappa Mu, and Sigma Tau Delta.

Students may also serve the university by joining the Kinesiology Club, National Association of Black Accountants, National Science Teachers Association (NSTA), American Marketing Association, Psychology Association, Golf Club, HIV Peer Educators, Business Club, Education Club, and the Honda Campus All-Star Challenge Club.

Greek sororities include Alpha Kappa Alpha, Delta Sigma Theta, Sigma Gamma Rho, Zeta Phi Beta. Fraternities include Alpha Phi Alpha, Omega Psi Phi, and Phi Beta Sigma.

SPORTS

Huston-Tillotson University is a member of the National Association of Intercollegiate Athletics (NAIA). The Rams participate in baseball, basketball, women's cross country, men's and women's soccer, track and field, volleyball, co-ed golf (club activity), and women's softball.

TUITION

$8,964

CONTACT INFORMATION

Enrollment Management
Huston-Tillotson University
900 Chicon Street
Austin, TX 78702
Phone: (512) 505.3027
Toll-free: (877) 505.3028
Fax: (512) 505.3192

Photo courtesy of Jarvis Christian College

JARVIS CHRISTIAN COLLEGE

ADDRESS: Highway 80 East P.R. 7631
Hawkins, TX 75765
(903) 769-5700

WEB SITE: www.jarvis.edu

FOUNDED: 1912

MASCOT: Bulldog

AFFILIATION: Disciples of Christ
(Christian Church)

TYPE: 4-Year Private

RATIO: 16:1

STUDENT BODY: 550

HISTORY

Jarvis Christian College was founded in 1912 from the efforts of the Christian Women's Board of Missions of the Disciples of Christ (CWBM) in Cincinnati, Ohio, which had a zeal for education. In 1904, its leadership entered into an alliance with the Negro Disciples of Christ, under the direction of Mrs. Mary Alphin, for the purpose of creating a Texas institution of learning for black youth.

The plan was for the Negro Disciples to raise the then-considerable sum of $1,000 and the CWBM would contribute $10,000. Three years after receiving a generous donation of land and funds from the Jarvis family, the Negro Disciples of Christ, in concert with the CWBM, began the task of building the physical plant of the school. Grand opening ceremonies for Jarvis Christian Institute were held January 14, 1913. The first class consisted of twelve students.

In 1914, high school subjects were added to the curriculum, and in 1916, junior college courses were added. The school was incorporated in 1928, and its name was changed to Jarvis Christian College in 1937. Two years later, in 1939, the first bachelor's degrees were awarded.

Today, Jarvis is a four-year, private, independent, coeducational liberal arts college that is affiliated with the Disciple of Christ (Christian Church). Jarvis Christian College is accredited regionally by the Commission on Colleges of the Southern Association of Colleges and Schools (SACS).

MISSION

Jarvis Christian College is committed to providing a quality education in the Judeo-Christian tradition. The mission of the college is to prepare each student intellectually, socially, spiritually, and personally to participate in and contribute to a global and technological society.

MOTTO

"Educating the Head, the Hand, and the Heart"

TRIVIA

The first major benefactors of Jarvis Christian were Major J.J. Jarvis and his wife, Ida, from Fort Worth, Texas. In 1910, they deeded 456 acres of land near Hawkins, Texas, to the Christian Women's Board of Missions on condition that it "keep up and maintain a school for the elevation and education of the Negro race … in which school there shall be efficient religious and industrial training." The land was to be used in the education of "head, hand and heart" and to produce "useful citizens and earnest Christians."

NOTABLES

- David "Fathead" Newman—Jazz great and saxophonist discovered by Ray Charles; session player for such greats as Aretha Franklin, B.B. King, Donny Hathaway, and Dr. John.

- Dr. Phelix Majiwa—Leading agricultural and biomedical researcher in South Africa

- Harold N. Woods—Diversion Investigator with the Department of Justice, Drug Enforcement Administration (DEA)

ACADEMIC PROGRAMS

Jarvis Christian College consists of two academic divisions: the Division of Business and Sciences and the Division of Education and the Arts.

A bachelor of arts degree is awarded in English, History, Music, and Religion. A bachelor of science degree is awarded in Biology, Chemistry, History, Human Performance, Mathematics, Music, and Sociology.

A bachelor of business administration is awarded in Accounting, Business Administration, Management, and Marketing.

Teaching certification programs are offered in Biology, Business, Chemistry, English, History, Mathematics, Music, Reading, and Special Education, and Coaching.

STUDENT ORGANIZATIONS

Jarvis Christian College offers social and group activities that include theater, praise dance, and gospel choir. Leadership opportunities can be found in the Student Government Association.

Greek-letter sororities include Alpha Kappa Alpha, Delta Sigma Theta, Sigma Gamma Rho, and Zeta Phi Beta. Fraternities include Alpha Phi Alpha, Kappa Alpha Psi, Omega Psi Phi, and Phi Theta Sigma. Honor societies include Alpha Kappa Mu, Beta Kappa Chi, and Sigma Tau Delta.

The college's publications include the *Jarvisonian,* a biannual publication for alumni and friends of the college. The *Jarvis Today* is a quarterly publication for friends of the college. *The Bulldog Life* is published by the Office of Student Affairs and Residential Life.

SPORTS

Jarvis Christian College's teams, the Bulldogs, are members of the National Association of Intercollegiate Athletics (NAIA) and the Red River Athletic Conference (RRAC). Men's sports include baseball and basketball; women's sports include basketball and volleyball.

TUITION

$16,323 (includes fees and room/board)

CONTACT INFORMATION

Mr. Chris Wooten
Office of Recruitment
Jarvis Christian College
P.O. Box 1470
Hawkins, TX 75765-1470
Phone: (903) 769-5734
Fax: (903) 769-4842

Photo courtesy of Paul Quinn College

PAUL QUINN COLLEGE

ADDRESS: **3837 Simpson Stuart Road**
Dallas, TX 75241
(214) 376-1000

WEB SITE: www.pqc.edu

FOUNDED: 1872

MASCOT: Tiger

AFFILIATION: AME Church

TYPE: 4-Year Private

RATIO: 10:1

STUDENT BODY: 450

HISTORY

Paul Quinn College was founded by a small group of African Methodist Episcopal preachers in Austin, Texas, on April 4, 1872. The school's original purpose was to educate freed slaves and their offspring. In 1877, the college moved from Austin to Waco, Texas, and was renamed Waco College. The college was housed in a modest one-building trade school where newly-freed slaves were taught the skills of blacksmithing, carpentry, tanning, and saddle work.

Later, under the direction of Bishop William Paul Quinn, AME districts were developed throughout the South and tasked with raising funds to improve the college. Under Bishop Quinn's direction, the college expanded its land ownership by purchasing more than twenty acres of property. The college's curriculum also expanded during

this time to include the subjects of Latin, mathematics, music, theology, English, carpentry, sewing, and household, kitchen, and dining room work.

In May 1881, the college was chartered by the State of Texas and changed its name to Paul Quinn College in commemoration of the contributions of Bishop William Paul Quinn.

In 1990, as a result of a gift from Dallas businessman Comer Cottrell, the college relocated to its present home in Dallas, Texas. The college now resides on 147 acres of beautiful rolling hills and trees just south of downtown Dallas.

MISSION

The mission of the college is to provide a quality, faith-based education that addresses the academic, social, and Christian development of students and prepares them to be servant leaders and agents of change in their communities. Academic excellence lies at the heart of the college's mission, along with the values of integrity, service, leadership, accountability, fiduciary responsibility, and an appreciation of cultural diversity.

MOTTO

"Greatness ... One Step at a Time"

TRIVIA

To construct the college's first building, a "Ten Cents a Brick" campaign was launched throughout the AME congregations in Texas.

2009-10 Presidential Scholar Yessika Aviles is the first Hispanic student to be elected president of the Student Government Association in the 137-year history of the college.

NOTABLES

- Frank Sims—Past chairman of the Federal Reserve Bank of Minneapolis

- Hiawatha Williams—Entrepreneur; owner of Williams Chicken

- 2008/2009 Freshmen Class— Recorded the highest cumulative grade point average in school history

ACADEMIC PROGRAMS

Paul Quinn College consists of three divisions: the Division of Arts & Sciences; the Division of Education; and the Division of Business & Professional Studies.

The Division of Arts & Sciences awards degrees in Biology; Computer Science; Engineering Technology; and Interdisciplinary Studies (with a concentration in English, History, Mathematics, Psychology, and Spanish).

The Division of Education awards degrees in Interdisciplinary Studies, Elementary Education, Secondary Education, Physical Education, and Human Performance & Wellness. Minors are available in Biology, Chemistry, Computer Science, Engineering Technology, English, History, Mathematics, Psychology, and Spanish.

The Division of Business & Professional Studies awards degrees in Business Administration (with a concentration in Accounting, Computer Information Systems, Entrepreneurship, Management, and Marketing), Legal Studies, and Organizational Management.

STUDENT ORGANIZATIONS

Paul Quinn College's social and cultural activities include ethnic, cultural, faith, social, political, and special interest clubs and organizations. Leadership opportunities can be found in the Student Government Association (SGA), as well as within various official National Pan-Hellenic Council recognized member fraternities and sororities and the National Council of Negro Women. Honor societies are also represented on campus.

SPORTS

Paul Quinn College's teams, the Tigers, are members of the National Association of Intercollegiate Athletics (NAIA) and participate in the Red River Athletic Conference. Men's sports include baseball, basketball, and track and field; women's sports include basketball, cross-country, and track and field.

TUITION

$18,500

CONTACT INFORMATION

Director of Enrollment Management
Paul Quinn College
3837 Simpson Stuart Road
Dallas, TX 75241-4331
Phone: (214) 379-5449
Fax: (214) 379-5448

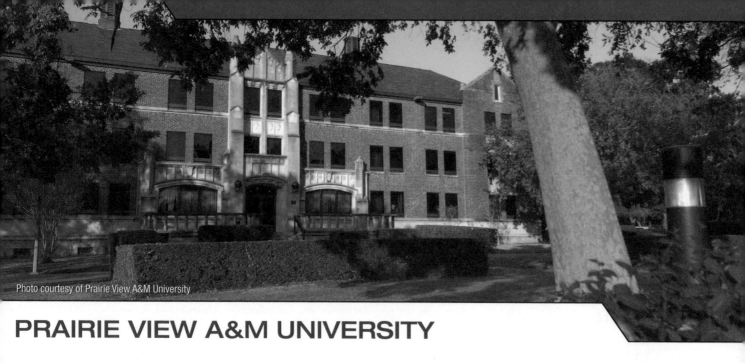

PRAIRIE VIEW A&M UNIVERSITY

ADDRESS: FM 1098 Road & University Drive
Prairie View, TX 77446
(877) PVAMU30

WEB SITE: www.pvamu.edu

FOUNDED: 1876

MASCOT: Panther

AFFILIATION: None

TYPE: 4-Year Public

RATIO: 16:1

STUDENT BODY: 8,200

HISTORY

Prairie View A&M University was founded during the Reconstruction Period after the Civil War as an agricultural and mechanical college whose goal was "preparation and training of colored teachers." The first state-supported college in Texas for African Americans, it was originally called the Alta Vista Agriculture & Mechanical College of Texas for Colored Youth for its location on the former Alta Vista Plantation.

The college opened its doors on March 11, 1878, with a curriculum that included home economics, mechanical arts, arts and sciences, and agriculture. Over the years, its name was changed several times: in 1879, the college became the Prairie View State Normal School; in 1945, Prairie View University; and finally, in 1973, Prairie View A&M University.

Prairie View A&M University is accredited by the Commission on Colleges of the Southern Association of Colleges and Schools (SACS).

MISSION

Prairie View A&M University is committed to providing excellence in teaching, research, and service.

MOTTO

"Prairie View Produces Productive People"

TRIVIA

Prairie View A&M University has produced more African-American flag rank military officers (9) than any other historically black university in the country.

The University's solar observatory is the only solar observatory in Texas and one of only nine in the nation.

Prairie View's marching band, the Marching Storm, have performed at President George W. Bush's inaugural parade, the Dallas Cowboys' Thanksgiving Day game, the Honda Battle of the Bands Invitational Showcase, and the Tournament of Roses Parade.

NOTABLES

- Charles Mose Brown—Legendary Blues singer

- Ann Ferrell Williams—Founder and artistic director of the world-renowned Dallas Black Dance Theatre

- Frederick Newhouse—Olympic gold medalist in men's track

- Emanuel Cleaver II—U.S. Congressman from the State of Missouri

ACADEMIC PROGRAMS

Prairie View A&M University offers baccalaureate degrees in 42 academic majors, 46 master's degrees, and four doctoral degree programs through its eight colleges and schools. Academic divisions consist of the College of the Agriculture and Human Sciences; the School of Architecture; the Marvin D. and June Samuel Brailsford College of Arts and Sciences; the College of Business; the Whitlowe R. Green College of Education; the Roy G. Perry College of Engineering; the College of Juvenile Justice and Psychology; and the College of Nursing.

Degrees are awarded in Accounting; Agriculture; Biology; Business Administration; Chemistry; Clinical Adolescent Psychology; Communications; Computer Science; Criminal Justice; Education; Engineering; Health; History; Human Sciences; Management; Marketing; Mathematics; Music; Nursing; Nursing Administration; Physics; Political Science; Psychology; Sociology; and Theatre.

STUDENT ORGANIZATIONS

Prairie View A&M University offers more than 100 honorary, professional, departmental, and social interest groups, including the Student Government Association, the Student Leadership Institute, and the student-run newspaper, *Panther.*

The university welcomes a very rich Greek life—all nine members of the National Pan-Hellenic Council are represented at PVAMU. Fraternities and sororities provide opportunities for students to develop leadership and organizational skills.

SPORTS

Prairie View A&M University teams, the Panthers and Lady Panthers, are charter members of the Southwestern Athletic Conference (SWAC), and compete in NCAA Division I-AA in football, and Division I in all other varsity sports.

Men's sports include baseball, basketball, cross-country, football, golf, tennis, and track and field. Women's sports include basketball, bowling, cross-country, soccer, softball, track and field, and volleyball.

TUITION*

$4,600/$14,000
(based on 15 hours)

CONTACT INFORMATION

Prairie View A&M University
P.O. Box 3089
Prairie View, TX 77446-0188
Phone: (877) PVAMU30
Fax: (936) 857-2699

Photo courtesy of St. Philip's College

ST. PHILIP'S COLLEGE

ADDRESS: 1801 Martin Luther King Drive
San Antonio, TX 78203
(210) 486-2700

WEB SITE: www.alamo.edu/spc

FOUNDED: 1898

AFFILIATION: Episcopal
Church

TYPE: 2-Year Public

RATIO: 19:1

STUDENT BODY: 10,300

HISTORY

St. Philip's College, founded in 1898, began as a sewing class in a house located in La Villita, an historic area of San Antonio. It was established by Bishop James Steptoe of St. Philip's Episcopal Church of the West Texas Diocese.

Artemisia Bowden, the daughter of a former slave, was a teacher who led the school for fifty-two years. During her tenure, the school evolved from a parochial day school to an industrial school to a fully accredited two-year college.

In 1917, the school moved to a new location in eastern San Antonio. In 1945, St. Philip's joined with San Antonio College to form the San Antonio Junior College District, which changed its name in 1982 to the Alamo Community College District.

St. Philip's College is accredited regionally by the Commission on Colleges of the Southern Association of Colleges and Schools (SACS).

TRIVIA

St. Philip's College is the only institution of higher education in the United States with dual designations as Historically Black and Hispanic Serving.

St. Philip's College's Southwest campus is located on land formerly owned by Kelly Air Force Base and serves as the business and industry hub for the college's technical programs.

NOTABLES

- Dr. Adena Williams Loston—President of St. Philip's College; inducted into San Antonio Women's Hall of Fame; awarded 2007 National Aeronautics and Space Administration's Exceptional Achievement Award

ACADEMIC PROGRAMS

St. Philip's College consists of four departments: the Department of Arts and Sciences; the Department of Applied Science and Technology; the Department of Health Sciences; and the Department of Continuing Education.

An associate of arts degree is offered with the following majors: Art 2D, Art 3D, Business Administration, Comic Book, Computer Science, Criminal Justice, Design, Digital Photography, Economics, English, Electronic, Foreign Languages/Spanish, Government, History, Humanities, Integrated Arts, Kinesiology, Liberal Arts, Mathematics, Music, Philosophy, Pre-Engineering, Pre-Law, Pre-Social Work, Psychology, Sociology, Speech, Stage Production & Technology, Teacher Education, and Theatre.

An associate of science degree is offered with the following majors: Allied Health, Biology, Chemistry, Environmental Science, Physics, Pre-Dentistry, Pre-Medicine, Pre-Nursing, and Pre-Pharmacy.

An associate of applied science degree is offered with the following majors: Accounting Technician; Administrative Assistant; Air Conditioning & Heating; Air Conditioning & Heating; Aircraft Technician Airframe; Aircraft Technician Powerplant; Automotive Technology; Baking and Pastry Arts; Business Administration; Business Management; CNC Manufacturing Technician; Collision/Refinishing Technician; Computer Aided Drafting (Architectural); Computer Maintenance Technology; Construction Business Management; Culinary Arts; Desktop Support Specialist; Diesel Construction Equipment Technician; Diesel/Heavy Equipment Technology; Early Childhood Studies; E-Business; Electrical Trades; Electrical Trades; Home Building Technology; Home Building Technology; Hospitality Event Management; Hotel Management; Industrial Maintenance Management; Legal Administrative Assistant; LVN; Medical Administrative Assistant; Network Administrator; Network Maintenance Specialization; Network Security Administrator; Precision Metal Workers: Manufacturing Operations Technician; Refrigeration Technology; Refrigeration Technology; Restaurant Management; Web Developer; and Welder/Welding Technologist.

Certificates are awarded in Department of Allied Construction Trades; Department of Allied Health; Department of Automotive Technology; Department of Business Information Solutions; Department of Drafting; Department of Early Childhood Studies; Department of Electronic and Information Technology; Department of Nursing Education; Department of Multi-Modal Transportation; Department of Repair and Manufacturing; and Department of Tourism, Hospitality, and Culinary Arts.

STUDENT ORGANIZATIONS

St. Philip's College offers students a health and fitness center and Kinesiology Club that promotes health and fitness and volunteers its healthy lifestyle expertise to service organizations in the San Antonio area.

SPORTS

St. Philip's College offers extramural sports activities that include men's basketball and women's volleyball.

TUITION*

$1,800/$4,000
*(based on two 15-hour semesters)

CONTACT INFORMATION

Director of Admissions
St. Philip's College
1801 Martin Luther King Drive
San Antonio, TX 78203
Phone: (210) 486-2333

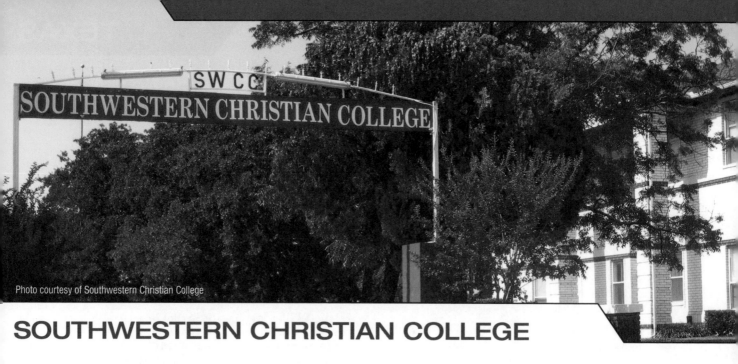

Photo courtesy of Southwestern Christian College

SOUTHWESTERN CHRISTIAN COLLEGE

ADDRESS: **200 Bowser Street**
Terrell, TX 75160
(972) 524-3341

WEB SITE: www.swcc.edu

FOUNDED: 1949

MASCOT: Ram

AFFILIATION: Church of Christ

TYPE: 4-Year Private

RATIO: 10:1

STUDENT BODY: 200

HISTORY

Southwestern Christian College was founded in 1948 when forty-five students met in Fort Worth, Texas. Originally called the Southern Bible Institute, the college had intended to remain in Fort Worth until an opportunity to purchase school property formerly owned by the Texas Military College in Terrell led to the college relocating to Terrell in 1949.

The college, founded and still supported by members of the Churches of Christ, is a four-year educational college whose guiding philosophy is to prepare students for effective and successful Christian living.

Southwestern Christian College is accredited by the Commission on Colleges of the Southern Association of Colleges and Schools (SACS) to award associate- and bachelor-level degrees.

MISSION

Southwestern Christian College is dedicated to the purpose of offering academic instruction that will prepare the student to effectively take his place in the business and social world, well-rooted and grounded in the Word of God.

MOTTO

"Where You Will Find Excellence in Christian Education"

TRIVIA

The Southwestern Christian College campus features the first dwelling ever erected in Terrell. This home, constructed in an octagonal shape to provide protection against Indians, is one of the twenty surviving Round Houses in the entire nation. The local chapter of the Historical Society has placed an historical marker at the Round House site.

NOTABLES

- Dr. Jack Evans, Sr.—President, Southwestern Christian College; longest-serving college president in the nation

- Dr. Adiaha Spinks—Physician

- Dr. Reba Williams White—Physician

- Clarence Stafford—Secret Service agent (retired)

ACADEMIC PROGRAMS

Southwestern Christian College associate of arts program includes instruction in Bible, Introduction to Computers, English, Foreign Language, History, Humanities, Mathematics, Physical Education, Psychology, and Speech.

The bachelor of arts program includes instruction in Bible, Introduction to Computers, English, History, Humanities, Mathematics, Physical Education, Psychology, Speech, Biblical Languages, Christian Ministry, Doctrinal/Historical Studies, Practical Ministry, and Textual Study.

The associate of science program includes instruction in Bible, Introduction to Computers, English, History, Humanities, Mathematics, Natural Science, Physical Education, Psychology, and Speech.

The bachelor of science program includes instruction in Bible, Introduction to Computers, English, History, Humanities, Mathematics, Natural Science, Physical Education, Psychology, Speech, Christian Ministry, Doctrinal/Historical Studies, Practical Ministry, Religious Education, and Textual Study.

STUDENT ORGANIZATIONS

Southwestern Christian College offers students several social and cultural activities, including theater, band, and chorale.

SPORTS

The Southwestern Christian College's teams, the Rams and Lady Rams, are members of the National Junior College Athletic Association (NJCAA).

Men's sports include basketball and track and field. Women's sports include basketball and track and field.

TUITION

$6,182

CONTACT INFORMATION

Admissions Department
Southwestern Christian College
P.O. Box 10
200 Bowser Street
Terrell, TX 75160
Phone: (214) 524-3341

Photo courtesy of Texas College

TEXAS COLLEGE

ADDRESS: 2404 N. Grand Avenue
Tyler, TX 75702
(903) 593-8311

WEB SITE: www.texascollege.edu

FOUNDED: 1894

MASCOT: Steer

AFFILIATION: Christian
Methodist
Episcopal Church

TYPE: 4-Year Private

RATIO: 20:1

STUDENT BODY: 750

HISTORY

Texas College was founded in 1894 by a group of ministers from the Colored Methodist Episcopal Church (now Christian Methodist Episcopal Church) as a training institute for teachers.

In 1909, the school was renamed Phillips University, but three years later reverted back to Texas College. It was accredited as a junior college in 1924, and as a four-year college in 1932.

The College is affiliated with the Christian Methodist Episcopal Church and is a member of the United Negro College Fund.

Texas College is accredited by the Commission on Colleges of the Southern Association of Colleges and Schools (SACS).

MISSION

The mission of Texas College is to ensure that graduates experience a balanced intellectual,

psycho-social, and spiritual development aimed at making them active and productive members of society. The College pursues the six core values of academic excellence, instills integrity, implants perseverance, promotes social responsibility, emphasizes tolerance, and encourages community service by its students as essential anchors in fulfilling its mission in an ever-changing world.

TRIVIA

Texas College was deeded the property on which sits the Emmett J. Scott High School, a symbol of segregation that was closed in 1970 by court order. The college hopes to use the property to showcase the historical perspectives of blacks, tell the story of Emmett J. Scott and other black institutions, serve as a repository of data for researchers, and host cultural events. Emmett J. Scott was personal secretary to Booker T. Washington for eighteen years, and was the highest-ranking African American in the Woodrow Wilson administration.

NOTABLES

- Dr. Jesse Jones—Texas State Representative; member of the Texas College Board of Trustees

- Mrs. Erma P. Hall—Actress, starred in the hit movie *Soul Food*

- Mrs. Billye Suber Aaron—First African-American woman in the southeast to co-host a daily television talk show; co-founder with her husband of the Hank Aaron Chasing the Dream Foundation

- Mr. Andrew Melontree—First African American to be elected County Commissioner of Smith County, Texas, since Reconstruction; first African American to be appointed as Election Judge by the Smith County Democratic Party; first African American to be nominated for United States Marshal for the Eastern Judicial District of Texas

ACADEMIC PROGRAMS

Texas College consists of four divisions: the Division of Business and Social Sciences; the Division of General Studies and Humanities; the Division of Natural and Computational Sciences; and the Division of Education.

Bachelor degrees are awarded in Art, Biology, Business Administration, Computer Science, Criminal Justice, English, History, Interdisciplinary Studies, Liberal Arts, Mathematics, Music, Physical Education, Political Science, Social Work, Sociology, and Religion. Associate of Arts degrees are awarded in General Studies and Early Childhood Education.

STUDENT ORGANIZATIONS

Texas College offers numerous organizations, departments, and special interest groups for students to join, including theater, band, chorale, religion, the Student Government Association, Pre-Alumni Club, the student newspaper (*The Steer*), and the yearbook (*The Texan*).

Greek-letter fraternities include Omega Psi Phi, Phi Beta Sigma, Alpha Phi Alpha, and Kappa Alpha Psi. Greek-letter sororities include Alpha Kappa Alpha, Delta Sigma Theta, Sigma Gamma Rho, and Zeta Phi Beta. Honor societies such as Alpha Kappa Mu are also represented on campus.

SPORTS

Texas College's teams, the Steers and Lady Steers, are members of the National Association of Intercollegiate Athletics (NAIA) and participate in the Red River Athletic Conference, with the exception of the football team, which competes in the Central States Football League.

Men's sports include football, baseball, basketball, soccer, and track. Women's sports include basketball, volleyball, softball, track and soccer.

In addition to the intercollegiate sport teams, the college has a host of intramural sports activities for non-student athletes.

TUITION

$7,992 ($3,996 per semester)

CONTACT INFORMATION

Enrollment Services
Texas College
P. O. Box 4500
2404 N. Grand Avenue
Tyler, TX 75702
Phone: (903) 593-8311 (Ext. 2297–Admissions)
Toll-free: (800) 306-6299
Fax: (903) 596-0001
E-mail: admissions@texascollege.edu
Web site: www.texascollege.edu

TEXAS SOUTHERN UNIVERSITY

ADDRESS: 3100 Cleburne Street
Houston, TX 77004
(713) 313-7011

WEB SITE: www.tsu.edu

FOUNDED: 1947

MASCOT: Tiger

AFFILIATION: None

TYPE: 4-Year Public

RATIO: 16:1

STUDENT BODY: 9,500

HISTORY

Texas Southern University was established as a result of the 1946 *Sweatt v. Painter* case in which Heman Marion Sweatt, an African American, was denied entrance to the University of Texas School of Law because integrated education was not allowed by the Texas State Constitution. Sweatt filed suit and the Texas court continued the case for six months, allowing the state time to create a law school for African Americans.

The result was the Texas State University for Negroes, which was founded on March 3, 1947. The university's Thurgood Marshall School of Law is named for the Supreme Court Justice who, as chief counsel for the NAACP Legal Defense Fund, successfully argued Heman Sweatt's case. The institution is the first HBCU to have a law school.

In 1951, Texas State University for Negroes was renamed Texas Southern University. Today, the university is accredited by the Southern Association of Colleges and Schools (SACS).

MISSION

Texas Southern University is committed to providing quality instruction, scholarly research, and socially responsible public service.

MOTTO

"Excellence in Achievement"

TRIVIA

Texas Southern University's NASA Research Center for Bionanotechnology and Environmental Research (C-BER) is closely aligned with NASA's Exploration Systems Mission Directorate. C-BER research focuses on key environmental factors such as microgravity, radiation, and other space travel-induced stress factors that affect manned flight missions.

NOTABLES

- Yolanda Adams—Award-winning gospel recording artist

- Michael Strahan—ESPN Sports commentator/analyst

- Dr. Kase Lawal—President and CEO of CAMAC

- Tony Wyllie—Vice president of Communications for the Houston Texans

- Patrick Trahan—Press secretary for the City of Houston

ACADEMIC PROGRAMS

Texas Southern University consists of the College of Liberal Arts and Behavioral Sciences; Jesse H. Jones School of Business; College of Education; College of Continuing Education; The Graduate School; Thurgood Marshall School of Law; College of Pharmacy and Health Sciences; School of Science and Technology; Barbara Jordan-Mickey Leland School of Public Affairs; and the Tavis Smiley School of Communications.

Degrees are awarded in Accounting; Administration of Justice; Airway Computer Science; Airway Science Management; Art; Biology; Business Administration; Chemistry; Civil Engineering Technology; Clinical Laboratory Science; Communication; Computer Science; Construction Technology; Design Technology; Dietetics; Economics; Educational Administration; Electronics Engineering Technology; Engineering Technology; English; Entertainment Management; Environmental Health; French; General Studies; Health Administration; Health Care Administration; Health Information Management; Health; History; Human Performance; Human Services and Consumer Sciences; Industrial Technology; Interdisciplinary Studies; Mass Communication; Mathematics; Military Science; Music; Physics; Political Science; Psychology; Public Affairs; Respira-

tory Therapy; Social Work; Sociology; Spanish; Theatre; Transportation Planning and Management; and Urban Planning.

STUDENT ORGANIZATIONS

Texas Southern University offers students more than 60 clubs and organizations, including the University Players (fine arts productions), Political Science Club, NAACP, Living Testimony Choir, International Students Organization, Environmental Health Club, and Association of Black Journalists.

Students may join the *Herald* (student-run newspaper), the *Tiger* yearbook, the Student Government Association, the legendary Debate Team, or the award-winning Ocean of Soul Marching Band and Jazz Ensemble. Communications majors or volunteers may work at student-run radio station, KTSU.

Greek fraternities include Alpha Phi Alpha, Kappa Alpha Psi, Omega Psi Phi, and Phi Beta Sigma; sororities include Alpha Kappa Alpha, Delta Sigma Theta, Sigma Gamma Rho, and Zeta Phi Beta.

SPORTS

Texas Southern University's teams, the Tigers, compete in the NCAA Division I-AA within the Southwestern Athletic Conference. Men's sports include baseball, basketball, cross-country, football, golf, and track and field. Women's sports include basketball, bowling, cross-country, golf, soccer, softball, track and field, and volleyball.

TUITION

$6,000

CONTACT INFORMATION

Enrollment Services Customer Service Center
Texas Southern University
3100 Cleburne Street
Houston, TX 77004-4598
Phone: (713) 313-6861
E-mail: admissions@tsu.edu

Photo courtesy of Wiley College

WILEY COLLEGE

ADDRESS: 711 Wiley Avenue
Marshall, TX 75670
(903) 927-3300

WEB SITE: www.wileyc.edu

FOUNDED: 1873

MASCOT: Wildcat

AFFILIATION: United Methodist Church

TYPE: 4-Year Private

RATIO: 15:1

STUDENT BODY: 967

HISTORY

Wiley College was founded in 1873 by medical missionary and educator Bishop Isaac Wiley, a minister in the Methodist Episcopal Church. The first HBCU west of the Mississippi River, the school opened with only two buildings housing its students.

During its history, Wiley has faced—and successfully cleared—several hurdles. The college managed to keep its doors open in spite of the racism and Jim Crow laws rampant during its first years. Five of the college's buildings that were destroyed in a 1906 fire were rebuilt; floods and cotton crop failures in 1915 did not discourage the college's leaders. Instead, Wiley remained strong and continued to expand.

Wiley College is accredited by the Commission on Colleges of the Southern Association of Colleges and Schools (SACS).

MISSION

Wiley College fosters an intellectually stimulating environment that encourages and supports spiritual, ethical, and moral development, an appreciation for the arts, global awareness, and concern for the common good in the global society in which it exits. Committed to the principles of educational access and opportunity, the college serves traditional and non-traditional students of diverse academic, social, geographic, economic, cultural, and religious backgrounds who demonstrate a desire and potential for learning in a Christian environment that is sensitive to the myriad of student needs.

MOTTO

"Achieving Excellence through Pride in Performance"

TRIVIA

The Civil Rights Movement was helped along

by the efforts of Wiley students. The first sit-ins in Texas—in the rotunda of the Old Harrison County Courthouse—were held by Wiley College and Bishop College students. James L. Farmer, Jr., a graduate of Wiley went on to become one of the "Big Four" of the Civil Rights Movement (with Roy Wilkins, Rev. Dr. Martin Luther King, Jr., and Whitney M. Young, Jr.).

NOTABLES

- James Farmer—Civil rights activist; co-founded the Congress of Racial Equality

- Heman Marion Sweatt—Plaintiff in the *Sweatt v. Painter,* U.S. Supreme Court case that ultimately helped found Texas Southern University

- Conrad O. Johnson—Musician and educator; inducted into Texas Bandmasters Hall of Fame in 2000

ACADEMIC PROGRAMS

Wiley College consists of four divisions: the Division of Arts & Sciences; the Division of Business & Technology; the Division of Education; and the Division of General Education & Special Studies.

The Division of Arts & Sciences awards degrees in Biology (with concentrations in Biological Sciences and Environmental Science), Chemistry, Criminal Justice, English, History, Religion, Mass Communications, Mathematics (with a concentration in Computer Science), Music, Sociology, and Spanish.

The Division of Business & Technology awards degrees in Business Administration (with concentrations in Accounting, Hospitality and Tourism Administration, and Organizational Management) and Computer Information Systems.

The Division of Education awards degrees in Early Childhood Education and Secondary Education (with concentrations in Biology, English, History, Mathematics, Music, Physical Education, and Spanish).

STUDENT ORGANIZATIONS

Wiley College offers students numerous clubs and organizations, including the A Cappella Choir, Gospel Choir, Accounting Club, Computer Club, Criminal Justice Club, Environmental Club, and the Students in Free Enterprise.

Students may work on the campus newspaper, the *Wiley Reporter,* or at the student-run radio station, KBWC. Leadership opportunities can be found in the Student Government Association.

Greek sororities include Alpha Kappa Alpha, Phi Chapter; Delta Sigma Theta, Alpha Iota Chapter; Sigma Gamma Rho, Beta Gamma Chapter; and Zeta Phi Beta, Theta Chapter; fraternities Alpha Phi Alpha, Alpha Sigma Chapter; Kappa Alpha Psi, Alpha Chi Chapter; Omega Psi Phi, Theta Chapter; and Phi Beta Sigma, Beta Chapter.

SPORTS

Wiley College's teams, the Wildcats, are members of the National Association of Intercollegiate Athletics (NAIA), and compete in the Red River Athletic Conference.

Men's sports include baseball, basketball, and track and field; women's sports include basketball, track and field, volleyball, and cheerleading.

TUITION

$15,590 per year

CONTACT INFORMATION

Director of Admissions
Wiley College
711 Wiley Avenue
Marshall, TX 75670
Phone: (903) 927-3222
Toll-free: (800) 658-6889

Photo courtesy of University of the Virgin Islands

UNIVERSITY OF THE VIRGIN ISLANDS

ADDRESS: 2 John Brewer's Bay
St. Thomas, VI 00802
(340) 693-1150

WEB SITE: www.uvi.edu

FOUNDED: 1962

MASCOT: Buccaneer

AFFILIATION: None

TYPE: 4-Year Public

RATIO: 14:1

STUDENT BODY: 2,500

HISTORY

The University of the Virgin Islands was established in 1961 when then-Governor Ralph M. Paiewonsky pledged to establish a college to serve the educational needs of the residents of the Virgin Islands. In March 1962, the College of the Virgin Islands was chartered as a center of higher learning.

In July 1963, the first campus was opened on the island of St. Thomas, built on land donated by the federal government. A second campus on St. Croix was built in 1964. The first baccalaureate degrees were awarded in 1970. By 1976, master's programs were added.

In 1972, the college was awarded land-grant status by Congress, allowing it to expand its programs and services. In 1986, the college was renamed the University of the Virgin Islands and designated by Congress as an HBCU. Today, it is considered the leading American institution of higher learning in the Caribbean.

The University of the Virgin Islands is accredited by the Commission on Higher Education of the Middle States Association of Colleges and Schools (MSACS).

MISSION

The University of the Virgin Islands is committed to being a learner-centered institution dedicated to the success of its students and committed to enhancing the lives of the people of the U.S. Virgin Islands and the wider Caribbean through excellent teaching, innovative research, and responsive community service.

MOTTO

"Historically American. Uniquely Caribbean. Globally Interactive."

TRIVIA

The university is the only HBCU located outside of the continental United States. Its campuses are located on St. Thomas and St. Croix.

NOTABLES

- Richard Skerritt—Rhodes scholar; businessman

- Dr. Granville Wrensford—Former chair of Albany State University's Department of Natural Sciences

ACADEMIC PROGRAMS

The University of the Virgin Islands consists of five academic divisions: Business; Education; Humanities and Social Services; Nursing; and Science and Mathematics.

Associate degrees are awarded in Accounting, Business Management, Computer Information Systems, Computer Science, Criminal Justice, Hotel and Restaurant Management, Inclusive Early Childhood Education, Nursing, Police Science and Administration, and Process Technology.

Bachelor of arts degrees are awarded in Accounting, Biology, Business Administration, Chemistry, Communication, Criminal Justice, Elementary Education, English, Humanities, Inclusive Early Childhood Education, Marine Biology, Mathematics, Music Education, Psychology, Social Sciences, Social Work, and Speech Communication and Theatre.

Bachelor of science degrees are awarded in Applied Mathematics, Biology, Chemistry, Computer Science, Criminal Justice, Marine Biology, Mathematics and Nursing.

Graduate degrees are awarded in School Psychology, Education, Mathematics for Secondary Teachers, Business Administration, Public Administration and Marine and Environmental Science.

STUDENT ORGANIZATIONS

The University of the Virgin Islands' 32 student organizations include the National Student Exchange Club, Debate Society, Student Nursing Association, Psychology Club, International Student Association, BUCS Dance Squad, Travel Club, Math Boosters, Environmental & Marine Science Club, Student Ambassadors Club, Accounting Association, "ABY" Always Believe in Yourself, Anguilla Student Association, Francophone Club, Future Business Leaders of America, Graduate Student Association, Paradise Players, and Senior Class Student Nurses Association.

National sororities and fraternities include Alpha Kappa Alpha Sorority Incorporated and Kappa Alpha Psi, Inc. Honor societies include Alpha Mu Gamma Foreign Language Honor Society and Golden Key Honor Society.

SPORTS

The University of the Virgin Islands' teams, the Buccaneers, are members of the LAI (Liga Atlética Interuniversitaria), a university league consisting of twenty American universities in the Caribbean and the Caribbean University Sports Association.

Men's sports include basketball, volleyball, track and field, cross-country, swimming, and table tennis. Women's sports include basketball, track and field, cross-country, swimming, table tennis, and dance.

TUITION

$3,600/$10,800

CONTACT INFORMATION

Director of Admissions
University of the Virgin Islands
2 John Brewer's Bay
St. Thomas, VI 00802
Phone: (340) 693-1224
Fax: (340) 693-1167

HAMPTON UNIVERSITY

ADDRESS: 530 East Queen Street
Hampton, VA 23668
(757) 727-5000

WEB SITE: www.hamptonu.edu

FOUNDED: 1868

MASCOT: Pirate

AFFILIATION: None

TYPE: 4-Year Private

RATIO: 16:1

STUDENT BODY: 5,700

HISTORY

Hampton University was established in 1868 as Hampton Normal and Agricultural Institute. Founded by Brigadier General Samuel Chapman Armstrong, the 29-year-old son of missionary parents, its purpose was to prepare promising young African-American men and women to teach and lead their newly-freed people.

During the early years of its existence, Hampton was supported by the Freedman's Bureau, Northern philanthropists, and religious groups. The first baccalaureate degrees were awarded in 1922, and in 1930, the school's name was changed to Hampton Institute to reflect its college-level accreditation. Its name was changed to Hampton University in 1984.

Hampton University is accredited by the Commission on Colleges of the Southern Association of Colleges and Schools (SACS).

MISSION

Hampton University is committed to the promotion of learning, building of character, and preparation of promising students for positions of leadership and service.

MOTTOS

"The Standard of Excellence" and "An Education for Life"

TRIVIA

The Emancipation Oak on Hampton University's campus was the site of the first Southern reading of President Lincoln's Emancipation Proclamation, an act which accelerated the demand for African-American education. The oak, which has been designated as one of the 10 Great Trees of the World by the National Geographic

Society, served as the first classroom for the newly freed men and women.

NOTABLES

- Booker T. Washington—Educator, author, and founder of Tuskegee Institute

- Charles Phillips—President, Oracle Corporation

- Wanda Sykes—Emmy Award-winning actress and comedienne

- Angela Burt-Murray—Editor-in-Chief, *Essence Magazine*

- Derrick Mahorn—Former NBA player

ACADEMIC PROGRAMS

Hampton University consists of seven schools: School of Business; School of Engineering and Technology; School of Liberal Arts; Scripps Howard School of Journalism and Communications; School of Nursing; School of Pharmacy; and School of Science. The university also has a Graduate College and a College of Education and Continuing Studies.

Undergraduate degrees are awarded in Accounting; Advertising; Architecture; Aviation; Banking and Finance; Biological Sciences; Broadcast Journalism; Business Management; Chemical Engineering; Chemistry; Communicative Sciences & Disorders; Computer Science; Economics; Education; Electrical Engineering; English; Entrepreneurship; Fine and Performing Arts; Health and Physical Education; Hotel and Restaurant Management; Management; Marine and Environmental Science; Marketing; Mathematics; Military Science; Modern Foreign Languages; Music; Nursing Education; Physics; Political Science and History; Print Journalism; Psychology; Public Relations; Religious Studies; and Sociology.

STUDENT ORGANIZATIONS

Hampton University offers students numerous clubs and organizations for students, including the university's Concert Choir, Leadership Institute, Terpsichorean Dance Company, International Students Association, Underwater Explorers Club, and Student Christian Association.

Greek fraternities include Alpha Phi Alpha, Iota Phi Theta, Kappa Alpha Psi, and Omega Psi Phi; sororities include Alpha Kappa Alpha, Delta Sigma Theta, Sigma Gamma Rho, and Zeta Phi Beta.

SPORTS

Hampton University's teams, the Pirates are members of National Collegiate Athletic Association (NCAA), Division I (I-AA for football) and participate in the Mid-Eastern Athletic Conference (MEAC).

Men's sports include basketball, cross-country, football, golf, tennis, and track and field; women's sports include basketball, bowling, cross-country, golf, tennis, softball, volleyball, and track and field.

TUITION

$15,464

CONTACT INFORMATION

Office of Admissions
Hampton University
Hampton, VA 23668
Phone: (757) 727-5328
Toll-free: (800) 624-3328
Fax: (757) 727-5095
E-mail: admissioncounselor@hamptonu.edu

Photo courtesy of Norfolk State University

NORFOLK STATE UNIVERSITY

ADDRESS: 700 Park Avenue
Norfolk, VA 23504
(757) 823-8600

WEB SITE: www.nsu.edu

FOUNDED: 1935

MASCOT: Spartan

AFFILIATION: None

TYPE: 4-Year Public

RATIO: 20:1

STUDENT BODY: 6,300

HISTORY

Norfolk State University is one of the largest predominantly black institutions in the United States.

It was founded in 1935 as the Norfolk Unit of Virginia Union University. In 1942, it became an independent institution, Norfolk Polytechnic College, and in 1944 became a part of Virginia State College.

In 1969, the Norfolk State College became fully independent. Ten years later, it attained university status and received authorization to grant graduate degrees.

Norfolk State University is accredited by the Commission on Colleges of the Southern Association of Colleges and Schools (SACS).

MISSION

Norfolk State University is committed to providing an affordable, high-quality education for an ethnically and culturally diverse student population, equipping them with the capability to become productive citizens who continuously contribute to a global and rapidly changing society.

MOTTO

"The Institution of Choice"

TRIVIA

Norfolk State University is located on the former site of the 50-acre Memorial Park Golf Course, which the city of Norfolk sold to the school for $1.

Norfolk State University's WNSB 91.1 FM signed on the air on February 22, 1980 as a 1000-watt noncommercial, educational radio station. In March 2000, it adopted an urban contemporary format with overnight satellite jazz programming.

NOTABLES

- Evelyn Fields—Rear admiral; former director of National Oceanic and Atmospheric Administration

- Bob Dandridge—Former NBA player with Milwaukee Bucks and Washington Bullets

- Yvonne Miller—First African-American woman to serve in both the Virginia House of Delegates and Senate

- Derrick Dingle—Executive editor of *Black Enterprise Magazine*

- Tim Reid—Television actor; producer

- Nathan McCall—Journalist; author

ACADEMIC PROGRAMS

Norfolk State University is comprised of the College of Liberal Arts; the College of Science, Engineering and Technology; the School of Business; the School of Education; the Ethelyn R. Strong School of Social Work; the Honors College; the Graduate School; and the School of Extended Learning.

Undergraduate degrees are awarded in Accounting, Finance Information Management; Tourism and Hospitality; Management, Marketing, Entrepreneurship; Secondary Education & School Leadership Development; Special Education; Early Childhood/Elementary Education; Health, Physical Education & Exercise Science; English and Foreign Languages; Military Science; Fine Arts; Music; History; Political Science; Interdisciplinary Studies; Psychology; Mass Communications & Journalism; Sociology; Allied Health; Mathematics; Biology; Nursing; Chemistry; Physics; Computer Science; Technology; Engineering; and Child Welfare Education.

STUDENT ORGANIZATIONS

Norfolk State University has more than 70 registered student organizations including Greek-letter fraternities and sororities, a Student Government Association, and a Graduate Student Organization.

SPORTS

Norfolk State University's teams, the Spartans, participate in National Collegiate Athletic Association Division I (NCAA) and the Mid-Eastern Athletic Conference (MEAC).

Men's sports include baseball, basketball, football, cross-country, tennis, and track and field. Women's sports include basketball, bowling, cross-country, softball, tennis, track and field, and volleyball.

TUITION*

$6,651/$12,680
(based on 15 credit hours)

CONTACT INFORMATION

Office of Admissions
Norfolk State University
700 Park Avenue
Norfolk, VA 23504
Phone: (757) 823-8396
Toll-free: (800) 274-1821
Fax: (757) 823-2078
E-mail: admissions@nsu.edu

Photo courtesy of Saint Paul's College

SAINT PAUL'S COLLEGE

ADDRESS: 115 College Drive
Lawrenceville, VA 23868
(434) 848-3111

WEB SITE: www.saintpauls.edu

FOUNDED: 1888

MASCOT: Tiger

AFFILIATION: Protestant
Episcopal
Church

TYPE: 4-Year Private

RATIO: 17:1

STUDENT BODY: 700

HISTORY

The Venerable Archdeacon James Solomon Russell, an Episcopal priest in the Diocese of Southern Virginia, founded the Saint Paul Normal and Industrial School on September 24, 1888, with fewer than one dozen students, most of whom were ex-slaves and/or children of ex-slaves. Archdeacon Russell realized the need for expansion and development as the enrollment increased. By an act of the General Assembly of Virginia, on March 4, 1890, the school was incorporated as the Saint Paul Normal and Industrial School. By authority of the Board of Trustees, the name of the institution was changed to Saint Paul's College in 1957 and bachelor of arts and bachelor of science degrees were added to the curriculum.

Throughout its history, the college has significantly impacted the surrounding com-

munity. During its early years of operation, the college supplied electricity for the towns of Lawrenceville and Southside Virginia. It also provided ice for the railroad. This rich tradition of community service continues as the school and its students today contribute hundreds of voluntary hours for a wide array of organizations within the community.

MISSION

Saint Paul's College's mission is to provide an intellectual atmosphere that meets the broad range of needs of its students and to provide leadership in an expanding social and technological society.

MOTTO

"An Education for Life"

TRIVIA

Notable programs on Saint Paul's campus include the Single Parent Support System

(SPSS), a residential academic program for single parents and their children; the Brown v. Board Scholars Program, a legislatively created program designed to provide educational opportunities to Virginia residents affected by public school closures during the period of Massive Resistance in Virginia; the James Solomon Russell Scholars Program, a program designed to recruit and encourage students to consider careers in church ministry; the Service Learning Program, a community outreach program that integrates community service with instruction to teach civic responsibility; and the Dominion Leadership Program, a grant-sponsored program for student ambassadors of the college.

NOTABLES

- Sidney Lowe—Former NBA player and head coach for North Carolina State University

- Darrell Green—Former NFL player for the Washington Redskins

- Dr. Helen Edmonds—Representative to the United Nations

ACADEMIC PROGRAMS

Saint Paul's College has four academic departments: the Department of Business Administration; the Department of Humanities and Behavioral Science; the Department of Natural Science and mathematics; and the Department of Teacher Education.

Bachelor of arts degrees are awarded in Criminal Justice; English; History/Social Science; Political Science; Religious Studies; and Sociology.

Bachelor of science degrees are awarded in Biology; Business Administration (with concentrations available in Accounting, General Business Administration, Management, Management Information Systems, and Marketing); Computer Science; Criminal Justice; General Studies; History/Social Science; Mathematics; Sociology/Criminal Justice; Sociology/Human Services; and Sociology/Social Work.

STUDENT ORGANIZATIONS

Saint Paul's College offers several student clubs and organizations that provide opportunities for personal development and campus involvement, including Pre-Alumni Council, NAACP, Poetry Club, Sunday School, Best Buddies, Choral Society, Lectors Guild, Canterbury Club, and Student Government Association. Greek fraternities and sororities are represented on campus.

SPORTS

Saint Paul's College's teams, the Tigers and Lady Tigers, are members of the National Collegiate Athletic Association (NCAA) and participate in the Central Intercollegiate Athletic Association (CIAA). Men's sports include baseball, basketball, cross-country, football, golf, indoor track, outdoor track, and tennis. Women's sports include basketball, cross-country, bowling, softball, indoor track, outdoor track, and volleyball.

TUITION

$13,210

CONTACT INFORMATION

Vice President for Student Affairs
Saint Paul's College
115 College Drive
Lawrenceville, VA 23868
Phone: (434) 848-6493
Toll-free: (800) 678-7071

VIRGINIA STATE UNIVERSITY

ADDRESS: 1 Hayden Drive
Petersburg, VA 23806
(804) 524-5000

WEB SITE: www.vsu.edu

FOUNDED: 1882

MASCOT: Trojan

AFFILIATION: None

TYPE: 4-Year Public

RATIO: 16:1

STUDENT BODY: 4,700

HISTORY

Virginia State University was founded in 1882 as the Virginia Normal and Collegiate Institute. It opened on October 1, 1883, and nine years later, after a legislative act ended its collegiate program, was renamed the Virginia Normal and Industrial Institute.

In 1920, the land-grant program that had been given to Hampton Institute was granted to the institute, and three years later the college program was restored. In 1930, it became the Virginia State College for Negroes.

In 1944, a branch of the college was added in Norfolk, Virginia; it later became the independent Norfolk State College. The college, which sits on a bluff overlooking the Appomattox River, was once again renamed in 1946 to Virginia State College; in 1979, Virginia State University was adopted as the name.

Virginia State University is accredited by the Commission on Colleges of the Southern Association of Colleges and Schools (SACS).

MISSION

Virginia State University is committed to promoting and sustaining academic programs that integrate instruction, research, and extension/public service in a design most responsive to the needs and endeavors of individuals and groups within its scope of influence.

MOTTO

"A Place to Grow"

TRIVIA

Virginia State University's first president, John Mercer Langston, was elected to Congress from Virginia and was the great-uncle of writer Langston Hughes.

NOTABLES

- James H. Coleman—First African-American to serve on the New Jersey Supreme Court

- Gaye Adegbalola—Blues singer; activist who founded the Harlem Committee on Self-Defense

- Shelia Baxter—Brigadier general of the U.S. Army

ACADEMIC PROGRAMS

Virginia State University consists of five schools: the School of Agriculture; the School of Business; the School of Engineering, Science and Technology; the School of Liberal Arts and Education; and the School of Graduate Studies, Research and Outreach.

Degrees are awarded in Accounting and Finance; Administrative System Management; Agriculture; Biology/Life Sciences; Career and Technical Studies; Chemistry; Computer Engineering; Computer Information Systems; Computer Science; Counselor Education; Criminal Justice; Economics; Education; Educational Administration & Supervision; Electrical and Electronic Engineering Technology; Engineering Technology; English/Languages and Literature; Family and Consumer Sciences; Health, Physical Education, and Recreation; History; Hospitality Management; Industrial Education and Technology; Interdisciplinary Studies/Teacher Education; Management; Manufacturing Engineering; Marketing; Mass Communications; Mathematics; Mechanical Engineering Technology; Music; Nursing; Nutrition and Dietetics; Physics; Plant Science; Political Science; Project Management; Psychology; Public Administration; Social Work; Sociology; Sports Management; and Visual Communication Art & Design.

STUDENT ORGANIZATIONS

Virginia State University offers organizations and clubs that include the VSU Concert Choir, Student Ambassadors, and the National Society of Pershing Angels. Departmental clubs include Biology Club, Business Management Club, Chemistry Club, Economic & Finance Club, Mass Communications Club, Philosophy Club, and Psychology Club.

Students can get involved in the student-run newspaper and radio station, WVST. Leadership opportunities can be found in the Student Government Association or the Institute for Leadership Development.

Greek fraternities include Alpha Phi Alpha, Kappa Alpha Psi, Omega Psi Phi, and Phi Beta Sigma; sororities include Alpha Kappa Alpha, Delta Sigma Theta, Sigma Gamma Rho, and Zeta Phi Beta.

SPORTS

Virginia State University's team, the Trojans, are members of the National Collegiate Athletic Association (NCAA), Division II and compete in the Central Intercollegiate Athletic Conference.

Men's sports include baseball, basketball, football, tennis, golf, indoor track, outdoor track, and cross-country. Women's sports include bowling, volleyball, tennis, softball, basketball, indoor track, outdoor track, cross-country, and cheerleading.

TUITION
$5,396/$12,926

CONTACT INFORMATION
Director of Admissions
Virginia State University
P.O. Box 9018
Petersburg, VA 23806-2096
Phone: (804) 524-5902
Toll-free: (800) 871-7611

VIRGINIA UNION UNIVERSITY

ADDRESS: 1500 North Lombardy Street
Richmond, VA 23220
(804) 257-5600

WEB SITE: www.vuu.edu

FOUNDED: 1865

MASCOT: Panther

AFFILIATION: American
Baptist Church
of USA

TYPE: 4-Year Private

RATIO: 15:1

STUDENT BODY: 1,500

HISTORY

Virginia Union University was founded in 1865 when members of the American Baptist Home Mission Society proposed providing education to freed slaves through a "National Theological Institute."

The purpose of the institute was to educate those desiring to enter into the Baptist ministry. However, the curricula was expanded to include courses at the preparatory, high school, and collegiate levels. One branch of the institute, the Wayland Seminary, was established in Washington, D.C. Another branch, the Colver Institute, was created in Richmond, Virginia.

In 1876, Colver became the Richmond Institute; ten years later, it became the Richmond Theological Seminary. In 1899, Wayland Seminary and Richmond Theological were merged into Virginia Union University. In 1932, Hart-

shorn Memorial College for Women became a part of Virginia Union. The fourth institution within the Virginia Union legacy became Storer College of Harper's Ferry, West Virginia, which merged with the university in 1964.

Virginia Union University is accredited by the Commission on Colleges of the Southern Association of Colleges and Schools (SACS).

MISSION

Virginia Union University is nourished by its African-American heritage and energized by a commitment to excellence and diversity. Its mission is to: 1) provide a nurturing intellectually challenging and spiritually enriching environment for learning; 2) empower students to develop strong moral values for success; and 3) develop scholars, leaders, and lifelong learners of a global society. To accomplish this mission, Virginia Union University offers a broad range of educational opportunities that advance liberal arts education, teaching, research, science, technology, continuing education, civic engagement, and international experiences.

TRIVIA

Virginia Union University houses the L. Douglas Wilder Collection featuring documents from the life and career of Virginia's 66th governor, the first elected African-American governor in U.S. history.

NOTABLES

- Douglas Wilder—First African American elected governor of a U.S. state

- Ben Wallace—NBA player; 4-time defensive player of the year

- Rev. Dr. Iyanla Vanzant—Motivational speaker and author

ACADEMIC PROGRAMS

Virginia Union University consists of four undergraduate academic schools: the Sydney Lewis School of Business; the School of Education & Interdisciplinary Studies; the School of Humanities and Social Sciences; and the School of Basic, Applied Sciences, and Technology.

The Sydney Lewis School of Business awards degrees in Accounting, Computer Information Systems, Entrepreneurial Management, Finance and Banking, and Marketing.

The School of Education & Interdisciplinary Studies awards degrees in Interdisciplinary Studies– Elementary Education, Interdisciplinary Studies– Exceptional Education, Secondary Education, Biology, English, Business, History, Chemistry, and Mathematics .

The School of Humanities and Social Sciences awards degrees in English, Media Arts, Political Science and Public Administration, Religious Studies, and Social Work.

The School of Basic, Applied Sciences, and Technology awards degrees in Biology, Chemistry, Criminology/Criminal Justice, Mathematics, Mathematics/Minor in Computer Science, and Psychology.

STUDENT ORGANIZATIONS

Virginia Union University offers more than 50 clubs and organizations, including the Akro-Vinci Modeling Troupe, Unique Image Dance Troupe, Biology Club, Pre-Law Society, Student Government Association, Panthers Claw Pep Squad, University Players Drama Club, and Rotaract Club. Students can work on the yearbook (*The Panther*) or the student newspaper (*The VUU Informer*). Communication students work at the campus television station. Greek-letter societies include Alpha Kappa Alpha, Delta Sigma Theta, Sigma Gamma Rho, and Zeta Phi Beta sororities; fraternities include Alpha Phi Alpha, Kappa Alpha Psi, Omega Psi Phi, Phi Beta Sigma, and Iota Phi Theta.

SPORTS

Virginia Union University's teams, the Panthers, are members of the National Collegiate Athletic Association (NCAA) and participate within the Central Intercollegiate Athletic Association (CIAA).

Men's sports include basketball, cross-country, football, golf, tennis, and track and field; women's basketball, bowling, cross-country, tennis, softball, track and field, and volleyball.

TUITION

$12,680

CONTACT INFORMATION

Director of Admissions
Virginia Union University
1500 North Lombardy Street
Richmond, VA 23220-1170
Phone: (804) 342-3570
Toll-free: (800) 368-3227

VIRGINIA UNIVERSITY OF LYNCHBURG

ADDRESS: 2058 Garfield Avenue
Lynchburg, VA 24501
(434) 528-5276

WEB SITE: www.vul.edu

FOUNDED: 1886

MASCOT: Dragon

AFFILIATION: Baptist

TYPE: 4-Year Private

RATIO: 5:1

STUDENT BODY: 274

HISTORY

Virginia University of Lynchburg was founded in 1886 by the Virginia Baptist State Convention as the Lynchburg Baptist Seminary, an institution of "self-reliance," "racial pride," and "faith."

The seminary was renamed Virginia Seminary in 1890 and began offering its first classes. In 1900, college-level courses were added and the seminary was reincorporated as the Virginia Theological Seminary and College. In 1962, it was renamed Virginia Seminary and College. In 1996, the college was incorporated and renamed Virginia University of Lynchburg.

Virginia University of Lynchburg is a member of the Transnational Association of Christian Colleges and Schools (TRACS) having been awarded Accredited status as a Category IV Institution by TRACS Accreditation Commission.

MISSION

Virginia University of Lynchburg seeks to recognize the possibilities in every human being and maximize the gifts of the individual within the context of a thoroughly Christian and nurturing environment, which offers students opportunities to develop into able leaders and scholars. The Mission of the school is to provide a solid Liberal Arts and Christian Education program for all students. The University continues to embrace our African-American heritage along with appreciation for other cultures and ethnic groups in our global community.

MOTTO

"Sibi Auxilium et Libertas"

TRIVIA

A Virginia University of Lynchburg student participated in the first HBCU 105 Voice Choir to perform at the John F. Kennedy Center in Washington, DC on September 7, 2008.

NOTABLES

- Vernon N. Johns—Noted preacher and forerunner of the modern civil rights movement

- Dr. Lawrence E. Carter—First and only dean of the Martin Luther King, Jr. International Chapel at Morehouse College

- Ed Hurt—Noted football, basketball, and track coach; first African American to serve on the International Olympic Committee

- Ann Spencer—Harlem Renaissance poet

- Ralph Reavis—President of Virginia University of Lynchburg; first African American to graduate from the University of Virginia, Department of Religious Studies with a Ph.D.

ACADEMIC PROGRAMS

Virginia University of Lynchburg consists of three schools: the School of Arts and Sciences, the School of Business, and the School of Religion.

The School of Arts and Sciences awards an Associate Degree in Arts and Sciences, a certificate in Ministry/Church Leadership, a Bachelor of Arts Degree in Sociology, Sociology/Criminology, and Religious Studies.

The School of Business awards a Bachelor of Arts Degree in General Business Administration, and in Organizational Management (online), and a Master of Arts Degree in Organizational Management (online).

The School of Religion awards a Master Degree in Divinity and a Doctor of Ministry Degree.

STUDENT ORGANIZATIONS

Leadership opportunities may be found in the Student Government Association.

TUITION

$3,950/$7,900

CONTACT INFORMATION

Director of Admissions
Virginia University of Lynchburg
2058 Garfield Avenue
Lynchburg, VA 24501-6417
Phone: (434) 528-5276

BLUEFIELD STATE COLLEGE

ADDRESS: 219 Rock Street
Bluefield, WV 24701
(304) 327-4000

WEB SITE: www.bluefieldstate.edu

FOUNDED: 1895

MASCOT: Blue Devil

AFFILIATION: None

TYPE: 4-Year Public

RATIO: 18:1

STUDENT BODY: 1,800

HISTORY

Bluefield State College was founded in 1895 as the Bluefield Colored Institute through an act of the West Virginia Legislature.

Originally a high school for Negro youth, the school was integrated in the 1950s. By the 1960s, it had evolved into a comprehensive four-year program offering teacher education, arts and sciences, and engineering technology. Since that time, a variety of two-year technical programs have been added in response to local needs.

Bluefield State College is accredited by the Higher Learning Commission and is a member of the North Central Association.

MISSION

Bluefield State College is committed to providing students an affordable, accessible opportunity for public higher education. An historically black institution, Bluefield State College prepares students for diverse professions, graduate study, informed citizenship, community involvement, and public service in an ever-changing global society. The college demonstrates its commitment to the student's intellectual, personal, ethical, and cultural development by providing a dedicated faculty and staff, quality educational programs, and strong student support services in a nurturing environment.

MOTTO

"Making Education Possible"

TRIVIA

Bluefield State College (then known as Bluefield Colored Institute) won consecutive Black Collegiate Football titles in 1927–28, outscoring its opponents 516–53 during that time.

NOTABLES

- Sylvester Myers—president of an internationally known construction cost-estimating management firm with offices at four locations in the United States

- William Bernard Robertson—Former U.S. Deputy Assistant Secretary of State for African Affairs and Director of the Peace Corps for Kenya and the Seychelles

- Maceo Pinkard—Harlem Renaissance musician and composer, whose most famous composition, "Sweet Georgia Brown," is a jazz classic

ACADEMIC PROGRAMS

Bluefield State College consists of five schools: the School of Arts and Sciences; the School of Engineering Technology & Computer Science; the School of Business; the School of Nursing and Allied Health; and the School of Education.

The School of Arts and Sciences awards bachelor of science degrees in Applied Science (Pre-Law and Interdisciplinary) and Criminal Justice Administration (Corrections and Law Enforcement), and a bachelor of arts degree in Humanities (English and Pre-Law) and Social Science (Geography, History, Political Science, Psychology and Sociology).

The School of Engineering Technology & Computer Science awards degrees in Architectural Engineering Technology, Civil Engineering Technology, Computer Science, Electrical Engineering Technology, Mechanical Engineering Technology, and Mining Engineering Technology.

The School of Business awards a bachelor of science degree in Accountancy and Business Administration (Accounting, Computer Science, Management, and Marketing).

The School of Nursing and Allied Health awards degrees in Nursing, Radiologic Technology, and Radiologic Sciences.

The School of Education awards a bachelor of science in Early/Middle Education and Elementary Education (K-6).

STUDENT ORGANIZATIONS

Bluefield State College offers more than forty social clubs and organizations for students, including the Accounting Club, Asclepius's Caduceus Pre-Med Society, Black Student Association, Blue Chicory Players, Blue Devil Press, College Republicans, Criminal Justice Club, Musician Guild, Riot Line, Stronghold Bible Club, Student Government Association, and the Thurgood Marshall Club.

Greek fraternities include Kappa Alpha Psi, Lambda Chi Omega, Phi Kappa Gamma, and Phi Sigma Phi; sororities include Alpha Kappa Alpha, Delta Chi Omega, Eta Omicron Tau, Phi Alpha Chi, and Phi Sigma Zeta.

SPORTS

Bluefield State College's athletic teams, the Big Blues and Lady Blues, are members of the National Collegiate Athletic Association (NCAA), Division II and participate in West Virginia Intercollegiate Athletic Conference (WVIAC). Men's sports include baseball, basketball, cross-country, golf, and tennis; women's sports include basketball, softball, cross-country, tennis, and volleyball.

TUITION

$4,596/$9,000

CONTACT INFORMATION

Bluefield State College
219 Rock Street
Bluefield, WV 24701
Phone: (304) 327-4000
Fax: (304) 325-7747
E-mail: bscadmit@bluefieldstate.edu

Photo courtesy of West Virginia State University

WEST VIRGINIA STATE UNIVERSITY

ADDRESS: P.O. Box 1000
Institute, WV 25112
(800) 987-2112

WEB SITE: www.wvstateu.edu

FOUNDED: 1891

MASCOT: Yellow Jacket

AFFILIATION: None

TYPE: 4-Year Public

RATIO: 19:1

STUDENT BODY: 3,300

HISTORY

West Virginia State University was originally founded in 1891 as the West Virginia Colored Institute. In its early years, the institute offered programs that provided the equivalent of a high school education. In 1915, college-level programs were added and it became known as the West Virginia Collegiate Institute. In 1929, it was renamed West Virginia State College.

In the 1950s, West Virginia State College lost the land-grant status it had been afforded by the Second Morrill Act in 1891 and became part of the West Virginia College System. During the desegregation years, the dynamics of the once all-black college changed dramatically, and today, the university has a greater number of white students.

In 2001, the land-grant status that was rescinded a half century earlier was returned to the college. Three years later, after the expansion of several programs and the addition of others, the school became West Virginia State University. West Virginia State University is accredited by the High Learning Commission of the North Central Association of Colleges and Schools.

MISSION

Founded in 1891, West Virginia State University is a public, land-grant, historically black university, which has evolved into a fully accessible, racially integrated, and multi- generational institution. The university, "a living laboratory of human relations," is a community of students, staff, and faculty committed to academic growth, service, and preservation of the racial and cultural diversity of the institution. Our mission is to meet higher education and economic development needs of the state and region through innovative teaching and applied research.

MOTTO

"A Living Laboratory of Human Relations"

TRIVIA

West Virginia State University's Reserved Officer Training Corps (ROTC) has produced more generals than any other ROTC program of an HBCU.

The NASA Educator Resource Center (ERC) at West Virginia State University is a satellite of the NASA resource center in Fairmont, West Virginia. The purpose of the program is to provide expertise and facilities to help educators access and utilize science, mathematics, geography, and technology instructional products.

NOTABLES

- Leon Howard Sullivan—Former pastor of Zion Baptist Church in Philadelphia; founded the Opportunities Industrialization Center (OIC); first African American to serve on the Board of Directors of General Motors Corporation

- Earl Francis Lloyd—First African-American athlete to play in an NBA game

- Catherine Coleman Johnson—Aerospace technologist in the Spacecraft Control Branch of NASA; helped calculate space vehicle navigation and guidance

- Tuskegee Airmen Mac Ross and George "Spanky" Roberts—Two of the first five African Americans to receive their wings as aviators in the Army Air Corps (1942)

ACADEMIC PROGRAMS

West Virginia State University consists of four academic colleges: College of Arts and Humanities; College of Business Administration and Social Sciences; College of Natural Sciences and Mathematics; and College of Professional Studies.

Undergraduate degrees are awarded in Art; Biology; Business Administration; Chemistry; Communications; Criminal Justice; Economics; Education; English; Health and Human Performance; History; Mathematics; Modern Foreign Languages; Music; Physics; Political Science; Psychology; ROTC; Social Work; and Sociology.

STUDENT ORGANIZATIONS

West Virginia State University offers forty organizations for students, including Angels, Inc., Criminal Justice Club, Ethiopian Organization, International Students Association, Math Club, and Women in Communication.

Students can work at the campus radio station, WVSU, or join the campus newspaper, *The Yellow Jacket,* which is published and edited by students. Greek organizations include Alpha Phi Alpha, Alpha Kappa Alpha, Kappa Alpha Psi, Omega Psi Phi, Delta Sigma Theta, Phi Beta Sigma, and Zeta Phi Beta.

SPORTS

West Virginia State University's teams, the Yellow Jackets, are members of the National Collegiate Athletic Association (NCAA), Division II and compete in the West Virginia Intercollegiate Athletic Conference. Men's sports include baseball, basketball, football, golf, tennis, and track and field. Women's sports include basketball, cheerleading, golf, softball, tennis, track and field, and volleyball.

TUITION

$2,173/$5,173

CONTACT INFORMATION

Admission Assistant
West Virginia State University
P.O. Box 1000
Institute, WV 25112-1000
Phone: (304) 766-3032
Toll-free: (800) 987-2112
Fax: (304) 766-4158

The Cultivators, 2000
Samuel L. Dunson, Jr.
Oil on canvas
38.5" x 26.5"

Part III:
HBCU Resources

Once you identify colleges that meet your educational criteria, the next steps are creating a timeline and organizing the materials you will need to begin the admission process.

This section provides a checklist of what you need to do during high school to prepare for entry into college. Information on various scholarships and HBCU tours is also provided.

The Notes pages provided at the end of this section will allow you to write down any scholarships or HBCU tours that interest you.

THE BASICS OF GETTING INTO COLLEGE

by Terry Wilfong

Colleges admit students on what they have done in their high school years. They look at a student's academic course load and type (college prep vs. technical or vocational), extracurricular activities (including volunteering in the community), and standardized test scores. Remember this:

The decisions you make during high school will determine which schools you will be eligible to attend.

School Environment

In beginning your search for colleges and universities, start first by finding those that offer the academic majors or disciplines that will support your life goals. Also consider the learning environment provided at the college, such as class size (student-to-faculty ratio), population makeup, and educational activities and organizations. Look at the geographic location as well. Are you a homebody or do you work well in a new environment? Narrow down your selection to no more than five colleges, and ensure that you visit each college before making your final decision.

Financial Aid

There are thousands of options available to students to finance a college education, but most students only concentrate on a very few, primarily scholarships and federal financial aid. "Packaging" is the real magic in financing college. It is the development and pulling together of various financial college payment options into one connected program, which reduces your financial responsibilities to pay for college. A package could consist of one or more of the following: scholarships, internships, work-study programs, family pitch-in systems, bargaining, merit-based scholarships, ROTC, reserve or national guard programs, federal financial aid, and many other creative options, including shortening your time in college.

Scholarships

There are three basic types of scholarships: need-based (background, financial need, ethnic, or gender considerations and basic skills), merit-based (standardized test scores, GPA, extracurricular activities, and academic major or discipline), and combination-based (a linking of the first two such as male student who wants to study nursing). There are also three main sources of scholarships: personal contacts (high school counselors, college financial aid officers, and local librarians), the Internet, and books/programs. More information can be gained by the Internet more quickly than by any other source. (See the partial list we have provided in this section.) Don't waste your time on web sites with outdated contact lists, broken application links, and discontinued programs. Do not use fee-based scholarship services. With a little work, you can find all the information that would be provided by such a service.

Once you have completed one scholarship application, the rest will be easy to complete. Most require your high school GPA, standardized test scores (SAT or ACT), a list of extracurricular activities, your class

It does not matter if you are the president of the senior class, the captain of the football team, have a 4.0 GPA and 1300 plus SATs—if you do not get the application in on the posted date, you will not get in.

ranking, and some form of essay with pictures. Once you collect these items, you can quickly put your scholarship applications together.

A quick note on scholarship application dates: It does not matter if you are the president of the senior class, the captain of the football team, have a 4.0 GPA and 1300 plus SATs—if you do not get the application in on the posted date, you will not get in. So be sure to pay special attention to these dates for the colleges you select.

Junior Colleges & Trade Schools

If you are not accepted to your first choice, consider attending a local junior college for one year or writing an appeal letter to the admissions director of the college you wanted to attend. Be sure to point out any special circumstances or skills that you think should be taken into consideration.

If you do not wish to pursue a college degree at all and would prefer to develop skills for business or industry, vocational and technical schools offer numerous opportunities.

If you have delayed researching colleges but would like to continue your education, look into programs such as Americorp or Habitat for Humanity, where you can build your academic and resume experience.

The most important thing to remember is that education is the door to all endeavors.

For more information about the college admissions process and paying for college, visit the College Success Program at www.urbanministries.com/College_Prep_s/134.htm. ᛫

Terry Wilfong is the author of The Complete Guide to College Financing and Admissions..

RESOURCES

APPLYING TO COLLEGE:
A Checklist

I t's never too early to begin planning for college, whether by keeping up your GPA, participating in extracurricular activities, or saving money for tuition. When you reach your junior year in high school, however, you'll need to start preparing in earnest. The following checklist can help you stay organized and on track as you pursue admission to the college or university of your choice.

Fall of Junior Year

✓ Make a list of the colleges you're interested in attending and begin to gather information online or by phone or mail.

  ▪ Find out if there are any college fairs in your area.

✓ Take the Preliminary Scholastic Assessment Test/National Merit Scholarship Qualifying Test (PSAT/NMSQT).

  ▪ This test helps you identify skills you need to hone before you take the Scholastic Assessment Test (SAT) or the American College Testing Assessment (ACT).

  ▪ The PSAT/NMSQT will also determine if you are eligible to compete for a National Merit Scholarship.

✓ Register for the Scholastic Assessment Test (SAT).

  ▪ You can take the SAT in November or December, but it's important to register early.

  ▪ You can find test dates and register online at www.collegeboard.com.

✓ Begin researching scholarships and other aid from both federal and private sources and from the schools you're interested in attending.

  ▪ Check out our list of resources on page 282.

  ▪ Most scholarship applications will require you to submit an essay, so start working on those now.

✓ Stay focused on academics!

  ▪ It's easy to get sidetracked, but colleges will look closely at your junior-year grades.

  ▪ Are you taking any AP classes? Find out when you can take Advanced Placement exams.

  ▪ Doing well on AP tests can earn you college credit and save money on tuition.

Spring of Junior Year

✓ Now's the time to start looking for a summer job to earn money for tuition.

✓ If you didn't take the SAT or ACT in the fall, make sure you register for the exam now.

✓ By mid-Spring, narrow your list of colleges to no more than 10.

✓ You'll need letters of recommendation for your college applications.

  ▪ Make a list of adults who know you well, such as teachers, coaches, church leaders, and employers.

  ▪ Provide everyone who agrees to write a letter with a stamped, addressed envelope.

  ▪ Don't forget to write thank-you notes!

Summer of Junior Year

✓ Schedule visits to as many college campuses as you can. Check out our list of HBCU tours on page 284.

✓ Request applications from the colleges you're interested in attending. Make a list of important dates and deadlines.

✓ Complete your application essays.

Fall of Senior Year

✓ Ask for feedback on your application essays from teachers, family, and friends. Make adjustments.

- ✓ Complete all your applications. Find out your high school's deadline for requesting transcripts to the appropriate colleges.

- ✓ If you want re-take the SAT, make sure you allow at least eight weeks for scores to be submitted to colleges.

- ✓ Mail your college applications and keep copies of everything you send.

  - Ask your high school to forward copies of your transcripts to the colleges to which you are applying.

- ✓ Find out if there are any financial aid informational events in your area.

- ✓ Begin to gather everything you'll need to complete the Free Application for Federal Student Aid (FAFSA).

  - You'll need copies of your family's most recent tax forms and bank statements, your driver's license, and W-2 forms.

- ✓ Your high school guidance office will receive copies of FAFSA by December. You can also file your application electronically at www.fafsa.ed.gov.

  - This not only saves a week or two in processing time, it makes it easier to track the status of your application.

- ✓ Mail or file FAFSA online as soon as possible after January 1.

- ✓ Depending on whether you filed FAFSA online or mailed it, processing takes two to four weeks.

  - Once processed, you'll receive your Student Aid Report (SAR) either in the mail or in an e-mail with a link to view it online.

  - Your SAR lists your Expected Family Contribution (EFC), which will determine the amount of aid you receive.

  - An electronic copy of your SAR is also made available to the schools you've listed on your FAFSA.

Spring of Senior Year

- ✓ Check your mailbox!

  - Acceptance letters usually arrive before May 1.

- You'll also receive a financial aid award letter from the financial aid office of each college that accepts you. This letter will outline the amount of aid you're eligible for and in what form—grants, loans, and/or work study.

- Different colleges may offer different award packages. You'll need to do your research and carefully compare each offer to make your final decision.

- Make sure you inform each college that sent you an acceptance or financial aid award letter of your decision.

- ✓ If you or your parents qualified for loans as part of your financial aid award, there's still work to be done!

  - If the school you're attending participates in the Federal Direct Loan Program, its financial aid office oversees the loan.

  - If your college of choice is part of the Federal Family Education Loan (FFEL) Program, they will provide you with a list of preferred lenders and you'll need to select a lender and work with the school to complete the application.

Summer of Senior Year

- ✓ Make a list of items you'll need to purchase or pack for your first year at college.

  - Check with your college's student residence or housing office for guidance on what to bring.

  - Get in touch with your new roommate by phone or e-mail and introduce yourself. Compare notes on how to design your "ideal college home" and to avoid duplication (you don't need two stereos!).

- ✓ Create a budget for your freshman year.

- ✓ Don't forget to spend some time with your high school friends and celebrate your accomplishments!

- ✓ If your college offers a freshman orientation program, make sure to participate. You'll make new friends and get a feel for the campus.

Congratulations, you're on your way! **ℍ**

RESOURCES

PAYING YOUR WAY:
Financing Your College Education

Going to college represents a huge financial commitment for many. The good news is that, on average, HBCUs cost much less than other institutions. Still, a college education is expensive, and most students must explore loans, scholarships, and grants to defray the costs of tuition.

Your high school guidance counselor can provide you with information on applying for financial assistance and also tell you about scholarship opportunities for residents of your city, county, or state. You may also qualify for a scholarship based on your academic performance or athletic ability.

The Internet offers endless resources to assist you in your search for financial assistance. You can visit www.fafsa.ed.gov for a free application for federal student aid. A searchable database of more than 2,300 sources of funding is available online at www.collegeboard.com.

Many scholarships and grants are specifically targeted to minority youth. The following list provides just a few of the resources available to help you begin your research.

Actuarial Foundation
www.actuarialfoundation.org

The Actuarial Foundation's Actuarial Diversity Scholarship is an annual scholarship program that encourages academic achievements for Black/African American, Hispanic, and Native American students.

American Architectural Foundation (AAF)
www.archfoundation.org

The AAF offers minority/disadvantaged scholarships to students who plan to study architecture at an NAAB-accredited program (National Architectural Accrediting Board).

American Chemical Society (ACS)
www.acs.org

The ACS offers scholarships to minority students who want to study chemistry or chemistry-related fields.

American Geological Institute (AGI)
www.agiweb.org

AGI, through its Minority Participation Program, offers Geoscience Student Scholarships to ethnic-minority students in the geosciences.

American Institute of Certified Public Accountants (AICPA)
www.aicpa.org/members/div/career/mini/smas.htm

The AICPA provides scholarships to minority students demonstrating exceptional academic achievement, leadership, and commitment to pursuing the CPA designation.

American Physical Society (APS)
www.aps.org

The APS Minority Scholarship provides funding and mentoring to minority physics students to increase the number of under-represented minorities obtaining degrees in physics.

American Planning Association (APA)
www.planning.org

The APA's Judith McManus Price Scholarship is awarded to women and minority students who are enrolled in a Planning Accreditation Board program and are interested in careers as practicing planners.

Aspen Institute
www.aspeninstitute.org

The Aspen Institute Program on Philanthropy and Social Innovation awards the William Randolph Hearst Endowed Fellowship to students of color with an interest in nonprofit organizations, philanthropy, and the social sector.

Boeing
www.boeing.com

Boeing offers scholarships to students who attend one of the colleges and universities with whom the company partners, including some HBCUs.

Congressional Black Caucus (CBC) Spouses

www.cbcfinc.org

Part of the Congressional Black Caucus Foundation, CBC Spouses provides scholarships to minority students.

Development Fund for Black Students in Science and Technology (DFBSST)

www.dfbsst.dlhjr.com

Established by a group of black technical professionals, DFBSST is an endowment fund that provides scholarships to African-American undergraduate students enrolled in scientific or technical fields of study HBCUs.

Gates Millennium Scholars Program (GMS)

www.gmsp.org

GMS provides scholarships to outstanding minority students with significant financial need.

Jackie Robinson Foundation (JRF)

www.jackierobinson.org

The JRF provides four-year scholarships for higher education to minority youths.

Microsoft

www.microsoft.com

The Microsoft Scholarship Program offers a scholarship to help minorities pursue education in computer science and related fields.

National Action Council for Minorities in Engineering (NACME)

www.nacme.org

The NACME Pre-Engineering Student Scholarship Program recognizes minority high school seniors who are committed to science and engineering.

National Association for the Advancement of Colored People (NAACP)

www.naacp.org

The NAACP offers a number of scholarships for minority youth to promote and ensure higher education opportunities.

National Association of Black Journalists (NABJ)

www.nabj.org

The NABJ awards scholarships to student members interested in pursuing careers in journalism.

National Association of Negro Business and Professional Women's Clubs, Inc. (NANBPWC)

www.charityadvantage.com/nanbpwc

The NANBPWC offers several scholarships as part of their mission to serve as a bridge for young people seeking to enter business and the professions.

National Black Nurses Association (NBNA)

www.nbna.org

The NBNA offers various scholarships to provide funding for continuing education.

National Black Police Association (NBPA)

www.blackpolice.org

The NBPA's Alphonso Deal Scholarship Award helps student pursue higher educational training in law enforcement or other related areas.

National Society of Black Engineers (NSBE)

www.national.nsbe.org

NSBE provides several scholarships to minority students studying engineering at both the undergraduate and graduate levels.

Ronald McDonald House Charities® (RMHC) The African-American Future Achievers

www.mcdonaldsnymetro.com

RMHC offers scholarships to students from disadvantaged communities who have at least one parent of African-American heritage.

Ron Brown Scholar Program

www.ronbrown.org

Named for the late Secretary of Commerce, the Ron Brown Scholar Program provides academic scholarships, service opportunities, and leadership experiences for young African Americans.

Thurgood Marshall College Fund

www.thurgoodmarshallfund.org

The Thurgood Marshall College Fund provides scholarships to students attending the nation's public HBCUs.

United Negro College Fund (UNCF)

www.uncf.org

The UNCF administers 400 scholarship and internship programs aimed at ensuring students from low- and moderate-income families can afford college tuition, books, and room and board. **⊞**

RESOURCES

TAKE AN HBCU TOUR:
Visiting College Campuses Helps You Make an Informed Decision

Choosing a college or university can be tough. One of the best ways to determine if a school is a fit for you is to visit the campus where you'll have the opportunity to ask professors and students about their experiences. There are plenty of college tours sponsored by a variety of black fraternities, sororities, and other organizations that will take you to several different schools in a single region. College tours are fun and informative ways to learn about life at HBCUs. Check out the tour web sites below for schedules and itineraries.

Alpha Phi Alpha Fraternity HBCU Tour
Xi Kappa Lambda Education Foundation
P.O. Box 1522
Missouri City, TX 77459
Roger McDonald: (713) 988-8440
Daryl Walton: (713) 773-0125
www.xikappalambda.org/HBCU

Annual HBCU Spring Break Tour
3630 N. Rancho #101
Las Vegas, NV 89130
Rev. Kelcey West, Founder and Tour Director
(702) 860-6638
k32west@aol.com

Annual Spring College Tour
Alpha Phi Alpha Fraternity, Inc.
Beta Lambda Educational Institute
5315 Cleveland Avenue
Kansas City, MO 64130
(816) 728-3548
events@betalambda.org
www.betalambda.org

Annual Brown/Parrish Black College Bus Tour
59th Street and Fifth Avenue
New York, NY 10001
(718) 670-3361 Ext. 2
www.blackcollegebustour.eventbrite.com

Arrow Collegiate College Tour
P.O. Box 1022
Temple Hills, MD 20757
(301) 505-2859
scrowder@arrowcollegiatetour.com
www.arrowcollegiatetour.com

Caring for Young Minds Black College Tour
P.O. Box 47336
Windsor Mill, MD 21244
caringforyoung@aol.com
www.caringforyoungminds.com

College Campus Tours
P.O. Box 355
Fayetteville, GA 30214
(770) 703-1509
shaun@collegecampustours.net
www.collegecampustours.net

College Choices 4 U Black College Tour
2145 Strang Avenue
San Leandro, CA 94578
(510) 276-7021 Ext. 2
collegechoices4u@aol.com
www.collegechoices4u.com

College Excursions USA
746 St. Nicholas Avenue, Suite 57
New York, NY 10031
(800) 715-9985
www.collegeexcursions.com

Delaware Valley College Tours, Inc.
P.O. Box 491
Bryn Mawr, PA 19010
(610) 527-3116
dvctinfo@aol.com
www.delawarevalleycollegetoursinc.com

Educational Student Tours

16850 Gresham Street
North Hills, CA 91343
(818) 891-8087
yasminde@aol.com
www.blackcollegetours.org

Gibbs Travel Historical Black College Tour

Gibbs Travel Agency
P.O. Box 300231
Houston, TX 77230
(713) 748-2242
gibbs_travel@yahoo.com
www.gibbstravelagency.com/collegetour.html

HBCA Black College Tour

HBCA Tour Committee
P.O. Box 1385
New London, CT 06320-1385
hbca_nl@yahoo.com
www.geocities.com/hbca_nl/

HBCU Campus Tours

9269 Utica Avenue, Suite 123
Rancho Cucamonga, CA 91730
(909) 466-4228
info@hbcucampustours.com
www.hbcucampustours.com

HBCU College Tour

Next Level Mentoring Program, Inc.
8459 US 42 #122
Florence, KY 41042
(859) 816-3031
info1@nlmp.org
www.nlmp.org

The National Black College Tour, Inc.

2303 Haflinger Circle
Conyers, GA 30012
contactus@thenationalblackcollegetour.com
www.nationalblackcollegetour.com

New Hope Missionary Baptist Church Youth Ministry Black College Tour

23455 West 9 Mile Road
P.O. Box 386
Southfield, MI 48034
(248) 353-0675
www.newhope-mbc.org/ministries/youth.htm

North Carolina Black College Tours

3200 Beechleaf Court, #100
Raleigh, NC 27604
(919) 232-2557
info@capitalcitytours.net
www.ncblackcollegetours.com

Pathways Educational Services College Tours

2900 Delk Road, #281, Suite 700
Marietta, GA 30067-5350
www.pathwayseducationalservice.org

Step Higher

P.O. Box 2306
Covington, KY 41012-2306
(859) 743-2907
edutours@mystephigher.org
www.mystephigher.org

Stepping in the Right Direction HBCU Tours

P.O. Box 6675
Altadena, CA 91003
(626) 676-7309
www.steppingintherightdirection.com

Theresa C. Suggs/Roy T. Lyons College Tour

NPHC Montgomery County
P.O. Box 454
Rockville, MD 20848-0454
(888) 235-8397
nphcmc20885@yahoo.com
www.nhpcmc.com

Thoroughbred College Tours, LLC.

P.O. Box 197445
Louisville, KY 40259-7445
(502) 386-6008
thoroughbredcollegetours@yahoo.com
www.thoroughbredcollegetours.com

Visions for Success

P. O. Box 18531
Fairfield, OH 45018-0531
(513) 607-8894
www.v-f-s.net

William E. Edwards Annual College Tour (WEE-ACT)

P.O. Box 11343
Stamford, CT 06911-3343
(203) 326-0029
aedwards@wee-act.org
www.wee-act.org

Notes

Notes

ABOUT THE KINSEY COLLECTION

The Kinsey Collection consists of the personal treasures of Bernard and Shirley Kinsey and includes paintings, sculptures, prints, books, historical documents, manuscripts, and vintage photographs.

The Kinseys began collecting to create memories of their travels, gradually building their "collection" into a narrative of African-American culture.

Collecting is now their passion, and they consider themselves to be stewards of history rather than owners of art. This includes securing historical documents and artifacts at auction, from slave shackles to Frederick Douglass' *I Must Mourn* speech.

Both graduates of an HBCU, they now live in California, where they showcase the collection in their home.

About the Artists

Hale Woodruff (p. xviii) was the first art instructor at the Atlanta University Center, where he began a national exhibition of black artists—held annually from 1942 to 1970—at Atlanta University.

Robert Scott Duncanson (p. 2) was born in 1821 to an African-American mother and Canadian father of Scottish descent. He traveled widely, studying in Italy and England, and became well-known for his portraits, still lifes, and landscapes before his death in 1872.

Hughie Lee–Smith (p. 20) served in the U.S. Navy from 1943–1945 as an official painter and went on to become an artist-in-residence at an HBCU, Howard University, from 1969–1971.

Bill Dallas (p. 44) received a BFA in painting from the University of California, Berkeley. Music is often featured in his work, as seen in his painting *Blue Jazz*. His work has been exhibited in California and New York.

Tina Allen (p. 64) is a sculptor and painter born in 1955. Her bust of Frederick Douglass was featured in the 2006 film *Akeelah and the Bee* and in the documentary *Story of a People—Expressions in Black*.

Samuel L. Dunson, Jr. (p. 276) was born in 1970 and began painting seriously during his second year at Tennessee State University, an HBCU. After graduating, he later returned to teach as an assistant art professor.

Bernard and Shirley Kinsey, 2002
Artis Lane
Oil on Canvas
41.75" x 31.75"

Artis Lane (above) was born in 1927, a descendant of educator and abolitionist Mary Ann Shadd. She was awarded a scholarship to the Ontario College of Art at age 15, and was the first woman admitted to Cranbrook Art Academy. She first became known for her portraits of such dignitaries as Jaqueline Kennedy, Nelson Mandela, and Ronald Reagan. In later years, she began to focus on social issues in her work, such as *The Beginning,* a painting of Rosa Parks seated on the historic bus, and *Tear on the Face of America.* The painting above is a portrait of Bernard and Shirley Kinsey, owners of the Kinsey Collection.